D1368602

WORDNET

Language, Speech, and Communication

WORDNET

AN ELECTRONIC LEXICAL DATABASE

edited by
Christiane Fellbaum

The MIT Press
Cambridge, Massachusetts
London, England

This book was set in Times New Roman on the Monotype "Prism Plus" Post-Script Imagesetter by Asco Trade Typesetting Ltd., Hong Kong

Printed and bound in the United States of America.

Library of Congress Cataloging-in-Publication Data

WordNet : an electronic lexical database / edited by Christiane Fellbaum.
    p.   cm. — (Language, speech, and communication)
Includes bibliographical references and index.
ISBN 0-262-06197-X (hc : alk. paper)
    1. WordNet. 2. Semantics—Data processing. 3. Lexicology—Data processing. 4. English language—Data processing. I. Fellbaum, Christiane. II. Series.
P325.5.D38W67   1998
423′.1—dc21
                                                              97-48710
                                                                 CIP

To the memory of Katherine James Miller and Derek Gross

Contents

Acknowledgments

The development of WordNet and its applications at Princeton University were supported in part by contract N00014-86-K-0492, with funding provided by the Navy Personnel Research and Development Center and the Manpower Personnel and Training Research Program of the Office of Naval Research; in part by contract N00014-91-J-1634-P00005 with the Office of Naval Research; in part by contract MDA 903-86-K-0242 with the Army Research Institute; in part by grant IRI-9528983 from the National Science Foundation; in part by contract N6601-94-C-6045 and contract N66001-95-C 8605, both with the Advanced Research Projects Agency; and in part by a grant from the James S. McDonnell Foundation. Opinions expressed are those of the authors and should not be attributed to any of these sponsors.

Contributors

Reem Al-Halimi Department of Computer Science, University of Waterloo

Robert C. Berwick Center for Biological and Computational Learning, Massachusetts Institute of Technology

J. F. M. Burg Department of Computer Science, Vrije Universiteit Amsterdam

Martin Chodorow Department of Psychology, Hunter College of CUNY

Christiane Fellbaum Cognitive Science Laboratory, Princeton University

Joachim Grabowski Lehrstuhl Psychologie III, Universität Mannheim

Sanda M. Harabagiu Artificial Intelligence Center, SRI International

Marti A. Hearst University of California, Berkeley

Graeme Hirst Department of Computer Science, University of Toronto

Douglas A. Jones Department of Linguistics, University of Maryland

Rick Kazman Software Engineering Institute, Carnegie Mellon University

Karen T. Kohl Artificial Intelligence Laboratory, Massachusetts Institute of Technology

Shari Landes Cognitive Science Laboratory, Princeton University

Claudia Leacock Cognitive Science Laboratory, Princeton University

George A. Miller Cognitive Science Laboratory, Princeton University

Katherine J. Miller Cognitive Science Laboratory, Princeton University

Dan I. Moldovan   Department of Computer Science and Engineering, Southern Methodist University

Naoyuki Nomura   JustSystems, Inc., Japan

Uta E. Priss   School of Library and Information Science, Indiana University

Philip Resnik   Department of Linguistics and Institute for Advanced Computer Studies, University of Maryland

David St-Onge   InfoWAN Datenkommunikation GmbH, Munich, Germany

Randee I. Tengi   Cognitive Science Laboratory, Princeton University

R. P. van de Riet,   Department of Mathematics and Computer Science, Vrije Universiteit, Amsterdam

Ellen M. Voorhees   National Institute of Standards and Technology

Foreword

It crystallized in 1985. Latent and inchoate for twenty years, in 1985 it became explicit, a project we could mention when asked what we were working on. But in 1985 WordNet was very different from what it became ten years later.

One of the project's original presuppositions was the *separability hypothesis*: that the lexical component of language can be isolated and studied in its own right. The history of lexicography suggests strongly that useful contributions can be made at the level of words. The lexicon is not independent of other components of language, of course, but it does seem to be separable from them. For example, whereas phonology and grammar are mastered once and for all in the early years of life, vocabulary continues to grow as long as a person stays intellectually active. Different cognitive processes seem to be involved.

Another presupposition was the *patterning hypothesis*: that people could not master and have readily available all the lexical knowledge needed to use a natural language unless they could take advantage of systematic patterns and relations among the meanings that words can be used to express. Those systematic mental patterns have been a subject for speculation at least since the time of Plato, and modern linguistic studies are beginning to suggest ways of identifying them in the semantic structures of natural languages. But much otherwise excellent work along these lines runs aground on the magnitude of the problem. An author might propose a semantic theory and illustrate it with some 20 or 50 English words (usually nouns), leaving the other 100,000 words of English as an exercise for the reader.

So a third presupposition was the *comprehensiveness hypothesis*: that computational linguistics, if it were ever to process natural languages as people do, would need to have available a store of lexical knowledge as extensive as people have. This observation was simply a language corollary of the growing interest at that time in knowledge-based systems in the field of artificial intelligence. Roger Schank and his colleagues were building language-processing systems having small vocabularies for well-defined topics, where word meanings were represented by a few hundred LISP programs, but it was becoming clear even in 1985 that this approach would have trouble scaling up. There seemed to be a need for a comprehensive lexical database that would include word meanings as well as word forms and that could be used under computer control.

Analyzing a word's meaning into semantic components that can be captured in LISP code is a form of componential lexical semantics. That is to say, componential semantics approaches the meaning of a word in much the same way it approaches the meaning of a sentence: the meaning of a sentence should be decomposable into the meanings of its constituents, and the meaning of a word should be similarly decomposable into certain semantic primitives, or conceptual atoms. Philip N. Johnson-Laird and I had explored componential semantics with much enthusiasm in our 1976 book, Language and Perception, but in 1985 we still did not have a definitive list of the conceptual atoms and it was beginning to look as if, whatever other virtues componential lexical semantics might have, it was not the best theory for natural language processing by computers.

Was there an alternative? In 1985 many cognitive psychologists and computational linguists were formulating word meanings in terms of networks, diagrams with nodes to represent meanings and darts to represent relations between the meanings. For example, *table* and *furniture* would label two nodes and a dart between them would represent the proposition that "a *table* is a kind of *furniture*." Is-A-KIND-OF is a semantic relation; no claim is made that the meaning of *furniture* is a component of the meaning of *table*. As workers became more self-conscious about the assumptions that are involved in these network representations, it became increasingly obvious that relational lexical semantics is one possible alternative to componential lexical semantics. And Jerry Fodor pointed out that many years earlier Rudolph Carnap had proposed a similar type of relational semantics.

In the early days of WordNet, therefore, we thought that we were testing whether or not a relational lexical semantics could be extended to a larger vocabulary than the toy illustrations of the day. By the time we had convinced ourselves that relational theories could scale up, we had created something that seemed to have intrinsic merit of its own. Thereafter, WordNet grew by the applications we made of it, each application showing the need for a new and better system. It is most appropriate, therefore, that the description of WordNet (version 1.5) in the first part of this book should be followed by an account of some uses that people have found for it.

In those early days, however, we had no plan to construct a complete lexicon. The initial idea was to identify the most important lexical nodes by character strings and to explore the patterns of semantic relations among them. If you wanted the definitions (or pronunciations or etymologies or usages) of a word form that labeled one of those nodes, you should look it up in an on-line, machine-readable dictionary. The theory we were testing assumed that, if you got the pattern of semantic relations right, a definition could be inferred from that—it seemed redundant to include definitions along with the network of semantic relations.

In 1978 I wrote a thought piece for the National Institute of Education in which I described the educational benefits that could follow from what I called an "automated dictionary." Many ideas formulated there have pervaded our thinking about WordNet, but in 1978 I was completely innocent of how to accomplish what I was talking about. With some modest help from the Sloan Foundation, the Spencer Foundation, and the IBM Thomas J. Watson Research Center, I was able to keep the ideas alive, and in 1984 I even managed to build a small semantic net of 45 nouns on an IBM PC. That tiny example, which I called a word net, was demonstrated at IBM and at Bellcore, where wise friends like Lance Miller, Roy Byrd, Michael Lesk, Donald Walker, Robert Amsler, and Stephen Hanson, among others, encourage me and guided me toward the technology that I needed.

Don Walker's group at Bellcore was particularly supportive and even hired some of my research associates to work jointly between Princeton University and Bellcore. In the summer of 1985 my wife Kitty and I, with the help of Pamela Wakefield and two undergraduate students, Ben Martin and Yana Kane, began to work seriously on what was to become WordNet. We achieved enough that Mike Lesk invited me to give a paper about it at the first conference of the University of Waterloo Centre for the New Oxford English Dictionary in November 1985. That talk explained the idea of using synonym sets (synsets) to represent lexical concepts and described the lexical matrix, a mapping between word forms and word meanings, important ideas that guided our early thinking.

Probably the most significant thing about the talk, however, was its title, which was provided by Lesk: "WordNet: A Dictionary Browser." WordNet was seen as a program ancillary to a machine-readable dictionary, a program that would allow users to explore an on-line dictionary on the basis of semantic, rather than alphabetic, similarities. Lesk automatically asked himself what the program might be good for and came up with an answer: browsing.

At the same time that WordNet was taking shape, some of us were collaborating to create a Program for Cognitive Studies at Princeton. Richard Cullingford visited Princeton from 1983 to 1985 and he, Gilbert Harman, and I persuaded Provost Neil Rudenstine to give us a mini-computer, which became the heart of the Cognitive Science Laboratory. With that facility in hand, I was able to persuade Susan Chipman, at the Office of Naval Research, to give us a contract to develop WordNet, and Cullingford and I together received a contract from the Army Research Institute to develop a computational theory of lexical semantics. In March 1986 the James S. McDonnell Foundation made a generous award to Princeton to support our work in cognitive science. Marie Bienkowski, Cullingford's graduate student and a proficient computer scientist, started working with us in 1985 and soon began to provide the software that was needed. Thus, WordNet became one of several active projects housed in Princeton's new Cognitive Science Laboratory.

The most important program used in building WordNet is one that we call, inelegantly, the Grinder. Lexicographers make their additions and changes in the lexical source files, and periodically the Grinder takes those files and converts them into a lexical database. Bienkowski wrote the first version of the Grinder in 1986 in LISP: Dan Teibel rewrote it in C in 1987; Antonio Romero rewrote it again in 1989; and Randee Tengi has been responsible for all versions and revisions since 1991. Any changes that are proposed in the content or form of WordNet imply changes to the Grinder, so it has been evolving steadily as WordNet has evolved.

People sometimes ask, "Where did you get your words?" We began in 1985 with the words in Kučera and Francis's Standard Corpus of Present-Day Edited English (familiarly known as the Brown Corpus), principally because they provided frequencies for the different parts of speech. We were well launched into that list when Henry Kučera warned us that, although he and Francis owned the Brown Corpus, the syntactic tagging data had been sold to Houghton Mifflin. We therefore dropped our plan to use their frequency counts (in 1988 Richard Beckwith developed a polysemy index that we use instead). We also incorporated all the adjective pairs that Charles Osgood had used to develop the semantic differential. And since synonyms were critically important to us, we looked words up in various thesauruses: for example, Laurence Urdang's little *Basic Book of Synonyms and Antonyms* (1978), Urdang's revision of Rodale's *The Synonym Finder* (1978), and Robert Chapman's 4th edition of *Roget's International Thesaurus* (1977)—in such works, one word quickly leads on to others. Late in 1986 we received a list of words compiled by Fred Chang at the Naval Personnel Research and Development Center, which we compared with our own list; we were dismayed to find only 15% overlap. So Chang's list became input. And in 1993 we obtained the list of 39,143 words that Ralph Grishman and his colleagues at New York University included in their common lexicon, COMLEX; this time we were dismayed that WordNet contained only 74% of the COMLEX words. But that list, too, became input. In short, a variety of sources have contributed; we were not well disciplined in building our vocabulary. The fact is that the English lexicon is very large, and we were lucky that our sponsors were patient with us as we slowly crawled up the mountain.

As the list of words grew progressively longer, the need for organization became increasingly pressing. The first division was by syntactic category: we created different files for nouns, verbs, and adjectives (adverbs were not added until 1992). But within each syntactic category there are still too many words to handle without further classification. Nouns were the worst problem—of the open classes of words, the noun class is the most open of all. So we stumbled into something that others have taught us to call an ontology. In the spring of 1987 Philip N. Johnson-Laird visited Princeton from the MRC Applied Psychology Unit in Cambridge, England, and became interested in the fact that WordNet had no obvious way to indicate changes in an adjective's meaning when it modifies different head nouns. He took 266 pairs of antonymous adjectives (all that WordNet contained at that time) and considered what classes of nouns each of them could appropriately modify. The result was a list of approximately 25 classes of nouns, which became the basic categories of the noun files. Our long list of nouns was then sorted into 25 categories; the individual files that resulted could be farmed out to different people to organize in terms of semantic relations, thus facilitating the work that had to be done. Christiane Fellbaum, who joined the team in the summer of 1987, took over the verbs and created a similar categorization for them.

Only the descriptive adjectives,which have been Kitty Miller's responsibility since the beginning, have remained grouped in one enormous file.

But how did WordNet evolve from a dictionary browser into a self-contained lexical database? A major advance occured when, early in 1989, Susan Chipman, dissatisfied with lexical browsing as the raison d'être for WordNet, asked us to develop a tool based on WordNet that would read a text file and report various kinds of information about the words in it, a tool that came to be called the Word Filter. Rare or otherwise undesirable words could be filtered out of naval documents and more familiar words could be suggested to replace them. This exercise made us immediately aware that we would have to do something about inflectional morphology. WordNet contains only base forms. If the word *ships* occurred in the text, WordNet did not recognize it. So Richard Beckwith and Michael Colon wrote a program, Morphy, that does lemmatization: if the word is not on a (long) list of exceptions, then suffixes are pruned until the lemma is found. By September 1989 it was possible to take input text and find the base forms in WordNet.

This possibility has led to a major project in which open-class words in text are associated with the appropriate sense in WordNet. Claudia Leacock, who joined the team in November 1991, and Brian Gustafson developed an interface, ConText, that will preprocess text (will tokenize, lemmatize, and syntactically tag words automatically) and display it along with WordNet entries for the target word (the word to be semantically tagged). In June 1993 Shari Landes took responsibility for assembling and supervising a large group of 'taggers'' who use ConText and do their best to give us disambiguated text as the output. The description of this work in chapter 8 need not be repeated here; suffice it to say that semantic tagging of text has greatly improved WordNet's coverage, both of words and of word meanings.

Another important change in the character of WordNet occurred in the spring of 1989 when Antonio Romero modified the Grinder to accept parenthetical definitions as part of any synset. As the number of words in WordNet increased, it became increasingly difficult for us, purely on the basis of synonyms, to keep all the different word senses distinct. In short, we learned the hard way what any lexicographer could have told us, namely, that definition by synonymy is not adequate. At first we kept our explanatory glosses as short as possible. Only after we had enjoyed the luxury of definitions for a year or so did we begin to write fuller glosses, even including (in quotation makes) illustrative phrases or sentences. The number of glosses has grown steadily. In April 1989 WordNet contained 37,409 synsets and no glosses; by July 1991 it contained 44,983 synsets and 13,688 glosses (30%); by January 1992 it contained 49,771 synsets and 19,382 glosses (39%); by January 1993 it contained 61,023 synsets and 36,880 glosses (60%); by January 1994 it contained 79,542 synsets and 58,705 glosses (74%); by January 1995 it contained 91,050 synsets and 75,389 glosses (83%). (As this book goes to press, the number of synsets is approximately 91,600.).

Our ambition, of course, is to reach 100%. Some of the applications being considered now assume that when a word is retrieved, WordNet will provide information about its meaning; if users look up *grandson* and find it defined simply as a kind of *grandchild*, they are not likely to feel that WordNet has served them well. So we have incorporated, and will continue to incorporate, more and more of the definitional information that modern dictionaries have educated their buyers to expect. In the course of incorporating this kind of explanatory information, we have all acquired greater respect for traditional lexicographers.

We have always considered WordNet to be an experiment, not a product. As soon as it became large enough to be useful, we offered it freely to the research community. Randee Tengi has supervised a series of releases: WordNet version 1.0 was released in June 1991; version 1.1 in August 1991; version 1.2 in April 1992; version 1.3 in December 1992; version 1.4 in August 1993; version 1.5 in March 1995. Interest in it has grown steadily. The 1995 release was announced to a mailing list of more than 500 individuals and laboratories all over the world; that number has now grown to almost 1,000.

Funding for this work has come from several sources, the most important being the Office of Naval Research, the Advanced Research Projects Agency, the James S. McDonnell Foundation, and, more recently, the Linguistic Data Consortium.

A small army of people have worked on it at one time or another. Most staff members have already been mentioned, but a large number of students have contributed—so many that it is not possible to list them all. A few stand out in our memory: Ben Martin, Amalia Bachman, Derek Gross, Michael Colon, Brian Gustafson, Ross Bunker, Robert Thomas, Anna Poplowski, Dan Markham, Joshua Schechter, and Paul Bagyenda have all made important contributions to the final product.

Finally, I want to express my gratitude to Christiane Fellbaum for accepting responsibility for organizing and editing this exposition of our work. In 1990 we published five papers on WordNet in the *International Journal of Lexicography*, and for a while that collection served well to inform interested parties what we had been up to. When these papers became outdated, we revised them a bit, but by now they are actually misleading. The problems of keeping documentation up to date are all too familiar, but this kind of expository documentation is a special case. I am deeply grateful to Christiane for this contribution to our joint effort, which is only one of many she has made over the years.

George A. Miller

Introduction

Christiane Fellbaum

A decade after the inception of WordNet seemed like a good time to take stock.[1] Everyone who has worked on WordNet is keenly aware of its shortcomings, and there has never been a moment when we felt that we were "done." Yet the fact that WordNet has been obtained by hundreds of researchers all over the world and applied in dozens of ways in a wide variety of areas has provided gratification along the way, and some applications have guided us in our thinking about the additions we made to the database.

WordNet has not only grown in size but also evolved in ways that we did not foresee when Miller 1990 appeared. One goal of publishing this book was to record these changes and provide an up-to-date account of the lexical database. (As the book goes to press, we are preparing version 1.6, but version 1.5 has been the standard on which most of the chapters are based.) Another goal is to explain the motivation for the painstaking construction of the database and the reasons for its particular design to readers who may be unfamiliar with WordNet altogether and to those users who may be unfamiliar with some of its components or its theoretical foundations. We also hope that the book will inspire further applications among linguists, psycholinguists, and researchers in artificial intelligence and natural language processing.

Of the four chapters in part I, the first three focus on the treatment of a particular syntactic category or a word class; chapter 4 describes in detail the design and implementation of the database and the associated software.

Parts II and III contain chapters contributed by colleagues outside of Princeton University's Cognitive Science Laboratory. Chapters 5 and 6 describe enhancements to WordNet, and chapter 7 considers WordNet through the lens of formal concept analysis. Chapters 8 through 16 discuss a variety of applications of WordNet. We are aware of many more, but the present selection intends to reflect the diversity and breadth of the applications and to highlight the potential that WordNet holds for advances in linguistics, natural language processing, and artificial intelligence research.

COMPUTERS AND THE LEXICON

The computer revolution has not only changed the way research is done but also opened up possibilities for new fields of investigation. In particular, greater accessibility to low-cost and powerful computers has spawned new efforts to understand the human mind, which is so large and complex that to gain a realistic understanding of it seems hopeless without a machine that can perform comparably large and complex tasks. Even if one does not accept the metaphor of the computer as the human mind, there is no doubt that computers provide an excellent modeling ground for testing theories of cognitive behavior. Language in particular has long been recognized as one of the most interesting aspects of human behavior and perhaps the most challenging manifestation of the complexities of the human mind. Linguistic theories attempt to model human grammar, or linguistic competence, but often these theories rely on data that are not well documented in actual use. Language corpora are now available that inform our theories and shape our understanding of the lexicon in particular, by providing solid evidence about such phenomena as polysemy, frequency of occurrence, and selectional preferences. On the less theoretical level, the union of computational resources and linguistic theory has evolved into a major area of research that has spawned a number of natural-language-processing projects. Language is also the vehicle through which humans express thoughts, and models of human cognitive processes, such as inferencing, must therefore include a lexicon. WordNet's hierarchical structure, which is motivated by theories of human knowledge organization, provides a useful component for artificial intelligence research projects.

Linguists have traditionally sliced up speakers' knowledge of language, or grammar, into phonology, morphology, syntax, semantics, and the lexicon. Those aspects of grammar that appear to be governed by clearly statable rules have been the subject of much work in computational linguistics. Thus, parsers, which identify the different constituents of phrases and sentences and assign a phrase structure to them, seem an ideal area for computational language modeling. By contrast, the lexicon, which is very large and seems far less "clean," presents an enormous challenge to those who attempt to capture its structure and properties in ways that truly reflect people's lexical knowledge. But the challenge of constructing realistically sized lexical databases for use in natural-language-processing projects ranging from information retrieval, to machine translation, to machine-based reasoning must be met, because "meaningful sentences are composed of meaningful words" (Miller 1995).

Independently of its needs, but with fortunate consequences for the natural-language-processing community, during the past decade linguists and psycholinguists have rediscovered the lexicon as an important area of investigation. The change from perceiving the lexicon as a wastebasket full of peripheral, irregular, and inelegant facts about language to perceiving it as a central component of grammar is due largely to the discovery that the lexicon is a highly structured repository of rules and principles that give it the status and prominence previously accorded only to syntax. In fact, the division between the different components of grammar is no longer as clear-cut as it once seemed, and the lexicon is now thought to contain, along with the semantic information for words, information that specifies and determines much of their syntactic behavior. Many of the discoveries about the lexicon's properties can now be tested on a large scale. Lexical semanticists, psycholinguists, and computational linguists can mutually benefit from the construction of lexical databases and the insights that can be gained from realistically sized models. Any linguistic or psycholinguistic theory of the lexicon must withstand the test of scale that is provided by the possibilities of computational treatments.

The demand for large, machine-tractable lexicons has raised a number of fundamental questions. First, how should the lexicon be constructed—by hand or automatically? Second, what kind of information should the lexicon contain? Third, what should the design of the lexicon be—that is, how should its contents be organized and made accessible? These questions are related; thus, the method for constructing one's dictionary determines its contents and their usefulness for research.

CONSTRUCTING THE LEXICAL DATABASE

There are essentially two methods for constructing an electronic dictionary. One is via automatic acquisition, that is, by scanning the text of a book format dictionary into the computer and then manipulating the contents so as to derive information that can be usefully applied for a variety of projects. Automatic acquisition is the method used for most of the lexical database projects described in Zernik 1991. It is clearly the fastest and least labor-intensive method and leaves one with the freedom to organize the data in accordance with one's particular goals or theory.[2]

The second method is to craft one's dictionary by hand. Manual construction is of course slow, expensive, and cumbersome, and hand-built dictionaries have tended to be too small to be of any use in natural-language-processing applications or to lend support for theories of lexical organization. However, the main advantage of a hand-built lexicon is that it allows one to create entries with the kinds of contents that one hopes will be useful for certain applications. These contents may be richer than the information one can extract from standard dictionaries. For example, Fillmore and Atkins's (1994) frame semantic lexicon is a resource whose contents will be valuable for sophisticated text analysis and automatic inferencing systems in ways that standard dictionaries probably cannot be. A second advantage is that the format of the entries can be controlled so that subsequent information extraction will require a minimum of manipulation.[3] Because WordNet was initially conceived as a test bed for a particular model of lexical organization that had never before been implemented on a large scale, it had to be manually constructed. As G. A. Miller states in his foreword, semantic networks containing more than a few dozen words did not exist, and we did not know what kinds of relations we would need to create a network linking the bulk of the English lexicon. Because WordNet represents an ongoing experiment without predecessors, it seemed advantageous to have the freedom to make changes and additions to its contents in the course of its development. We have often taken advantage of this freedom, and the version of WordNet described in most chapters here—version 1.5—includes several changes that were implemented after the publication of what came to be known informally as the "Five Papers" (Miller 1990).

THE CONTENTS OF WORDNET

Although WordNet contains compounds, phrasal verbs, collocations, and idiomatic phrases, the word is the basic unit. WordNet does not decompose words into smaller meaningful units, though a comparison with componential analyses reveals some common aspects. For example, the CAUSE relation that links many verb pairs (Fellbaum, chapter 3) is considered a semantic primitive in analyses such as Jackendoff's (1983) that decomposes meanings in terms of Lexical Conceptual Structures. Priss (chapter 7) examines WordNet in the framework of formal concept analysis, where objects are structured on the basis of their attributes into concept lattices that can be diagrammatically represented. This powerful analysis, which has a number of advantages for representing conceptual and lexical structures, is based on the formal representation of concepts according to their objects and attributes, that is, aspects of meaning of the concepts in question. Priss's analysis, though relying on meaningful units below the concept/word level, has yielded some interesting insights and comparisons with WordNet's present structure.

WordNet also does not contain organizational units larger than words, such as scripts (Schank and Abelson 1977) or frames (Fillmore and Atkins 1992), which have been proposed as building blocks for lexicons. Frames contain all those lexicalized concepts that are relevant to certain kinds of situations, such as an economic transaction. They include both verbs and nouns and the structural and semantic relations that hold among them in a particular situation. A framelike semantics is precluded by WordNet's strict separation of its entries according to their syntactic category membership (Noun, Verb, Adjective, and Adverb). However, the relational semantics of WordNet reflect some of the structure of frame semantics. For example, WordNet relates verbs like *buy* and *sell*, which are part of a common frame (the "commercial transaction" frame) in Fillmore and Atkins's analysis. In fact, both frame semantics and the relational semantics in WordNet share a great deal with semantic field analysis in that they all naturally relate words and concepts from a common semantic domain. The absence of relations that would allow the construction of frames or scripts and yield topical information about a text or discourse—which in turn would make possible inferencing and anaphoric reference resolution—is addressed in several chapters in part II.

The division into four separate semantic nets, one for each open word class, also entails that WordNet contains no information about the syntagmatic properties of the words. This aspect of word meaning is instead the focus of semantic concordances (Landes, Leacock, and Tengi, chapter 8), naturally occurring texts that provide the contexts for specific word senses. Resnik (chapter 10) addresses the more specific question of verb-noun co-occurrences.

Unlike dictionaries in book format, WordNet contains short phrases, such as *bad person*, that are not paraphrasable by a single word. These phrases reflect lexical gaps and are a product of WordNet's relational structure, which may link two concepts via a third that happens not to be lexicalized in English. But these gaps are not always structural artifacts; they are often lexicalized in other languages, and they reveal conceptual structures as distinct from lexical structures.

People often draw the distinction between word (or lexical) knowledge and world (or encyclopedic) knowledge. Two kinds of books reflect this distinction: dictionaries are generally the repository of word knowledge, and encyclopedias the repository of world knowledge. The boundaries between the two are in fact fuzzy. We can probably all agree that knowing that *hitting* someone is a hostile act constitutes world knowledge, whereas knowing that the verb *hit* is a strong verb, that it is more or less synonymous with *strike*, and that it takes a direct argument constitutes word knowledge. It is less clear how knowing that the direct argument of *hit* must be a solid object (as opposed to, say, a gas) should be classified. But there is no question that understanding the meaning and uses of a word requires both kinds of knowledge. Kay (1989) points out that our mental lexicons must contain both word and world knowledge, and that only those lexicons that contain both kinds of knowledge are likely to yield successful applications. Encyclopedic knowledge is vast and difficult to assemble, although Lenat and his colleagues (Lenat and Guha 1990) have been working for a number of years on constructing an intelligent system that has all facts pertaining to words and concepts at its disposition. WordNet does not attempt to include encyclopedic knowledge, although the definitions that accompany the synonym sets (synsets) provide information about the concepts that is not strictly part of their lexical structure. G. A. Miller points out in the foreword that, although WordNet's synsets were initially intended to contain no information other than pointers to other synsets, it was found that definitions and illustrative sentences were needed to distinguish closely related synsets whose members were polysemous. And in the case of many technical concepts, such as uncommon plants and animals, lexical and encyclopedic knowledge are merged in the definitions, which are likely to constitute all the knowledge everyday speakers need to access.

Knowledge beyond that usually given in dictionaries is needed for reasoning and making inferences about states and events referred to by sentences. Harabagiu and Moldovan (chapter 16) show how the information in WordNet can be augmented to create a knowledge base that can be successfully used for inferencing.

THE DESIGN OF WORDNET

Until recently the lexicon of a language was represented by dictionaries in printed book format only. These are not meant to show the lexicon's structure; rather, they facilitate the looking up of words and enable the user to find information about their spelling, meaning, and use. Access to particular words is through their spelling, so dictionaries and lexicons must fulfill their purpose via an organization based on orthographic principles. However, a word's spelling is often an accidental or conventional feature. If one takes the main purpose of dictionaries and lexicons to be that of giving information about the meaning of words and the semantic structure of the language, then clearly it would be more desirable to construct these reference works so that their entries can be accessed via their semantic properties. On-line dictionaries, which are not constrained by the alphabetized format of books, present exciting possibilities for novel arrangements of lexical information. Unlike a book, a computational lexicon allows a searcher to access information along more than one path, semantics being among them. How one wants to exploit the potential of electronic reference resources depends on one's ideas of the salient properties of words and the lexicon as well as on the applications one has in mind. As G. A. Miller explains (chapter 1), WordNet is a semantic dictionary that was designed as a network, partly because representing words and concepts as an interrelated system seems to be consistent with evidence for the way speakers organize their mental lexicons.

The first lexical reference book that took meaning as its organizing principle was Roget's thesaurus. Thesauruses are built around concepts and are designed to help users find the "right" word when they have a concept in mind. By contrast, dictionaries are books designed to give users information about words and to help them understand the concepts behind unfamiliar words they have encountered. WordNet is neither a traditional dictionary nor a thesaurus but combines features of both types of lexical reference resources.

WORDNET AS A THESAURUS

WordNet's design resembles that of a thesaurus in that its building block is a synset consisting of all the words that express a given concepts (see G. A. Miller, chapter 1). Thus, the user of WordNet who has a given concept in mind can find, by calling up one of the words expressing this concept, other words that lexicalize the same concept. But WordNet does much more than list concepts in the form of synsets. The synsets are linked by means of a number of relations, including hyponymy, meronymy, and entailment (see chapters 1–3 by G. A. Miller, K. J. Miller, and Fellbaum). Different kinds of semantic opposition, lumped together in the antonymy relation, link words only, rather than concepts. WordNet thus clearly separates the conceptual and the lexical levels, and this distinction is reflected in the one between semantic-conceptual and lexical relations that hold among synsets and words, respectively.

Unlike in a thesaurus, the relations between concepts and words in WordNet are made explicit and labeled; users select the relation that guides them from one concept to the next and choose the direction of their navigation in conceptual space.

Words express concepts, and the lexicon is constrained by the kinds of concepts that are available to us by virtue of our perception of, and interaction with, the world around us. These limitations on our conceptual inventory may well be innate and universal. The majority of lexicalized concepts are shared among languages, although most, if not all, languages have words for some concepts that are not lexicalized in other languages. Although words depend on the existence of concepts, the inverse is not true: concepts can, and do, lead a life independently of words. In the process of constructing the network of words and concepts, we found that in many cases it was necessary to postulate concepts that happen not to be lexicalized in English. Consider the example cited earlier, *bad person*, which has a number of subordinates including *offender* and *libertine*. If *bad person* did not intervene between its superordinate *person* and such hyponyms as *offender* and *libertine*, these words would be (infelicitous) sisters to *adventurer*, *lover*, and *worker*. Similarly, Fellbaum (chapter 3) describes how apparently related verbs turn out to fall into distinct groups on the basis of certain semantic and syntactic properties. Such groups are not always headed by a superordinate verb, yet the unlexicalized concept under which existing words can be subsumed arguably exists, as shown by the verbs' distinct properties. WordNet's particular structure therefore reveals a conceptual inventory that is only partially mapped onto the lexicon of English: in this respect, WordNet differs from thesauruses, where only lexicalized concepts are accounted for.

WORDNET AS A DICTIONARY

In some respects, WordNet resembles a traditional dictionary. For example, WordNet gives definitions and sample sentences for most of its synsets. A definition is valid for all the synonyms in a synset, since it expresses the meanings of the concept. The sample sentences may not be felicitous for all synonyms, and often different sentences are given for different members of the synset. Like a dictionary, WordNet also contains information about morphologically related words. Relational adjectives, often listed as run-ons in conventional dictionaries, are connected to specific nouns (see K. J. Miller, chapter 2). For example, the link between the adjective *behavioral* and the corresponding noun *behavior* exists merely for these two word forms—it does not relate *behavioral* to *conduct*, a synonym of *behavior*.

RELATIONS IN WORDNET

WordNet makes the commonly accepted distinction between conceptual-semantic relations, which link concepts, and lexical relations, which link individual words (Evens 1988, and papers therein). Evens (1988, 5) points out that researchers aspiring to model memory and the mental lexicon tend to build semantic networks with conceptual-semantic relations, whereas workers focusing on lexical aspects use primarily lexical, word-word relations. However, as K. J. Miller (chapter 2) points out, there is solid evidence that speakers associate an adjective with its antonym on a word form basis rather than on a conceptual basis. Also, experimental data have shown that a substantial proportion of speakers' associations to word stimuli are syntagmatic (Fillenbaum and Jones 1965; Cramer 1968; Rosenweig 1970); this indicates further the existence of word-specific mental links. It seems, then, that the difference in the nature of the relations does not coincide neatly with the distinction between the mental organization of words and a purely lexical or linguistic organization.

WordNet does not contain syntagmatic relations linking words from different syntactic categories.[4] One reason is that the four major syntactic categories (Noun, Verb, Adjective, Adverb) are treated separately. The separation is due to the semantic differences between the relations that link words and concepts from the four syntactic categories, as G. A. Miller (chapter 1), K. J. Miller (chapter 2), and Fellbaum (chapter 3) show. For example, although both nouns and verbs are organized hierarchically, the hyponymy relation that links nouns differs from the troponymy relation that links verbs, as Fellbaum argues. Similarly, entailment relations linking verbs bear some resemblance to meronymy relations linking nouns, yet they are clearly different (Fellbaum and Miller 1990; Fellbaum, chapter 3). WordNet respects the semantic distinctions between relations for the different parts of speech, although the number of relations in WordNet has been kept small and limited to those that appear to be salient for speakers. Among nouns, the polysemy of the meronymy relation, first pointed out by Chaffin, Hermann, and Winston (1988), is acknowledged in three kinds of subrelations subsumed under meronymy. Other lexical semanticists have undertaken careful analyses of semantic and lexical relations and proposed subtle distinctions (Cruse 1986). These distinctions are valid in the context of a semantic analysis of conceptual relations, but they do not seem to be reflected in speakers' minds, where relatively few relations are salient.[5] Probably the largest number of relations—53—has been proposed by Mel'čuk and Zholkovsky (1988), who call them "lexical functions." Many of these include relations among morphologically related word forms.

THE TENNIS PROBLEM

WordNet links words and concepts through a variety of semantic relations based on similarity and contrast. Because it focuses on the semantics of words and concepts rather than on semantics at the text or discourse level, WordNet contains no relations that indicate the words' shared membership in a topic of discourse. For example, WordNet does not link *racquet, ball,* and *net* in a way that would show that these words, and the concepts behind them, are part of another concept that can be expressed by *court game.* Connecting *racquet, ball, net,* and *court game,* or *physician* and *hospital,* is a challenge for electronic dictionaries that Roger Chaffin (personal communication) has called the "tennis problem." The tennis problem is addressed in a number of the chapters in this volume. Several chapters explore the possibilities for deriving topical information from the lexical and conceptual relations encoded in WordNet. Hirst and St-Onge (chapter 13) describe an application of "lexical chains" (Morris and Hirst 1991), which are sequences of nouns in a context constructed on the basis of the semantic relations among the nouns; Al-Halimi and Kazman (chapter 14) construct "lexical trees" on a similar basis to derive topical information. Harabagiu and Moldovan (chapter 16) propose disambiguating the content words in the definitions of WordNet's synsets and describe a way to increase the semantic connections among the words; the resulting dense network allows them to extract topical information and establish text coherence.

NEW PERSPECTIVES, ENHANCEMENTS, AND APPLICATIONS

Besides semantic networks, there of course exist other ways of representing concepts and their semantic content. Priss, a mathematician working in the framework of formal concept analysis, casts WordNet in this format and takes it from there into relational concept analysis (chapter 7). Priss's approach is useful in a number of ways. Because it allows her to examine conceptual structures apart from lexical structures, formal concept analysis reveals differences between the two in the form of lexical gaps (Priss 1996). Her chapter demonstrates for the case of meronymy how the theoretical framework she adopts can be useful in finding irregularities in WordNet.

Many users of WordNet have lamented the lack of syntactic information that would match the detail of the semantic treatment in WordNet. Indeed, WordNet contains very little syntax, because it was conceived as a semantic database only. However, syntactic restrictions on adjectives are indicated (their position with respect to the head noun and attributive use only; see K. J. Miller, chapter 2). Syntax is most important for verbs, which can subcategorize for a variety of noun arguments, prepositional phrases, and sentential complements. Currently, frames providing basic information about transitivity and argument type are part of every verb synset, but little detail about the nature of these arguments is given. Applications in knowledge engineering (Burg and van de Riet, chapter 15) and inferencing (Harabagiu and Moldovan, chapter 16) especially would benefit from information linking verbs and nouns. Some users of WordNet rely on a syntactic database like COMLEX (Macleod, Grishman, and Meyers 1994) to complement the semantic information provided by WordNet. A strict division of these two aspects of the grammar of verbs is certainly artificial. Levin (1985, 1993) has amassed impressive evidence showing that the semantic makeup of verbs is intimately linked with their syntactic behavior.

Kohl, Jones, Berwick, and Nomura (chapter 6) have worked out an enhancement of the syntactic frames in WordNet by adopting Levin's (1993) classification of English verbs on the basis of syntactic alternations.

Kohl et al. focused on over 200 distinct sentence patterns. Their program generates more than 10,000 example sentences for over 2,600 word forms (over 3,000 senses) in WordNet. A particularly attractive feature of Kohl et al.'s work is that example sentences that are "bad" for a particular verb are generated as well (and marked as bad); these sentences indicate that verbs that are semantically similar in WordNet do not always share the same syntactic behavior. Kohl et al.'s work shows that the kind of semantic similarity on which WordNet is built differs from that which is regularly reflected in syntax, although there is significant overlap.

Another valuable addition to WordNet is Kohl et al.'s assignment of thematic roles to the nouns that occur in the sample sentences; the absence of thematic or semantic roles associated with nouns that are selected by verbs often presents an obstacle to applying WordNet to knowledge engineering or inferencing (for example, Burg and van de Riet (chapter 15) note that they manually added lists with full specifications for the semantic roles associated with the nouns in the verb frames). The next version of WordNet is expected to incorporate Kohl et al.'s work and make WordNet a more useful resource for linguistic research and natural language processing.

We are frequently asked why WordNet contains the particular conceptual-semantic and lexical relations that it does and not others. Some of the reasons for our choice or relations are discussed here and by G. A. Miller (chapter 1); WordNet is not likely to incorporate new relations in the future. But there is no reason to exclude the possibility of other relations in a WordNet that is customized for a particular purpose. Hearst (chapter 5) describes a method by which new relations can be automatically acquired from naturally occurring text. It is based on the examination of specific phrasal patterns like *such as* ... and *or other* ... that link hyponymically related nouns. Hearst's work is important not only in uncovering relations through textual analyses but also in showing some syntagmatic co-occurrence patterns of paradigmatically related words.

WORDS AND THEIR CONTEXTS

WordNet itself does not give any information about the context in which the word forms and senses occur. However, as Miller and Charles (1991) have pointed out, speakers' knowledge of words must consist not only of the meaning of the words but also of the contexts in which they can occur.

Knowing how a word interacts with other words in context is a requirement for knowing a word.

In order to provide contextual information about word forms and senses, a semantic concordance was created at the Princeton Cognitive Science Laboratory (Landes, Leacock, and Tengi, chapter 8). A semantic concordance is a database combining a text and a lexicon so that words in the text are linked to the appropriate senses in the lexicon. The semantic concordance can be viewed either as a text whose words are annotated with syntactic and semantic information, or as a lexicon containing example sentences for (most) word senses. In the case of the concordance described by Landes, Leacock, and Tengi, the lexicon is WordNet (version 1.5), and the texts are parts of the Standard Corpus of Present-Day Edited American English (the Brown Corpus; Kučera and Francis 1967) as well as the complete text of a novella. The concordance is a research tool that holds great potential for educational applications as well as for sense disambiguation.

Fellbaum, Grabowski, and Landes (chapter 9) describe some aspects of the semantic annotation process resulting in the concordance. They note that the fine-grainedness of WordNet's sense distinctions presented serious challenges to linguistically naive "taggers" who had to choose, from among the various senses of a polysemous word, the sense that applied to a given context in the Brown Corpus or the novella. Fellbaum, Grabowski, and Landes found that the taggers' confidence in selecting a sense generally matched the level of their performance. Performance was measured in terms of the agreement between the taggers' choice of the most appropriate sense for a given occurrence of a word and the choice of two experienced lexicographers. The naive taggers' performance, and their degree of confidence, depended on the number of senses of the polysemous words, their syntactic class membership, and the order in which the senses were presented.

The possible contexts in which a given word can occur are part of a word's meaning and therefore of speakers' knowledge about that word. Speakers make use of this contextual knowledge in disambiguating polysemous words. Thus, speakers interpret the meaning of *eat* in *What are you eating for dinner?* differently than in *What is eating you?* Resnik (chapter 10) addresses the question of selectional preferences of verbs for their direct arguments. He looks at the kinds of nouns that co-occur with verbs and classes these as members of a WordNet taxonomy, which is by definition a semantically unified domain. Selectional preferences can be characterized in terms of the probable class (WordNet hierarchy) membership of the nouns that co-occur with a given verb. Resnik finds that some verbs (such as *drink*) place stronger selectional constraints on their arguments than others, such as *enjoy*, which accepts a wide variety of nouns. In fact, Pustejovsky (1995) argues that the meaning of verbs like *enjoy* in a given sentence is partially determined by the nouns they co-occur with; he points out that *enjoy a cigar* denotes a different activity from *enjoy a meal* and *enjoy a book*.

SENSE DISAMBIGUATION

Although it is clear that speakers assign meanings to polysemous words on the basis of the contexts in which these words occur, the process of disambiguation is not yet precisely understood. Computers that are programmed to disambiguate can do reasonably well but fall short of performing at the same level as humans. Is topical context more important than local context? How large a local context do speakers need? That is, how big a "window" on either side of the polysemous word is required to disambiguate it? Leacock and Chodorow (chapter 11) test different approaches to automatic sense disambiguation on the polysemous verb *serve*. In three experiments involving local context, they compared the success of different classifiers in the disambiguation task. First, they found that a local context of six open-class words on either side of the target word yielded the best performance when both test and training data were large. In a second experiment they included in their test data words that are semantically related to words in the training data. Semantic similarity is measured in terms of distance between hierarchically related synsets in WordNet. Although the results here were less encouraging than in the first experiment, a third experiment combining local context and WordNet similarity measures yielded improved results.

INFORMATION RETRIEVAL

Sense disambiguation is crucial for a range of applications, such as automatic text or information retrieval. As Voorhees (chapter 12) explains, finding the desired document(s) in a large heterogeneous pool requires a successful match between the words in the search query and the document titles or abstracts. Voorhees explored WordNet's usefulness for matching words, but found that the difficulties presented by the need for sense resolution precluded any successful exploitation of the semantic information in WordNet. Only when the concepts (as expressed by WordNet synsets) were chosen manually so that the intended sense was known did the semantic relations encoded in WordNet improve correct retrieval.

SEMANTIC RELATIONS AND TEXTUAL COHERENCE

Hirst and St-Onge (chapter 13) are also concerned with context, in particular with the question of what constitutes a coherent context. On the assumption that a discourse tends to contain semantically related concepts, these authors use the notion of "lexical chain" (Morris and Hirst 1991) as a measure of coherence; a lexical chain is a cluster of nouns in a text that are linked via the relations in WordNet. Hirst and St-Onge apply the notion of lexical chain to the detection of malapropisms, defining a malapropism as a word referring to a concept that is not related to the other concepts referred to in the text. Using a measure of strength for the links in a chain, Hirst and St-Onge suggest that the greater the semantic distance between words in a text, the greater the likelihood of a malapropism.

Al-Halimi and Kazman, too, are interested in the question of information storage, indexing, and retrieval (chapter 14). They describe a method for automatically indexing transcripts of videoconferences by topics, rather than by keywords, and retrieving particular segments of the transcripts by matching them to queries using topical indexing. Al-Halimi and Kazman characterize topical information in terms of "lexical trees," a modification of Morris and Hirst's (1991) lexical chains. One of their innovations is the evaluation of the relative informativeness of semantic relations.

Hirst and St-Onge are among the many users of WordNet who have pointed out its lack of information about the semantic distance between two related words; WordNet makes no effort to weight the meaning differences. The authors cite the example *more stew than steak*, in which the pattern *more . . . than . . .* links semantically related words (similar patterns are discussed by Hearst in chapter 5). In this particular example, the two nouns are separated in WordNet by six synsets, which clearly does not reflect their true semantic distance. Speakers know that two of the hyponyms of *good person*, {*saint, holy man, holy person, angel*}, and {*plaster saint*} are very similar to each other, but that they are not as similar to a third hyponym, {*square shooter, straight arrow*}. Distinguishing and measuring the semantic relatedness of concepts is an area with important consequences for semantic disambiguation, for example. Hirst and St-Onge review work aimed at quantifying semantic distance between WordNet synsets. Their own work examines lexical chain links whose varying strengths depend on the relation between words in WordNet.

KNOWLEDGE ENGINEERING

Perhaps the most ambitious use to which WordNet has been put is knowledge engineering, represented by two chapters in this volume. Work in artificial intelligence requires large databases with rich lexical representations. As the contributions by Burg and van de Riet and by Harabagiu and Moldovan make clear, WordNet has the potential for significantly contributing to problems such as conceptual modeling and automatic inferencing; however, both pairs of authors had to substantially augment the information in WordNet to meet their goals. But the enhancements they require may point in the direction of future developments of the database.

Burg and van de Riet (chapter 15) explore the usefulness of WordNet for their linguistically based conceptual modeling environment, taking as an example a library and the objects and events associated with it. To achieve their ambitious goal of creating conceptual models, which requires sense disambiguation and language generation, Burg and van de Riet had to significantly augment WordNet, adding more subtly distinguished relations, function words, and thematic roles, and enriching the morphology. The authors distinguish three levels of linguistic and conceptual knowledge: a lexical level, which contains information about the synonyms, antonyms, and so on, of a word or concept; a domain level, which refers to the topic of the discourse; and an application-specific level, which relates objects and events. Thus, the domain level in their example is *library*; the lexical level tells us that a *book* is a *volume*; and the application-specific level contains the information that books can be lent. Presently, WordNet gives information only about the lexical level, and its usefulness for knowledge engineering is still limited.

Harabagiu and Moldovan (chapter 16) point out that modeling commonsense reasoning requires an extensive knowledge base with a very large number of concepts and relations. WordNet provides the former, but Harabagiu and Moldovan find its connection density insufficient to support inferencing. Their solution is to disambiguate the open-class words in the glosses that are part of most synsets and to establish relations among them, transforming the glosses into semantic networks, which include relations between different syntactic categories. The glosses become defining features along which "smart" markers propagate and generate inferences. In their example, a path between *hungry* and *refrigerator* is established because the markers collide at the node *food*, which is part of the semantic network of both *hungry* and *refrigerator*. Thus, an inference between being hungry and going to the refrigerator can be made.

We hope that the chapters discussing the theoretical foundations and contents of WordNet, as well as the applications highlighted here, will stimulate further research into the nature of conceptual and lexical relations and semantic networks, and inspire workers in linguistics, psycholinguistics, and all areas of natural language processing to test WordNet's usefulness as a research tool.

Notes

1. I am grateful to Rick Lewis for helpful advice and comments, and to Shari Landes and Randee Tengi for technical assistance.

2. Wilks, Slator, and Guthrie (1996) discuss some of the important questions concerning the automatic acquisition and subsequent exploitation of lexical data, in particular with reference to Procter's *Longman Dictionary of Contemporary English* (1978).

3. Wilks, Slator, and Guthrie (1996, 122) point out that, when lexicons are based on linguistic or psychological theories, the lexical representations tend to conform to the preexisting theories rather than vice versa. Clearly, though, some lexicons are built precisely to test certain theories and are therefore preferable to theory-free lexicons. Moreover, although Wilks, Slator, and Guthrie's criticism of theoretically biased lexicons specifically includes WordNet, we believe that its particular lexical contents do not differ substantially from those of standard dictionaries that are automatically acquired for language-understanding systems. Many of the lexical representations in WordNet turn out to conform to generally accepted, mainstream notions of the structure of the lexicon, although we arrived at them via different routes. Thus, the hierarchical structure of WordNet is contained in most standard dictionaries (Amsler 1980). Moreover, there is much evidence that people store conceptual knowledge in ways that resemble inheritance systems. See chapters 1 through 4 for detailed discussions of these points.

4. The exceptions are the relations between denominal adjectives and the nouns from which they are derived (*legal-lawyer*), and between adjectives such as *big* and the corresponding attribute (SIZE). Both these relations are described by K. J. Miller (chapter 2).

5. Burg and van de Riet (chapter 15) point out that distinguishing different kinds of semantic oppositions among verbs would allow one to relate not only verbs like *borrow* and *lend*, but also ones like *borrow* and *return*; these authors point out that both kinds of opposition (conversive and reversive) yield verb pairs with a salient connection.

References

Amsler, R. A. (1980). *The structure of the Merriam-Webster pocket dictionary.* Unpublished doctoral dissertation, University of Texas, Austin.

Chaffin, R., Hermann, D. J., and Winston, M. (1988). An empirical taxonomy of part-whole relations: Effects of part-whole relation type on relation identification. *Language and Cognitive Processes, 3,* 17–48.

Cramer, P. (1968). *Word association.* New York: Academic Press.

Cruse, D. A. (1986). *Lexical semantics.* Cambridge, England: Cambridge University Press.

Evens, M. (Ed.). (1988). *Relational models of the lexicon.* Cambridge, England: Cambridge University Press.

Fellbaum, C., and Miller, G. A. (1990). Folk psychology or semantic entailment? A reply to Rips and Conrad. *The Psychological Review, 97,* 565–570.

Fillenbaum, S., and Jones, L. V. (1965). Grammatical contingencies in word association. *Journal of Verbal Learning and Verbal Behavior, 4,* 248–255.

Fillmore, C. J., and Atkins, B. T. S. (1992). Towards a frame-based lexicon: The semantics of RISK and its neighbors. In A. Lehrer and E. Feder Kittay (Eds.), *Frames, fields, and contrasts,* 75–102. Hillsdale, NJ: Erlbaum.

Fillmore, C. J., and Atkins, B. T. S. (1994). Starting where the the dictionary stops: The challenge for computational lexicography. In B. T. S. Atkins and A. Zampolli (Eds.), *Computational approaches to the lexicon,* 349–393. New York: Oxford University Press.

Jackendoff, R. (1983). *Semantics and cognition.* Cambridge, MA: MIT Press.

Kay, M. (1989). The concrete lexicon and the abstract dictionary. In *Proceedings of the Fifth Annual Conference of the UW Centre for the New Oxford English Dictionary,* 35–41. Waterloo, Ontario, Canada: University of Waterloo, Centre for the New OED.

Kučera, H., and Francis, W. N. (1967). *The standard corpus of present-day edited American English* [the Brown Corpus]. (Electronic database.) Providence, RI: Brown University.

Lenat, D. B., and Guha, R. V. (1990). *Building Large Knowledge-based systems: Representation and inference in the CYC project.* Reading, MA: Addison-Wesley.

Levin, B. 1985. Introduction. In B. Levin (Ed.), *Lexical semantics in review,* 1–62. Cambridge, MA: MIT, Center for Cognitive Science.

Levin, B. (1993). *English verb classes and alternations.* Chicago: University of Chicago Press.

Macleod, C., Grishman, R., and Meyers, A. (1994). the Comlex syntax project: The first year. In *Proceedings of the ARPA Human Language Technology Workshop*, 8–12. San Francisco: Morgan Kaufmann.

Mel'čuk, I., and Zholkovsky, A. (1988). The explanatory combinatorial dictionary. In M. Evens (Ed.), *Relational models of the lexicon*, 41–74. Cambridge, England: Cambridge University Press.

Miller, G. A. (Ed.). (1990). *WordNet: An on-line lexical database.* Special issue of *International Journal of Lexicography*, 3(4).

Miller, G. A. (1995). WordNet: A lexical database for English. *Communications of the ACM, 38*(11), 39–41.

Miller, G. A., and Charles, W. G. (1991). Contextual correlates of semantic similarity. *Language and Cognitive Processes, 6*, 1–28.

Morris, J., and Hirst, G. (1991). Lexical cohesion computed by thesaural relations as an indicator of the structure of text. *Computational Linguistics, 17*, 21–48.

Priss, U. E. (1996). *Relational concept analysis: Semantic structures in dictionaries and lexical databases.* Unpublished doctoral dissertation, Technische Hochschule Darmstadt, Germany.

Procter, P.(Ed.). 1978. *Longman dictionary of contemporary English.* Harlow, Essex, England: Longman Group.

Pustejovsky, J. (1995). *The generative lexicon.* Cambridge, MA: MIT Press.

Rosenweig, M. R. (1970). International Kent-Rosanoff word association norms, emphasising those of French male and female students and French workmen. In L. Postman and G. Keppel (Eds.), *Norms of word association*, 95–176. New York: Academic Press.

Schank, R. C., and Abelson, R. P. (1977). *Scripts, plans, goals, and understanding.* Hillsdale, NJ: Erlbaum.

Wilks, Y., Slator, B., and Guthrie, L. (1996). *Electric words: Dictionaries, computers, and meanings.* Cambridge, MA: MIT Press.

Zernik, U. (Ed.). (1991). *Lexical acquisition: Exploiting on-line resources to build a lexicon.* Hillsdale, NJ: Erlbaum.

PART I
THE LEXICAL DATABASE

Chapter 1

Nouns in WordNet

George A. Miller

WordNet (version 1.5) contains almost 80,000 noun word forms organized into some 60,000 lexicalized concepts. Many of these nouns are
collocations; a few are artificial collocations invented for the convenience
of categorization. No special attempt has been made to include proper
nouns; on the other hand, since many common nouns once were names,
no serious attempt has been made to exclude them. In terms of coverage,
WordNet's goals differ little from those of a good standard college-level
dictionary, and the semantics of WordNet is based on the notion of word
sense that lexicographers have traditionally used in writing dictionaries.
It is in the organization of that information that WordNet aspires to
innovation.

WordNet is not a conventional dictionary that has been made readable
by a computer, although it contains much of the same information that is
found in the entries of machine-readable dictionaries. The lexical entries
of a conventional dictionary contain spelling, pronunciation, inflected and
derivative forms, etymology, part of speech, definitions and illustrative
uses of the alternative senses, synonyms and antonyms, special usage
notes, occasional line drawings or plates—a good dictionary is a remarkable store of information. Much of this information is usually omitted
when a dictionary is made machine readable, and even more is omitted in
WordNet. WordNet does not give pronunciation, derivative morphology,
etymology, usage notes, or pictorial illustrations. WordNet does, however, try to make the semantic relations between word senses more
explicit and easier to use.

The basic semantic relation in WordNet is synonymy. Sets of synonyms
(synsets) form the basic building blocks. Some progress has been made in
extracting sets of synonyms from thesauruses (Ravin 1992), but this work
has been done manually in WordNet. The notion of synonymy used in

WordNet does not entail interchangeability in all contexts; by that criterion, natural languages have few synonyms. The more modest claim is that WordNet synonyms can be interchanged in some contexts. To be careful, therefore, one should speak of synonymy relative to a context, but in order to facilitate the discussion this qualification will usually be presupposed, not asserted.

A synset is essentially what Sparck Jones (1964, 1986) calls a "run," which is the basic element in her theory of semantic classification. Sparck Jones selects a particular word form in a sentence and searches for other word forms that can be substituted for it without changing the way the sentence can be employed; a set of word forms that are interchangeable in some context constitutes a run. She uses this basic element differently, however. Sparck Jones builds a "synonymy system" on the assumption that two runs are similar if they have a word form in common. For example, *pellet* and *injection* would be similar because, given appropriate contexts, both can be substituted for *shot*. She speculates that some chain of runs might be found connecting any two words in the same part of speech. In WordNet, on the other hand, synsets are linked by semantic relations. Thus, the structure of the two systems is very different. In WordNet, for example, it happens to be the case that there is no path connecting the synset {shot, pellet} with the synset {shot, injection}.

Most synsets are accompanied by the kind of explanatory gloss that is provided in conventional dictionaries. But a synset is not equivalent to a dictionary entry. In particular, dictionary entries for polysemous words (words that can be used to express more than one meaning) have several different glosses, whereas a synset has only a single gloss. Thus, a dictionary entry can contain semantic information that, in WordNet, would be distributed over several distinct synsets, one for each meaning. It is convenient to think of a synset as representing a lexicalized concept of English. That is to say, a lexicalized concept is represented in WordNet by the set of synonyms that can be used (in an appropriate context) to express that concept.

Although synonymy is a semantic relation between word forms, the semantic relation that is most important in organizing nouns is a relation between lexicalized concepts. It is the relation of subordination (or class inclusion or subsumption), which in this context we will call *hyponymy*. For example, the noun *robin* is a hyponym (subordinate) of the noun *bird*, or, conversely, *bird* is a hypernym (superordinate) of *robin*. It is this semantic relation that organizes nouns into a lexical hierarchy.

1.1   LEXICAL HIERARCHY

Information about hyponymic relations between nouns is given in the definitional phrases of conventional dictionaries (Amsler 1980). As a simplified example, consider the North American sense of the noun *robin*. A conventional dictionary might define this sense by some such phrase as 'a migratory bird that has a clear melodious song and a reddish breast with gray or black upper plumage'. This exemplifies a common definitional formula for a noun. It consists of a hypernym or genus term (*bird*, in this example), preceded by adjectives or followed by relative clauses that describe how this instance differs from all other instances of that hypernym. (Note that the purpose of a lexical definition is to distinguish among hyponyms, not to enumerate all features of the word's referent.)

If this example is pursued, the appropriate sense for the noun *bird* might be defined as 'a warm-blooded egg-laying animal having feathers and forelimbs modified as wings'. Continuing, *animal* might be defined as 'an organism capable of voluntary movement and possessing sense organs and cells with noncellulose walls'. And *organism* might be defined as 'a living entity'. Thus, each hypernym leads on to a more generic hypernym. When we come to represent these relations in WordNet, however, we find that hypernymy cannot be represented as a simple relation between word forms. For example, when we say that *tree* is a kind of *plant*, we are not talking about tree graphs or manufacturing plants. Hypernymy is a relation between particular senses of words. That is to say, hypernymy is a relation between lexicalized concepts, a relation that is represented in WordNet by a pointer between the appropriate synsets.

Thus, a lexical hierarchy can be reconstructed by following the trail of hypernymically related synsets: {*robin*, *redbreast*} @→ {*bird*} @→ {*animal*, *animate_being*} @→ {*organism*, *life_form*, *living_thing*}, for example, where the brackets indicate a synset and @→ is the transitive, asymmetric, semantic relation that can be read 'IS-A' or 'IS-A-KIND-OF'. (By convention, @→ is said to point upward.) This design creates a sequence of levels, or a hierarchy, going from many specific terms at the lower levels to a few generic terms at the top.

A valuable consequence of representing hypernymy in this manner is that for each hypernymic relation we can add a corresponding hyponymic relation that points in the opposite direction. The hypernymic semantic relation that is represented in the WordNet source files by @→ goes from specific to generic and so is a generalization. Whenever it is the case that a noun synset S_s @$\rightarrow$ another noun synset S_g, there is always an inverse relation, $S_g \sim\rightarrow S_s$. That is to say, if S_g is the hypernym of S_s, then S_s is the hyponym of S_g. The inverse semantic relation, $\sim\rightarrow$, which can be read 'SUBSUMES', goes from generic to specific (from hypernym to hyponym) and so is a specialization.

Since a noun usually has a single hypernym, lexicographers include it in the definition; since a noun can have many hyponyms, lexicographers seldom list them. Similarly, in WordNet the generalization relation is coded explicitly in the source files by the labeled pointer, @$\rightarrow$, between synsets. When the WordNet source files are converted automatically into a lexical database, one step in this process is to insert inverse pointers for the specialization relation, $\sim\rightarrow$. In WordNet, therefore, moving toward more specific terms is as easy as moving toward more generic terms. Not only is the synset {*bird*} connected to its hypernym, but it will also return a list of all the different kinds of birds. By combining a generic step and a specific step, it is possible to find a list of terms coordinate with *bird*.

All of the information required to construct these relations is available in a conventional dictionary, but it is not presented there in a way that makes it easy to find. Given a machine-readable dictionary, however, it is possible for a computer to do much of the work of finding hypernyms and inferring hyponyms (Chodorow, Byrd, and Heidorn 1985). One program can be written to locate the genus terms in noun definitions and another program can grow a taxonomic tree from any root term by consulting the index of genus terms. In WordNet, however this work has been done manually.

What emerges from this manner of representing hyponymy and hypernymy is a lexical hierarchy, or tree diagram. It is a defining property of tree graphs that they branch from a single stem without forming circular loops. Of course, loops sometimes do arise inadvertently in conventional dictionaries. Every dictionary probably contains a few vacuous circles, instances where word W_a is used to define word W_b and W_b is also used to define W_a, and the pair of synonyms is left unrelated to anything else. But circularity is the exception, not the rule. The fundamental design that lexicographers try to impose on the semantic organization of nouns is not a circle, but a hierarchy.

Hierarchies of this sort are widely used by computer scientists as a means of representing knowledge (Sowa 1991). They have the advantage that information common to many items in the database need not be stored with every item. Computer scientists call such hierarchies inheritance systems, because they think of specific items inheriting information from their generic superordinates. That is to say, all of the properties of the superordinate are assumed to be properties of the subordinate as well; instead of being listed redundantly with both items, those properties are listed only with the superordinate.

Inheritance is most easily appreciated for names. If you are told that someone has a collie named Rex, *Rex* immediately inherits all the properties of collies. Consequently, it would be distinctly odd to ask whether Rex is capable of voluntary movement. Since you have been told that Rex is a collie and you know that collies are animals, you are expected to understand that Rex inherits all the properties that define *collie*, and voluntary movement is one of the attributes that *collie* inherits from *animal*. However, this lexical structure implies that a (linear) reasoning process must be a part of the process of lexical retrieval: "If Rex is a collie, then Rex is a dog; and if Rex is a dog, then Rex is an animal; and if Rex is an animal, then Rex is capable of voluntary movement."

A surprising amount of information can be inherited in this manner. For example, the detailed hypernyms of the North American robin in WordNet are *robin* @→ *thrush* @→ *oscine* @→ *passerine* @→ *bird*, so perching can be inherited from *passerine*, singing from *oscine*, and flying and migration from *thrush*. Not all of these features of robins need to be specified as features of *robin* (although in the mental dictionary of most people they probably are, since few people are familiar with these intermediate terms).

The nouns in WordNet form a lexical inheritance system; a systematic effort has been made to connect hyponyms with their hypernyms (and vice versa). WordNet assumes that a distinction can always be drawn between synonymy and hyponymy (but cf. Sparck Jones 1986). In practice, of course, this distinction is not always clear, although that lack of clarity causes no problem in conventional dictionaries. For example, a conventional dictionary can include in its entry for *board* the information that this word can be substituted for *surfboard* in some sentences. In addition to the generic meaning of *board*, there are hyponyms of this generic meaning that a conventional dictionary may treat as synonyms of different senses of *board*. If the information were entered this way in WordNet, a request for information about the hypernyms of {*board*} would elicit the same path twice, the only difference being that one path would be prefaced by {*surfboard, board2*} @→ {*board1*}. In WordNet, therefore, an effort has been made to avoid cases where a noun is its own hyponym; it is not made explicit that *board* is frequently used to refer to specific kinds of boards (surfboards, skateboards, chessboards, etc.).

WordNet presupposes a linguistic knowledge of anaphoric relations; for example, an anaphor can be a hypernym of its antecedent, as in *I thought it was a <u>robin</u> but the <u>bird</u> flew away before I could get close enough to be sure*. More generally, a hypernym can replace a more specific term whenever the context ensures that the substitution will not produce confusion.

1.2   UNIQUE BEGINNERS

One way to construe the hierarchical principle is to assume that all nouns are contained in a single hierarchy. In principle, it is possible to put some empty synset at the top: to make $\{\Lambda\}$ the hypernym of every synset that does not have a hypernym, thus pulling all nouns together into a single hierarchical structure. Then every synset but one would have a hypernym, and the single exception would be the unique beginner for all the others. This device is sometimes convenient when using the hierarchy to estimate semantic distances, since a path can then be traced between any two words or any two synsets. The lexical justification is tenuous, however, because these abstract generic concepts carry so little semantic information; it is doubtful that people could agree on appropriate words to express them.

WordNet divides the nouns into several hierarchies, each with a different unique beginner. These multiple hierarchies correspond to relatively distinct semantic fields, each with its own vocabulary. Since the features that characterize a unique beginner are inherited by all of its hyponyms, a unique beginner corresponds roughly to a primitive semantic component in a compositional theory of lexical semantics. Partitioning the nouns has one important practical advantage: it reduces the size of the files that lexicographers must work with and makes it possible to assign the writing and editing of different files to different people.

The problem, of course, is to decide what the primitive semantic components should be. Different workers make different choices; one important criterion is that, collectively, they should provide a place for every English noun. The lexical source files in WordNet use the set of 25 unique beginners that are listed in table 1.1. These hierarchies vary widely in size and are not mutually exclusive—some cross-referencing is required—but on the whole they cover distinct conceptual and lexical domains. They

Table 1.1
List of 25 unique beginners for noun source files

{act, activity}	{food}	{possession}
{animal, fauna}	{group, grouping}	{process}
{artifact}	{location}	{quantity, amount}
{attribute}	{motivation, motive}	{relation}
{body}	{natural object}	{shape}
{cognition, knowledge}	{natural phenomenon}	{state}
{communication}	{person, human being}	{substance}
{event, happening}	{plant, flora}	{time}
{feeling, emotion}		

were selected after considering the possible adjective-noun combinations that could be expected to occur (an analysis that was carried out by Philip N. Johnson-Laird).

Once these 25 unique beginners had been chosen, however, some natural groupings among them became apparent. For example, 8 were concerned with nouns denoting tangible things; 5 could be grouped as abstractions, and 3 more as psychological features. They could be arranged hierarchically as in figure 1.1. Accordingly, a small noun.Tops file was created in order to include these semantic relations in the system, which reduced the number of unique beginners to 11.

It is of interest that the 25 lexical source files are relatively shallow, that is to say, seem to have a limited number of levels of specialization. In theory, of course, there is no limit to the number of levels an inheritance system can have. Lexical inheritance systems, however, seldom go more than 10 or 12 levels deep, and the deepest examples usually contain technical distinctions that are not part of the everyday vocabulary. For example, a Shetland pony is a pony, a horse, an equid, an odd-toed ungulate, a placental mammal, a mammal, a vertebrate, a chordate, an animal, an organism, and an entity: 12 levels, half of them technical.

1.3 SOME PSYCHOLINGUISTIC ASSUMPTIONS

Although the general structure of noun hierarchies is generated by the hyponymy/hypernymy relations, it is not obvious how this knowledge is represented in a person's lexical memory. It seems reasonable to suppose that conceptual details are given by the features that distinguish one concept from another. For example, a robin is a bird that is colorful, sings,

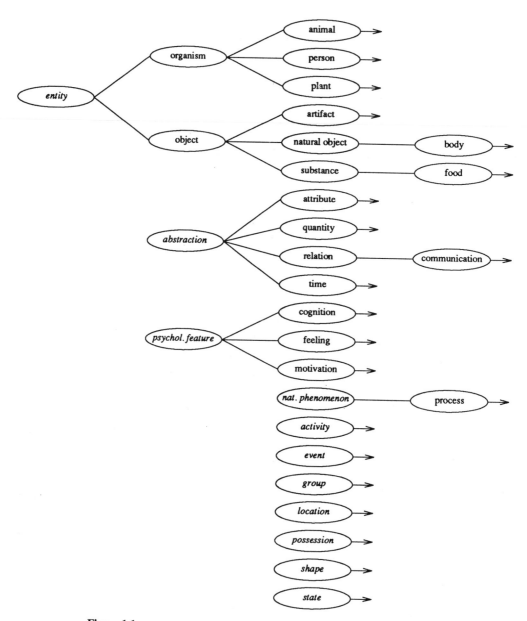

Figure 1.1
Diagrammatic representation of relations that reduce the 25 noun source files to 11 unique beginners. The unique beginners are italicized.

and flies, so not only must the word form *robin* be entered as a hyponym of *bird*, but the attributes of color and singing and flying must somehow be associated with *robin*. Moreover, {*robin*} must inherit from {*bird*} the fact that birds are warm-blooded vertebrates that have beaks, wings, and feathers, and that they lay eggs—so those features must somehow be associated with (or inherited by) {*bird*}. In order to make all of this information available when {*robin*} is activated, it must be possible to associate {*robin*} appropriately with at least three different kinds of distinguishing features (Miller 1991):

1. attributes: is redbreasted, (warm-blooded, vertebrate);
2. parts: has (beak, feathers, wings); and
3. functions: sings, flies, (lays eggs).

Although each kind of distinguishing feature should be treated differently (e.g., attributes are adjectives, parts are nouns, functions are verbs), most cognitive theories of how this knowledge is represented treat all features the same way. Given lists of such features associated with each synset, the simple approach is to define hyponymy as follows: when the features characterizing synset {*A*} are all included among the features characterizing synset {*B*}, but not vice versa, then {*B*} is a hyponym of {*A*}.

If hyponymy is defined in terms of features, then features become centrally important. For any given synset, its defining features must be individually necessary and jointly sufficient, and checking that one list of features is included in another list must be a basic cognitive operation. Many cognitive psychologists have doubted that all words can be so easily characterized by such lists of defining features.

Although most lexicographers and computer scientists find lexical hierarchies to be a natural way to represent the organization of nominal meanings, many cognitive scientists have expressed serious doubts about it. The doubts are not so much about the existence of hyponymic relations between lexicalized concepts as they are about the cognitive processes whereby such relations are realized in human lexical memory. The problems start to arise when one looks for experimental evidence that inclusion relations between lists of features actually exist in the minds of people who know and use these words.

In 1969 Collins and Quillian reported that the time required to verify the statement *A robin is a bird* is shorter than the time required to verify *A robin is an animal*. They suggested that their observation provided psychological evidence for the effect of distance in a lexical hierarchy: longer distances in the hierarchy take longer to traverse in thought. This possibility stimulated considerable research, in the course of which a number of problems arose that eventually led to serious questions about the cognitive reality of lexical hierarchies.

The objections were carefully summarized in 1981 by Smith and Medin, who referred to the featural explanation of hyponymy as the "classical view." It was found, for example, that the time required to verify that a chicken is a bird is significantly longer than the time required to verify that a robin is a bird, even though *chicken* and *robin* stand in the same taxonomic relation to *bird*. The problem is not that *robin* occurs more frequently than *chicken* (it does not), but simply that robins are more typical birds than chickens are. The classical view makes no allowance for typicality. Moreover, it is not even clear whether the classical theory should predict faster verification with immediate or with remote hypernyms; the immediate hypernym seems more similar (has more features in common), but fewer common features need to be verified with a remote hypernym. Experimental data collected subsequent to Collins and Quillian's (1969) experiment have been inconclusive.

Studies in which people are asked to rate typicality (Rips, Shoben, and Smith 1973; Rosch 1973) show that people agree consistently about typical instances and that the ratings have little to do with frequency or familiarity. Rosch argued that a concept is represented, not by a list of distinguishing features, but by the focal instances (or prototypes) that are the best examples of the concept. This point of view has been developed most extensively by Lakoff (1987), who makes it the basis for a general theory of human cognition.

Prototypicality theory need not be limited to a single exemplar. The lexicalized concept of "animal," for example, could hardly rest on a single prototype animal; one supposes that category membership must depend on a match to either a prototypical mammal or a prototypical bird or a prototypical fish. Thus, prototypicality theory accommodates disjunctive concepts, which are not allowed under the classical theory. Lakoff exemplifies this situation with the Dyirbal concept "balan," which includes women, fire, dangerous things, and several other items. Lakoff argues that disjunctive concepts are the rule, not the exception, and that they provide evidence for an alternative to the classical view.

Attacks on the classical explanation of lexical hierarchies were so persuasive in the mid-1980s when WordNet was first conceived that it seemed a reasonable prediction that we might discover some principled reason why such a scheme will not work. Indeed, we quickly convinced ourselves that verbs, adjectives, and adverbs are organized differently. But the hierarchical structure of the noun lexicon seems to fit linguistic facts despite the lack of a good explanation.

For example, the sentence *A pistol is more dangerous than a rifle* states a sensible comparison, but *A pistol is more dangerous than a gun* and *A gun is more dangerous than a pistol* are both uninterpretable (Bever and Rosenbaum 1970). There is apparently some linguistic prohibition against comparative constructions linking hypernyms and hyponyms. But such a prohibition could work only if the grammatical rule could apply to lexical hierarchies generally and if the hyponym-hypernym relation were immediately available to the linguistic processor.

Or, again, the sentence *I gave him a good novel, but the book bored him* is easily understood, whereas *I gave him a good novel, but the catsup bored him* is a puzzler. Because it is lexical knowledge that a novel is a book, the anaphoric coreference is acceptable. But a novel is not catsup, so the second sentence is unacceptable. There is apparently a linguistic convention that accepts anaphoric nouns that are hypernyms of the antecedent. But such a convention could not work unless knowledge of hypernymy were easily available.

Or, still again, there are selectional constraints for some verbs that hold for all hyponyms of a given noun (Resnik 1993). The direct object of the verb *drink*, for example, can be any hyponym of the noun *beverage*— which implies that the necessary hyponymic knowledge must be stored in a quickly retrievable manner.

So the hierarchical organization of nominal concepts appears to be a necessary feature of the mental dictionary. In spite of strong attacks on it as a cognitive theory, the hierarchical principle is important for the noun lexicon. But what about typicality? Perhaps typicality and hierarchy coexist. That is to say, more information must be stored with every lexicalized concept than is required to establish its position in a lexical hierarchy. Imagery or other mental models might be associated with lexicalized nouns without disrupting their hierarchical organization.

Undoubtedly hyponyms and hypernyms do share features of meaning, but associations based on shared features of meaning are only part of the associative structure of lexical knowledge. In addition to the associations between words that are interchangeable in a context, the mental dictionary includes associations between words that frequently occur together. In terms popular in the 1950s and 1960s (Jenkins 1954), WordNet provides a good account of paradigmatic associations, but contains almost nothing about syntagmatic associations. Since theories of association have always explained learning by co-occurrence more easily than learning by substitutability, this neglect of syntagmatic relations is hard for cognitive psychologists to accept.

To put the matter differently, WordNet suffers from what Roger Chaffin has called the "tennis problem" (Miller 1993). Suppose you wanted to learn the specialized vocabulary of tennis and asked where in WordNet you could find it. The answer would be everywhere and nowhere. Tennis players are in the `noun.person` file, tennis equipment is in `noun.artifact`, the tennis court is in `noun.location`, the various strokes are in `noun.act`, and so on. Nouns that co-occur in discussions of tennis are scattered around WordNet with nothing to pull them together. Other topics have similarly dispersed vocabularies. At least part of the dissatisfaction with a purely hierarchical organization of nouns can be attributed to this neglect of co-occurrence relations. If we knew how to add to each noun a distinctive representation of the contexts in which it is used (Miller and Charles 1991), WordNet would be much more useful. Although WordNet 1.5 lacks such information, the work on semantic tagging of text (see Landes, Leacock, and Tengi, this volume) is an attempt to remedy that deficiency. But the fact that there is more to know about a word than its location in a hierarchy of lexicalized concepts does not mean that lexical hierarchies are an unimportant part of the mental dictionary.

The organization of WordNet is provided by pointers that represent semantic relations, not by lists of features. As described so far, nouns in WordNet consist of synsets that are organized into hierarchies by pointers representing hyponymy and hypernymy. The relation {robin} @→ {bird} says merely *A robin is a kind of bird*. The featural information that plays such an important role in the classical view is provided in WordNet only by the explanatory glosses that accompany (nearly all) synsets. In WordNet, featural information does not define hyponymy or contribute to the noun hierarchy in any explicit way.

1.4 SOME THINGS NOT IN WORDNET

Though evidence exists for the cognitive reality of lexical hierarchies of nouns, it is still necessary to examine critically some of the ways a noun hierarchy has been realized. Various kinds of information that are available in a person's mental dictionary are not available in WordNet. For example, most people have information about exceptions: *A whale is not a fish*, *A penguin is not a bird that flies*, *A spider is not an insect*, and so on. The IS-NOT-A-(KIND-OF) relation is not used in WordNet, which is monotonic in the sense that adding a new lexical fact will not cause a contradiction.

A more serious problem, however, is that @→ actually represents more than one semantic relation. Wierzbicka (1984) has distinguished five kinds of hyponymic relations, but two of them seem particularly salient. One is the IS-A-KIND-OF relation that has been discussed in terms of *robin* and *bird*. When human artifacts are involved, however, another semantic relation, IS-USED-AS-A-KIND-OF, comes into play. Wierzbicka calls these hyponymies "taxonomic" and "functional," respectively; Pustejovsky (1991) has called them "formal" and "telic." For example, a poker (formally) is a metal rod that (telically) is used to stir burning logs. Sometimes the hypernym is purely formal (e.g., *A thrush is a bird*), and sometimes the hypernym is purely telic (e.g., *An adornment is a decoration*), but the puzzling cases are those in which both a formal and a telic hypernym are available.

There are three possibilities for dealing with this situation.

1. The most frequent case is to let @→ represent both formal and telic relations at the same time. For example, in the case of {*poker*} @→ {*fire_iron*}, both form and function are represented.

2. Another possibility is to point to more than one hypernym. For example, {*written_agreement*} @→ {*legal_document*} represents a formal relation and {*written_agreement*} @→ {*agreement*} represents a telic relation. Multiple hypernyms create what is sometimes called a "tangled" hierarchy (Fahlman 1979); something more than linear reasoning is required in order to infer that *written_agreement* is both a document and an agreement.

3. Finally, sometimes the hyponym can be split into two different synsets, one with a formal hypernym and the other with a telic hypernym. For example, {*chicken*} @→ {*bird*} is formal and {*chicken*} @→ {*food*} is telic. Together, they can be paraphrased as *Chicken is a bird that is used for food*, but again, something more than linear reasoning is required to derive that proposition.

Unfortunately, the noun files in WordNet were well developed before we realized the importance of this distinction.

WordNet draws no explicit distinctions between proper and common nouns, or between mass and count nouns. After reading the excellent discussion by Quirk et al. (1985, chap. 5), we decided that so many nouns can be reclassified in context that the task of coding their status was too difficult for inclusion.

Moreover, WordNet does not attempt to identify what have been called "basic-level" categories or "generic" concepts (Berlin, Breedlove, and Raven 1966, 1973). Rosch (1975; Rosch et al. 1976) extended and elaborated this generalization: for concepts at the basic level, which is usually somewhere in the middle of the lexical hierarchy, people can list many distinguishing features. Above the basic level, descriptions are brief and general. Below the basic level, little is added to the features that distinguish basic concepts. For example, *furniture* has only the most general definition, whereas *chair* can be defined in great detail, and *throne* differs from *chair* only in minor ways. Thus, "chair" would be a basic-level concept. These observations have been made largely for the names of concrete, tangible objects, but some cognitive scientists have argued that a basic or primary level should be a feature of every lexical hierarchy (Hoffmann and Ziessler 1983; Lakoff 1987).

Some claims have been made that the basic level is where the parts of something can be specified (Tversky and Hemenway 1984), which might explain why tests of this hypothesis have been concerned primarily with words denoting physical objects. Unfortunately, we were not always able to identify a basic-level concept, even for hyponyms of {*entity*}, and nothing similar seems to hold for nouns subsumed under the other unique beginners.

Finally, there are not enough different semantic relations in WordNet. Other accounts (Cruse 1986; Mel'čuk and Zholkovsky 1988) have employed many more. WordNet was limited to what were believed to be the semantic relations of broadest applicability and greatest familiarity. At the same time it was hoped that the chosen set of semantic relations would suffice to individuate the meaning of each synset. When WordNet was first conceived, therefore, it was not intended to include definitional glosses. It was hoped that synonyms would disambiguate one another and that, for nouns, information about hypernyms and hyponyms would provide additional disambiguating information. For good measure, pointers representing the semantic relations of meronymy (part-whole relations) and antonymy (opposition of meaning) would also be included. The (somewhat idealistic) hope was that the definition of any word could be inferred from its position in this network of semantic relations and that definitional glosses would be redundant.

As WordNet grew and finer distinctions were required, it became obvious that we had not included enough different kinds of semantic relations to characterize all of the differentiae that are needed. Moreover, it was much easier to read a definitional gloss than to try to infer it from the array of pointers associated with each synset. Therefore, explanatory phrases have been added to most synsets. These are marked off from the rest of the synset by parentheses. The parenthetical glosses serve to keep the several senses of polysemous words distinct, but redundancy is apparent, for example, between the hypernymic concepts, indicated by @→, and the genus words of the defining gloss. If more distinguishing features could be indicated by pointers representing additional semantic relations, the glosses would become even more redundant. An imaginable test of the system would then be to write a computer program that would synthesize glosses from the information provided by the pointers.

1.5 PARTS AND MERONYMY

In addition to the formal and telic roles of nouns, Pustejovsky (1991) proposes what he calls a "constitutive" role, which deals with the relation between an object and its constituents or proper parts. Since the constitutive relation is one between a noun that denotes the whole and the nouns that denote its parts, this noun-noun relation is readily represented in WordNet's noun files.

The part-whole relation between nouns is generally considered to be a semantic relation, called *meronymy* (from the Greek *meros* 'part'; Cruse 1986), comparable to synonymy, antonymy, and hyponymy. This relation also has an inverse: if S_m is a meronym of S_h, then S_h is said to be a *holonym* of S_m. The conventional test phrases are *is a part of* or *has a*. If W_m *is a part of* W_h is acceptable, then W_m is a meronym of W_h; if W_h *has a W_m (as a part)* is acceptable, then W_h is a holonym of W_m.

In WordNet meronymy is found primarily in the noun.body, noun.artifact, and noun.quantity files. For concrete objects like bodies and artifacts, meronyms can help to define a basic level. No such level is apparent for terms denoting quantities, however, where small units of measurement are parts of larger units at every level of the hierarchy.

Meronymy is often compared to hyponymy: both are asymmetric and (with reservations) transitive, and both can relate terms hierarchically (Miller and Johnson-Laird 1976). That is to say, parts can have parts: a finger is a part of a hand, a hand is a part of an arm, an arm is a part of a body. If one starts with some complex whole, like {*automobile*} or {*human_body*}, it can be broken down into several levels of meronyms, but many of those meronyms will also be meronyms of other wholes. That is to say, some components serve as parts of many different things: think of all the different mechanisms that have gears. Tangled hierarchies are relatively rare when hyponymy is the semantic relation; in meronymic hierarchies, on the other hand, they are common. *Point*, for example, is a meronym of *arrow, awl, dagger, fishhook, harpoon, icepick, knife, needle, pencil, pin, sword*, and *tine*, and *handle* has an even greater variety of holonyms. Since the points and handles involved are so different from one holonym to the next, it is remarkable that this situation causes as little confusion as it does.

Since meronyms are distinguishing features that hyponyms can inherit, meronymy and hyponymy become intertwined in complex ways. For example, if {*beak*} and {*wing*} are meronyms of {*bird*}, and if {*robin*} is a hyponym of {*bird*}, then, by inheritance, {*beak*} and {*wing*} must also be meronyms of {*robin*}. Although the connections may appear complex when dissected in this manner, they are rapidly deployed in language comprehension. For example, most people do not even notice the inferences required to establish a connection between the following sentences: *It was a robin. The beak was injured.*

The relations between meronymy and hyponymy are further complicated by the fact that parts are hyponyms as well as meronyms. For example, {*beak, bill, neb, nib*} is a not only a meronym of {*bird*}, it is a hyponym of {*jaw*}, which in turn is a meronym of {*skull*} and a hyponym of {*skeletal_structure*}. A frequent problem in establishing the proper relation between hyponymy and meronymy arises from a general tendency to attach parts too high in the hierarchy. For example, if {*wheel*} is said to be a meronym of {*vehicle*}, then sleds cannot be vehicles. In WordNet a special synset was created for the intermediate concept, {*wheeled_vehicle*}.

An important caveat is that the *is a part of* construction is not always a reliable test of meronymy. People will accept the test frame W_m *is a part of* W_h for a variety of part-whole relations. For example, in many instances transitivity is limited. Thus, Lyons (1977) notes that *handle* is a meronym of *door* and *door* is a meronym of *house*, yet it sounds odd to say *The house has a handle* or *The handle is a part of the house*. Winston, Chaffin, and Hermann (1987) take such failures of transitivity to indicate that different part-whole relations are involved in the two cases. For example, *The branch is a part of the tree* and *The tree is a part of the forest* do not imply *The branch is a part of the forest* because the *branch/tree* relation is not the same as the *tree/forest* relation. For Lyons's example, they suggest, following Cruse (1986), that *is a part of* is sometimes used where *is attached to* would be more appropriate: *is a part of* should be transitive, whereas *is attached to* is clearly not. *The house has a door handle* is acceptable because it negates the implicit inference in *The house has a handle* that the handle is attached to the house.

Such observations raise questions about how many different IS-A-PART-OF relations there are. Winston, Chaffin, and Hermann (1987) differentiate six types of meronyms: component-object (*branch/tree*), member-collection (*tree/forest*), portion-mass (*slice/cake*), stuff-object (*aluminum/airplane*), feature-activity (*paying/shopping*), and place-area (*Princeton/New Jersey*). Chaffin, Hermann, and Winston (1988) add a seventh: phase-process (*adolescence/growing up*). But Iris, Litowitz, and Evens (1988) distinguish only four: functional part (*wheel/bicycle*), segment (*slice/loaf*), member (*sheep/flock*), and subset (*meat/food*). Meronymy is obviously a complex set of semantic relations, and there is considerable disagreement about how to distinguish among them.

Only three types of meronymy are coded in WordNet:

$W_m \#p \rightarrow W_h$ indicates that W_m is a component part of W_h,
$W_m \#m \rightarrow W_h$ indicates that W_m is a member of W_h, and
$W_m \#s \rightarrow W_h$ indicates that W_m is the stuff that W_h is made from.

Of these three, the IS-A-COMPONENT-OF relation, represented by $\#p$ in WordNet, is by far the most frequent, and so it has been used as the default when the type of meronymy is not obviously one of these three.

1.6 ANTONYMY

The strongest psycholinguistic indication that two words are antonyms is that each is given on a word association test as the most common response to the other (Deese 1965). For example, if people are asked for the first word they think of (other than the probe word itself) when they hear *victory*, most will respond *defeat*; when they hear *defeat*, most will respond *victory*. Such oppositions are most common for deadjectival nouns: the nouns *happiness* and *unhappiness* are antonyms because they derive from the antonymous adjectives, *happy* and *unhappy*. These deadjectival nouns occur primarily as hyponyms of {*attribute*}, and their relation to the adjectives that provide values of the attributes is discussed below.

Semantic opposition is not a fundamental organizing relation between nouns, but it does exist and so merits its own representation in WordNet. For example, both [{*man*} !→ {*woman*}] and [{*woman*} !→ {*man*}] are entered in the source files; the exclamation point represents the antonymy relation and the square brackets indicate the particular word forms that enter into this semantic relation. However, this opposition is not inherited by all the hyponyms of {*man*} and {*woman*}; the opposition must be entered separately for every male/female pair of words.

Perhaps the most interesting observation about antonymous nouns is that noun antonyms nearly always have the same hypernym, often the same immediate hypernym.

1.7   ATTRIBUTES AND MODIFICATION

Values of attributes are expressed by adjectives. For example, SIZE and COLOR are attributes of robins: the size of robins might be described by the adjective *small*, and the color associated with robins can be described by the adjective *red*. There is a stable association between the nouns *size* and *color*, which denote attributes, and the adjectives *small* and *yellow*, which provide values of those attributes. Nouns can be said to serve as arguments for attributes: SIZE(*robin*) = *small*, or COLOR(*robin*) = *red*. The value of the attribute SIZE when applied to robins is *small*; the value of the attribute COLOR when applied to robins is *red*.

It might be possible to incorporate into WordNet an association between {*robin*} and {*red*} that would constitute a kind of selectional restriction for the adjective *red*. Such associations have not been incorporated, since they are semantically complex. What is straightforward, however, is the connection between the attribute and the adjectives that express values of that attribute: between the noun *size* and the adjectives *large* and *small*; between the noun *color* and the adjectives *red*, *yellow*, *green*, and so on. Many of those associations have been incorporated into WordNet.

Although we have not undertaken the project, it should be possible to collect a large corpus of adjective-noun pairs and, using the adjective-attribute connections encoded in WordNet, induce the important attributes of various nouns. For example, a dog can be friendly or unfriendly because friendliness is an attribute of dogs, but *stingy dog* or *shallow dog* must be interpreted figuratively, since generosity and depth are not normal canine attributes. Keil (1979, 1983) has proposed that children learn the hierarchical structure of nominal concepts by observing what can and cannot be predicated at each level. For example, children may learn the important semantic distinction between animate and inanimate nouns by observing that the adjectives *dead* and *alive* can be predicated of one class of nouns but not the other.

Where adjectival modification plays a major role in WordNet is in the formation of collocations or compounds that differentiate lexical concepts that are more specific than the basic level. For example, adjectives can elaborate the basic concept {*chair*} as *easy chair, electric chair, straight chair*, or *high chair*. Modification by nouns that are pressed into service as adjectives is even more productive: *barber chair, beach chair, camp chair, deck chair, lawn chair*, and so on. It is generally the case that a collocation of the form *modifier + noun* will be a hyponym of that noun, although there are many exceptions. Even though the supply of such collocations seems inexhaustible, an effort has been made to include them in WordNet because they are nearly always less polysemous than their hypernym.

1.8   SIMILAR MEANINGS OF POLYSEMOUS NOUNS

In most dictionaries similar meanings of a polysemous word, or meanings that have similar etymologies, are grouped together. The result is that alternative meanings are organized in a tree having two or three levels. One advantage of such groupings is that they permit some control over the degree of refinement in drawing sense distinctions. If gross distinctions are all you need, you can consider only the main headings; if fine distinctions are required, use the whole set of alternative definitions.

The interface to WordNet 1.5 orders the meanings of polysemous nouns according to their relative frequencies of occurrence in the passages that have been semantically tagged (see Landes, Leacock, and Tengi, this volume). It would be possible, of course, to go through the polysemous nouns in WordNet (some 15,000 of them) and manually insert connections between similar meanings, thus creating two levels of meaning refinement. Not only would that be an enormous task, but it would require very delicate semantic judgments that no two people would be likely to agree about—one of the major differences between conventional dictionaries lies in the way they distinguish and group the senses of polysemous words (Atkins and Levin 1991).

In this situation, Philip N. Johnson-Laird (personal communication) proposed a principled way to group similar meanings. He pointed out that if two meanings of a word are similar, then the meanings of their hyponyms should also be similar in the same way. For example, if two senses of the noun *fish* are related as an animal and as a food, then all the matching hyponyms for these two senses of *fish* (which includes *perch*, *sole*, *bass*, etc.) will also bear that relation. That is to say, since one sense of *perch1* is a hyponym of the animal *fish1* and another sense of *perch2* is a hyponym of the food *fish2*, it should be the case that these two senses of *perch* are also related as an animal and its edible flesh. A pair of hyponyms related in this way were called *cousins*.

The task, then, is to identify nodes holding similarity relations as high up in the noun hierarchy as possible. In the case of { *fish1* } and { *fish2* }, we can go still higher, up to the *food* and *animal* nodes. Any matching hyponyms of these two nodes are candidates for classification as similar meanings. A preliminary list of about a dozen candidates illustrating cousinhood was prepared to test the idea, and Claudia Leacock assumed responsibility for implementing this suggestion in WordNet.

It soon became clear that a mechanism for marking exceptions would be necessary. To continue with the same example, one hyponym of *animal* is *coral*, which grows into ocean reefs; *coral* is also a hyponym of *food*, referring to lobster roe. Clearly, these two matching hyponyms of *animal* and *food* are not instances of an animal and its edible flesh. Therefore, once a productive rule governing cousinhood is found, the matching hyponyms are checked manually, exceptions are noted, and a list of exceptions is created.

Once the notion of grouping by rule had been proposed, two other bases for grouping seemed worth adding. One is called *sisters*, the other, *twins*. The sister relation is the usual one encountered when working with tree structures: sisters are word forms (either simple words or collocations) that are both immediate hyponyms of the same node. The assumption is that if two identical strings share the same hypernym, then their meanings are similar. For example, the noun *flounder* can refer to different kinds of flatfish, so two senses of *flounder* are grouped together as having similar meanings.

The second basis for grouping, the twins, is based on the assumption that if two synsets share the same word forms, then their senses are similar. Twins are defined as synsets that have three or more words in common. For example, one sense of *duo* is a musical group and another is a musical composition. Both synsets contain {*duo, duet, duette*}.

The grouping of similar meanings is a recent addition to WordNet; it has been implemented only for nouns, and coverage is by no means complete. As with every aspect of WordNet, the work continues. In WordNet 1.5, cousin relations for over 100 node pairs have been identified. The interface provides grouped meanings as an option and is an alternative to ordering the meanings by frequency of occurrence. For example, the fish and food meanings of *sole* are grouped together, distinct from the meaning of *sole* as a part of the foot. Transitivity is used to combine groups of similar senses.

This strategy does not provide as much grouping of meanings in WordNet as is found in most conventional dictionaries, but it does have the advantage of being relatively well defined.

1.9   CONCLUSION

In earlier descriptions of WordNet (Beckwith et al. 1991; Miller et al. 1990), it was suggested that WordNet is based on psycholinguistic principles in the same sense that the *Oxford English Dictionary* is based on historical principles. That claim has not borne the fruit that was expected at the time it was first made. The fact is that WordNet has been largely ignored by psycholinguists; computational linguists have found it far more interesting. Since both groups have been primarily interested in the semantics of nouns, the different reception is interesting.

First, however, the claim is not false. WordNet is organized conceptually, not alphabetically, and its realization as a computer database resembles a dynamic system more closely than does a printed book. The basic analysis of the vocabulary seems to match evidence from selective impairments in brain-damaged subjects (Caramazza et al. 1994). No one has denied the existence of the hierarchical families of lexicalized concepts that nouns can be used to express, and there is good behavioral evidence that people appreciate and use the semantic relations of synonymy, antonymy, hypernymy, and meronymy in spoken and written communication.

Psycholinguists, however, do not regard these features of WordNet as principles that can be used to explain the psychological bases of human language. They are, rather, something that needs to be explained— presumably in terms of more basic cognitive processes. There may even be a tendency to feel that if some particular psychological theory does not explain one of these features, that feature is not really important. Computational linguists, on the other hand, see WordNet as a promising component of systems that will be able to process language in useful ways, perhaps even to understand it. The ontology implicit in the noun hierarchies has received special attention from computational linguists, whereas most psycholinguists tend to emphasize additional word knowledge that is not explicit in a lexical hierarchy.

Development of the nouns in WordNet has therefore been driven far more by potential applications to computational linguistics than by advances in theories of cognitive psychology. Perhaps this outcome should have been foreseen. After all, a dictionary based on historical principles contributed little to the study of history.

References

Amsler, R. A. (1980). *The structure of the Merriam-Webster pocket dictionary.* Unpublished doctoral dissertation, University of Texas, Austin.

Atkins, B. T. S., and Levin, B. (1991). Admitting impediments. In U. Zernik (Ed.), *Lexical acquisition: Exploiting on-line resources to build a lexicon*, 233–262. Hillsdale, NJ: Erlbaum.

Beckwith, R., Fellbaum, C., Gross, D., and Miller, G. A. (1991). WordNet: A lexical database organized on psycholinguistic principles. In U. Zernik (Ed.), *Lexical acquisition: Exploiting on-line resources to build a lexicon*, 211–232. Hillsdale, NJ: Erlbaum.

Berlin, B., Breedlove, D., and Raven, P. H. (1966). Folk taxonomies and biological classification. *Science, 154*, 273–275.

Berlin, B., Breedlove, D., and Raven, P. H. (1973). General principles of classification and nomenclature in folk biology. *American Anthropologist, 75*, 214–242.

Bever, T. G., and Rosenbaum, P. S. (1970). Some lexical structures and their empirical validity. In R. A. Jacobs and P. S. Rosenbaum (Eds.), *Readings in English transformational grammar*, 3–50. Waltham, MA: Ginn.

Caramazza, A., Hillis, A., Leek, E. C., and Miozzo, M. (1994). The organization of lexical knowledge in the brain: Evidence from category- and modality-specific deficits. In L. Hirschfeld and S. Gelman (Eds.), *Mapping the mind: Domain specificity in cognition and culture*, 68–84. New York: Cambridge University Press.

Chaffin, R., Hermann, D. J., and Winston, M. (1988). An empirical taxonomy of part-whole relations: Effects of part-whole relation type on relation identification. *Language and Cognitive Processes, 3,* 17–48.

Chodorow, M. S., Byrd, R. J., and Heidorn, G. E. (1985). Extracting semantic hierarchies from a large on-line dictionary. In *Procedings of the 23rd Annual meeting of the Association for Computational Linguistics,* 299–304. Association for Computational Linguistics.

Collins, A. M., and Quillian, M. R. (1969). Retrieval time from semantic memory. *Journal of Verbal Learning and Verbal Behavior, 8,* 240–247.

Cruse, D. A. (1986). *Lexical semantics.* New York: Cambridge University Press.

Deese, J. (1965). *The structure of associations in language and thought.* Baltimore: Johns Hopkins Press.

Fahlman, S. E. (1979). *NETL: A system for representing and using real-world knowledge.* Cambridge, MA: MIT Press.

Hoffmann, J., and Ziessler, C. (1983). Objektidentifikation in künstlichen Begriff-shierarchien. *Zeitschrift für Psychologie, 191,* 135–167.

Iris, M. A., Litowitz, B. E., and Evens, M. (1988). Problems of the part-whole relation. In M. Evens (Ed.), *Relational models of the lexicon,* 261–288. New York: Cambridge University Press.

Jenkins, J. J. (1954). Word associations in the study of language structure. In C. E. Osgood and T. A. Sebeok (Eds.), *Psycholinguistics: A survey of theory and research problems,* 114–116. Memoir 10 of the *International Journal of American Linguistics.*

Keil, F. C. (1979). *Semantic and conceptual development: An ontological perspective.* Cambridge, MA: Harvard University Press.

Keil, F. C. (1983). On the emergence of semantic and conceptual distinctions. *Journal of Experimental Psychology: General, 121,* 357–385.

Lakoff, G. (1987). *Women, fire, and dangerous things: What categories reveal about the mind.* Chicago: Univeristy of Chicago Press.

Lyons, J. (1977). *Semantics.* 2 vols. New York: Cambridge University Press.

Mel'čuk, I., and Zholkovsky, A. (1988). The explanatory combinatorial dictionary. In M. Evens (Ed.), *Relational models of the lexicon,* 41–74. New York: Cambridge University Press.

Miller, G. A. (1991). Lexical echoes of perceptual structure. In G. R. Lockhead and J. R. Pomerantz (Eds.), *The perception of structure,* 249–261. Washington, DC: American Psychological Association.

Miller, G. A. (1993). The association of ideas. *The General Psychologist, 29,* 69–74.

Miller, G. A., Beckwith, R., Fellbaum, C., Gross, D., and Miller, K. J. (1990). Introduction to WordNet: An on-line lexical database. *International Journal of Lexicography, 3,* 235–244.

Miller, G. A., and Charles, W. G. (1991). Contextual correlates of semantic similarity. *Language and Cognitive Processes, 6,* 1–28.

Miller, G. A., and Johnson-Laird, P. N. (1976). *Language and perception.* Cambridge, MA: Harvard University Press.

Pustejovsky, J. (1991). The Generative Lexicon. *Computational Linguistics, 17,* 409–441.

Quirk, R., Greenbaum, S., Leech, G., and Svartvik, J. (1985). *A comprehensive grammar of the English language.* London: Longman.

Ravin, Y. (1992). Synonymy from a computational point of view. In A. Lehrer and E. Feder Kittay (Eds.), *Frames, fields, and contrasts: New essays in semantic and lexical organization,* 397–419. Hillsdale, NJ: Erlbaum.

Resnik, P. S. (1993). *Selection and information: A class-based approach to lexical relationships.* Unpublished doctoral dissertation, University of Pennsylvania, Philadelphia.

Rips, L. J., Shoben, E. J., and Smith, E. E. (1973). Semantic distance and the verification of semantic relations. *Journal of Verbal Learning and Verbal Behavior, 12,* 1–20.

Rosch, E. (1973). On the internal structure of perceptual and semantic categories. In T. E. Moore (Ed.), *Cognitive development and the acquisition of language,* 111–144. New York: Academic Press.

Rosch, E. (1975). Cognitive representations of semantic categories. *Journal of Experimental Psychology, 104,* 192–233.

Rosch, E., Mervis, C. B., Gray, W., Johnson, D., and Boyes-Braem, P. (1976). Basic objects in natural categories. *Cognitive Psychology, 8,* 382–439.

Smith, E. E., and Medin, D. L. (1981). *Categories and concepts.* Cambridge, MA: Harvard University Press.

Sowa, J. F. (Ed.). (1991). *Principles of semantic networks: Explorations in the representation of knowledge.* San Mateo, CA: Morgan Kaufmann.

Sparck Jones, K. (1964). *Synonymy and semantic classification.* Unpublished doctoral dissertation, Univeristy of Cambridge, England.

Sparck Jones, K. (1986). *Synonymy and semantic classification.* Edinburgh: Edinburgh University Press.

Tversky, B., and Hemenway, K. (1984). Objects, parts, and categories. *Journal of Experimental Psychology: General, 113,* 169–193.

Wierzbicka, A. (1984). Apples are not a "kind of fruit." *American Ethnologist, 11,* 313–328.

Winston, M. E., Chaffin, R., and Hermann, D. J. (1987). A taxonomy of part-whole relations. *Cognitive Science, 11,* 417–444.

Chapter 2
Modifiers in WordNet

Katherine J. Miller

All languages provide some means of modifying or elaborating the meanings of words, although they differ in the syntactic forms that such modification can assume. In English such modification is primarily associated with the syntactic categories Adjective and Adverb. Adjectives modify the senses of nouns. Adverbs are left with the responsibility for modifying everything else: verbs, adjectives, other adverbs, and entire clauses or sentences.

2.1 ADJECTIVES

Adjectives are words whose sole function is to modify nouns (e.g., *large* and *comfortable* in *a large chair, a comfortable chair*). In addition, English allows words belonging to other syntactic categories to function as adjectives. Nouns are frequently used as adjectives (*kitchen chair, barber chair*), as are present and past participles of verbs (*the creaking chair, the overstuffed chair*). Nouns can also be modified by prepositional phrases (*chair by the window, chair with green upholstery*) and even by entire clauses (*the chair that you bought at the auction*).

WordNet (version 1.5) contains 16,428 adjective synsets (synonym sets), including many nouns, participles, and prepositional phrases that function frequently as modifiers (e.g., *home*, as in *home cooking* or *home office*). WordNet divides adjectives loosely into two categories. *Descriptive adjectives* (e.g., *big, beautiful, interesting, possible, married*) constitute by far the larger category. The second category is called *relational adjectives* simply because they are related by derivation to nouns. (For example, *electrical* in *electrical engineer* is related to the noun *electricity*.) Each class of adjectives, descriptive and relational, displays typical semantic and syntactic properties, but the distinctions are not always clear-cut and in WordNet the categories tend to overlap.

2.1.1. Descriptive Adjectives

Descriptive adjectives are what one usually thinks of when adjectives are mentioned. Put somewhat simplistically, a descriptive adjective typically ascribes to a noun a value of an attribute. That is to say, x *is Adj* presupposes that there is an attribute A such that $A(x) = Adj$. To say *The package is heavy* presupposes that there is an attribute WEIGHT such that WEIGHT($package$) = $heavy$. Thus, *heavy* and *light* are values for the attribute WEIGHT. WordNet contains pointers between descriptive adjectives and the nouns by which appropriate attributes are lexicalized.

2.1.1.1 Antonymy   The semantic organization of descriptive adjectives is unique to them and entirely different from that of the other major categories. Nothing like the hyponymic relation that generates nominal hierarchies is available for adjectives: it is not clear what it would mean to say that one adjective "is a kind of" some other adjective. Instead, the basic semantic relation among descriptive adjectives is antonymy. The importance of antonymy first became obvious from results obtained with word association test: when the probe is a familiar adjective, the response commonly given by adult speakers is its antonym. For example, to the probe *good*, the common response is *bad*; to *bad*, the most frequent response is *good*. This mutuality of association is a salient feature of the data for descriptive adjectives (Deese 1964, 1965). It seems to be acquired as a consequence of these pairs of words being used together in the same phrases and sentences (Charles and Miller 1989; Justeson and Katz 1991a, b).

This importance of antonymy in the organization of descriptive adjectives is understandable when one recognizes that the function of these adjectives is to express values of attributes and that attributes tend to be bipolar. Antonymous adjectives express opposing values of an attribute. For example, the antonym of *heavy* is *light*, which expresses a value at the opposite pole of the WEIGHT attribute. In WordNet this binary opposition is represented by reciprocal labeled pointers meaning 'IS-ANTONYMOUS-TO' and is displayed to the WordNet user as *heavy* (*vs. light*) and *light* (*vs. heavy*).

This account suggests two closely related questions, which can serve to organize the following discussion.

1. When two adjectives have closely similar meanings, why do they not have the same antonym? For example, why do *heavy* and *weighty*, which are closely similar in meaning, have different antonyms, *light* and *weightless*, respectively?

2. If antonymy is so important, why do many descriptive adjectives seem to have no antonym? For example, continuing with WEIGHT, what is the antonym of *ponderous*? To the suggestion that *light* is the antonym of *ponderous*, the reply must be that the antonym of *light* (in the appropriate sense) is *heavy*. Is some different semantic relation (other than antonymy) involved in the subjective organization of the rest of the adjectives?

The first question caused serious problems for WordNet, which was initially conceived as using labeled pointers between synsets in order to represent semantic relations between lexical concepts. But it is not appropriate to introduce antonymy by labeled pointers between the synsets, for example, between {*heavy, weighty, ponderous*} and {*light, weightless, airy*}. People who know English judge *heavy/light* to be antonyms, and perhaps *weighty/weightless*, but they pause and are puzzled when asked whether *heavy/weightless* or *ponderous/airy* are antonyms. The concepts are opposed, but the word forms are not familiar antonym pairs. Antonymy, like synonymy, is a semantic relation between word forms.

A qualification is necessary here: saying that antonymy is a relation between word forms implies that a word form with two different meanings is two different word forms. Accordingly, in WordNet that difference is represented by digits: if *hard* meaning 'unyielding' is *hard1* and *hard* meaning 'difficult' is *hard2*, then the antonym of *hard1* is *soft* and the antonym of *hard2* is *easy*.

The problem is that the antonymy relation between word forms is not the same as the conceptual opposition between word meanings. Aside from a number of frequently used adjectives (many of which are Anglo-Saxon), most antonyms of descriptive adjectives are formed by a morphological rule that changes the polarity of the meaning by adding a negative prefix (most often the Anglo-Saxon *un-* or the Latinate *in-* and its allomorphs *il-, im-, ir-*). Morphological rules apply to word forms, not to word meanings; they generally have a semantic reflex, of course, and in the case of antonymy the semantic reflex is so striking that it deflects attention away from the underlying morphological process. But the important consequence of the morphological origin of antonyms is that word form antonymy is not primarily a relation between meanings—thus precluding the simple representation of antonymy by pointers between synsets.

If the familiar semantic relation of antonymy holds only between selected pairs of words like *heavy/light* and *weighty/weightless*, then the second question arises: what is to be done with *ponderous, massive,* and *airy*, which seem to have no appropriate antonyms? The simple answer is to introduce a similarity pointer and use it to indicate that the adjectives lacking antonyms are similar in meaning to adjectives that do have antonyms. The term *similar* as used here typically indicates a kind of specialization; that is to say, the class of nouns that can be modified by *ponderous*, for example, is included in—is smaller than—the class of nouns that can be modified by *heavy*.

Gross, Fischer, and Miller (1989) proposed that adjectives are organized in clusters of synsets associated by semantic similarity to a focal adjective that relates the cluster to a contrasting cluster at the opposite pole of the attribute. Thus, *ponderous* is similar to *heavy* and *heavy* is the antonym of *light*, so a conceptual opposition of *ponderous/light* is mediated by *heavy*. Gross, Fischer, and Miller distinguish direct antonyms like *heavy/light*, which are conceptual opposites that are also lexical pairs, from indirect antonyms, like *heavy/airy*, which are conceptual opposites that are not lexically paired. Under this formulation, all descriptive adjectives have antonyms; those lacking direct antonyms have indirect antonyms (i.e., are similar in meaning to adjectives that have direct antonyms).

In WordNet direct antonyms are represented by the antonymy pointer *!*; indirect antonyms are inherited through similarity, which is indicated by the similarity pointer *&* meaning 'IS SIMILAR TO'. The configuration that results is illustrated in figure 2.1 for the cluster of adjectives around the direct antonyms *fast/slow*. For example, *prompt* does not have a direct antonym, but its indirect antonym can be found via the path "*Prompt* is similar to *fast* is antonymous to *slow*."

This strategy has been successful with the great bulk of English adjectives, but particular adjectives have posed some interesting problems. Among the adjectives that have no satisfactory antonym are some of the strongest and most colorful in the language. *Angry* is an example. The related attribute ANGER is gradable from no anger to extreme fury, but unlike most attributes it does not seem to be bipolar. Many terms are similar in meaning to *angry: enraged, irate, wrathful, incensed, furious.* But none of them has a direct antonym, either. For such adjectives the usual strategy is to search for a related antonym pair and to code it as similar in

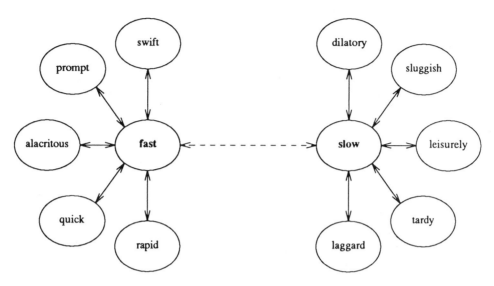

Figure 2.1
Bipolar adjective structure. ($\longrightarrow$ = similarity; $\dashrightarrow$ = antonymy)

meaning to a member of that pair. In the case of *angry*, the best related pair seems to be *pleased/displeased*, but coding *angry* as similar to (i.e., a special sense of) *displeased* misses the passion inherent in its meaning. The solution adopted for *angry* was to use *not angry* for *unangry* (a word form not attested in most dictionaries) to mark the zero point on a monopolar continuum.

The recognition that there are exceptions to the predominating bipolar antonymy around which descriptive adjectives are organized is unavoidable. In particular, some "non" antonyms are prime candidates as zero-point indicators—which does not make them any less meaningful or useful in the language (consider *nonaddictive* vs. *addictive* or *noncombustible* vs. *combustible*). Moreover, the case of *angry* calls attention to the fact that for other pairs in which the antonym is formed by a negative prefix, it is possible that the apparent bipolarity might represent two opposing monopolar continua conjoined.

The semantic organization illustrated in figure 2.1 is realized by organizing adjectives into bipolar clusters, which can be likened to the subject files for nouns and verbs. WordNet 1.5 contains over 1,732 of these clusters, one for each pair of antonyms; thus, there are 3,464 half clusters of closely similar senses.

The cluster for *fast/slow*, which defines the attribute SPEED, consists of two half clusters, one for senses of *fast* and one for senses of *slow*. Each half cluster is headed by what is called a *head synset*, in this case *fast* and its antonym *slow*, along with a parenthetical gloss and example phrases. Following the head synset is what are called *satellite synsets*, which represent senses that are similar to (in most cases, specializations of) the sense of the head adjective. The other half cluster is headed by the reverse antonymous pair *slow/fast*, followed by satellite synsets for senses of *slow*.

An interesting problem was posed by antonymous pairs expressing the same sense or closely related senses and representing values of the same attribute. In such cases the same set of satellite synsets can be related to two different antonymous pairs. For example, *big/little* and *large/small* are equally salient as antonyms defining the attribute SIZE. Many synsets could just as well be coded as similar to *big* as to *large*. Therefore, in order to avoid unnecessary redundancy, a single cluster was created headed by both pairs and displayed to the WordNet user as *large* (*vs. small*), *big* (*vs. little*) for one half cluster and by *small* (*vs. large*), *little* (*vs. big*) for the other half cluster.

A final word about *large/small* and *big/little*: although the concept *large* is clearly opposed to the concept *little*, the pair *large* and *little* are simply not accepted as antonyms. Overwhelmingly, association data and co-occurrence data indicate that *big* and *little* are considered a pair and *large* and *small* are considered a pair. These two pairs demonstrate that antonymy is a semantic relation between words rather than between concepts.

2.1.1.2 Gradation   Most discussions of antonymy distinguish between contradictory and contrary terms. This terminology originated in logic, where two propositions are said to be contradictory if the truth of one implies the falsity of the other and are said to be contrary if only one proposition can be true but both can be false. Thus, *alive* and *dead* are said to be contradictory terms because the truth of *Kennedy is dead* implies the falsity of *Kennedy is alive*, and vice versa. And *fat* and *thin* are said to be contrary terms because *Kennedy is fat* and *Kennedy is thin* cannot both be true, although both can be false if Kennedy is of average weight. However, Lyons (1977, vol. 1) has pointed out that this definition of contrary terms is not limited to opposites, but can be applied so broadly as to be almost meaningless: for example, *Kennedy is a tree* and *Kennedy is a dog* cannot both be true, but both can be false, so *dog* and *tree* must be contraries. Lyons argues that gradability, not truth func-

Table 2.1
Examples of graded adjectives

SIZE	LIGHTNESS	QUALITY	BODY WEIGHT	TEMPERATURE
astronomical	snowy	superb	obese	torrid
huge	*white*	great	*fat*	*hot*
large	ash-gray	*good*	plump	warm
——	gray	mediocre	——	tepid
small	charcoal	*bad*	slim	cool
tiny	*black*	awful	*thin*	*cold*
infinitesimal	pitch-black	atrocious	gaunt	frigid

tions, provides the better explanation of these differences. Contraries are gradable adjectives, contradictories are not.

Gradation, therefore, must also be considered as a semantic relation organizing lexical memory for adjectives (Bierwisch 1989). For some attributes gradation can be expressed by ordered strings of adjectives, all of which point to the same attribute noun in WordNet. Table 2.1 illustrates lexicalized gradations for SIZE, LIGHTNESS, QUALITY, BODY WEIGHT, and TEMPERATURE. The most difficult grade to find terms for is the neutral middle of each attribute; in some cases it is simply not lexicalized, whereas extremes are extensively lexicalized.

The grading in table 2.1 is the exception, not the rule; surprisingly little gradation is lexicalized in English. Gradation is usually accomplished in other ways, much of it by means of adverbs of degree, such as *very, decidedly, extremely, rather, quite, somewhat* (Cliff 1959). But most grading is done by morphological rules for the comparative and superlative degrees, which can be extended if *less* and *least* are used to complement *more* and *most*. Since this conceptually important relation of gradation does not play a central role in the organization of adjectives, it has not been coded in WordNet.

2.1.1.3 Markedness Most attributes have an orientation. It is natural to think of them as dimensions in a hyperspace, where one end of each dimension is anchored at the point of origin of the space. The point of origin is the expected or default value; deviation from it merits comment and is called the marked value of the attribute.

The antonyms *deep/shallow* illustrate this general linguistic phenomenon known as markedness. In an important paper on German adjectives,

Bierwisch (1967) noted that only unmarked spatial adjectives can take measure phrases. For example, *The pool is five feet deep* is acceptable; the measure phrase, *five feet*, describes the DEPTH of the pool. But when the antonym is used, as in **The pool is five feet shallow*, the result is not acceptable. Thus, the primary member, *deep*, is the unmarked term; the secondary member, *shallow*, is marked and does not take measure phrases, except in special circumstances. Note that the unmarked member, *deep*, lends its name to the attribute, DEPTH.

Measure phrases are not appropriate with many attributes, yet markedness is a general phenomenon that characterizes nearly all direct antonyms. In nearly every case one member of a pair of antonyms is primary: more customary, more frequently used, less remarkable, or morphologically related to the name of the attribute. The primary or unmarked term is the default value of the attribute, the value that would be assumed in the absence of information to the contrary. In a few cases (e.g., *wet/dry*, *easy/difficult*) it may be arguable which term should be regarded as primary, but for the vast majority of pairs the marker is morphologically explicit in the form of a negative prefix: *un+pleasant*, *in+decent*, *im+patient*, *il+legal*, *ir+resolute*, *a+symmetrical*, *mal+adroit*, *dis+similar*, for example.

Markedness has not been explicitly coded in WordNet. But the noun that names an attribute—for example, DEPTH—and the adjectives expressing values of that attribute (in this case, *deep*, *shallow*, etc.) are linked in WordNet by a pointer.

2.1.1.4 Polysemy and Selectional Preferences   Justeson and Katz (1993) found that the different senses of polysemous adjectives (*old*, *right*, *short*) occur with specific nouns (or specific senses of polysemous nouns). For example, the sense of *old* meaning 'not young' frequently modifies hyponyms of *person*—nouns like *man*—whereas *old* meaning 'not new' frequently modifies hyponyms of *artifact*. Justeson and Katz note that the noun context therefore often serves to disambiguate polysemous adjectives.

An alternative view, put forth by Murphy and Andrew (1993), holds that adjectives are monosemous but have different extensions; Murphy and Andrew assert that speakers compute the appropriate meanings in combination with the meanings of the nouns that the adjectives modify. They further argue against the claim that antonymy is a relation between two word forms on the basis of the fact that speakers generate different antonyms for an adjective like *fresh* depending on whether it modifies *shirt* or *bread*. WordNet takes the position that these facts point to the polysemy of adjectives like *fresh*; this view is also adopted by Justeson and Katz (1993), who point out that the different antonyms (whether direct or indirect) can help to disambiguate polysemous adjectives. In WordNet the different senses of an ambiguous word frequently have different antonyms: for example, *old1/new* (for *an old car*) and *old2/young* (for *old people*). In the case of *fresh*, the sense in *fresh bread* has the direct antonym *stale*; the sense in *a fresh shirt* is similar to *clean* and so has the indirect antonym *dirty* in the pair *clean/dirty*.

Adjectives—whether polysemous or not—are selective about the nouns they modify. The general rule is that if the referent denoted by a noun does not have the attribute whose value is expressed by the adjective, then that adjective-noun combination requires a figurative or idiomatic interpretation. For example, a building or a person can be tall because buildings and persons have HEIGHT as an attribute, but streets and stories do not have HEIGHT, so *tall street* and *tall story* do not admit literal readings. Nor do antonymy relations hold when nouns lack the pertinent attribute. Compare *short story* with *tall story*, or *short order* with *tall order*. It is really a comment on the semantics of nouns, therefore, when it is said that adjectives vary widely in their breadth of application. Adjectives expressing evaluations (*good/bad, desirable/undesirable*) can modify almost any noun; those expressing activity (*active/passive, fast/slow*) or potency (*strong/ weak, intense/mild*) also have wide ranges of applicability (cf. Osgood, Suci, and Tannenbaum 1957). Other adjectives are strictly limited with respect to the range of nouns they can modify (*pious/impious, abridged/ unabridged, edible/inedible,* or *endogamous/exogamous*).

The semantic contribution of adjectives is secondary to, and dependent on, the nouns that they modify. Edward Sapir (1944) seems to have been the first linguist to point out explicitly that many adjectives take on different meanings when they modify different nouns. Thus, *tall* denotes one range of heights for a building, another for a tree, and still another for a person. It appears that part of the meaning of each of the nouns *building, tree,* and *person* is a range of expected values for the attribute HEIGHT. *Tall* is interpreted relative to the expected height of objects of the kind denoted by the head noun: a tall person is someone who is tall for a person.

Therefore, in addition to containing a mere list of its attributes, a nominal concept is usually assumed to contain information about the expected values of those attributes: for example, both buildings and persons have the attribute HEIGHT, but the expected height of a building is much greater than the expected height of a person. Such information has not been coded in WordNet.

How adjectival information modulates nominal information is not a question to be settled in terms of lexical representations. For WordNet the assumption is that the interactions between adjectives and nouns are not prestored but are computed as needed by some on-line interpretive process. As suggested by Miller and Johnson-Laird (1976, 358), "The nominal information must be given priority; the adjectival information is then evaluated within the range allowed by the nominal information."

2.1.1.5 Color Adjectives One large and intensively studied group of adjectives deserves special comment. English color terms are exceptional in several ways. They can serve as either nouns or adjectives, yet they are not nominal adjectives (i.e., nouns used as adjectives): they can be graded, nominalized, and conjoined with other descriptive adjectives, and they can appear in predicate position, as nouns used as modifiers cannot (*the apple is red* for *the red apple* but not **Cooking is home* for *home cooking*). Nevertheless, except for *black/white*, the pattern of direct and indirect antonymy that is observed for other descriptive adjectives does not hold for them.

Only one color attribute is clearly described by direct antonyms: LIGHTNESS, whose polar values are expressed by *white/black*. Students of color vision can produce evidence of oppositions between red and green, and between yellow and blue, but those are not treated as direct antonyms in lay speech. The organization of color terms is given by the dimensions of color perception: lightness (sometimes called value), hue, and saturation, which define the well-known color solid. In WordNet the names of hues are coded as similar to *colored* in the opposition *colored/colorless* (cross-referenced to *chromatic/achromatic*); names for the shades of gray from white to black are coded as similar to *white*, *gray*, or *black*, in a tripartite cluster cross-referenced to *achromatic*. It has become obvious that it might be better and certainly more systematic to code the hues to *chromatic* rather than to *colored* and the grays to *achromatic* rather than to *colorless*. Such a realization is anticipated for WordNet 1.6.

There is reason to believe that the elaborate color terminology available in the languages of industrialized countries is a consequence of technological progress and not a natural linguistic development. Speculation about the evolution of color terminology (Berlin and Kay 1969) suggests that it begins with a single, conventional attribute, LIGHTNESS. Some languages still spoken have only two color terms to express values of that attribute, and it has been shown that this lexical limitation is not a consequence of perceptual deficits (Heider 1972; Heider and Olivier 1972). As technology develops and makes possible the manipulation and control of color, the need for greater terminological precision grows and more color terms appear in the language. They are always added along lines determined by innate mechanisms of color perception rather than by established patterns of linguistic modification.

2.1.1.6   Quantifiers   The term *quantifier* is borrowed from logic, where it refers to an operator that specifies the quantity of a term. In grammar the term is applied to an ill-defined class of words or expressions such as *all, some, many, few, less, both,* that also specify quantities. Two of these terms, *all* and *some,* are in many of their uses essentially linguistic equivalents of, respectively, the universal quantifier $\forall x f(x)$, indicating 'for all x, $f(x)$', and the existential quantifier $\exists x f(x)$, indicating 'for some x, $f(x)$'. For example, in the expressions *All professors wear glasses* and *Some professors wear glasses,* both *all* and *some* function much the way logical quantifiers function.

Some linguists include quantifiers in the class of determiners (*the, this, their,* etc.), whose function is to determine the reference of a noun phrase. Quantifiers, too, help determine the reference of a noun phrase. For example, when the expression *some professors* is used in contrast with *other professors, some* functions much as a determiner does. Moreover, quantifiers share other characteristics with determiners. Syntactically, they appear in prenominal position (*some books, the books*) and even in preadjectival position (*some large books, the large books*). Nevertheless, whereas a determiner "tells us which member ... of a set of entities is being referred to [,] a quantifier tells us how many entities or how much substance is being referred to" (Lyons 1977, vol. 2, 455). WordNet, therefore, distinguishes quantifiers from determiners.

In many respects, quantifiers resemble descriptive adjectives. Like adjectives, quantifiers typically have antonyms (*much/little* and *many/ few*). Even *some* and *all* enter into a three-way contrast with *no.* Like adjectives, many quantifiers are gradable: by degree adverbs (*very much food* and *very many books,* but not *very some food or *very no food), and in some cases by inflection for comparative and superlative degrees (*much, more1, most1,* and *many, more2, most2*). For these gradable quantifiers the antonyms also are gradable: *little, less, least,* and *few, fewer, fewest.*

One notable characteristic of many quantifiers is that they can modify only one of the two major classes of nouns, "count nouns" (*apple*, *book*, *town*) and "mass or noncount nouns" (*traffic*, *sugar*, *furniture*). For example, *many* modifies only count nouns (*many apples* but not *many sugar), whereas *much* modifies only mass nouns (*much sugar* but not *much apples). But because the distinction between these two noun classes is not always clear-cut, neither the noun categories nor the limitation on quantifiers is coded in WordNet.

Because of the ways in which quantifiers resemble adjectives—in particular, because they have antonyms and readily form themselves into bipolar clusters—WordNet follows the practice of considering quantifiers a subclass of adjectives and includes them in the descriptive adjective file.

2.1.1.7 Participial Adjectives   A subclass of descriptive adjectives consists of forms ending in *-ing* and *-ed*. Most of these adjectives are the participle forms of verbs. The adjectives in *an obliging waiter*, *elapsed time*, and *his accustomed thoroughness* are what we are calling *participial adjectives*. They typically occur in prenominal position, and they typically have stative meanings something like 'being in or having achieved a state as specified (by the verb)'.

Many participial adjectives do not fit comfortably into the cluster structure of descriptive adjectives, primarily because they lack antonyms, either direct or indirect. Therefore, WordNet maintains a separate file of such adjectives. In this file each adjective (or synset) is entered individually rather than as part of a cluster. In order to relate them semantically to other words in the language, each adjective is cross-referenced to the appropriate verb by means of a pointer meaning 'PRINCIPAL-PART-OF': for example, the entry for *breaking* has a pointer to the appropriate sense of the verb *break*, and *elapsed* has a pointer to the verb *elapse*. WordNet 1.5 contains 88 such participle synsets.

On the other hand, a great number of participial adjectives do have direct or indirect antonyms: the adjectives in, for example, *boiling water* (indirect antonym, *cold*), *laughing children* (indirect antonym, *unhappy*), *retired teachers* (indirect antonym, *active*), and *married couples* (direct antonym, *unmarried*). Because adjectives like these are completely at home in the cluster structure of descriptive adjectives, they are included in that category in WordNet rather than being cross-referenced to verbs.

Numerous *-ed* forms, however, have no corresponding verbs and are consequently not participles. Consider *skilled*, *foliaged*, *downhearted*, and *un-* words like *unexcited* or *unabridged*. *Skilled* and *foliaged* are related to nouns rather than verbs and mean 'having skill' and 'having foliage', respectively. *Downhearted* is derived by way of the combining form *-hearted*, meaning 'having a heart (or spirit) as specified'. And *unexcited* and *unabridged* are derived from the respective adjectives *excited* and *abridged* rather than from nonexistent verbs **unexcite* and **unabridge*. These too we call participial adjectives because they resemble participles. They are included in the descriptive adjective category in WordNet.

No theoretical import should be attached to whether an adjective is placed in the participle subfile or in the main descriptive adjective file. The decision is purely pragmatic, based on whether a particular adjective fits readily into the cluster structure; those in the participle file do not.

2.1.2   Relational Adjectives

The second large and open adjective class consists of adjectives that are related semantically and morphologically to nouns, though the morphological relation is not always direct. We refer to them as *relational adjectives* (Levi 1978). Typically, such an adjective plays a role similar to that of a modifying noun and functions as a classifier. For example, *musical* in *musical instrument* is related to *music* and *dental* in *dental hygiene* is related to *tooth*, and they serve to identify kinds of instruments and hygiene, respectively. Frequently a noun can be modified by both the relational adjective and the noun from which it is derived, as in *atomic bomb* and *atom bomb*; even *tooth hygiene* would be acceptable as an informal expression for *dental hygiene*. (Note that the morphological relation of *dental* to *tooth* is indirect, by way of the Latin word for 'tooth', *dens*.)

There is also a semantic relation between the adjective and the noun it modifies, and the relation may differ with different head nouns. For example, *agricultural equipment* means 'equipment used in agriculture' whereas *agricultural college* means 'a college teaching the science of agriculture'.

In some cases a noun gives rise to two homonymous adjectives, one a relational adjective, the other descriptive. For example, the adjective in *criminal law* is not the same as that in *criminal behavior*, as reflected in the fact that only in the second case can the adjective be used predicatively (*His behavior is criminal* but not **The law is criminal*).

Relational adjectives differ from descriptive adjectives in a number of ways. They do not refer to a property of the nouns they modify and so do not relate to an attribute. Typically they are not gradable (**the extremely* *atomic bomb* and **the very dental hygiene* are not acceptable). Typically they occur only in attributive position, as modifying nouns do. And typically (but not always) they lack direct antonyms. Consequently, most do not fit comfortably into the cluster arrangement of descriptive adjectives. However, when a relational adjective does have an antonym, and especially if the antonym is direct and the pair can serve as a bipolar focus for related senses (e.g., *physical/mental*), then they are placed in the descriptive adjective file. For those that do not lend themselves to the cluster arrangement, WordNet maintains a separate file, with pointers to the corresponding nouns. The decision about which file an adjective is to be listed in is, in the end, pragmatic. In WordNet 1.5 the relational adjective file contains 2,832 adjective synsets.

2.2 ADVERBS

Most adverbs belong to the large open class derived from adjectives by suffixation. Of these, the great majority are derived by adding the suffix *-ly* and typically specify manner (*beautifully, oddly, quickly, wickedly, interestingly, hurriedly*) or degree (*extremely, barely, intensely, decidedly*). Others are derived by adding any of a number of other suffixes, especially *-ward, -wise, -ways*, having directional senses (*northward, forward*) or dimensional senses (*crosswise, lengthways*) as well as manner senses (*crabwise, clockwise, sideways*).

In WordNet derived adverbs are linked to adjective senses by means of a pointer meaning 'DERIVED-FROM'. Because so many adjectives are polysemous and a derived adverb usually inherits the sense of the base adjective, particular adverbs are linked to particular adjective senses in WordNet.

Some adverbs are homomorphous with their adjectives. For example, *fast*, not **fastly*, is the adverb meaning 'rapidly' or 'quickly' (*ran as fast as he could*); and *hard*, not **hardly*, is the adverb meaning, among other things, 'with effort' (*hit the ball hard, worked hard*) or 'with difficulty' (*Prejudices die hard*). Other adverbs that are homomorphous with adjectives differ in meaning from them: *pretty*, as in *He did pretty well*. And some adjective + *-ly* forms are not semantically related to adjectives at all: *scarcely* and *hardly* for example.

Adverbs derived from adjectives frequently inherit from their related adjectives such properties as antonymy or gradation. For example, the antonymous relation between the adjectives *specific* and *general* is found also between the related adverbs, *specifically* and *generally*. And an adjective's gradability is reflected in its related adverb, which can take adverbs of degree just as the adjective can: *played very beautifully, danced extremely poorly.*

In addition, a number of lexical adverbs are gradable by means of inflections for comparative and superlative degrees: *near, nearer, nearest,* and *soon, sooner, soonest.*

Adverbs are a heterogeneous group made even more heterogeneous by the numerous phrases used adverbally, some of which are included in WordNet. In order to keep WordNet to a manageable size, however, an effort is made to enter only those frozen phrases that are used widely enough to be attested in standard dictionaries. WordNet 1.5 contains 3,242 adverb synsets.

The semantic organization of adverbs is simple and straightforward. There is no tree structure, as for nouns and verbs; nor is there a cluster structure as for adjectives. Aside from the relation between a derived adverb and its adjective, only synonymy and sometimes antonymy are recognized. Nor has any attempt been made to categorize adverbs: whether derived from an adjective or not, whether consisting of a single word or a phrase, whether used primarily to modify a verb or another modifier or a sentence, whether indicating manner or time or place or degree—or whatever—all adverbs are listed individually in a single adverb file. Each synset consists of an adverb, its related adjective (if any) marked by the derivational pointer, any synonyms or antonyms, and a parenthetical gloss including example phrases (most of which remain to be supplied in a later version of WordNet).

2.3   THE WORDNET INTERFACE

Modifiers in WordNet are coded by means of various structural features and relational pointers mentioned earlier; these features and pointers are interpreted by the interface, which presents the information to the user in a straightforward way (see Tengi, this volume).

2.3.1   Descriptive Adjectives

In WordNet the descriptive adjectives are entered in a file whose name, `adj.all`, is a relic from the time when all adjectives in WordNet were in a single file. This is the file in which adjectives are organized in clusters, as described earlier and illustrated in figure 2.1. The user finds the cluster

```
fast (vs. slow)
    => alacritous, prompt -- (quick in responding: "prompt
        obedience")
    => blistering, red-hot -- (very fast: "a blistering
        pace"; "a red-hot line drive")
    => double-quick -- (of a marching cadence; very quick)
    => fast-flying, hurrying, speedy -- (moving or
        functioning quickly and energetically: "a fast-
        flying messenger"; "affection for this hurrying
        driving ... little man"; "a speedy errand boy")
    => fleet, swift -- (moving with great speed: "fleet of
        foot"; "a swift current")
    => hot, high-speed -- ("in hot pursuit"; "a high-speed
        chase")
    => instantaneous, instant(prenominal) -- (with no
        delay: "Relief was instantaneous"; "instant
        gratification")
    => meteoric -- (like a meteor in speed: "a meteoric
        rise to fame")
    => quick, rapid, speedy -- (occurring in a brief
        period of time: "a quick inspection"; "a rapid
        rise through the ranks")
Also See-> expedited, hurried, sudden
```

Figure 2.2
One sense of the adjective *fast*.

organization displayed on the monitor a half cluster at a time: the head synset for the target adjective appears on the first line of the display, followed by synsets for each of the satellite senses.

For example, the cluster for the sense of *fast/slow* meaning 'acting or moving quickly' is so coded that the synsets in the half cluster for *fast* appear on the monitor as in figure 2.2. (Note that with a head adjective the interface always displays the antonym. One reason is that antonymy is the organizing principle for descriptive adjectives; another is that the antonym helps to define the head word, particularly when it is polysemous.)

As shown further in figure 2.2, many head synsets contain SEE ALSO pointers to related clusters; those pointer words appear on the monitor below the list of satellite synsets. Finally, in the source files a head synset usually includes a pointer to the noun that names the attribute for which the adjective gives a value. To find this information (say, for *fast*), the WordNet interface window offers the menu choice fast is a value

```
breaking -- ("the breaking waves")
    Participle of verb break (Sense 16)
    => break -- (curl over and fall apart in surf or foam,
        of waves)
    => collapse, fall in, cave in, give way, -- (literally
        or metaphorically: "The wall collapsed"; "The
        business collapsed")
```

Figure 2.3
Sense of the participial adjective *breaking*.

of ____; if this choice is selected, the monitor again displays the target adjective followed this time by the requested attribute name and information about it:

```
=> speed, swiftness--(a rate (usually rapid) at
which something happens: "The project advanced with
gratifying speed")
```

2.3.2 Participial Adjectives

For most participial adjectives, the coding and interface representation are the same as for other descriptive adjectives. But for those in the participle subfile, called adj.ppl, the coding is such that the interface presents the participle (with gloss and example phrases) followed by the related verb and information about the sense of the verb. For the participial adjective *breaking*, as in *the breaking waves*, figure 2.3 shows how the information is represented.

2.3.3 Relational Adjectives

The file for relational adjectives is called adj.pert, for 'pertaining or relating to'. The coding of adjectives in this file is different from that of descriptive adjectives. Rather than being part of a cluster, each synset is entered individually, so coded that the interface will present the adjective with its related noun and information about the sense of the noun. For the occasional case of antonymy, the adjective is followed by its antonym in parentheses, just as for descriptive adjectives: *extracellular* (*vs. intracellular*). The entry for the relational adjective *stellar*, for example, is realized on the user's monitor as in figure 2.4.

As already mentioned, many adjectives, both descriptive and relational, are limited as to the syntactic positions they can occupy. Such a limitation is usually coded in WordNet, and because it is a word form limitation it

```
stellar, astral -- (relating to or resembling or emanating
    from or consisting of stars or constellations: "an
    astral body"; "stellar light")
  Pertains to noun star (Sense 1)
  => star
  => celestial body, heavenly body -- (natural objects
      visible in the sky)
```

Figure 2.4
Sense of the relational adjective *stellar*.

is coded for individual adjectives rather than for synsets. Consider the half cluster *awake*(*predicate*) (*vs. asleep*). Although the head word is limited to predicate position, as indicated, the limitation does not hold for all of the synonyms in the cluster. Only those individual words so coded are limited, as in the synset *astir*(*predicate*), *up*(*predicate*): *The boys are astir* and *The woman is up*, but not **the astir boys*, **the up woman*.

Limitation to prenominal (or attributive) position is indicated by *prenominal* in parentheses. For example, when the adjective *previous* is in prenominal position, as in *We regretted our previous condemnation of him*, it refers to what is past. But if *previous* appears in predicate position, it has a very different sense, meaning 'premature': *Our condemnation of him was a bit previous*. Therefore, the form *previous* must be specifically marked for position: *previous*(*prenominal*) for its 'past' sense, and *previous*(*predicate*) for the 'premature' sense.

For those few adjectives that can appear only immediately following a noun, the marking is *postnominal* in parentheses: *galore*(*postnominal*), as in *daffodils galore*; *elect*(*postnominal*), as in *president elect*; and *aforethought*(*postnominal*), as in *malice aforethought*. In many of these cases the adjective constitutes part of what is essentially a frozen construction.

2.3.4 Adverbs

The coding of adverbs is as straightforward and uncomplicated as their semantic organization. To begin with, all adverbs are listed in a single file, called adv.all.

For lexical adverbs (in the closed class of underived adverbs) the coding involves no pointers of any kind between synsets other than the occasional antonym pointer. Therefore, an adverb synset is displayed on the monitor almost exactly as entered in the source files. For example, WordNet contains three senses of *then*, distinguished in the source files by numerals. They appear on the monitor as shown in figure 2.5.

```
Sense 1
subsequently, then, thereupon, therewithal, and then, after
that -- ("And then he left")

Sense 2
then, in that case, that being so -- ("Then you'll be
rich")

Sense 3
Then, at that time, at that point in time, at the time --
("then I was young")
```

Figure 2.5
Three senses of the adverb *then*.

```
Sense 1
clearly, plainly, plain -- ("They were clearly lost"; "You
    are plainly wrong")
  Derived from adj plain (Sense 1)
  => apparent, clear, evident, manifest, patent, plain --
      (readily seen or understood: "angry for no
      apparent reason"; "a clear and present danger";
      "evident hostility"; "manifest disapproval";
      "patent advantages"; "made his meaning plain")

Sense 2
simply, plainly -- ("dressed plainly")
  Derived from adj plain (Sense 2)
  => modest, plain, simple -- (free from pomp or
      affectation: "modest cottages"; "a plain blue
      suit"; "a simple rectangular brick building")
```

Figure 2.6
Two senses of the adverb *plainly*.

The coding for derived adverbs is a bit more elaborate. Because derived adverbs are related morphologically and semantically to their base adjectives, their coding is similar to that of relational adjectives (which are related morphologically and semantically to nouns). The adverb is entered along with the appropriate adjective marked by a derivational pointer, each derived synonym (if any) is followed by its appropriate adjective similarly marked; all followed by a parenthetical gloss and example phrases. The representation on the monitor includes all this information. For example, the entry for *plainly* is represented as in figure 2.6.

If an adverb has an antonym, the antonym is coded with the antonym pointer, just as for adjectives. But because antonymy is not as important an organizing principle for adverbs as it is for adjectives, adverbs are not organized into clusters headed by pairs of antonyms. Nor are adverb antonyms displayed directly by the interface as is the case for adjectives. Instead, the antonym has to be requested separately by means of a menu choice, `antonyms of . . .`; if this choice is selected, the antonym synset is then presented on a separate line following the target synset.

2.4   CONCLUSION

The semantic organization of modifiers in WordNet is unlike that of either nouns or verbs. There is nothing like the tree structures created by hyponymy for nouns or troponymy for verbs.

WordNet divides adjectives into two major classes, descriptive and relational, each with its own typical kind of organization. Descriptive adjectives constitute by far the larger class. Because they ascribe to the nouns they modify values of (typically) bipolar attributes, their striking feature is that the vast majority have explicit antonyms; those that do not are considered to have indirect antonyms by virtue of their similarity to adjectives that do have direct antonyms. Descriptive adjectives are there-fore organized into clusters on the basis of binary opposition (antonymy) and similarity of meaning. Participial adjectives are considered a subclass of descriptive adjectives, even though not all of them fit into the cluster structure; those that do not are cross-referenced to the verbs of which they are participles. Quantifiers also are included in the descriptive adjective file.

Relational adjectives, on the other hand, which are assumed to be sty-listic variants of modifying nouns, are cross-referenced to the noun files. The particular relation between such an adjective and its corresponding noun varies enormously from instance to instance. If that relation is not specified in an accompanying gloss, the rather loose definition 'RELATING-OR-PERTAINING-TO' is typically considered adequate. The function such adjectives play is usually that of classifying their head nouns.

The structure of the adverb file is little more than a list of synsets. Derived adverbs are cross-referenced to their base adjectives, from which they inherit their meaning. Otherwise, only the occasional case of anto-nymy, among both lexical and derived adverbs, is recognized in WordNet.

We believe that the model presented here accounts for the majority of English modifiers. We do not claim complete coverage.

References

Berlin, B., and Kay, P. (1969). *Basic color terms: Their universality and evolution.* Berkeley and Los Angeles: University of California Press.

Bierwisch, M. (1967). Some semantic universals of German adjectives. *Foundations of Language, 3,* 1–36.

Bierwisch, M. (1989). The semantics of gradation. In M. Bierwisch and E. Lang (Eds.), *Dimensional adjectives: Grammatical structure and conceptual interpretation,* 51–74. Berlin: Springer-Verlag.

Charles, W. G., and Miller, G. A. (1989). Contexts of antonymous adjectives. *Applied Psycholinguistics, 10,* 357–375.

Cliff, N. (1959). Adverbs as multipliers. *Psychological Review, 66,* 27–44.

Deese, J. (1964). The associative structure of some English adjectives. *Journal of Verbal Learning and Verbal Behavior, 3,* 347–357.

Deese, J. (1965). *The structure of associations in language and thought.* Baltimore: Johns Hopkins Press.

Gross, D., Fischer, U., and Miller, G. A. (1989). The organization of adjectival meanings. *Journal of Memory and Language, 28,* 92–106.

Heider, E. R. (1972). Universals in color naming and memory. *Journal of Experimental Psychology, 93,* 10–20.

Heider, E. R., and Olivier, D. C. (1972). The structure of color space in naming and memory for two languages. *Cognitive Psychology, 3,* 337–354.

Justeson, J. S., and Katz, S. M. (1991a). Co-occurrences of antonymous adjectives and their contexts. *Computational Linguistics, 17,* 1–19.

Justeson, J. S., and Katz, S. M. (1991b). Redefining antonymy: The textual structure of a semantic relation. In *Proceedings of the Seventh Annual Conference of the UW Centre for the New Oxford English Dictionary and Text Research,* 138–154. Waterloo, Ontario, Canada: University of Waterloo, Centre for the New OED and Text Research.

Justeson, J. S., and Katz, S. M. (1993). *Principled disambiguation: Discriminating adjective senses with modified nouns. Unpublished manuscript,* IBM Thomas J. Watson Research Center, Yorktown Heights, NY.

Levi, J. N. (1978). *The syntax and semantics of complex nominals.* New York: Academic Press.

Lyons, J. (1977). *Semantics.* 2 vols. New York: Cambridge University Press.

Miller, G. A., and Johnson-Laird, P. N. (1976). *Language and perception.* Cambridge, MA: Harvard University Press.

Murphy, G. L., and Andrew, J. M. (1993). The conceptual basis of antonymy and synonymy in adjectives. *Journal of Memory and Language, 32,* 301–319.

Osgood, C. E., Suci, G. J., and Tannenbaum, P. H. (1957). *The measurement of meaning.* Urbana: University of Illinois Press.

Sapir, E. (1944). Grading: A study in semantics. *Philosophy of Science, 11,* 83–116.

Chapter 3

A Semantic Network of English Verbs

Christiane Fellbaum

Over the past decade or so, the verb lexicon has become the focus of attention for many linguists and psychologists working with a variety of frameworks and assumptions. One common goal is to characterize the structure of the verb lexicon and its representation as a part of speakers' linguistic knowledge. Although aspiring to very similar goals, WordNet distinguishes itself from many other efforts in examining not just particular verb classes, but the entire verb lexicon. Constructing WordNet therefore represents an experiment that will show whether a particular model of the lexicon will fit all verbs. The network design of WordNet and its deliberate limitation to paradigmatic relations and whole lexical items—rather than atomic meaning units—distinguish it from most current models of the lexicon. Yet WordNet contains much implicit information about verb classes and their semantic and syntactic properties that can be uncovered within the web structures. The effort to examine virtually the entire verb lexicon has paid off in some interesting discoveries about the properties of verb classes and semantic domains.

3.1 THE ORGANIZATION OF VERBS IN WORDNET

3.1.1 Breaking Up the Lexicon into Semantic Domains

A well-tested approach to the lexicon, popular especially among semanticists and anthropological linguists, is to view it in terms of semantic fields that contain the lexicalized concepts of conceptual fields. For the purpose of organizing the English verb lexicon as a relational network, dividing up the lexicon into semantic fields seemed like a good idea for two reasons. First, it provided an initial, semantically based organization of the thousands of polysemous verbs in the English lexicon. Second, researchers who have studied such fields have pointed out that words that are linked by semantic and lexical relations usually belong to the same semantic domain. Thus, a relational analysis is necessarily also an analysis of the lexicon in terms of semantic fields.

Semantic domains that have been the subject of intensive study, such as vegetables and color terms, have been shown to be organized by relations like hyponymy: *red* belongs to the semantic field of color because it is a kind of *color*. Similarly, *sprint* and *run* can be said to belong to the semantic domain of motion verbs, because *to sprint* is *to run* in some way (and *to run* is *to move* in some way); the relation between *red* and *color* seems quite similar to that between *sprint* and *run*, or between *run* and *move*.

Because most work on semantic networks has focused on nouns, no established lexical and semantic relations were readily available for verbs. But whatever relations one might choose to link verb concepts, the intuition that such relations will primarily connect verbs from the same semantic domain seems reasonable. Dividing the verb lexicon into semantic domains initially on a purely intuitive basis then might lead one to discover relations that organize verbs and verb concepts.

A first cut was made between verbs headed by verbs denoting actions and events on the one hand, and states on the other hand. Most verbs are of the former kind, and these were subdivided into 14 more specific semantic domains (called "files" in WordNet; see G. A. Miller, this volume): verbs of motion, perception, contact, communication, competition, change, cognition, consumption, creation, emotion, perception, possession, and bodily care and functions, and verbs referring to social behavior and interactions. This classification was based partly on some of the perceptually based semantic verb classes discussed in Miller and Johnson-Laird 1976 and partly on a semantic classification that seemed appropriate because it could accommodate virtually all verbs. Of course, another group of researchers faced with the same task would likely have carved up the verb lexicon in a different way. However, neither the number of groups nor the particular labels attached to them plays an important role for the kind of analysis of the verb lexicon that is undertaken here.

The verbs that are arguably elaborations of the concept "be," including *resemble*, *belong*, and *suffice*, do not fit into any of the 14 semantic domains we distinguished. These stative verbs constitute a semantically heterogeneous class and are therefore the only group that does not constitute a semantic domain. Also included in this group are auxiliaries and control verbs like *want, fail, prevent,* and *succeed,* as well as aspectual verbs like *begin.*

The 15 groups have turned out to be adequate for accommodating all the verb synsets (synonym sets) that have been added over the years (WordNet 1.5 contains over 11,500 verb synsets). But it must be stressed that the borders between the verb domains are vague. For example, many verbs cannot be unequivocally classified as either cognition or communication verbs (*wonder, speculate, confirm, judge,* etc.). Similarly, a verb like *whistle* in *The bullet whistled past him* can be classified both as a verb of sound emission and as a verb of motion (Atkins and Levin 1991). If such verbs were represented as monosemous, they would be linked to verbs from more than one semantic field. In WordNet we have tended to treat them as polysemous words that are found in more than one semantic domain. However, what particular group a verb belongs to is of no great consequence, since in WordNet the meaning of a given verb is expressed primarily by its relations to other verbs and synsets.

3.1.2   Unique Beginners

The division of the verb lexicon into semantic domains not only gives one a grip on organizing a large amount of data, but is also necessitated by the absence of a single root verb or "unique beginner" that could head the entire verb lexicon. Noting this absence, Lyons (1977, 294) proposes a set of root verbs including *act, move, get, become, be, make.* Pulman (1983) suggests just *be* and *do,* which amounts to a division between activity and stative verbs, reflecting Jackendoff's (1983, 170) major conceptual categories EVENT and STATE.[1] Although such primitives appear to be good candidates for root verbs, we found that, for WordNet, adopting verbs like *be* and *do* as unique beginners did not seem entirely appropriate.

To begin with, even these semantically unelaborated concepts are polysemous. WordNet distinguishes 12 senses each for *do* and *be* (this is not an excessive number, as a check of a conventional dictionary will confirm). Of course, some of these senses would not qualify as unique beginners—*do* in *do my hair* or *do my room in blue* clearly expresses semantically very specific and elaborate concepts—but there are still too many basic senses to make it possible to single out one as the topmost sense from which all others descend. Second, we found that the particular semantic relations we settled on to create our network made it awkward to link such abstract verbs as *do* to the next level of subordinates such as *communicate* and *move.* For example, whereas a hierarchical link between *communicate* and *chat* seemed entirely appropriate, the same link between *do* and *communicate* appeared less felicitous—the two concepts seem farther removed from each other than do *communicate* and *chat*. Similarly, *move* and *run* can easily be related, but *do* and its immediate subordinate, *move*, appear semantically much farther apart. Third, there seems to be no psycholinguistic evidence that people link *do* and activity verbs like *move* in their minds, whereas there is evidence that people associate pairs like *move* and *run* (Chaffin, Fellbaum, and Jenei 1994). Adopting a set of unique beginners such as those proposed by Lyons (1997) and Pulman (1983) seemed to be inconsistent with WordNet's aspiration to reflect speakers' lexical organization. Therefore, we settled on more meaningful unique beginners for the 14 semantic domains.

Within a single semantic field it is frequently the case that not all verbs can be grouped under a single unique beginner; some semantic domains can be represented only by several independent trees. Motion verbs, for example, have two homophonous top nodes, expressing two distinct concepts: *move1* and *move2*, expressing translational movement and movement without displacement, respectively. Verbs of possession go upward to three concepts, expressed by the synsets {*give, transfer*}, {*take, receive*}, and {*have, hold*}; for the most part, their subordinates encode ways in which society has ritualized the transfer of possessions: *bequeath, donate*; *inherit, usurp*; *own, stock*; and so on. Communication verbs are headed by the verb *communicate* but immediately divide into two independent trees expressing verbal and nonverbal (gestural) communication; these are not lexicalized in English. The subdomain of verbal communication neatly splits further into verbs denoting the communication of spoken and written language. Other semantic domains, such as the verbs of bodily care and functions, consist of a number of independent hierarchies that form a coherent semantic field by virtue of the fact that most of the verbs (*wash, comb, shampoo, make up*; *ache, atrophy*) select for the same kinds of noun arguments (kinds of body parts). Verbs of social interaction, though constituting a coherent semantic field, encompass a number of different semantic subdomains, including politics (*elect, depose*), work (*hire, subcontract, strike*), and interpersonal relations (*court, marry*).

3.1.3 Verb Synsets

3.1.3.1 Synonyms and Near-Synonyms   Just like the nouns and adjectives in WordNet, verbs are grouped together as sets of synonyms. However, if one adopts the definition of synonyms as words that can be substituted for each other in most contexts, few truly synonymous verbs, such as *shut* and *close*, can be found in the English lexicon. Many Anglo-Saxon/Greco-Latinate word pairs express the same concept but do not easily tolerate substitution in a given speech register or context: *begin-commence, end-terminate, rise-ascend, blink-nictate, behead-decapitate*, and so on (Cruse 1986). In general, the Greco-Latinate verbs are used in more formal registers (*buy* vs. *purchase*), or they are euphemistic substitutions for words that may be considered offensive or that express bodily activities and functions (*pass away* vs. *die* vs. *kick the bucket*; *shave* vs. *epilate*, *sweat* vs. *perspire, spit* vs. *expectorate*). WordNet does not account for such usage differences by means of relations among synsets, and lexical pairs like these are generally members of the same synset. However, the information given in parentheses (a gloss and one or more sample sentences) often spells out the specific usage restrictions associated with individual verbs.[2]

Subtle meaning differences between apparent synonyms sometimes show up in different selectional restrictions. For example, *rise* and *fall* can select as an argument such abstract entities as *the temperature* or *prices*, but their close synonyms *ascend* and *descend* cannot. We have generally avoided placing verbs that differ significantly with respect to their selectional restrictions into the same synset. Because many apparently synonymous words exhibit such distributional differences, glosses and sample sentences are helpful here, too, in drawing the appropriate distinctions.

3.1.3.2 Idioms and Metaphors   Frozen idiomatic verb phrases like *kick the bucket* and *keep an eye on* are included in the appropriate synsets, as are verbs that have metaphorical senses in addition to their literal meaning(s). For example, *die* is included as a synonym of *break* and *break down* (as of a car, computer, etc.).

Metaphorical sense extensions of verbs often share not only the meanings but also the syntax of their literal synonyms, expressed in WordNet by sentence frames (see section 3.6.2). Thus, the verbs *break* and *break down* and their metaphorical synonym *die* are all unaccusatives. Similarly, *fall* (*sick, in love*) is an unaccusative verb, just like its literal synonym *become*. And many unaccusative verbs with nonliteral meanings do not have simple synonyms, but can be paraphrased by passives, a syntactically related construction. For example, *fall* (as in *This task fell to me*) lacks a synonym, but can be glossed by *be assigned. Go* in *The building went up* means *be erected*; in *This prize went to Mary*, it means *was awarded*. When a book *comes out* or *appears*, it *is issued*, and when it *goes to press* or *goes on the block*, it *is printed* or *auctioned*. *Come* in *This shoe comes in three colors* means *is found/available*. When something *comes* or *springs* to mind, it *is associated* or *remembered*. If a word *escapes* someone's lips, it inadvertently *is articulated*. And so on.

3.2 EVIDENCE FOR LEXICAL AND SEMANTIC RELATIONS AMONG VERBS

Before WordNet, semantic networks of nouns had been attempted on a small scale, but little effort had been made to explore a relational organization of the verb lexicon. Notable exceptions are the work of Evens (1988, and references therein) and Mel'čuk (Mel'čuk and Zholkovsky 1984), whose relational lexicons extend beyond nouns to verbs. However, their work argues for a fairly large number of relations, including not only semantic but also morphologically and syntactically based ones. Furthermore, these networks do not make any claims to modeling speakers' lexical organization.

3.2.1 Psycholinguistic Evidence for the Organization of Semantic Memory for Verbs

Although a fair amount of research has been done to study speakers' semantic memory for nouns and adjectives, psycholinguists have paid much less attention to how speakers store and access verbs in their mental lexicon. Word association data for verbs are sparse. Moreover, the results of association data where verbs are given as the stimulus show that at most half the responses are verbs, pointing to a syntagmatic organization that exists in parallel with a paradigmatic one (Cramer 1968, 67; Rosenweig 1970, 102; Fillenbaum and Jones 1965; Chaffin, Fellbaum, and Jenei 1994). However, the design of WordNet is based on paradigmatic relations and does not accommodate direct links between words from different syntactic categories.

Besides word associations, substitution errors are a source of data for studying the mental organization of words and concepts. Garrett (1992) reports data from verb substitution errors, drawn from his and Shattuck-Hufnagel's large corpus of errors. Garrett cites verbs that speakers have erroneously substituted for one another, such as *ask* and *tell*, and *go* and *come*. Clearly, these verb pairs come from the same semantic domain, and they select for the same or semantically related subjects. These and other substitution errors are classified by Garrett as pairs of opposites: *start-stop, remember-forget, believe-doubt, ask-tell, precede-follow, fill-empty, love-hate, heard-said, taken-given*. These verb pairs resemble those that constitute the stimulus-response pairs in association experiments (Palermo and Jenkins 1964; Chaffin, Fellbaum, and Jenei 1994), where opposition is a major link between stimulus and response. Such psycholinguistic evidence indicates that semantic opposition is an important organizer of speakers' mental lexicons, and in WordNet it links many verb pairs.

Garrett (1992) cites further substitution errors, where he classifies the relation between intended and actual utterance as one of "weak functional contrast": *answer-dial, drink-breathe, eat-cook*. However, the relation between the verbs in these pairs seems less one of contrast than one of (in our terms) lexical entailment: for someone to *answer* (a telephone call), (some)one must have *dialed*; when *drinking*, one *breathes* in air; and when one *eats*, (some)one must have *cooked*.

Other examples of substitution errors cited by Garrett (1992) are *drink-eat, watch-listen, written-published, looks-sounds, smells-sounds, barks-meows*. The verbs in these pairs come from the same semantic domain, and they select for either the same or semantically related arguments. They are either co-hyponyms or sisters (i.e., daughters of a shared superordinate).

3.2.2 Evidence from Typicality and Category Membership Judgments

Data obtained from typicality and membership gradation judgments are a good source for insights into which words and concepts are related in speakers' minds. Again, though, most work in this area has been done with nouns only (Rosch 1975; Markowitz 1988). A notable exception is the work of Pulman (1983), who asked whether there is a prototype effect for verbs, similar to that obtained for nouns by Rosch (1973). His subjects consistently judged some verbs to be better category members than others. For example, they rated *murder* as both highly similar to, and a prototypical member of, the category *kill*; similarly, they judged *survey* to be very closely related to *look*. On the other hand, of the six verbs given with each category, *sacrifice* and *squint* were considered not very similar to, or prototypical members of, the categories *kill* and *look*, respectively. Such results could be helpful for constructing a model of the mental lexicon; however, Pulman's data are limited to eight categories with six member verbs each, and we do not know of large-scale experiments on proto-typicality ratings that could have supplied an empirical basis for the classification of verbs.

3.2.3 Dictionary Definitions as a Heuristic for Discovering Semantic Relations

A richer source for insight into the representation of words and concepts is provided by traditional dictionaries, where words are defined in terms of other words, reflecting the way in which speakers specify their meanings. For example, nouns are typically defined in terms of their superordinates, by means of formulas like (*x is*) *a kind of*.[3] Dictionary definitions can also give evidence about semantic relations among verbs and indicate how verb taxonomies might be constructed. Thus, the verb *shuffle* is defined in *Webster's Third* as 'to move or walk in a sliding, dragging manner without lifting the feet'; *shout* is defined as 'to utter in a loud voice'. Definitions of this kind indicate that some verbs are manner elaborations of other, more general, verbs. Other verbs, for which there is no identifiable superordinate, are glossed with definitions like 'fail to . . . ' Thus, one sense of *lose* is defined in dictionaries like *Collins* and *Webster's Third* as 'fail to sustain, maintain, or keep'. We interpret formulas with a negating control verb like *fail* as containing two semantically opposed verb concepts, analogously to the way dictionaries define many adjectives in terms of their antonyms (i.e., by means of the formula *not x*).

Many verbs are defined by means of the formula *to x while y-ing*. This definition helped to inspire much of our entailment relation (see section 3.3.1). Finally, many verbs that have both a transitive and an inchoative sense are defined in dictionaries like *Collins* by means of the formula *to become or make x* (e.g., *melt* is glossed as 'to become or make liquid'). In WordNet these two senses are distinguished and linked by a pointer labeled CAUSE.

These examples show that dictionary definitions can provide a good heuristic for discovering verb pairs linked by various semantic relations, including a manner elaboration, semantic opposition, entailment, and causation. Unlike psycholinguistic experiments, dictionaries provide evidence for representing tens of thousands of words.

3.3 LEXICAL AND SEMANTIC RELATIONS AMONG VERBS AND SYNSETS

The number of relations in WordNet was kept deliberately small, and lumping together several subrelations as well as ignoring certain semantic distinctions seemed justified for several reasons.[4] Chaffin, Fellbaum, and Jenei (1994) show that subjects do not distinguish between different types of manner relation (path, instrument, direction, etc.) or semantic opposition (converse, contradictory, reversives, etc.). When asked to write a sentence expressing the relation between verb pairs linked by different kinds of manner relation, subjects generated the same sentence for all pairs; the same was true for pairs linked by different kinds of semantic opposition.

Semantically opposed verbs have been found to co-occur in text with frequencies far higher than expected by chance (Fellbaum 1995). This high co-occurrence rate is independent of the particular kind of opposition (see Mettinger 1994 for a classification and analyses of different kinds of semantic opposition).

Finally, keeping the number of relations small has meant that they can be conveniently displayed on a pull-down menu in the WordNet interface (see Tengi, this volume).

3.3.1 Entailment

The different relations that organize the verbs can be cast in terms of one overarching principle, lexical entailment. *Entailment* is used here to refer to the relation between two verbs V_1 and V_2 that holds when the sentence *Someone V_1* logically entails the sentence *Someone V_2*. For example, *snore* lexically entails *sleep* because the sentence *He is snoring* entails *He is sleeping*; the second sentence necessarily holds if the the first one does.

Lexical entailment is a unilateral relation: if a verb V_1 entails another verb V_2, then it cannot be the case that V_2 entails V_1. When two verbs can be said to be mutually entailing, they must be synonyms; that is, they must have the same sense. Negation reverses the direction of entailment: *not sleeping* entails *not snoring*, but *not snoring* does not entail *not sleeping*. The converse of entailment is contradiction: if the sentence *He is snoring* entails *He is sleeping*, then *He is snoring* also contradicts the sentence *He is not sleeping* (Kempson 1977).

The entailment relation between verbs resembles meronymy between nouns, but meronymy is better suited to nouns than to verbs. To begin with, in order for sentences based on the formula *An x is part of a y* to be acceptable, both *x* and *y* must be nouns. The gerundive form of the verbs converts them into nouns, and as nouns they should be related by the HAS-A relation. For example, Rips and Conrad (1989) obtained consistent results when they asked subjects to judge questions like *Is thinking a part of planning?* versus *Is planning a part of thinking?* But this change in syntactic category does not overcome fundamental meaning differences between nouns and verbs. Fellbaum and Miller (1990) argue that, first, verbs cannot be taken apart in the same way as nouns, because the parts of the activities, events, or states that verbs refer to are not analogous to the parts of the referents of nouns. Most noun parts have distinct, delimited referents. Activities, states, and events, on the other hand, do not have the same kind of distinct parts that characterize objects, groups, or substances. Breaking up verbs into semantic components (as in a Lexical Conceptual Structure) shows that verbs cannot easily be decomposed into referents denoted solely by verbs; Lexical Conceptual Structures are typically made up of verbs, nouns, and prepositions. Second, the relations among parts of activities, events, and states differ from those found among the referents of noun parts. Any acceptable statement about part relations between two verbs always involves the temporal relation between the activities that the verbs denote. One activity or event is part of another activity or event only when it is part of, or a stage in, its temporal realization.[5]

People will accept part-whole statements involving verb pairs like *drive-ride*. Although neither activity is a discrete part of the other, the two are connected in that when you drive a vehicle, you necessarily also ride in it. Similarly, *snoring* or *dreaming* can be a part of *sleeping*, in the sense that the two activities are, at least partially, temporally coextensive: the time that you spend snoring or dreaming is a proper part of the time you spend sleeping. And it is true that when you stop sleeping, you also necessarily stop snoring or dreaming (but you may continue sleeping without snoring). The differences between pairs like *drive* and *ride* and *snore* and *sleep* are due to the temporal relations between the members of each pair. The activities can be simultaneous (as with *drive* and *ride*), or one can include the other (as with *snore* and *sleep*). For both pairs, engaging in one activity necessitates engaging in the other activity. Therefore, the first activity in each pair entails the second.

The two semantic relations subsumed under lexical entailment that we have considered so far share the feature of temporal inclusion. That is to say, the sets of verbs related by entailment have in common that one member temporally includes the other. A verb V_1 will be said to include a verb V_2 if there is some stretch of time during which the activities denoted by the two verbs co-occur, but no time during which V_2 occurs and V_1 does not. If there is a time during which V_1 occurs but V_2 does not, V_1 will be said to properly include V_2.

Temporal inclusion may go in either direction. Verb pairs like *buy* and *pay* differ from those like *snore* and *sleep* in that whereas *snore* entails *sleep* and is properly included by it, *buy* entails *pay* but properly includes it. That is to say, either the entailing or the entailed verb may properly include the other.

3.3.1.1 Hyponymy among Verbs

The sentence frame used to test hyponymy between nouns, *An x is a y*, is not suitable for verbs, because it requires that *x* and *y* be nouns: *To amble is kind of to walk* is not a felicitous sentence. Lyons (1977, 294) notes that verbs cannot be fit into the formula *x is a kind of y* without prior nominalization. But even in their gerundive form, verbs and nouns differ. In the case of nouns, *kind of*, which makes the hierarchical relation explicit, can be omitted from the formula. Thus, speakers are quite comfortable with statements like *A horse is an animal* or *A spade is a garden tool*. However, they are likely to reject such statements as *Ambling is walking* or *Mumbling is talking*, where the superordinate is not accompanied by some qualification. This indicates that the semantic distinction between two verbs is different from the features that distinguish two nouns in a hyponymic relation.

An examination of "verb hyponyms" and their superordinates shows that lexicalization involves many kinds of semantic elaborations across different semantic fields. For example, Talmy's (1985) analysis of motion verbs treats them as conflations of *move* and such semantic components as MANNER and CAUSE, exemplified by *slide* and *pull*, respectively. To these components could be added SPEED (encoded in *run, stroll*) or the CONVEYANCE of displacement (*bus, truck, bike*). Similarly, English verbs denoting different kinds of *hitting* express the DEGREE OF FORCE used by the agent (*chop, slam, whack, swat, rap, tap, peck*, etc.). Some verbs refer to different degrees of INTENSITY of the action or state (*drowse, doze, sleep; whisper, shout*).

In WordNet the many different kinds of elaborations that distinguish a "verb hyponym" from its superordinate have been merged into a manner relation that Fellbaum and Miller (1990) have dubbed *troponymy*. The troponymy relation between two verbs can be expressed by the formula *To V_1 is to V_2 in some particular manner. Manner* is interpreted here more loosely than in Talmy's work, for example, and troponyms can be related to their superordinates along many semantic dimensions. Subsets of particular kinds of manners tend to cluster within a given semantic field. Among competition verbs, for example, many troponyms are conflations of the basic verb *fight* with nouns denoting the occasion for, or form of, the fight: *battle, war, tourney, joust, duel, feud*, and so on. Troponyms of communication verbs often encode the speaker's INTENTION or motivation for communicating, as in *examine, confess,* or *preach,* or the MEDIUM of communication, as in *fax, e-mail, phone,* or *telex.*

3.3.1.2 Troponymy and Entailment Troponymy is a particular kind of entailment. First, every troponym V_1 of a more general verb V_2 also entails V_2. Thus, *march* is a troponym of *walk,* but *marching* also entails *walking.* Second, the activities referred to by a troponym and its more general superordinate are always temporally coextensive; for example, one must necessarily be walking every instant that one is marching (though one need not be marching every instant that one is walking). Troponymy therefore represents a special case of entailment: pairs that are always temporally coextensive and are related by entailment.

In contrast with pairs like *march-walk,* a verb like *walk* entails and is included in *step,* but is not a troponym of *step; snore* entails *sleep,* but is not a troponym of *sleep.* The verbs in these pairs are related only by entailment and proper temporal inclusion; verbs related by entailment and proper temporal inclusion cannot also be related by troponymy.

3.3.1.3 Verb Taxonomies Verb hierarchies constructed by means of the troponymy relation tend to have a more shallow, bushy structure than nouns; in most cases the number of hierarchical levels does not exceed four. Moreover, virtually every verb taxonomy shows what might be called a bulge, that is to say, a level with far more verbs than the other levels in the same hierarchy. Call this layer L, the layer above it $L + 1$, and the layer below it $L - 1$. Certain parallels can be drawn between L and what has been called the basic level in noun hierarchies (Rosch et al. 1976). Consider, for example, the taxonomy arising from (one sense of) the verb *talk*: the highest-level ($L + 2$) verb is *communicate*; the next lower level $L + 1$ contains relatively few verbs, including *talk* and *write.* However, *talk* (L) has many troponyms, including *babble, mumble, slur, murmur,* and *bark.* Although a statement relating $L + 1$ to $L + 2$—*To talk is to communicate in some manner*—is perfectly acceptable, statements relating L to $L + 1$—*To babble/mumble/slur/murmur … is to talk in some manner*—seem more felicitous; these verbs elaborate the concept "talk" in distinct ways, yet the features of *talk* are still clearly present. *Talk,* on the other hand, seems semantically more remote from its superordinate, *communicate.* And $L - 1$ has few members, which tend to be compounded (such as *telecommunicate*).[6]

As one descends in a verb hierarchy, the variety of nouns that the verbs on a given level can take as potential arguments decreases. This seems to be a function of the increasing elaboration and meaning specificity of the verbs. Thus, figures or pictures can *communicate* and *talk*; they can even *deceive* or *lie*; but they cannot *fib* or *perjure themselves*, as only human speakers can.

Occasionally, it is difficult to assign a verb to a single superordinate. (The same is true of nouns; *piano* in WordNet is both a kind of "stringed instrument" and a kind of "percussion instrument.") For example, *sprawl* may mean either to sit or to lie with one's limbs extended. Pulman (1983) notes that many verbs denoting manners of killing (*hang, strangle, shoot,* etc.) can be both manners of killing and manners of executing someone (i.e., killing someone as a form of punishment that is sanctioned by society). Although (as here) the existence of two appropriate superordinates might indicate a tangled hierarchy, in other cases, such as the verb *whistle* discussed earlier, it might argue for the polysemy of the verb.

Artificial intelligence researchers have argued for a semantic network model of lexical memory on the grounds that it is economical: thinking of a *poodle* as a *dog* means storing all the information about dogs via the inheritance principle (see G. A. Miller, this volume). In the case of verbs, too, some knowledge about a verb concept is inherited from its superordinate. For example, the troponyms of (one sense of) the verb *communicate* inherit their argument structure from their superordinate (three arguments linked to nouns denoting a communicator (a source), a message, and a recipient). Similarly, although troponyms of *speak* may differ widely in the particular manners of speaking they denote, they all share the aspects of meaning associated with *speak* (vibration of the vocal cords, movement of the lips and tongue, etc.).

3.3.2   Semantic Opposition among Verbs

The pointer labeled OPPOSITION in the verb lexicon in fact expresses a complex relation encompassing several distinct subtypes of semantic opposition. For example, converses are opposites that are associated with no common superordinate or entailed verb: *give/take, buy/sell, lend/ borrow, teach/learn*, and so on. They have in common that they occur within the same semantic field: they refer to the same activity, but the thematic roles associated with them (SOURCE and GOAL) are mapped differently in the surface structure of the sentences in which they occur. The fact that both verbs refer to the same action would lead one to surmise that their strong lexical association is probably due to their frequent co-occurrence in usage.[7]

Most antonymous verbs are stative or change-of-state verbs that can be expressed in terms of attributes. Among stative verbs there are many contradictory pairs, which do not tolerate degree adverbs: *live/die, exclude/include, differ/equal, wake/sleep.* Opposition relations are also frequent among change verbs. Virtually no other relation (other than synonymy) holds these verbs together. Thus, the organization of this suburb of the lexicon is flat rather than hierarchical: there are no superordinates (except the generic *change* and *be* or *have*) and virtually no troponyms. Change verbs and stative verbs generally have a structure resembling that of direct antonymous adjectives, with only synonymy and opposition relations. Many deadjectival verbs of change formed with a suffix such as *-en* or *-ify* inherit opposition relations from their root adjectives: *lengthen/shorten, strengthen/weaken, prettify/uglify,* for example.

As in the case of adjectives, much of the opposition among verbs is based on the morphological markedness of one member of an opposed pair, as in the pairs *tie/untie* and *appear/disappear.* Semantic opposition among verbs is a lexical relation holding among particular verb forms. Thus, the members of the pairs *fall/descend* and *rise/ascend* seem identical in meaning, yet they are distinguished by the way they pick out their direct antonyms: *rise/descend* and *ascend/fall* are conceptually opposed, but are not direct antonyms; only *rise/fall* and *ascend/descend* form salient oppositions. The strong lexical, rather than conceptual, associations may be partly based on the contexts in which these verbs occur (i.e., on the differences in their selectional restrictions).

Many semantically opposed verb pairs are co-troponyms (sisters) whose opposition is contained in the manner that differentiates them from their shared superordinate. For example, *rise/fall* and *walk/run* differ with respect to the direction and the speed of the motion they refer to, respectively. Other semantically opposed pairs share an entailed verb. For example, *fail* and *succeed* both entail *try,* because one must necessarily try in order to either fail or succeed; *forget* (a fact, a name, etc.) entails *know,* because one can only forget something that one has known. In contrast to the kinds of entailment discussed earlier, these verbs are related not by temporal inclusion but by a kind of backward presupposition, where the activity denoted by the entailed verb always precedes the activity denoted by the entailing verb. Entailment via backward presupposition also holds between certain verb pairs linked by a result or purpose relation, such as *fatten-feed.*

Some opposition relations interact with the entailment relation in a systematic way. Cruse (1986) distinguishes an opposition relation that holds between verb pairs like *damage* and *repair*, and *remove* and *replace*. One member of these pairs, Cruse states, constitutes a "restitutive." This kind of opposition also always includes entailment, in that the restitutive verb always presupposes what one might call the "deconstructive" one. Many reversive *un-* or *de-* verbs also presuppose their unprefixed, opposed counterpart: in order to *untie, unwrap*, or *unscrew* something, (some)one must have *tied, wrapped*, or *screwed* it first.

3.3.3   The Cause Relation

The cause relation picks out two verb concepts, one causative (like *give*), the other what might be called "resultative" (like *have*). English has lexicalized causative pairs like *show-see* and *fell-fall*, which are linked in WordNet by the appropriate pointer.

In addition, WordNet contains CAUSE pointers from causative, transitive verbs to the corresponding anticausative (inchoative), intransitive sense of the same word; most of these are found among the verbs of change. Examples are *blacken, develop, break*, and *shrink*. Most anticausative verbs imply either an animate agent or an inanimate cause (*The glass door broke—The storm/The children broke the glass door*). A few verbs are compatible only with an inanimate cause: *The wooden deck molded—All that rain molded the wooden deck* is acceptable, but *The house sitter molded the wooden deck* is not.

The cause relation also shows up systematically among the motion verbs: *bounce, roll, blow*, and the like, alternate between a causative and an anticausative usage (*She blew a soap bubble in his face* vs. *The soap bubble blew in his face*). Whereas the causative variants of these verbs usually require an inanimate object, some unergative verbs like *run, jump, gallop, walk, race*, which select for an animate agent, can also have a causative reading, as in the sentences *He raced the horse past the barn* and *The father walked his son to school*. (See Levin 1985 and Pinker 1989 for a conceptual analysis of these verbs and its implications for language acquisition.)

Carter (1976) notes that causation is a specific kind of entailment: if V_1 necessarily causes V_2, then V_1 also entails V_2. He cites the entailment relation between verb pairs like *expel* and *leave*, or *bequeath* and *own*, where the entailing verb denotes the causation of the state or activity referred to by the entailed verb. Like all entailment relations, cause is

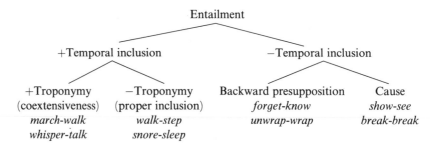

Figure 3.1
Four kinds of entailment relations between verbs.

unidirectional: *feeding* somebody causes that person to *eat*, but some-body's *eating* does not entail that someone *feeds* that person. An excep-tion is that when the subject of *eat* is not a potentially independent agent, such as a baby or a confined animal, then *eating* does entail the causative act of *feeding*. But this belongs to the realm of world knowledge, not word knowledge.

The four different kinds of lexical entailment that systematically interact with the semantic relations coded in WordNet are related in figure 3.1.

3.4 POLYSEMY

English has far fewer verbs than nouns, and verbs are approximately twice as polysemous as nouns (Fellbaum 1990). In the course of creating the semantic concordance (Landes, Leacock, and Tengi, this volume), we encountered many extended uses of verbs that do not follow straight-forwardly from standard dictionary definitions. In order to fit the partic-ular context in which a verb was found in either the Standard Corpus of Present-Day Edited American English (the Brown Corpus; Kučera and Francis 1967) or *The Red Badge of Courage*, we have tended to split rather than lump senses; that is, fine sense distinctions are explicitly drawn rather than subsumed under a more broadly interpretable, but underspecified, single verb.

The most frequently used verbs (*have, be, run, make, set, go, take*, and others) are also highly polysemous, and their meanings often depend heavily on the nouns with which they co-occur. Even when they function as light verbs (Grimshaw and Mester 1988), these verbs have several distinct meanings. For example, *make* in *Make love, not war* means 'to engage in', whereas in *make a stink* it has a creation sense. This kind of polysemy often can be discerned only if one examines the noun classes that constitute the arguments of the verbs, and a sufficient number of examples can be found only in a large text such as the ones that were tagged during the creation of the semantic concordance.

The importance of the noun's contribution to the meaning of a verb is at the core of much recent work in lexical semantics. Pustejovsky (1991, 1995) argues against static, bounded word senses and proposes instead the notion of a more flexible "Generative Lexicon." He points out the polysemy of some aspectual verbs like *begin*, experiencer verbs like *enjoy*, and many causatives, whose specific meanings depend largely on the particular context in which they occur. For example, *finish* and *enjoy* in (1) mean 'finish/enjoy smoking', whereas in (2) they mean 'finish/enjoy drinking':

(1) Paul finished/enjoyed the cigar.

(2) Paul finished/enjoyed the beer.

Here *the cigar* and *the beer* "coerce" the meaning of the verbs. Pustejovsky proposes a mechanism whereby the contribution of the verb's arguments to its meaning is captured in a systematic fashion. This attractive proposal could be captured in WordNet if nouns and verbs were linked; nouns could be related to verbs expressing characteristic functions (see G. A. Miller, this volume). However, it is not clear at which level the links should be made if one strives for maximal economy in the lexicon but wants to avoid large numbers of exceptions.

3.4.1 Polysemy and Troponymy: Autohyponymy

A look at the verb lexicon as a semantic network shows that it shares certain properties with the noun lexicon. For example, there are "autorelations"; that is, some of the senses of a number of polysemous verb are linked by the semantic relations usually found only between distinct word forms. For example, there are polysemous verbs whose senses are related by troponymy; that is to say, a semantically more elaborate verb is sometimes expressed by the same surface form as its more general superordinate. Thus, *behave* in its broader sense means 'conduct oneself'; in another, more specific sense, it means 'conduct oneself well':

(3) The children behaved {terribly/well} last night.

(4) The children behaved last night.

The superordinate subcategorizes for an adverb, as (3) shows. For the second sense of *behave*, illustrated in (4), the superordinate sense of the verb has been conflated with a particular adverb, *well*. Because the adverb has been incorporated into that verb, the subcategorization requirement is satisfied. The two senses of *behave* are distinct not only semantically but also syntactically; whereas the more specific sense of *behave* can never be followed by an adverb, the semantically less elaborate sense requires an adverb.

Polysemy among hierarchically related verbs always involves a conflation of the constituent that distinguishes the semantically richer subordinate from its superordinate. Other verbs (e.g., *dress* and *fit*) behave similarly and show the same difference in semantic structure with respect to the absence or presence of an incorporated adverb (Fellbaum, to appear).

Some polysemous verbs have an incorporated noun argument. For example, the transitive superordinate *drink* takes noun arguments that are hyponyms of *liquid* or *beverage*. The intransitive subordinate verb has the more specific sense of 'to drink alcoholic beverages', with a conflated noun (representing an entire noun class) implied. This sense is illustrated in (5):

(5) We were up drinking all night.

Another intransitive, closely related subordinate sense is 'be an alcoholic/drink alcohol regularly'; here, both a noun class and an adverb have been conflated with the verb:

(6) The pilot lost her job because she drinks.

Another example of a polysemous verb pair where one sense incorporates a specific noun (class) is *furnish*:

(7) They now furnish the area with electricity. (= 'provide')

(8) They furnished the apartment. (= 'provide with furniture')

In (8) the elaborated sense of *provide* incorporates the noun *furniture*; only specific subordinates of this noun (such as *Danish furniture*) can be expressed on the surface:

(9) They furnished the house with *(Danish) furniture.

In the superordinate verb, on the other hand, a MATERIAL argument of *provide* must be expressed.

The more semantically specific member of a homomorphous poly-semous verb pair often expresses that the action is carried out in a success-ful way. Thus, *guess* can mean either 'make a guess' or 'guess correctly/right'—the latter sense conflates the superordinate and an adverbial adjunct:

(10) I guessed the number of beans in the jar. (= 'guess successfully')

(11) How did you figure out the number of beans? I guessed. (= 'make a guess')

Here, the more general sense is intransitive, whereas the transitive sense has an incorporated adverb (*successfully* or *correctly*). Similarly, the sense of *handle* without a surface manner adjunct means 'handle successfully'; *fit* without an adverb means 'fit right'; *impress* signifies 'impress favor-ably'; and so on. Other examples include *behave* and *suit*; here, the more specific sense includes an adverbial sense like *well*, *appropriately*, or *favorably*. The adverbs here all seem to come from one end of an anto-nymic scale.

Clark and Clark (1979) studied the meaning relations between nouns and the homomorphous verbs derived from them, such as *tailor*, *parent*, and *master* (also see Lehrer 1990 on the limited productivity of this and similar patterns). Some denominal verbs have several related meanings, only one of which carries a meaning element referring to the noun:

(12) We sailed to Southampton (on the *QE II*/a big steamer). (= 'travel on a boat')

(13) We sailed on the lake *in a motorboat. (= 'travel in a sailboat')

(14) The committee forged a new policy. (= 'make')

(15) The smith forged the metal *at a forge. (= 'make at a forge')

The superordinate sense in (12) means 'travel on water'; as the possible adjuncts show, this sense of *sail* is not in contrast with a hyponym such as *steam*. Similarly, the verb in (14) is the superordinate of the verb in (15). In both (13) and (15), the subordinate, more restricted sense is the denominal one.

3.4.2 Polysemy and Entailment

There appear to be a few polysemous verbs whose senses are related by the kind of entailment that holds between verb pairs like *snore* and *sleep*. *Webster's Third* lists the following two senses of *drive*:

(16) 'to operate and steer a vehicle'

(17) 'to have oneself carried in a vehicle'

This distinction is no longer clear in a sentence like (18), where the president may or may not be the driver. In the former case, his driving (operating the car) necessarily entails his driving (being a passenger):

(18) The president drove on to the Capitol.

Similarly, *sew* in a sentence like (19)

(19) She sewed her dress.

is ambiguous between a sense meaning 'fasten or join (fabric) by stitching' and another sense meaning 'make or create by sewing', where the second sense entails the first. Thus, if (19) means 'She made a dress', then it entails that 'She fastened together pieces of fabric by stitching'.

3.4.3   Polysemy and Opposition: Autoantonymy

A semantic split resulting in a verb's acquiring a second sense that is more elaborate than the first does not seem totally surprising. However, that a verb could also mean its opposite would appear contrary to sound lexical principles. Nevertheless, Horn (1988), citing examples given by Clark and Clark (1979), discusses cases where the different senses of polysemous verbs stand in a relation of semantic opposition:

(20) These manufacters now bone their shirt collars. (= 'provide with bones, stays')

(21) She boned the turkey. (= 'remove the bones from')

(22) The violinist strung his instrument. (= 'provide with strings')

(23) Could you string these beans, please? (= 'remove the strings from')

The semantic distinction between the verbs can be seen in sentences like (24) and (25):

(24) *We strung the beads and the beans.

(25) *She seeded the clouds and the grapes.

Horn (1988) points out that under one reading the verb selects a GOAL argument (as in (20) and (22)), whereas under the opposite reading it selects a SOURCE (as in (21) and (23)). (24) and (25) are bad because they contain both kinds of objects, which are semantically incompatible. In the cases where the direct object is a SOURCE, such verbs have synonyms with a negative prefix: *debone a turkey*, *unpit a cherry*, and so on. Horn states that this prefixation is redundant and occurs only in cases where both GOAL and SOURCE readings are plausible, or where the speaker wants to be absolutely certain to avoid ambiguity. The avoidance of redundancy, then, provides the language with polysemous verbs, whose two senses are in a relation of semantic opposition. Other examples (from Horn 1988) are *seed a lawn/grapes*, *dust the crops/furniture*, and *milk the tea/cow*.

3.5   TESTING THE PSYCHOLOGICAL VALIDITY OF THE WORDNET MODEL

It turns out that the semantic organization of verbs in WordNet has some psychological validity. Chaffin, Fellbaum, and Jenei (1994) conducted several experiments that were specifically intended to test the psychological reality of the relations in WordNet.

First, Chaffin, Fellbaum, and Jenei (1994) wanted to see whether linguistically naive subjects could identify different relations among a number of verb pairs. Subjects were presented with three different tasks involving the four kinds of entailment relations (troponymy, proper inclusion, backward presupposition, and cause). In an analogy task, 48 subjects were shown one verb pair (the stem) and asked to choose from among six other pairs the one whose members bear the same relation to each other as the members of the stem (the key). Subjects selected the key pairs at almost three times the level expected by chance, but almost half the answers disagreed with the WordNet classification.

In a sorting experiment, a different group of 12 subjects were asked to sort examples of the four relations, a task that allowed more latitude for subjects to impose their own classifications. A hierarchical clustering analysis revealed that subjects identified four main groups of relations corresponding to the WordNet classification of four kinds of entailment.

Finally, a third group of 40 subjects were given verb pairs illustrating the different kinds of entailment relations. They were asked to write a rationale sentence explicating the relation between the verb pairs. The results showed that subjects agreed with the WordNet classification of the relations, although there was little overlap in the particular sentences that subjects used to describe the relations. In this task, there was greatest agreement about troponymy. Troponymy was also the relation for which subjects were most accurate in the analogy task, and for which the highest agreement was found in the sorting task. The least amount of agreement was found, in all three experiments, in the cases involving proper inclusion and presupposition. These relations seem intuitively less obvious than troponymy and cause.

In the experiments described above, the subjects were given verb pairs linked by WordNet relations. It could be argued that this constrained and possibly biased the subjects' responses. Forcing the subjects to consider only verb pairs that were linked by WordNet relations may not reflect how verbs are in fact organized in speakers' mental lexicons. Therefore, Chaffin, Fellbaum, and Jenei examined data from association experiments, which are a good source of evidence of speakers' mental organization of the lexicon. In such experiments, participants are given a word and asked to respond with the first word that comes to mind. The hypothesis is that the response word is stored in close proximity to the stimulus word. Chaffin, Fellbaum, and Jenei analyzed the existing association data gathered by Palermo and Jenkins (1964), who presented 1,000 students with 200 stimuli, of which 23 were unambiguously verbs. Of the responses to these verb stimuli, only 38.1% were other verbs; 93.3% of these verb responses could be classified as being related to the stimulus via one of the WordNet relations. Troponymy and opposition were most frequently represented, pointing to the psychological salience of these relations.

Chaffin, Fellbaum, and Jenei also collected their own association data, using verbs from different semantic domains as stimuli. First, responses to 75 verb stimuli from 14 subjects were analyzed. Only 30.4% of the responses were verbs; of those, 91% were related to the stimulus via one of the relations coded in WordNet. As in the case of Palermo and Jenkins's data, troponymy and opposition related most of the stimulus-response pairs, with synonymy being somewhat less frequent, and presupposition, inclusion, and cause linking stimulus and response least often. As in other experiments of this kind. more than half of the responses were nouns. Chaffin, Fellbaum, and Jenei classified about 90% of these noun responses as typical members of the semantic class of nouns that express the arguments of the verb stimuli. For example, common stimulus-response pairs were *eat-food*, *eat-dinner*, *sing-soprano*, and *open-key*. Moreover, for transitive and unaccusative verbs, subjects produced nouns that typically express the internal arguments of these verbs, whereas for unergative and activity verbs with transitive-intransitive alternations, they produced frequently occurring subject nouns. The fact that about half of the responses to verbs are nouns suggests that verbs are not only related to other verbs in semantic memory, but also represented as parts of states, events, and activities, denoted by the kind of noun-verb pairs that emerge from association experiments.

Similar results were obtained when Chaffin, Fellbaum, and Jenei asked subjects to respond to 25 verb stimuli with verbs only. In this case 82.6% of all responses, and 91.7% of first responses, were verbs linked to the stimulus via a WordNet relation, with troponymy, opposition, and synonymy being most frequently represented.

These results support the notion that the relations organizing the verb lexicon in WordNet also serve to link some verbs and verb concepts in speakers' minds. Troponymy, which is the most frequently coded relation in WordNet, was identified most often as linking stimulus-response pairs. However, it seems clear that verbs and nouns are at least as strongly related.

3.6 ALTERNATIVE MODELS OF THE VERB LEXICON

A relational network like WordNet represents but one particular approach to the lexicon. Linguists, psychologists, and anthropologists have devised different representations of the lexicon depending on which aspects of the language they focused on. WordNet does not constitute an attempt to capture all the knowledge that comes with knowing a word. However, much of the information that is explicit in other models of the verb lexicon is implicitly contained in WordNet. WordNet could be augmented with additional information without disturbing its particular weblike design.

3.6.1 Semantic Fields

A view of the structure of the lexicon in terms of semantic fields (Lehrer and Feder Kittay 1992, and papers therein) somewhat resembles that of WordNet with its fieldlike domains. A semantic field analysis is based on the belief that the meaning of a word in a given field arises from similarity and contrast relations between it and other words in that field. In contrast to WordNet, however, semantic field analyses usually employ both paradigmatic and syntagmatic relations. In WordNet the information about a word's selectional preferences is not part of the network structure, but instead tends to be part of the parenthetical material accompanying most synsets; for verbs, this information often specifies what kinds of nouns occur as typical arguments of the verbs in the synset.

3.6.2   Schemata and Frame Analysis

Some linguists and lexicographers argue that a purely relational analysis is not sufficient to describe speakers' representation of the verb lexicon. They propose a theory based on cognitive frames or knowledge schemata that encompass speakers' experiences and beliefs and provide a conceptual foundation for the meaning of words (e.g., Schank and Abelson 1977). Words and the concepts they stand for are not directly interrelated, but share membership in common frames or schemata.

Fillmore and Atkins (1992) propose a "frame-based" dictionary in which word senses are linked with cognitive structures, or frames, whose knowledge is presupposed for the concepts expressed by the lexical items. A lexical item is associated with a "valence description," which specifies both the syntactic and the semantic contribution of the word in its contexts. Fillmore and Atkins discuss in detail the commercial transaction frame. They distinguish the categories (MONEY, BUYER, SELLER, GOODS) and the verbs (*buy, sell, charge, cost,* etc.) associated with this frame and show how different sentences and syntactic constructions referring to commercial transaction events can be derived in an elegant and economical fashion.

Although WordNet does not link verbs with specific nouns, it provides syntactic frames for each verb, indicating the number of noun arguments that the verb subcategorizes for. However, the noun slots in these syntactic frames are not at present linked to either thematic roles or semantic categories like BUYER.[8] WordNet could be augmented in such a way that semantic and thematic roles are linked to the noun arguments in the frames that accompany each synset. In that case the opposition relation between verb pairs like *buy* and *sell* would be reflected in the reversal of the noun arguments as well (the BUYER and SELLER arguments that are mapped onto the subject and the oblique object in the case of *buy*, respectively, are mapped onto the indirect object and the subject in the case of *sell*). Further, *buy* and *pay* are related in WordNet by entailment, and linking the noun arguments specified in the syntactic frames to thematic roles would show clearly that the BUYER argument in one case is also the argument expressing the one who pays.

3.6.3   Compositional Analyses

Most approaches to verb semantics have been attempts at decomposition in one form or another. Early proponents of semantic decomposition (e.g., Katz and Fodor 1963; Katz 1972; Gruber 1976; Lakoff 1970; Jackendoff 1972; Schank 1972; Miller and Johnson-Laird 1976), whether in a generative or an interpretive framework, argued for the existence of a finite set of universal semantic-conceptual components (or primes, or primitives, or atomic predicates, or, in the case of nouns, markers) into which all lexical items could be exhaustively decomposed. Among the best-known examples of the decomposition of a verb is McCawley's (1968) analysis of *kill* into CAUSE TO BECOME NOT ALIVE, which has been much discussed (e.g., Fodor 1970; Shibatani 1972).

These early attempts at semantic decomposition were much criticized as an inadequate theory of semantic representation (e.g., Chomsky 1972) and subsequently abandoned. However, more recent approaches to verb semantics have taken a similar line by representing the meaning of a verb in terms of its Lexical Conceptual Structure (LCS) (e.g., Hale and Laughren 1983; Jackendoff 1983; Talmy 1985). An LCS typically consists of conceptual categories such as PATH, MANNER, and PLACE, in addition to irreducible verb concepts such as BECOME, DO, and CAUSE. For example, Jackendoff (1983) represents the verb *lose* (as in *Beth lost her doll*) as a possession going on an abstract PATH, namely, (away) from the possessor.

An analyis of verbs in terms of their LCS (e.g., Jackendoff 1983) can reveal patterns of lexical structure. Thus, Talmy's (1985) work illustrates how English motion verbs differ from their counterparts in the Romance languages in terms of the particular combinations of meaning components that compose the field of motion verbs. A semantic analysis of verbs in terms of LCSs also explains their syntactic behavior. For example, Hale and Keyser (1987) and Levin and Rapoport (1988) argue that only verbs whose LCS contains a CAUSE component can undergo middle formation. Moreover, many aspects of how children acquire the syntax and semantics of verbs can be explained in terms of the verbs' semantic components (e.g., Pinker 1989).

In contrast to a decompositional approach, a relational analysis like WordNet's takes only other verbs as the smallest unit of analysis. This has the advantage that the units can be thought of as entries in speakers' mental dictionaries. However, the relational analysis adopted in WordNet shares some aspects of decomposition.

First, some categories that make up LCSs are verb concepts (CHANGE, GO, STAY, BE, DO, and others). These correspond to either unique beginners or high-level verbs in the WordNet hierarchies. Verbs whose LCSs are made up of these components are troponyms in WordNet. Second, at least one element of many verbs' LCSs, CAUSE, has the status of a semantic relation in WordNet. Thus, in the LCS of a verb like *give*, CAUSE is an explicit component, whereas in WordNet this semantic aspect of *give* is expressed only via the CAUSE relation to *have*. Third, semantic components of some verbs, such as Talmy's (1985) PATH, found in many verbs of motion, are implicit in the troponymy relation linking verbs like *move* and *traverse*. PATH, like SPEED, is arguably a subrelation of troponymy in the domain of motion verbs.

Although a compositional treatment of verbs differs formally from a relational one, there are significant points of overlap, and the representation of verb meanings in WordNet shares some aspects of a compositional analysis.

3.6.4   Lexical Subordination

Levin and Rapoport (1988) show that many verbs are semantically composed of other verbs. They cite as an example the different meanings of *brush* in phrases like the following:

(26) brush the tangles out

(27) brush a hole in one's coat

(28) brush the coat clean

Levin and Rapoport point out that each use of *brush* here has a paraphrase in which *brush* is not the main verb. Thus, (26) means 'remove the tangles by brushing'; (27) can be paraphrased as 'create a hole by brushing'; and (28) has the meaning 'cause to become clean by brushing'.

Verbs of communicating by bodily gestures (*He nodded his assent*) are similar examples of verbs with extended meanings. Levin and Rapoport (1988) argue that the different types of extended meaning constructions form a natural class of verbs derived by a process they call lexical subordination, which creates a new, more complex LCS through the incorporation of a semantic component.

In WordNet the compositional meanings of verbs like *brush* and *nod* are represented as distinct senses of these polysemous verbs. They are troponyms of the different basic verbs that Levin and Rapoport describe. Thus, users can access the different senses of a verb like *nod*, including the one glossed as 'express by nodding', and note its meaning extension as a communication verb. Alternatively, users can view the troponyms of the superordinate verb, *gesture* ('communicate nonverbally'), which include *nod*, *shrug*, and *wink*. The troponym list displays the class of verbs that can undergo the particular meaning extensions noted by Levin and Rapoport (1988). Thus, the multiple access to these verbs' meanings permitted by WordNet captures not only the polysemy of the individual verbs, but also their membership in a class of such verbs, as pointed out by Levin and Rapoport.

3.7 SEMANTIC RELATIONS AND SYNTACTIC REGULARITIES

An analysis of verbs in terms of their semantic and conceptual components can reveal many of the verbs' syntactic properties. Verbs whose LCSs are identical in terms of specific meaning components tend to share syntactic behavior, for example, with respect to syntactic diatheses. Probably the most comprehensive exploration of parallel syntactic-semantic patterns in the English verb lexicon is that of Levin (1985, 1993), who examines a large number of semantically based verb classes and shows how syntactic patterns systematically accompany the semantic classification. Although discovering semantically coherent verb classes through shared syntactic behavior is a very different approach from the one taken by WordNet—which is trying to uncover the semantic organization of the lexicon in terms of lexical and semantic relations—the two endeavors share many results. Many of Levin's verb classes, which share certain syntactic properties, also constitute verb "trees" in WordNet, which are formed on purely semantic grounds by the MANNER relation. In fact, thinking about the verb lexicon in terms of hierarchies yields some syntactic generalizations.

3.7.1 Distinguishing Subtrees

An exploration of the syntactic properties of co-troponyms occasionally provides the basis for distinguishing semantic subgroups of troponyms.

As a case in point, consider verbs like *weave* and *mold*, which are members of the creation verb class. Many creation verbs participate in a syntactic alternation that Levin (1993) terms the Material/Product alternation, illustrated by the following examples:

(29) She wove a rug from the black sheep's wool.

(30) She wove the black sheep's wool into a rug.

(31) They molded a head from the clay.

(32) They molded the clay into a head.

Some verbs, like *fabricate* and *compose*, which are also members the creation verb class, do not participate in this syntactic alternation, despite their semantic similarity to verbs like *weave* and *mold*:

(33) The reporter fabricated a story out of the girl's account.

(34) *The reporter fabricated the girl's account into a story.

(35) She composed a quartet out of the old folk song.

(36) *She composed the old folk song into a quartet.

In discussing these verbs, Fellbaum and Kegl (1988) point out that the data suggest a need for a fine-grained subclassification of creation verbs that distinguishes verbs referring to acts of mental creation (such as *fabricate* and *compose*) from verbs denoting creation from raw materials (such as *weave* and *mold*). Such a distinction would account for the systematic difference among the verbs in most cases. Thus, Levin (1993) distinguishes these verbs in terms of membership in one of two classes: the BUILD class, which comprises verbs like *bake*, and the CREATE class, which comprises verbs like *compose* and *fabricate*. In WordNet we have drawn this distinction by means of two generic verb concepts, "create from raw material" and "create mentally." Although they are not lexicalized in English, these artificial top nodes heading two distinct trees make it possible to capture the generalization discussed above by means of different superordinates whose troponyms differ syntactically. The syntactic phenomena therefore justify postulating the two concepts in WordNet.

This example demonstrates how syntactic differences between apparently similar verbs can be cast in terms of the particular way in which the meanings of words are represented in WordNet.

3.7.2 Syntactic Reflexes of the Verb's Position within a Tree Structure

Viewing verbs in terms of semantic relations can also provide clues to understanding the verbs' syntactic behavior. Fellbaum and Kegl (1989) studied a class of English verbs that participate in the following transitive-intransitive alternation:

(37) Mary ate a bag of pretzels.

(38) Mary ate.

Previous analyses of these verbs have explained the alternation in terms of aspect (Mittwoch 1982). However, an analysis of the troponyms of the verb *eat* showed that they fall into two syntactic classes: those that must always be used transitively, and those that are always intransitive. The first class includes the verbs *gobble, guzzle, gulp,* and *devour*; the second class includes verbs like *dine, graze, nosh,* and *snack*. Fellbaum and Kegl suggest that this syntactic difference is not just a transitivity alternation characteristic of a single verb; rather, they suggest, it is semantically motivated. They show that English has two verbs *eat* and that each verb occupies a different position in the network; that is to say, each verb is part of a different taxonomy. Intransitive *eat* has the sense of 'eat a meal'. In some troponyms of this verb, such as the denominals *dine, breakfast, picnic,* and *feast,* the verb *eat* has become conflated with hyponyms of the noun *meal.* These verbs are intransitive because they are all lexicalizations of the verb *eat* that means 'eat a meal'. Other intransitive troponyms of this verb are *munch, nosh,* and *graze.* Although these verbs are not conflations of *eat* and a noun, they are semantically related in that they refer to eating informal kinds of meals or repasts. By contrast, the transitive verb *eat* has the sense of 'ingest in some manner', and its troponyms all refer to a specific manner of eating: *gobble, gulp, devour.* Thus, the semantics of the troponyms in each case provide a classification in terms of two distinct hierarchies matching the syntactic distinction between the two verb groups.

3.7.3   Restrictions on Middle Formation

Viewing the verb lexicon in terms of taxonomic trees can also shed light on a particular syntactic constraint that appears to be semantically based. One of the hallmarks of the middle construction is that it usually requires the presence of an adverb or adverbial:

(39) Her new novel sells *(fast/like hotcakes).

(40) This car drives *(easily/like a dream).

However, there are cases where the adverb requirement is relaxed:

(41) This vegetable microwaves (easily).

(42) This suitcase zips shut (in a flash). (note: *shut* is a resultative adjective)

The conditions for the relaxation of the adverb requirement can be explained if the verbs are viewed in terms of the hierarchical (troponymic) organization. Apparent synonyms then are in fact not synonyms, but troponyms or superordinate verbs that are semantically more or less elaborated. For example, the verb *cook* has a number of troponyms, including *fry, broil, braise,* and *microwave.* These verbs express different manners of cooking. Similarly, the troponyms of *close,* including *velcro, button, zip* and *snap,* refer to specific ways of closing something.

It turns out that the troponyms can occur in middles without adverbs (see (41) and (42)), whereas the superordinate, semantically less specific verbs must be accompanied by an adverb in the middle:

(43) This vegetable cooks *(quickly).

(44) This suitcase closes *(easily).

An adverb is required in the middle when the verb is a "basic"-level verb referring to an expected property of the subject.[9] Thus, the assertions that vegetables can be cooked and suitcases can be closed do not seem particularly interesting and, hence, natural; however, stating in what manner a certain vegetable can be cooked (or a certain suitcase can be closed) does convey real information. Note that the sentence stress in these middles must fall on the adverb.

By contrast, the middle sentences containing the troponyms refer to properties of the vegetable/suitcase that cannot necessarily be assumed a priori. Thus, the verbs here may carry new information. In that case they receive sentence stress and do not require an adverb. These verbs are in fact conflations of the superordinate and a manner adverbial: *microwave* means 'cook in a microwave oven'; *zip* means 'close with a zipper'; and so on. If this manner is asserted, rather than assumed, the need for an overt adverbial is obviated.

The transitive-intransitive alternations and the adverb requirement in middles demonstrate that viewing verbs in terms of semantic relations can also provide clues to understanding their syntactic behavior.

Ackerman and Goldberg (1996) provide another example for the usefulness of a hierarchical perspective on the verb lexicon. They note that certain deverbal past participles are infelicitous in prenominal (attributive) position:

(45) *a killed man

(46) *a changed design

(47) *a told secret

By contrast, participles based on semantically similar but more specific verbs (troponyms) can occur in these contexts:

(48) a murdered man

(49) an altered design

(50) a divulged secret

Ackerman and Goldberg conclude that the infelicitous adjectives do not supply sufficient information about their head nouns, and they propose the following principle:

(51) An adjectival past participle is not felicitous if it is based on a basic-level verb that contrasts with semantically more specific predicates.

3.8   CONCLUSION

A relational analysis of English verbs has revealed some striking ways in which verbs differ from nouns. The semantics of verbs are generally more complex. This chapter has discussed the different lexical and semantic relations among verbs, and some of the lexicalization patterns in various semantic domains that emerge from the particular organization imposed on the lexicon in WordNet. A semantic network of verbs can provide a useful perspective on syntactic patterns as well.

Notes

1. Such semantically unelaborated concepts, as well as others like *change* and *move*, have played a role in decompositional semantic analyses (e.g., Katz and Fodor 1963; Katz 1972; Gruber 1976; Lakoff 1970; Schank 1972; Miller and Johnson-Laird 1976), where they are thought to be members of a finite set of universal semantic-conceptual components (or primes, or primitives, or atomic predicates, or, in the case of nouns, markers) into which all lexical items can be exhaustively decomposed. Dowty (1979) claims that all verbs are ultimately composable as stative predicates, which, by means of aspectual connectives and operators such as DO, yield other verb classes. With the exception of the statives, Dowty additionally assigns to all verbs the operator BECOME as part of their lexical makeup. His analysis shows that all (nonstative) verbs can be classified as verbs of change, either as intransitives (stative predicates plus the operator BECOME) or as transitives (with the additional operator DO).

2. Cruse (1986, 1992) discusses the modulatory effect that accompanies the activation of the concept "die" when users encounter such emotively colored idioms as *snuff it* and *pass away*. He refers to the relation between the plain word *die* and "charged" idioms like *snuff it* as "nano-hyponymy," pointing out that although it is like hyponymy, it is not truth-conditional.

3. Researchers have tried to exploit the fact that there seem to be a limited number of canonical formulae for glossing word meanings in dictionaries. For example, Chodorow, Byrd, and Heidorn (1985) have used definitions to automatically extract noun hierarchies from dictionaries.

4. But see Cruse 1986 for detailed discussions of the semantics of interitem relations and subrelations, and their polysemy.

5. Some activities can be broken down into sequentially ordered subactivities. For the most part, these are complex activities that are said to be mentally represented as scripts (Schank and Abelson 1977). They tend not to be lexicalized in English: *eat at a restaurant, clean an engine, get a medical checkup,* and so on. The analysis into lexicalized subactivities that is possible for these verb phrases is, however, not available for the majority of simple verbs in English.

6. Rifkin (1985) cites interesting experimental evidence for the existence of basic levels in event taxonomies. However, his investigation focuses both on simple verbs and on verb phrases denoting complex events that comprise several sub-activities, such as *studying for a test* and *reading a book.* Many of his complex categories are lexicalized as nouns, like *meals* and *sports.* Therefore, his results cannot be directly compared with the kinds of verb taxonomies that seem to exist in the lexicon.

7. In Fellbaum 1995 it is shown that the co-occurrence phenomenon of antonymous words, hypothesized and confirmed for adjectives by Miller and Charles (1991) and Justeson and Katz (1991a,b), respectively, is independent of lexical category. Thus, semantically opposed verbs, too, co-occur in text with frequencies far higher than would be predicted by chance.

8. The syntactic frames in WordNet 1.5 are clearly not sufficient to fully characterize the verbs' lexical behavior. Karen Kohl has greatly enriched the syntactic information for verbs in WordNet (Kohl et al., this volume) by means of a program that generates sentences and sentence alternations based on Levin 1993 for the verbs; moreover, her program generates thematic roles for the nouns in these sentences.

9. For the notion of basic-level nouns, see Rosch et al. 1976. This notion also appears to be useful in examining certain properties of the verb lexicon (Fellbaum 1990).

References

Ackerman, F., and Goldberg, A. E. (1996). Constraints on adjectival past participles. In A. E. Goldberg (Ed.), *Conceptual structure, discourse and language,* 17–30. Stanford, CA: CSLI Publications.

Atkins, B. T. S., and Levin, B. (1991). Admitting impediments. In U. Zernik (Ed.), *Lexical acquisition: Exploiting on-line resources to build a lexicon,* 233–262. Hillsdale, NJ: Erlbaum.

Carter, R. (1976). Some constraints on possible words. *Semantikos, 1,* 27–66.

Chaffin, R., Fellbaum, C., and Jenei, J. (1994). *The paradigmatic organization of verbs in the mental lexicon.* Unpublished manuscript, Trenton State College.

Chodorow, M., Byrd, R., and Heidorn, G. (1985). Extracting semantic hierarchies from a large on-line dictionary. In *Proceedings of the 23rd Annual Meeting of the Association for Computational Linguistics,* 299–304. Association for Computational Linguistics.

Chomsky, N. (1972). *Studies on semantics in generative grammar.* The Hague: Mouton.

Clark, E. V., and Clark, H. H. (1979). When nouns surface as verbs. *Language*, *55*, 767–811.

Cramer, P. (1968). *Word association*. New York: Academic Press.

Cruse, D. A. (1986). *Lexical semantics*. New York: Cambridge University Press.

Cruse, D. A. (1992). Antonymy revisited: Some thoughts on the relationship between words and concepts. In A. Lehrer and E. Feder Kittay (Eds.), *Frames, fields, and contrasts*, 289–306. Hillsdale, NJ: Erlbaum.

Dowty, D. (1979). *Word meaning and Montague Grammar*. Dordrecht: Reidel.

Evens, M. (Ed.). (1988). *Relational models of the lexicon*. Cambridge, England: Cambridge University Press.

Fellbaum, C. (1990). English verbs as a semantic net. *International Journal of Lexicography*, *3*, 278–301.

Fellbaum, C. (1995). Co-occurrence and antonymy. *International Journal of Lexicography*, *8*, 281–303.

Fellbaum, C. (to appear). The syntax and semantics of some polysemous verbs. In. Y. Ravin and C. Leacock (Eds.), *Polysemy*. Cambridge, England: Cambridge University Press.

Fellbaum, C., and Kegl, J. (1988). *Taxonomic hierarchies in the verb lexicon*. Paper presented at the EURALEX Third International Congress, Budapest, Hungary.

Fellbaum, C., and Kegl, J. (1989). Taxonomic structures and cross-category linking in the lexicon. In *Proceedings of the Sixth Eastern States Conference on Linguistics*, 93–104. Columbus: Ohio State University, Department of Linguistics.

Fellbaum, C., and Miller, G. A. (1990). Folk psychology or semantic entailment? A reply to Rips and Conrad. *The Psychological Review*, *97*, 565–570.

Fillenbaum, S., and Jones, L. V. (1965). Grammatical contingencies in word association. *Journal of Verbal Leaning and Verbal Behavior*, *4*, 248–255.

Fillmore, C. J., and Atkins, B. T. S. (1992). Towards a frame-based lexicon: The semantics of RISK and its neighbors. In A. Lehrer and E. Feder Kittay (Eds.), *Frames, fields, and contrasts*, 75–102. Hillsdale, NJ: Erlbaum.

Fodor, J. A. (1970). Three reasons for not deriving "kill" from "cause to die." *Linguistic Inquiry*, *1*, 429–438.

Garrett, M. (1992). Lexical retrieval processes. In A. Lehrer and E. Feder Kittay (Eds.), *Frames, fields, and contrasts*, 377–395. Hillsdale, NJ: Erlbaum.

Grimshaw, J., and Mester, A. (1988). Light verbs and theta-marking. *Linguistic Inquiry*, *19*, 205–232.

Gruber, J. (1976). *Lexical structures in syntax and semantics*. New York: North-Holland.

Hale, K., and Keyser, S. J. (1987). *A view from the middle* (Lexicon Project Working Paper 10). Cambridge, MA: MIT, Center for Cognitive Science.

Hale, K., and Laughren, M. (1983). *The structure of verbal entries: Preface to dictionary entries of verbs* (Warlpiri Lexicon Project). Cambridge, MA: MIT, Department of Linguistics and Philosophy.

Horn, L. (1988). Morphology, pragmatics, and the *un-* verb. In *Proceedings of the Fifth Eastern States Conference on Linguistics*, 210–233. Columbus: Ohio State University, Department of Linguistics.

Jackendoff, R. S. (1972). *Semantic interpretation in generative grammar.* Cambridge, MA: MIT Press.

Jackendoff, R. S. (1983). *Semantics and cognition.* Cambridge, MA: MIT Press.

Justeson, J. S., and Katz, S. M. (1991a). Co-occurrences of antonymous adjectives and their contexts. *Computational Linguistics, 17,* 1–19.

Justeson, J. S., and Katz, S. M. (1991b). Redefining antonymy: The textual structure of a semantic relation. In *Proceedings of the Seventh Annual Conference of the UW Centre for the New OED and Text Research*, 138–154. Waterloo, Ontario, Canada: University of Waterloo, Centre for the New OED and Text Research.

Katz, J. J. (1972). *Semantic theory.* New York: Harper and Row.

Katz, J. J., and Fodor, J. A. (1963). The structure of a semantic theory. *Language, 39,* 170–210.

Kempson, R. (1977). *Semantic theory.* Cambridge, England: Cambridge University Press.

Kučera, H., and Francis, W. N. (1967). *The standard corpus of present-day edited American English* [the Brown corpus]. (Electronic database.) Providence, RI: Brown University.

Lakoff, G. (1970). *Irregularity in syntax.* New York: Holt, Rinehart and Winston.

Lehrer, A. (1990). Polysemy, conventionality, and the structure of the lexicon. *Cognitive Linguistics, 1,* 207–246.

Lehrer, A., and E. Feder Kittay (Eds.). (1992). *Frames, fields, and contrasts.* Hillsdale, NJ: Erlbaum.

Levin, B. (1985). Introduction. In B. Levin (Ed.), *Lexical semantics in review*, 1–62. Cambridge, MA: MIT, Center for Cognitive Science.

Levin, B. (1993). *English verb classes and alternations.* Chicago: University of Chicago Press.

Levin, B., and Rapoport, T. (1988). Lexical subordination. In *Papers from the 24th Regional Meeting of the Chicago Linguistic Society*, 275–289. Chicago: University of Chicago, Chicago Linguistic Society.

Lyons, J. (1977). *Semantics.* 2 vols. New York: Cambridge University Press.

Markowitz, J. (1988). The nature of lexical relations. In M. Evens (Ed.), *Relational models of the lexicon*, 237–260. Cambridge, England: Cambridge University Press.

McCawley, J. D. (1968). Lexical insertion in a transformational grammar without deep structure. In *Papers from the Fourth Regional Meeting of the Chicago*

Linguistic Society, 71–80. Chicago: University of Chicago, Chicago Linguistic Society.

Mel'čuk, I., and Zholkovsky, A. (1984). *Explanatory combinatorial dictionary of modern Russian*. Wiener Slawistischer Almanach, Sonderband 14. Vienna.

Mettinger, A. (1994). *Aspects of semantic opposition in English*. Cambridge, England: Cambridge University Press.

Miller, G. A., and Charles, W. G. (1991). Contextual correlates of semantic similarity. *Language and Cognitive Processes, 6*, 1–28.

Miller, G. A., and Fellbaum, C. (1991). Semantic networks of English. *Cognition* [special issue, B. Levin and S. Pinker (Eds.)], 197–229. Reprinted in B. Levin and S. Pinker (Eds.), *Lexical and conceptual semantics*, 197–229. Cambridge, MA: Blackwell.

Miller, G. A., and Johnson-Laird, P. N. (1976). *Language and perception*. Cambridge, MA: Harvard University Press.

Mittwoch, A. (1982). On the difference between *eating* and *eating something:* Activities vs. accomplishments. *Linguistic Inquiry, 13*, 113–122.

Palermo, D. S., and Jenkins, J. J. (1964). Word association norms: Grade school through college. Minneapolis: University of Minnesota Press.

Pinker, S. (1989). *Learnability and cognition: The acquisition of argument structure*. Cambridge, MA: MIT Press.

Pulman, S. G. (1983). *Word meaning and belief*. London: Croom Helm.

Pustejovsky, J. (1991). The Generative Lexicon, *Computational Linguistics, 17*, 409–441.

Pustejovsky, J. (1995). *The Generative Lexicon: A theory of computational semantics*. Cambridge, MA: MIT Press.

Rifkin, A. (1985). Evidence for a basic level in event taxonomies. *Memory and Cognition, 13*, 538–556.

Rips, L., and Conrad, F. (1989). Folk psychology of mental activities. *Psychological Review, 96*, 187–207.

Rosch, E. (1973). On the internal structure of perceptual and semantic categories. In T. E. Moore (Ed.), *Cognitive development and the acquisition of language*, 111–144. New York: Academic Press.

Rosch, E. (1975). Cognitive representations of semantic categories. *Journal of Experimental Psychology, 104*, 192–233.

Rosch, E., Mervis, C. B., Gray, W., Johnson, D., and Boyes-Braem, P. (1976). Basic objects in natural categories. *Cognitive Psychology, 8*, 382–439.

Rosenweig, M. R. (1970). International Kent-Rosanoff word association norms, emphasising those of French male and female students and French workmen. In L. Postman and G. Keppel (Eds.), *Norms of word association*, 95–176. New York: Academic Press.

Schank, R. C. (1972). Conceptual dependency: A theory of natural language understanding. *Cognitive Psychology, 3*, 552–631.

Schank, R. C., and Abelson, R. P. (1977). *Scripts, goals, plans, and understanding.* Hillsdale, NJ: Erlbaum.

Shibatani, M. (1972). Three reasons for not deriving "kill' from "cause to die" in Japanese. In J. Kimball (Ed.), *Syntax and semantics*, vol. 1, 125–137. New York: Academic Press.

Talmy, L. (1985). Lexicalization patterns: Semantic structure in lexical forms. In T. Shopen (Ed.), *Language typology and syntactic description*, vol. 3, 57–149. Cambridge, England: Cambridge University Press.

Chapter 4

Design and Implementation of the WordNet Lexical Database and Searching Software

Randee I. Tengi

In developing WordNet, it has been convenient to divide the work into two interdependent tasks that bear a vague similarity to the traditional tasks of writing and printing a dictionary. One task was to write the source files that contain the basic lexical data—the contents of those files are the lexical substance of WordNet. The second task was to create a set of computer programs that would accept the source files and do all the work leading ultimately to a display for the user.

The WordNet system falls naturally into four parts (see figure 4.1): the lexical source files; the software (the Grinder) used to convert these files into the lexical database; the WordNet lexical database; and the software tools used to access the database. This chapter discusses features of the design and implementation of WordNet: the process of creating the lexical source files, their conversion to the WordNet database, the organization and format of the database files, and the user software for retrieving information from the database. Issues such as portability and the distribution of WordNet are also addressed.

4.1 LEXICAL FILES

WordNet's source files are written by lexicographers. They are the product of a detailed relational analysis of lexical semantics: a variety of lexical and semantic relations are used to represent the organization of lexical knowledge (see chapters by G. A. Miller, K. J. Miller, and Fellbaum, this volume).

In WordNet, nouns, verbs, adjectives, and adverbs are organized into synsets (synonym sets), which are further arranged into a set of lexical source files by syntactic category and other organizational criteria. Nouns

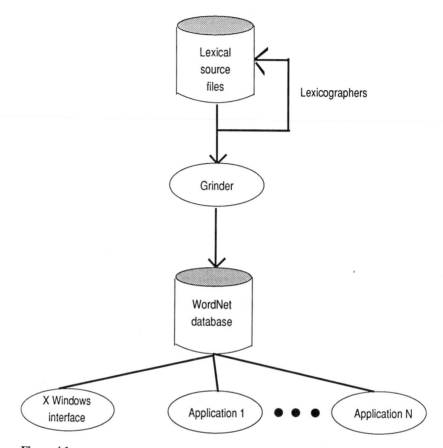

Figure 4.1
The WordNet system.

and verbs are grouped according to semantic fields. Adjectives are divided among three files (one for descriptive adjectives, one for relational adjectives, and one for participal adjectives), although these categorizations may not be strictly enforced. A single file contains all the adverbs. Each lexical file is assigned a file number for use within the database.

A lexical file contains synsets from only one syntactic category. A synset consists of synonymous words, relational pointers, a gloss, and example sentences. Comments for use by the lexicographers can be entered in a lexical file, outside of a synset, by enclosing the text of the comment in parentheses. Comments are discarded when the database is built.

4.1.1 Word Forms and Senses

A word form in the WordNet database is either the orthographic representation of an individual word or a string of individual words joined with underscore characters. A string of words so joined is referred to as a *collocation* (also called a *compound* or *phrase*) and represents a single concept, such as the compound noun *fountain_pen*. Lexicographers may enter word forms in upper- or lowercase, and hyphenation may be used. Functions in the searching software attempt to map word forms specified by users to word forms found in the database.

A word form may be augmented with information necessary for the correct processing and interpretation of the data. An integer "identification number" must be added by the lexicographer if the same word form appears more than once in a lexical file. Since each occurrence of a word form indicates a different sense of the word, this provides a mechanism for uniquely identifying each sense within a lexical file. Word forms in adjective clusters constitute an exception to this rule: identification numbers only need to be appended to identical word forms within a single cluster, since a satellite is identified as being attached to a cluster (see K. J. Miller, this volume). When the use of a descriptive adjective is limited to a specific syntactic position in relation to the noun that it modifies ("predicate," "prenominal," or "immediately postnominal"), the word form is followed by a syntactic marker code. Syntactic markers are not used by the searching software, but are retained in the database and are presented to the user with search results.

A word in a synset (a "word/sense pair") is represented by its orthographic word form, syntactic category, semantic field (lexical file name), and identification number. Together, these items make a "sense key" that uniquely identifies each word/sense pair in the database. The name of the lexical file containing the synset determines the syntactic category and semantic field. For example, two senses of *paper*, 'a composition or report' and 'a newspaper', are both in the file noun.communication. The 'report' sense has been assigned (by the lexicographer) the identification number 1 and the 'newspaper' sense the number 3. Table 4.1 lists the items necessary for uniquely identifying these senses and one other sense: 'stuff that we write on'.

4.1.2 Relational Pointers

The relations found in WordNet help distinguish it from standard lexical resources and dictionaries. In constructing a synset, the lexicographer

Table 4.1
Sense key information

Word form	ID	Syntactic category	Semantic field
paper	1	Noun	Communication
paper	3	Noun	Communication
paper	0	Noun	Substance

identifies the relevant relations and encodes them in the synset as relational pointers. Synonymy of words is implicit by inclusion in the same synset. Other relations are represented by either semantic (between synsets) or lexical (between individual word forms) pointers. Some relations, such as attributes, cross syntactic categories. Many relations are reflexive, meaning that a relational pointer from one synset to another implies a pointer in the opposite direction. Depending on the relation, the reflexive pointer may be for the same relation (antonymy) or for one that is opposite in meaning (hyponymy/hypernymy). The Grinder automatically generates missing reflexive pointers in the database.

A pointer is constructed by specifying a word form from the target synset, followed by a comma, followed by the symbol corresponding to the desired relation. For a semantic relation, any word form in the target synset can be specified. Selection of the target word form in a lexical relation is determined by the source word form and the relation between the two. Lexical and semantic pointers are entered using different syntax; therefore, a synset can be built that contains both. A pointer to a target synset residing in a different lexical file from the source has the name of the lexical file prepended to it.

Table 4.2 lists the relational pointer types and symbols by syntactic category. Meronymy is further specified by appending one of the following characters to the meronymy pointer: p to indicate a part of something; s to indicate the substance of something; m to indicate a member of some group (see G. A. Miller, this volume). Holonymy is specified in the same manner, each pointer representing the semantic relation opposite to the corresponding meronymy relation. Reflexive relations are listed in table 4.3.

4.1.3   Verb Sentence Frames

Each verb synset has a list of sentence frames illustrating the types of simple sentences in which the verbs in the synset can be used. A list of

Table 4.2
Relations and pointer symbols

Noun		Verb		Adjective		Adverb	
Antonym	!	Antonym	!	Antonym	!	Antonym	!
Hyponym	~	Troponym	~	Similar	&	Derived from	\
Hypernym	@	Hypernym	@	Relational adj.	\		
Meronym	#	Entailment	*	Also see	^		
Holonym	%	Cause	>	Attribute	=		
Attribute	=	Also see	^	Participle	<		

Table 4.3
Reflexive relations

Relation	Reflexive relation
Antonym	Antonym
Hyponym	Hypernym
Hypernym	Hyponym
Holonym	Meronym
Meronym	Holonym
Similar to	Similar to
Attribute	Attribute

verb frames can be restricted to a single verb in a synset or can be applicable to all the verbs in a synset. Verb sentence frames are represented by frame numbers in both the lexical source files and the database files.

4.1.4 Synset Syntax

Strings in the lexical source files that conform to the following syntactic rules are recognized by the Grinder as synsets:

1. Each synset begins with a left curly bracket ({).
2. Each synset is terminated with a right curly bracket (}) and a newline.
3. Each synset contains a list of one or more word forms, each followed by a comma and a space.
4. To code semantic relations, the list of word forms is followed by a list of relational pointers specified using the following syntax: a word form from the target synset (optionally preceded by *filename:* to indicate a word form in a different lexical file), followed by a comma, followed by a relational pointer symbol and a space.

Sample synsets for noun *apple* and its hypernym

```
{ apple, edible_fruit,@ (fruit with red or yellow or
green skin and crisp whitish flesh)}

{ edible_fruit, produce,@ noun.plant:fruit,@ (edible
reproductive body of a seed plant esp. one having
sweet flesh)}
```

Sample synset for verb *eat*

```
{ [ eat, verb.contact:eat_at,ˆ eat_into,ˆ ] take_in,
consume,@ chew,* swallow,* frames: 8 (take in solid
food) }
```

Figure 4.2
Sample synsets.

5. For verb synsets, `frames:` is followed by a comma-separated list of applicable verb frame numbers. The list of verb frames follows all relational pointers.

6. To code lexical relations, a word form and its following list of elements from 4 and/or 5 are all enclosed in square brackets (`[...]`).

7. An optional gloss, enclosed in parentheses, precedes 2.

8. To code adjective clusters, each part of a cluster (a head synset, optionally followed by satellite synsets) is separated from other parts of a cluster by a line containing only hyphens. Each cluster is enclosed in square brackets.

In figure 4.2 subsets from the lexical source files `noun.food` and `verb.consumption` illustrate the synset syntax used.

4.2 ARCHIVE SYSTEM

The lexical source files are maintained in an archive system based on the Unix Revision Control System (RCS) for managing multiple revisions of text files. The archive system has been established for several reasons: to allow the reconstruction of any version of the WordNet database, to keep a history of all the changes to lexical files, to prevent lexicographers from making conflicting changes to the same file, and to ensure that it is always possible to produce an up-to-date version of the WordNet database. The programs in the archive system are Unix shell scripts that envelop RCS commands in a manner that maintains the desired control over the lexical source files while providing a simple interface for the lexicographers.

The `reserve` command extracts from the archive the most recent revision of a file and "locks" it for as long as a lexicographer is working on it. This prevents anyone else from making changes to the file until it is unlocked. The `review` command extracts a file from the archive for the purpose of examination only. To avoid accidental changes, a review copy of a file does not have write permission, and the suffix `.r` is appended to the filename. The `restore` command verifies the integrity of a reserved file and returns it to the archive system, making the returned copy the most recent version. The `release` command is used to break a lock placed on a file with the `reserve` command. This is generally used if the lexicographer decides that changes should not be returned to the archive. The `whose` command is used to find out whether files are currently reserved, and if so, by whom.

4.3 THE WORDNET LEXICAL DATABASE

At the heart of the WordNet system is the lexical database. A simple ASCII format was chosen for the database files to facilitate access from different programming languages such as C, Perl, and awk. The database can also be viewed with an editor or text-based Unix tools such as `grep` and `more`. Several interfaces have been developed that, in response to user queries, extract raw data from the database and format it for display to the user. Simple tools can be constructed that search the entire database for items such as all noun synsets having more than one hypernym and all words with more than a specified number of senses. Users outside of Princeton University have incorporated the WordNet database into applications as diverse as information retrieval systems and crossword puzzle generators (see part II for descriptions of several applications). The ease with which WordNet is enveloped into other systems reinforces the felicity of this approach.

One shortcoming of the database's ASCII format is that the files are editable and therefore in theory extensible. However, in practice this is almost impossible. One of the Grinder's primary functions is the calculation of addresses for the synsets in the data files. Editing any of the database files would almost certainly create incorrect byte offsets, derailing most searching strategies. At the present time, building a WordNet

database requires the use of the Grinder to process all of the lexical source
files at the same time.

4.3.1 Ordering of Senses

The different senses of a given word form are ordered from most to least
frequently used, with the most common sense numbered 1. This ordering
is determined by frequency of use in semantically tagged corpora (see
Landes, Leacock, and Tengi, this volume). Senses that have not occurred
in the tagged text are presented in random order. At this time, no indication is given in the database as to which sense numbers are based on a
count of semantic tags and which are haphazard. However, for each
tagged word, a corresponding line can be found in the `cntlist` file
(provided with the database) listing the number of times the sense occurs.
Checking for a word sense in this file indicates whether a sense number is
based on frequency of use or not—if a word sense is present, the sense
number is based on frequency data.

4.3.2 Index of Familiarity

One of the best-known and most important psycholinguistic facts about
the mental lexicon is that some words are much more familiar than others.
The familiarity of a word is known to influence a wide range of performance variables: speed of reading, speed of comprehension, ease of
recall, probability of use. The effects are so ubiquitous that experimenters
who hope to study anything else must take great pains to equate the
words they use for familiarity. To ignore this variable in a lexical database that is supposed to reflect psycholinguistic principles would be
unthinkable.

In order to incorporate differences in familiarity into WordNet, a syntactically tagged *index of familiarity* is associated with each word form.
Frequency of use is usually assumed to be the best indicator of familiarity.
The closed-class words that play an important syntactic role are the most
frequently used, of course, but even within the open-class words there are
large differences in frequency of occurrence that are assumed to correlate
with—or to explain—the large differences in familiarity. The frequency
data that are readily available in the technical literature and semantically
tagged corpora, however, are inadequate for a database as extensive as
WordNet.

Fortunately, an alternative indicator of familiarity is available. It
is known that frequency of occurrence and polysemy are correlated

Table 4.4
Hypernyms of *bronco* and their index values

Word	Polysemy
bronco	1
@ → mustang	1
@ → pony	5
@ → horse	14
@ → equine	0
@ → odd-toed ungulate	0
@ → placental mammal	0
@ → mammal	1
@ → vertebrate	1
@ → chordate	1
@ → animal	4
@ → organism	2
@ → entity	3

(Jastrezembski 1981; Jastrezembski and Stanners 1975; Zipf 1945). That is to say, on the average, the more frequently a word is used, the more different meanings it will have in a dictionary. An intriguing finding in psycholinguistics (Jastrezembski 1981) is that polysemy seems to predict lexical access times as well as frequency does. Indeed, if the effect of frequency is controlled by choosing words of equivalent frequencies, polysemy is still a significant predictor of lexical decision times.

WordNet uses polysemy as an index of familiarity. This measure can be determined from a machine-readable dictionary. If an index value of 0 is assigned to words that do not appear in the dictionary, and if values of 1 or more are assigned according to the number of senses a word has, then an index value can be made available for every word in every syntactic category. Associated with every word form in WordNet, therefore, is an integer that represents a count of the number of senses that word form has when it is used as a noun, verb, adjective, or adverb.

A simple example of how the familiarity index might be used is shown in table 4.4. If, say, the superordinates of *bronco* are requested, WordNet can respond with the sequence of hypernyms shown in the table. Now, if all the terms with a familiarity index (polysemy count) of 0 or 1 are omitted, which are primarily technical terms, the hypernyms of *bronco* include simply *bronco @→ pony @→ horse @→ animal @→ organism*

$@\rightarrow$ *entity*. This shortened chain is much closer to what a layperson would expect.

4.3.3 Index and Data Files

The database is periodically constructed from the lexical source files. It is essentially a reformulation of the synsets from the form suitable for editing by the lexicographers to an interrelated set of searchable files in which relational pointers are "resolved" and sense numbers and polysemy counts assigned. The division of synsets by syntactic category is maintained, but the data for each syntactic category are represented by two files: an index file and a data file.

The information for each synset begins at a specific byte offset ("synset address") in a data file and continues until a newline character is reached. Relational pointers are represented in the data files by their pointer symbols and target synset addresses. The index files are alphabetized lists of all the word forms in WordNet; they are the primary paths into the data files. Each index file entry for a word form contains a list of the synset addresses for all the senses of the word. A search for all senses of a word involves doing a binary search for the base form of the word in the index file for a syntactic category and moving down the list of synset addresses. For each address, the synset is read from the corresponding data file. Pointers are traced through a data file by moving from a source synset to a target via the synset addresses.

In the index files, word forms are represented in lowercase only, regardless of how they were entered in the lexical files (this folds various orthographic representations of a word into one line, enabling database searches to be case insensitive). The files are sorted according to the ASCII character set collating sequence and can be searched quickly with a binary search.

An index file begins with several lines containing a copyright notice, version number, and license agreement. Each remaining line contains the following information: a word form; the polysemy count; a list of symbols for all pointers used in the synsets containing the word (this is used by the retrieval software to indicate to a user which searches are applicable); a list of synset addresses, one for each sense of the word. The sense numbers for the different senses of a word are obtained from the word's entry in an index file. Sense numbers are assigned sequentially to the synset addresses beginning with 1 (i.e., the third address points to the synset containing sense 3 of the word form).

A data file begins with the same preamble as an index file, followed by a list of the lexical file names. Each remaining line corresponds to a synset and is an encoding of the information entered by the lexicographer with pointers resolved to synset addresses. Word forms match their orthographic representation in the lexical files.

The first piece of information on each line is the synset address. (This is redundant, since a computer program that reads a synset from a data file generally knows the byte offset it was read from. However, this piece of information is helpful when using Unix utilities such as grep to trace synsets and pointers without the use of sophisticated software. It also provides a unique "key" for each synset, which is useful to programming systems like Prolog and Oracle.) The integer corresponding to the name of the lexical file containing the synset is next. A list of word forms, relational pointers, and verb sentence frame numbers follows. The textual gloss is the final item, if the synset has one.

Relational pointers are represented by several pieces of information. The pointer symbol is first, followed by the address of the target synset and its syntactic category (necessary for pointers from one syntactic category to another), followed by a field that differentiates lexical and semantic pointers. For a lexical pointer, this field indicates the word number in the target synset of the word form pointed to. A semantic pointer is indicated by a 0.

4.3.4   The Sense Index

The WordNet sense index provides an alternative method for accessing synsets and words in the WordNet database. It is useful to programs that are interested in retrieving synsets or information related to a specific word/sense pair in WordNet. It can also be used with Unix tools like grep to find all senses of a word in one or more syntactic categories.

The file is a sorted list of all words in all synsets in the WordNet database—all the word/sense pairs, represented as sense keys, described earlier, with each line containing the synset address and sense number corresponding to the sense of the word. A binary search of the file quickly retrieves this information and allows direct access to a synset via the synset address. For many applications, this is preferable to retrieving a synset using the index file as a means of finding byte offsets into the data file, especially if the sense key is known. The sense index is not used by the WordNet searching software, but writers of applications that look for specific senses often find this file extremely useful.

4.4 GRINDER UTILITY

The Grinder is a versatile utility with the primary purpose of compiling the lexical source files into a database format that facilitates machine retrieval of the information in WordNet. It is also used as a verification tool to ensure the syntactic integrity of a lexical file when returned to the archive system with the `restore` command. To build a WordNet database, all of the lexical files must be processed together.

The Grinder program is a multipass compiler for synsets. Several command line options control the operation of the program and determine which passes are run. The first pass uses a parser, developed using the Unix `lex` lexical analysis program and `yacc` parsing program generator, to verify that the syntax of the lexical files conforms to the specification of lexical items and the input grammar, and builds an internal representation of the parsed synsets. Additional passes refer only to this internal representation of the lexicographic data.

The first pass attempts to find as many syntactic and structural errors as possible. Syntactic errors occur when the input file fails to conform to the input grammar's specification. Structural errors refer to relational pointers that cannot be resolved for some reason, usually because the lexicographer has made a typographical error, such as constructing a pointer to a nonexistent file or failing to specify an identification number when referring to an ambiguous word form. At this point only structural errors in pointers to files that are processed together can be detected. When the Grinder is used as a verification tool, as called from `restore`, only this pass is run, and structural errors are ignored.

In its second pass the Grinder resolves the semantic and lexical pointers. The pointers that were specified in each synset are examined in turn, and the target of each pointer (either a synset or a word form in a synset) is found. The source pointer is then resolved by adding an entry to the internal data structure that notes the "location" of the target. In the case of reflexive pointers, the target pointer's synset is then searched for a corresponding reflexive pointer. If one is found, the data structure that represents it is modified to note the "location" of its target, the original source pointer. If a reflexive pointer is not found, the Grinder automatically creates one with all the pertinent information.

A subsequent pass travels down the list of word forms, assigning to each the polysemy count for each syntactic category. Words not found in the corresponding syntactic category of the machine-readable dictionary are assigned 0. Next, the `cntlist` file is read to obtain the frequency counts for word senses, and sense numbers are assigned accordingly.

The Grinder's final pass generates the WordNet database files. First the byte offset of each synset is determined and the internal data structures are updated with the synset addresses; then the data, index, and sense index files are output. A command line option can be specified to generate database statistics such as the number of synsets in each syntactic category.

4.5   RETRIEVING LEXICAL INFORMATION

To give a user access to information in a database, an interface is required. When considering the role of the interface, it is important to recognize the difference between a printed dictionary and a lexical database. WordNet's interface software creates its responses to a user's requests on the fly. Unlike an on-line version of a printed dictionary, where information is stored in a fixed format and displayed on demand, WordNet's information is stored in a format that would be meaningless to an ordinary reader. The interface provides a user with a variety of ways to retrieve and display lexical information. Different interfaces can be created to serve the purposes of different users, but all of them will draw on the same underlying lexical database, and they may use the same software functions that interface to the database files.

User interfaces to WordNet can take many forms. Window-based interfaces have been developed for X Windows, Microsoft Windows, and the Macintosh operating system. An alternative command line interface retrieves the same data, with exactly the same output as the window-based interfaces, although the specification of the retrieval criteria is more cumbersome, and the whole effect is less impressive. Nevertheless, the command line interface is extremely useful since some users do not have access to windowing environments. Shell scripts and other programs can also be written around the command line interface, resulting in powerful database retrieval programs that can work over large sets of queries.

The information retrieval process is the same regardless of the type of search requested. The first step is to read the entry for the search word from the appropriate index file to obtain the synset addresses of all senses of the word. Next, each of the synsets in the data file is searched for the requested information. Searching is complicated by the fact that each synset containing the search word also contains pointers to other synsets in the data file that may need to be retrieved and displayed, depending on the search type. For example, each synset in a hypernymic pathway points to the next synset up in the hierarchy. If a user requests a recursive search on hypernyms, a recursive retrieval process is repeated until a synset is encountered that contains no further hypernym pointers.

The WordNet user interfaces and other software tools rely upon a library of functions to manipulate the database files and their contents. The structured, flexible design of the library provides a simple programming interface to the WordNet database. A comprehensive set of functions is provided: they perform searches and retrievals, morphological transformations, and other general-purpose functions. Functions can be classified as "complex," "low-level," or "utility." This hierarchical approach allows programmers to write applications without having to deal with the nuts and bolts of the database files. Complex functions are built from low-level and utility functions. New complex functions can be developed from existing functions and new code specific to the task. The standard user interfaces depend upon the complex functions to perform the actual data retrieval, morphological transformations, and formatting of the search results for display to the user. Low-level functions provide access to the lexical information in the index and data files, while shielding the programmer from the details of reading files and parsing data. These functions return the requested information in data structures that can be interpreted and used as desired by the application. Utility functions allow manipulations of the search strings, open and close database files, and the like.

The basic searching function (findtheinfo()) receives as its input four arguments: a word form, a syntactic category, a code corresponding to a search type, and a sense number (this can be set to ALLSENSES to retrieve information about all senses; otherwise, a specific sense number is passed to limit the search). Most searches correspond to a relational pointer, and for many the user may request a hierarchical search, or a search that traverses only one level of the tree. (See table 4.5 for a list of the different types of searches available in the library.) When a synset is retrieved from the database, it is formatted, as determined by the search type, into an output buffer. The resulting buffer, containing all of the formatted synsets for all of the requested senses of the search word, is returned to the caller—the calling function simply has to print the contents of the buffer returned. The search code expects the word form passed

Table 4.5
Searches available from WordNet library

Noun searches	Verb searches	Adjective searches	Adverb searches
Synonyms (ordered)	Synonyms	Synonyms	Synonyms
Synonyms (grouped)			
Antonyms	Antonyms	Antonyms	Antonyms
Coordinate terms			
Is a kind of			
Kinds of			
Kinds of (hierarchical)			
Is a part of			
Is a part of (hierarchical)			
Parts of			
Parts of (hierarchical)			
	Manner of		
	Ways to		
	Entailment		
	Cause		
	Sentence frames		
Values for (attribute)		Is a value of (attribute)	
Familiarity	Familiarity	Familiarity	Familiarity
Grep*	Grep	Grep	Grep

*Grep is a Unix utility for extracting lines from files that match a specified regular expression.

to be a base form that is present in WordNet in the designated part of speech. Other library functions allow a program to determine the base form of a string (see section 4.7) and in which syntactic categories it exists in the database.

This general search-and-retrieval algorithm is used in several different ways to implement the user interfaces to WordNet. The window-based interfaces determine all syntactic categories and possible searches for a word, allowing selection only from valid choices. The command line interface requires the user to supply a search word and search type (the syntactic category is encoded in each search type). Valid searches can be determined in advance by entering a word without any options—a list of all possible searches in all syntactic categories is returned. Multiple searches on a word can be done with a single command, but a separate command line must be constructed for each search word.

4.6 X WINDOWS INTERFACE

The command xwn starts the X Windows interface in the background, freeing the window from which it was started for other tasks.[1] The WordNet Window provides full access to the database. The standard X Windows mouse functions are used to open, close, and move the window and to change its size. Help on the general operation of the program is obtained by pressing the middle mouse button with the cursor in the top part of the window. The top part of the window provides an area for entering a search string, and buttons corresponding to syntactic categories and options. Beneath this area a status line indicates the type of search results presently displayed in the large buffer below.

4.6.1 Searching the Database

Retrieval of information from the lexical database is accomplished in two steps. First the user moves the cursor into the horizontal box below "Enter Search Word:" and types a search string followed by a carriage return. A single word, hyphenated word, or collocation may be entered. The program determines the syntactic categories the string is found in, and which searches are possible in each. When required, the base form of the string in each syntactic category is found. The part-of-speech button corresponding to each applicable syntactic category is highlighted. A search can now be selected by holding any mouse button on a highlighted part-of-speech button, revealing a pull-down menu of searches for the syntactic category. All of the searches available for the search string are highlighted. Figure 4.3 shows the searches available for the noun *snake*. Selection of a search is accomplished by scrolling through the menu with the mouse button pressed until the desired search is in reverse video. When the button is released, the synsets required to satisfy the search are retrieved from the database, formatted, and displayed in the lower window. The status line shows the type of search that was selected. By default, all of the senses found in WordNet that match the query are displayed. Searches may be limited by entering a list of sense numbers in the "Senses:" box. When the search string is changed, the box is automatically cleared, defaulting back to all senses.

Selecting the Options button displays a menu of functions that are not directly associated with WordNet searches. Menu selections determine the following: the display of user help messages; the display of synset

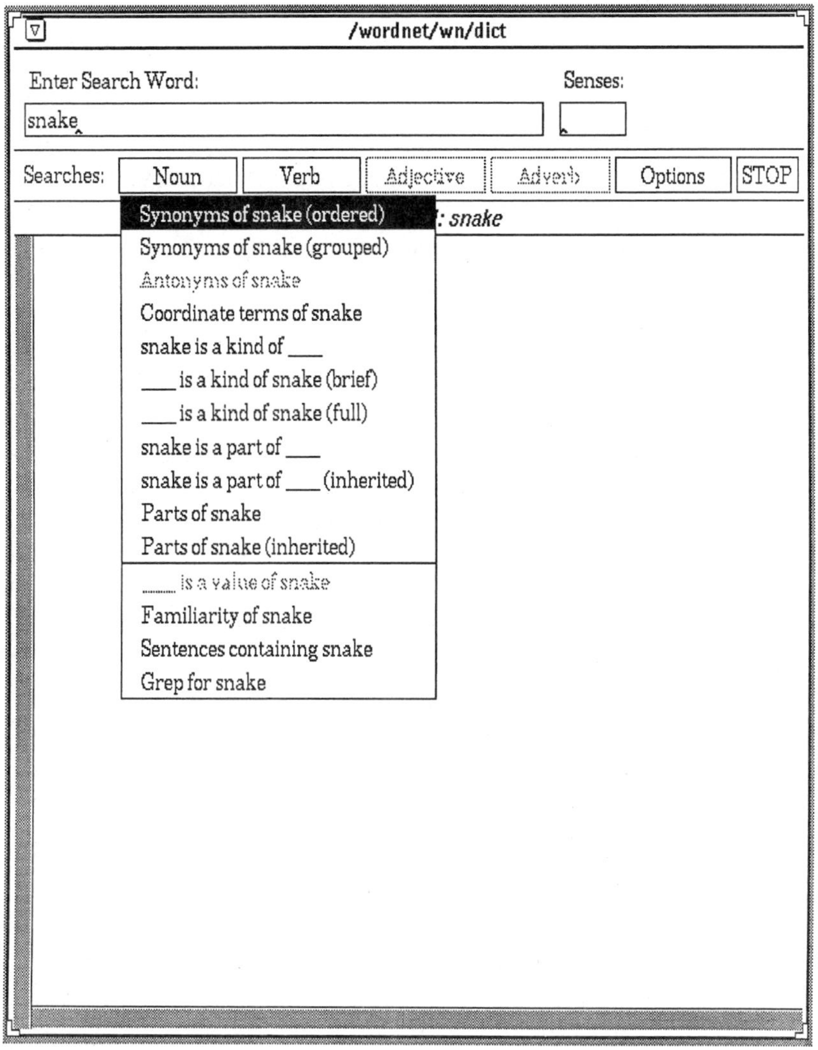

Figure 4.3
Searches for noun *snake*.

glosses; the logging of search results to a disk file; the display of the WordNet license. The final menu item is used to quit the application.

4.6.2 Search Results

The output generated by the standard WordNet interfaces is intended to be self-explanatory. Visual cues, such as indentation to represent levels in the hierarchies, aid a user in interpreting the formatted search results. The complex nature of the adjective structure makes for less straightforward output of retrieved adjective synsets. In an attempt to clarify the display of adjective synsets and clusters, direct antonyms, which are represented only by head synsets, are always displayed together. This allows head synsets to be easily distinguished from satellites, as well as from each other (see K. J. Miller, this volume).

The information retrieved is formatted and displayed in the large buffer below the status line. Horizontal and vertical scroll bars are used to view text that exceeds the window's borders. The output consists of a one-line description of the search type, followed by the formatted search results for all senses matching the query. Each sense is displayed in the following manner: a line containing the sense number, followed by a line with the synset for that sense, followed by the search results for the sense. In most cases, each line of search results is preceded by a marker (usually =>), then a synset. If a search traverses more than one level of a tree, subsequent synsets are indented by spaces corresponding to their level in the hierarchy. If a search does not apply to all senses of the search string, the output is headed by a line that indicates how many out of the total number of senses match the search criteria.

For most searches, senses that match the query are output in sense number order, based on frequency of occurrence in previously tagged corpora whenever possible (see Landes, Leacock, and Tengi, this volume). Noun senses can be grouped by similarity of meaning, rather than by frequency of use (see G. A. Miller, this volume). When this search is selected, all senses that are close in meaning are displayed together, with a line of dashes indicating the end of a group.

When "Sentence frames for verb ____" is selected, syntactic frames that are appropriate for all verbs in a synset are preceded by the marker *>. If a frame is acceptable for the search string only, it is preceded by the marker => (see Fellbaum, this volume).

When an adjective is printed, its direct antonym, if it has one, is also printed in parentheses. When a sense is in a head synset, all of the satellite

```
┌─────────────────────────────────────────────────────────────────┐
│ ▽                        /wordnet/wn/dict                         │
│                                                                   │
│ Enter Search Word:                        Senses:                 │
│ snake                                                             │
│                                                                   │
│ Searches:  │ Noun │ │ Verb │ │Adjective│ │Adverb│ │Options│ │STOP││
│─────────────────────────────────────────────────────────────────│
│       Synonyms / Hypernyms (Ordered by Frequency) of Noun snake   │
│───────────────────────────────────────────────────────────────── │
│ 5 senses of snake                                                 │
│                                                                   │
│ Sense 1                                                           │
│ snake, serpent, ophidian –– (limbless scaly elongate reptile; some are venomous) │
│    => diapsid, diapsid reptile –– (reptile having a pair of openings in the skull behind each eye) │
│                                                                   │
│ Sense 2                                                           │
│ snake, snake in the grass –– (a deceitful or treacherous person)  │
│    => bad person –– (a person who does harm to others)            │
│                                                                   │
│ Sense 3                                                           │
│ Snake, Snake River –– (a tributary of the Columbia River)         │
│    => river –– (a large natural stream of water (larger than a creek); "the river was navigable for 50 miles") │
│                                                                   │
│ Sense 4                                                           │
│ Hydra, Snake –– (a long faint constellation near the equator stretching between Virgo and Cancer) │
│    => constellation –– (a configuration of stars as seen from the earth) │
│                                                                   │
│ Sense 5                                                           │
│ snake, plumber's snake, auger –– (a long flexible steel coil for dislodging stoppages in curved pipes) │
│    => hand tool –– (a tool used with workers' hands)              │
│                                                                   │
└─────────────────────────────────────────────────────────────────┘
```

Figure 4.4
Synonym search for noun *snake*.

synsets are also displayed. When present, syntactic restrictions are noted in parentheses (see K. J. Miller, this volume).

Some lexical pointers relate synsets from different syntactic categories. In the case of verbal (past or present) adjectives, the output indicates the verb and displays the corresponding synset. For an adverb derived from an adjective, the specific adjectival sense on which the adverb is based is indicated. The same is true of a relational adjective: the synset for the related noun is printed.

Figure 4.4 shows the results of a synonym search listing the four senses of the noun *snake* found in WordNet. By default, glosses are displayed and synsets are printed, along with their first-level hypernyms.

Table 4.6
Morphy suffixes and endings

Noun		Verb		Adjective	
Suffix	Ending	Suffix	Ending	Suffix	Ending
s		s		er	
ses	s	ies	y	est	
xes·	x	es	e	er	e
zes	z	es		est	e
ches	ch	ed	e		
shes	sh	ed			
		ing	e		
		ing			

4.7 MORPHOLOGY

Many dictionaries hang their information on uninflected headwords without separate listings for inflectional (or many derivational) forms of the word. In a printed dictionary, that practice causes little trouble; with a few highly irregular exceptions, morphologically related words are generally similar enough in spelling to the reference form that the eye, aided by boldface type, quickly picks them up. In an electronic dictionary, on the other hand, when an inflected form is requested, the response is likely to be a frustrating announcement that the word is not in the database; users are required to know the base form of every word they want to look up. In WordNet only base forms of words are generally represented. In order to spare users the trouble of affix stripping, and to assist with the creation of programs that use WordNet to automatically process natural language texts, the WordNet software suite includes functions that give WordNet some intelligence about English morphology.

The library of WordNet morphological processing functions, Morphy, handles a wide range of morphological transformations. Morphy use two processes to try to convert a word into a form that is found in the Word-Net database: rules of detachment and exception lists. Applying the rules of detachment involves checking lists of inflectional endings, based on syntactic category, that are detached from individual words (see table 4.6). These rules work well for regular inflections. The exception list for each syntactic category consists of a sorted list of inflected forms of words, followed by one or more base forms, and is used for irregular inflections. Morphy tries to use these two processes in an intelligent manner to translate the word passed into a form found in WordNet. It first checks for exceptions, then uses the rules of detachment. Morphy is passed two items: a word form and a syntactic category.

4.7.1 Single Words

Single words (as opposed to collocations or compounds) are relatively easy to process. Morphy first looks for the word form in the exception list corresponding to the part of speech. If it is found, then the first (usually only) base form is returned. Subsequent lookups for the same word return alternative base forms, as long as they are found. For example, for the inflected form of the noun *bases*, both *base* and *basis* would be returned sequentially as base forms. If the word is not in the exception list, the rules of detachment for the syntactic category are applied in the following manner: whenever a matching suffix is found, a corresponding ending is added, if necessary, and WordNet is consulted to see if the resulting word is found in the database. The first word form found in the database is returned.

4.7.2 Compounds and Phrases

A collocation or compound can be quite challenging to transform into a base form that is present in WordNet. In general, only base forms of words, even those making up compounds such as *attorney general*, are stored in WordNet. Transforming the plural compound *attorneys general* is then simply a matter of finding the base forms of the individual words making up the string. This usually works for nouns; therefore, nonconforming noun compounds, such as *customs duties*, are entered in the noun exception list (a transformation on each word results in the base form *custom duty*, which is not in WordNet).

Verb phrases that include prepositions, such as *acted in concert*, are more difficult. As with single words, the exception list is searched first. If the phrase is not found, Morphy determines whether it includes a preposition. If it does, an attempt is made to find the base form in the following manner. It is assumed that the first word in the phrase is a verb and that the last word is a noun. The algorithm then builds a search string with the base forms of the verb and noun, leaving the remainder of the phrase (usually just the preposition, but more words may be involved) in the middle. For example, if passed *acted in concert*, the database would be searched for *act in concert*, which is found in WordNet. If a verb phrase does not contain a preposition, the base form of each word in the phrase is found, and WordNet is searched with the resulting string.

4.7.3 Hyphenation

The insertion of hyphens into a string also presents difficulties for searching the database. It is often a subjective decision whether a word is hyphenated, joined as one word, or a collocation of several words, and which of the various forms are entered into WordNet. When Morphy breaks a string into "words," it looks for both spaces and hyphens as delimiters. It also looks for periods in strings and removes them if an exact match is not found in the database. A search for an abbreviation, such as *P.M.*, returns synsets such as {*P.M. post meridiem*}. Not every pattern of hyphenation or collocation is searched for properly, so it is advantageous to query several strings if the results of one search seem incomplete.

4.8 PORTABILITY AND DISTRIBUTION

4.8.1 Portability

WordNet is developed on a network of Sun SPARCstations. The software programs and tools are written using the ANSI C programming language, Unix utilities, Perl scripts, and Bourne shell scripts. The database and interface software were designed to be easily ported to many computer architectures and operating systems. The WordNet 1.5 Unix package includes binaries for SunOS, Solaris, Linux, Silicon Graphics, and NeXT platforms. Source code is included, allowing users to port the system to other platforms and to incorporate the WordNet library into applications as needed. The PC and Macintosh interfaces are distributed in binary form only, and the source code is available upon request.

The obvious trade-off between the ASCII database format and a binary format is one of size. The database is very large (version 1.5 is approximately 24 megabytes). This is one of the major difficulties when using WordNet on smaller computer platforms such as the PC and Macintosh. However, most academic and commercial systems used for running "real" applications or software development are reasonably powerful and have substantial disk space, so this should not be a significant problem. The database files are also available in a Prolog loadable format, with some sample queries provided.

4.8.2   Distribution

Once WordNet grew large enough to be generally useful, the next step was to make it available to other users. Distribution of a database the size of WordNet with its associated searching interfaces and tools needed to be accomplished in a manner that was workable for a small development group and an even smaller systems staff. Distribution has grown considerably: version 1.2 (April 1992) ran on four computer platforms and contained 102,000 words in 52,000 synsets. We had fewer than 100 users. WordNet now has a worldwide user community approaching 1,000 members, with FTP sites in both the Untied States and Europe (thanks to Oliver Christ at the University of Stuttgart, Germany). The database released with version 1.5 has grown to 91,600 synsets containing 168,000 words. The Cognitive Science Laboratory and the WordNet project are sites on the World Wide Web, and remote users can access WordNet with a World Wide Web interface (see the appendix to this volume, "Obtaining and Using WordNet").

Notes

1. This section is intended to give the reader an idea of the look and feel of the X Windows interface to the WordNet database. The Microsoft Windows and Macintosh interfaces are very similar.

References

Jastrezembski, J. E. (1981). Multiple meanings, number of related meanings, frequency of occurrence, and the lexicon. *Cognitive Psychology, 13*, 278–305.

Jastrezembski, J. E., and Stanners, R. F. (1975). Multiple word meanings and lexical search speed. *Journal of Verbal Learning and Verbal Behavior, 14*, 534–537.

Zipf, G. K. (1945). The meaning-frequency relationship of words. *Journal of General Psychology, 33*, 251–256.

PART II

EXTENSIONS, ENHANCEMENTS, AND NEW PERSPECTIVES ON WORDNET

Chapter 5

Automated Discovery of WordNet Relations

Marti A. Hearst

5.1 INTRODUCTION

The WordNet lexical database is now quite large and offers broad coverage of general lexical relations in English. As is evident in this volume, WordNet has been employed as a resource for many applications in natural language processing and information retrieval. However, many potentially useful lexical relations are currently missing from WordNet. Some of these relations, although useful for natural-language-processing and information retrieval applications, are not necessarily appropriate for a general, domain-independent lexical database. For example, WordNet's coverage of proper nouns is rather sparse, but proper nouns are often very important in application tasks.

The standard way lexicographers find new relations is by looking through huge lists of concordance lines. However, culling through long lists of concordance lines can be a rather daunting task (Church and Hanks 1990), so a method that picks out those lines that are very likely to hold relations of interest should be an improvement over more traditional techniques.

This chapter describes a method for the automatic discovery of WordNet-style lexicosemantic relations by searching for corresponding lexicosyntactic patterns in large text collections. Large text corpora are now widely available and can be viewed as vast resources from which to mine lexical, syntactic, and semantic information. This idea is reminiscent of what is known as "data mining" in the artificial intelligence literature (Fayyad and Uthurusamy 1996); however, in this case the ore is raw text rather than tables of numerical data. The Lexicosyntactic Pattern Extraction (LSPE) method is meant to be useful as an automated or semi-automated aid for lexicographers and builders of domain-dependent knowledge bases.

The LSPE technique is lightweight; it does not require a knowledge base or complex interpretation modules in order to suggest new WordNet relations. Instead, promising lexical relations are plucked out of large text collections in their original form. LSPE has the advantage of not requiring the use of detailed inference procedures. However, the results are not comprehensive; that is, not all missing relations will be found. Rather, suggestions can only be made based on what the text collection has to offer in the appropriate form.

Recent work in the detection of semantically related nouns via, for example, shared argument structures (Hindle 1990) and shared dictionary definition context (Wilks et al. 1990) attempts to infer relationships among lexical items by determining which terms are related using statistical measures over large text collections. LSPE has a similar goal but uses a quite different approach, since only one instance of a relation need be encountered in a text in order to suggest its viability. It is hoped that this algorithm and its extensions, by supplying explicit semantic relation information, can be used in conjunction with algorithms that detect statistical regularities to add a useful technique to the lexicon development toolbox.

It should also be noted that LSPE is of interest not only for its potential as an aid for lexicographers and knowledge-base builders, but also for what it implies about the structure of English and related languages: namely, that certain lexicosyntactic patterns unambiguously indicate certain semantic relations.

Section 5.2 describes the lexicosyntactic patterns and the LSPE acquisition technique. Section 5.3 investigates the results obtained by applying this algorithm to newspaper text and analyses how these results map onto the WordNet noun network. Sections 5.4 and 5.5 discuss related work and summarize the chapter.

5.2   THE ACQUISITION ALGORITHM

Surprisingly useful information can be found by using only very simple analysis techniques on unrestricted text. Consider the following sentence, taken from Grolier's *Academic American Encyclopedia*:

(1) Agar is a substance prepared from a mixture of red algae, such as Gelidium, for laboratory or industrial use.

Most readers who have never before encountered the term *Gelidium* will nevertheless infer from this sentence that Gelidium is a kind of red algae.

This is true even if the reader has only a fuzzy conception of what red algae is. Note that the author of the sentence is not deliberately defining the term, as would a dictionary or a children's book containing a didactic sentence like *Gelidium is a kind of red algae*. However, the semantics of the lexicosyntactic construction indicated by the pattern shown in (2a) are such that they imply (2b):

(2) a. NP_0 *such as* NP_1 {, $NP_2 \ldots$, $(and|or)NP_i$} $i \geq 1$
    b. *for all* NP_i, $i \geq 1$, HYPONYM (NP_i, NP_0)

Thus, from sentence (1) we conclude (3):

(3) HYPONYM(*Gelidium, red algae*)

This chapter assumes the standard WordNet definition of *hyponymy*; namely, a concept represented by a lexical item L_0 is said to be a hyponym of the concept represented by a lexical item L_1 if native speakers of English accept sentences constructed from the frame *An L_0 is a (kind of)* L_1. Here L_1 is the *hypernym* of L_0 and the relationship is transitive.

Example (2) illustrates a simple way to uncover a hyponymic lexical relationship between two or more noun phrases in a naturally occurring text. This approach is similar in spirit to the pattern-based interpretation techniques used in the processing of machine-readable dictionaries (e.g., Alshawi 1987; Markowitz, Ahlswede, and Evens 1986; Nakamura and Nagao 1988). Thus, the interpretation of sentence (1) according to (2) is an application of pattern-based relation recognition to general text.

There are many ways that the structure of a language can indicate the meanings of lexical items; the difficulty lies in finding constructions that frequently and reliably indicate the relation of interest. It might seem that because free text is so varied in form and content (as compared with the somewhat regular structure of the dictionary), it may not be possible to find such constructions. However, there is a set of lexicosyntactic patterns, including the one shown in (2a), that indicate the hyponym relation and that satisfy the following desiderata:

1. They occur frequently and in many text genres.
2. They (almost) always indicate the relation of interest.
3. They can be recognized with little or no pre-encoded knowledge.

Item 1 indicates that the pattern will result in the discovery of many instances of the relation, item 2 that the information extracted will not be erroneous, and item 3 that making use of the pattern does not require the tools that it is intended to help build.

5.3   LEXICOSYNTACTIC PATTERNS FOR HYPONYMY

This section illustrates the LSPE technique by considering the lexico-syntactic patterns suitable for the discovery of hyponym relations. Since only a subset of the possible instances of the hyponymy relation will appear in a particular form, we need to make use of as many patterns as possible. The lexicosyntactic patterns in (4)–(8) (like the one in (2)) indicate the hyponym relation, followed by illustrative sentence fragments and the predicates that can be derived from them (detail about the environment surrounding the patterns is omitted for simplicity):

(4) *such NP as* $\{NP\,,\}^*\{(or|and)\}$ *NP*
   ... works by such authors as Herrick, Goldsmith, and Shakespeare.
   $\Longrightarrow$ HYPONYM(*author, Herrick*),
   HYPONYM(*author, Goldsmith*),
   HYPONYM(*author, Shakespeare*)

(5) *NP* $\{,NP\}^*\{,\}$ *or other NP*
   Bruises, ..., broken bones, or other injuries ...
   $\Longrightarrow$ HYPONYM(*bruise, injury*),
   HYPONYM(*broken bone, injury*)

(6) *NP* $\{,NP\}^*\{,\}$ *and other NP*
   ... temples, treasuries, and other important civic buildings.
   $\Longrightarrow$ HYPONYM(*temple, civic building*),
   HYPONYM(*treasury, civic building*)

(7) *NP* $\{,\}$ *including* $\{NP\,,\}^*$ $\{or|and\}$ *NP*
   All common-law countries, including Canada and England ...
   $\Longrightarrow$ HYPONYM(*Canada, common-law country*),
   HYPONYM(*England, common-law country*)

(8) *NP* $\{,\}$ *especially* $\{NP\,,\}^*$ $\{or|and\}$ *NP*
   ... most European countries, especially France, England, and Spain.
   $\Longrightarrow$ HYPONYM(*France, European country*),
   HYPONYM(*England, European country*),
   HYPONYM(*Spain, European country*)

When a relation HYPONYM(NP_0, NP_1) is discovered, aside from some lemmatization and removal of unwanted modifiers, the noun phrase is left as an atomic unit, not broken down and analyzed. If a more detailed interpretation is desired, the results can be passed on to a more intelligent or specialized language analysis component.

5.4   DISCOVERY OF NEW PATTERNS

Patterns (2) and (4)–(5) were discovered by hand, by looking through text and noticing the patterns and the relationships indicated. However, to make this approach more extensible, a pattern discovery procedure is needed. Such a procedure is sketched below:

1. Decide on a lexical relation that is of interest (e.g., meronymy).
2. Decide a list of word pairs from WordNet in which this relation is known to hold (e.g., *house-porch*).
3. Extract sentences from a large text corpus in which these terms both occur, and record the lexical and syntactic context.
4. Find the commonalities among these contexts and hypothesize that the common ones yield patterns that indicate the relation of interest.

This procedure was tried out by hand using just one pair of terms at a time. In the first case indicators of the hyponomy relation were found by looking up sentences containing *England* and *country*. With just this pair new patterns (6) and (7) were found, as well as patterns (2) and (4)–(5) that were already known. Next, trying *tank-vehicle* led to the discovery of a very productive pattern, pattern (8). (Note that for this pattern, the fact that it has an emphatic element does not affect the fact that the relation indicated is hyponymic.)

Initial attempts at applying steps 1–3, by hand, to the meronymy relation did not identify unambiguous patterns. However, an automatic version of this algorithm has not yet been implemented and so the potential strength of step 4 is still untested. There are several ways step 4 might be implemented. One candidate is a filtering method like that of Manning (1993), to find those patterns that are most likely to unambiguously indicate the relation of interest; another is the transformation-based approach of Brill (1995). Alternatively, a set of positive and negative training examples, derived from the collection resulting from steps 1–3, could be fed to a machine-learning categorization algorithm, such as C4.5 (Quinlan 1986).

On the other hand, it may be the case that in English only the hyponym relation is especially amenable to this kind of analysis, perhaps because of its "naming" nature. This question remains open, however.

5.5   PARSING ISSUES

For detection of local lexicosyntactic patterns, only a partial parse is necessary. This work makes use of a regular-expression-based noun phrase recognizer (Kupiec 1993), which builds on the output of a part-of-speech tagger (Cutting et al. 1991).[1] Initially, a concordance tool based on the Text DataBase (TDB) system (Cutting, Pedersen, and Halvorsen 1991) is used to extract sentences that contain the lexical items in the pattern of interest (e.g., *such as* or *or other*). Next, the noun phrase recognizer is run over the resulting sentences, and their positions with respect to the lexical items in the pattern are noted. For example, for pattern (5), the noun phrases that directly precede *or other* are recorded as candidate hyponyms, and the noun phrase that follows these lexical items is the candidate hypernym.[2] Thus, it is not necessary to parse the entire sentence; instead, just enough local context is examined to ensure that the nouns in the pattern are isolated, although some parsing errors do occur.

Delimiters such as commas are important for making boundary determinations. One boundary problem that arises involves determining the referent of a prepositional phrase. In the majority of cases the final noun in a prepositional phrase that precedes *such as* is the hypernym of the relation. However, there are a fair number of exceptions, as can be seen by comparing (9a) and (9b):

(9) a. The component parts of flat-surfaced furniture, such as chests and tables, . . .

 b. A bearing is a structure that supports a rotating part of a machine, such as a shaft, axle, spindle, or wheel.

In (9a) the nouns in the hyponym positions modify *flat-surfaced furniture*, the final noun of the prepositional phrase, whereas in (9b) they modify *a rotating part*. So it is not always correct to assume that the noun directly preceding *such as* is the full hypernym if it is preceded by a preposition. It would be useful to perform analyses to determine modification tendencies in this situation, but a less analysis-intensive approach is to simply discard sentences in which an ambiguity is possible.

Pattern type (6) requires the full noun phrase corresponding to the hypernym *important civic buildings*. This illustrates a difficulty that arises from using free text as the data source, as opposed to a dictionary—often the form that a noun phrase occurs in is not the form that should be recorded. For example, nouns frequently occur in their plural form but should be recorded in their singular form (although not always—for example, the algorithm finds that *cards* is a kind of *game*—a relation omitted from WordNet 1.5, although *card game* is present). Adjectival quantifiers such as *other* and *some* are usually undesirable and can be eliminated in most cases without making the statement of the hyponym relation erroneous. Comparatives such as *important* and *smaller* are usually best removed, since their meaning is relative and dependent on the context in which they appear.

The amount of modification desired depends on the application for which the lexical relations will be used. For building up a basic, general-domain thesaurus, single-word nouns and very common compounds are most appropriate. For a more specialized domain, more modified terms have their place. For example, noun phrases in the medical domain often have several layers of modification that should be preserved in a taxonomy of medical terms.

5.6 SOME RESULTS

In an earlier discussion of this acquisition method (Hearst 1992), hyponymy relations between simple noun phrases were extracted from Grolier's *Academic American Encyclopedia* and compared with the contents of an early version of WordNet (version 1.1). The acquisition method found many useful relations that had not yet been entered into the network (they have all since been added). Relations derived from encyclopedia text tend to be somewhat prototypical in nature and should in general correspond well to the kind of information that lexicographers would expect to enter into the network. To further explore the behavior of the acquisition method, this section examines results of applying the algorithm to six months' worth of text from The *New York Times*.

When a result HYPONYM(N_0, N_1) is compared with the contents of WordNet's noun database, three outcomes are possible:

1. Both N_0 and N_1 are in WordNet, and the relation HYPONYM(N_0, N_1) is already in the database (possibly through transitive closure).
2. Both N_0 and N_1 are in WordNet, and the relation HYPONYM(N_0, N_1) is not (even through transitive closure); a new hyponym link is suggested.
3. One or both of N_0 and N_1 are not present; these noun phrases and the corresponding hyponym relation are suggested.

As an example of the second outcome, consider the following sentence and derived relation, automatically extracted from The *New York Times*:

(10) Felonies such as stabbings and shootings, ...
$\implies$ HYPONYM(*shootings, felonies*),
HYPONYM(*stabbings, felonies*)

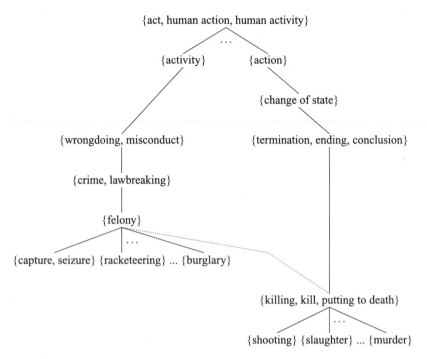

Figure 5.1
A portion of WordNet 1.5 with a new link (dotted line) suggested by an auto-matically acquired relation: HYPONYM(*shooting, felony*). Many hyponym links are omitted in order to simplify the diagram.

The text indicates that a shooting is a kind of felony. Figure 5.1 shows the portion of the hyponymy relation in WordNet 1.5's noun hierarchy that includes *felony* and *shooting*. In the current version, despite the fact that there are links between *racketeering, ..., burglary* and *felony*, there is no link between *shooting, ..., murder* and *felony* or any other part of the crime portion of the network. Thus, the acquisition algorithm suggests the addition of a potentially useful link, as indicated by the dotted line. This suggestion may in turn suggest still more changes to the network, since it may be necessary to create a different sense of *shooting* to distinguish "shooting a can" or "hunting" (which are not necessarily crimes) from "shooting people."

Not surprisingly, the relations found in newspaper text tend to be less taxonomic or prototypical than those found in encyclopedia text. For example, the relation HYPONYM(*milo, crop*) was extracted from the *New*

York Times. WordNet classifies *milo* as a kind of sorghum or grain, but grain is not entered as a kind of crop. The only hyponyms of the appropriate sense of *crop* in WordNet 1.5 are *catch crop, cover crop,* and *root crop.* One could argue that hyponyms of *crop* should only be refinements on the notion of crop, rather than lists of types of crops. But in many somewhat similar cases, WordNet does indeed list specific instances of a concept as well as refinements on that concept. For example, hyponyms of *book* include *trade book* and *reference book,* which can be seen as refinements of *book,* as well as *Utopia,* which is a specific book (by Sir Thomas More).

When information is extracted directly from text in this way, relations like HYPONYM(*milo, crop*) are at least brought up for scrutiny. It should be easier for a lexicographer to take note of such relations if they are represented explicitly rather than trying to spot them by sifting through huge lists of concordance lines.

Often the import of relations found in newspaper text is more strongly influenced by the context in which they appear than is the import of those found in encyclopedia text. Furthermore, these relations tend more often to reflect subjective judgments, opinions, or metaphorical usages than do the more established statements that appear in the encyclopedia. For example, the assertion that the movie *Gaslight* is a *classic* might be considered a value judgment (although encyclopedias state that certain actors are stars, so perhaps this isn't so different), and the statement that *AIDS* is a *disaster* might be considered more a metaphorical statement than a taxonomic one.

Tables 5.1 and 5.2 show the results of extracting 50 consecutive hyponym relations from six months' worth of the *New York Times* using pattern (2a), the *such as* pattern. The first group in table 5.1 corresponds to the situation in which the noun phrases and relation are already present in WordNet. The second group corresponds to the situation in which the noun phrases are present in WordNet but the hyponymy relation between them is absent. The third group corresponds to the situation in which at least one noun phrase is absent and the corresponding relation is necessarily absent as well. In this example these relations all involve proper noun hyponyms.

Some interesting relations are suggested. For example, the only hyponyms of *euphemism* in WordNet 1.5 are *blank, darn,* and *heck* (euphemisms for curse words). *Detainee* also exists in WordNet, as a hyponym of *prisoner, captive,* which in turn is a hyponym of *unfortunate, unfortu-*

Table 5.1
Examples of useful relations suggested by the automatic acquisition method, derived from the *New York Times*

Description	Hypernym	Hyponym(s)
Relation and terms already appear in WordNet 1.5	fabric	silk
	grain	barley
	disorders	epilepsy
	businesses	nightclub
	crimes	kidnappings
	countries	Brazil India Israel
	vegetables	broccoli
	games	checkers
	regions	Texas
	assets	stocks
	jurisdictions	Illinois
Terms appear in WordNet 1.5, relation does not	crops	milo
	wildlife	deer raccoons
	conditions	epilepsy
	conveniences	showers microwaves
	perishables	fruit
	agents	bacteria viruses
	felonies	shootings stabbings
	euphemisms	restrictees detainees
	goods	shoes
	officials	stewards
	geniuses	Einstein Newton
	gifts	liquor
	disasters	AIDS
	materials	glass ceramics
	partner	Nippon
At least one term (and therefore relation) does not appear in WordNet 1.5 (proper noun)	companies	Volvo Saab
	institutions	Tufts
	airlines	Pan USAir
	agencies	Clic Zoli
	companies	Shell

Table 5.2
Examples of less felicitous relations also derived from the *New York Times*

Description	Hypernym	Hyponym(s)
Relation does not appear in WordNet 1.5 but is perhaps too general	things	exercise
	topics	nutrition
	things	conservation
	things	popcorn peanuts
	areas	Sacramento
Context-specific relations, so probably not of interest	others	Meadowbrook
	facilities	Peachtree
	categories	drama miniseries comedy
	classics	*Gaslight*
	generics	Richland
Misleading relations resulting from parsing errors (usually not detecting the full NP)	tendencies	aspirin anticoagulants
	competence	Nunn
	organization	Bissinger
	children	Headstart
	titles	*Batman*
	companies	sports
	agencies	Vienna
	jobs	computer
	projects	universities

nate person. If nothing else, this discovered relation points out that the coverage of euphemisms in WordNet 1.5 is still rather sparse, it also suggests another category of euphemism, namely, government-designated terms that act as such. The final decision on whether or not to classify *detainee* in this way rests with the lexicographers.

Another interesting example is the suggestion of the link between *Einstein* and *genius*. Both terms exist in the network (see figure 5.2), and *Einstein* is recorded as a hyponym of *physicist*, which in turn is a hyponym of *scientist* and then *intellectual*. One of the hypernyms of *genius* is also *intellectual*. Thus, the lexicographers have made *genius* and *scientist* siblings rather than specifying one to be a hyponym of the other. This makes sense, since not all scientists are geniuses (although whether all scientists are intellectuals is perhaps open to debate as well). The figure indicates that *philosopher* is also a child of *intellectual*, and individual philosophers appear as hyponyms of *philosopher*. Hence, it does not seem

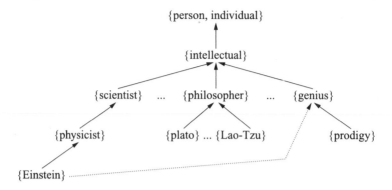

Figure 5.2
A portion of WordNet 1.5 with a new link (dotted line) suggested by an automatically acquired relation: HYPONYM(*Einstein, genius*). Many hyponym links are omitted in order to simplify the diagram.

unreasonable to propose a link between *genius* and particular intellectuals so known.

Table 5.2 illustrates some of the less useful discovered relations. The first group lists relations that are probably too general to be useful. For example, various senses of *exercise* are classified as *act* and *event* in WordNet 1.5, but *exercise* is described as a *thing* in the newspaper text. Although an action can be considered to be a thing, the ontology of WordNet assumes they have separate originating synsets. A similar argument applies to the *conservation* example.

The next group in table 5.2 refers to context-specific relations. For example, there most likely is a facility known as the *Peachtree facility*, but this is important only to a very particular domain. Similarly, the relationship between *others* and *Meadowbrook* most likely makes sense when the reference of *others* is resolved, it is not important out of context. On the other hand, although the HYPONYM(*Gaslight, classic*) relation is inappropriate in this exact form, it may well be suggesting a useful omitted concept, "classic films." Of course, the main problem with such a concept is the subjective and time-sensitive nature of its membership.

Most of the terms of WordNet's noun database are unmodified nouns or nouns with a single modifier. For this reason, the analysis presented here only extracts relations consisting of unmodified nouns in both the hypernym and hyponym roles (although determiners are allowed and a very small set of quantifier adjectives: *some, many, certain,* and *other*).

Table 5.3
Results from 200 sentences containing the term *or other*

Frequency	Explanation
38	Some version of the NPs and the corresponding relation were found in WordNet.
31	The relation did not appear in WordNet and was judged to be a very good relation (in some cases both NPs were present, in some cases not).
35	The relation did not appear in WordNet and was judged to be at least a pretty good relation (in some cases both NPs were present, in some cases not).
19	The relation was too general.
8	The relation was too subjective or contained unresolved or inappropriate referents (e.g., *these*).
34	The NPs involved were too long, too specific, and/or too context specific.
12	The relations were repeats of cases counted above.
22	The sentences did not contain the appropriate syntactic form.

This restriction is also useful because, as touched on above, the procedure for determining which modifiers are important is not straightforward. Furthermore, for the purposes of evaluation, in most cases it is easier to judge the correctness of the classification of unmodified nouns than of modified ones.

Although not illustrated in this example, the algorithm also suggests many multiword term relations (e.g., HYPONYM(*data base search*, *disk-intensive operation*). To further elucidate the performance of the algorithm, 200 consecutive instances of pattern (5), the *or other* pattern, were extracted and evaluated by hand. Sentences that simply contained the two words *or other* (or *or others*) were extracted initially, regardless of syntactic context. The most specific form of the noun phrase was looked up first; if it did not occur in WordNet, then the leftmost word in the phrase was removed and the phrase that remained was looked up. This process was repeated until only one word was left in the phrase. In each case the words in the phrase were first looked up as is and then reduced to their root form using the morphological analysis routines bundled with WordNet.

The results were evaluated in detail by hand and were placed into one of eight categories, as shown in table 5.3. The judgments of whether the relations were "very good" or "pretty good" are meant to approximate the judgment that would be made by a WordNet lexicographer about whether or not to place the relation into WordNet. Of course, this evaluation is very subjective, so an attempt was made to err on the side of conservativeness. Using this conservative evaluation, 104 out of the 166 eligible sentences (those that had the correct syntax and did not repeat already listed relations), or 63%, were either already present or strong candidates for inclusion in WordNet.

As seen in the examples from *New York Times* text, many of the suggested relations are more encyclopedic, and less obviously valid as lexicosemantic relations. Yet as WordNet continues to grow, the lexicographers may choose to include such items.

In summary, these results suggest that automatically extracted relations can be of use in augmenting WordNet. As mentioned above, the algorithm has the drawback of not guaranteeing complete coverage of the parts of the lexicon that require repair, but it can be argued that some repair is better than none. When the algorithm is applied to newspaper text, which tends to be more unruly than well-groomed encyclopedia text, a fair number of uninteresting relations are suggested, but if a lexicographer or knowledge engineer makes the final decision about inclusion, the results should be quite helpful for winnowing out missing relations.

5.7   RELATED WORK

Extensive work has been done on the use of partial parsing for various tasks in language analysis. For example, Kupiec (1993) extracts noun phrases from encyclopedia texts in order to answer closed-class questions, and Jacobs and Rau (1990) use partial parsing to extract domain-dependent knowledge from newswire text. The discussion of related work in this section will focus on efforts to automatically extract lexical relation information, rather than general knowledge.

5.7.1   Hand-Coded and Knowledge-Intensive Approaches

Several knowledge-intensive approaches have been taken to automated lexical acquisition. In describing the procedure his group followed in order to build a lexicon/knowledge base for natural-language-processing analyzer of a medical text, Hobbs (1984) notes that much of the work was done by looking at the relationships implied by the linguistic presuppositions in the target texts. One of his examples, "[the phrase] 'renal dialysis units and other high-risk institutional settings' tells us that a renal dialysis unit is a high-risk setting" is a version of pattern (6) described earlier. This analysis was done by hand; it might have been aided or accelerated by an automatic analysis like that described here.

Coates-Stephens (1991, 1992) describes FUNES, a system that acquires semantic descriptions of proper nouns using detailed frame roles, a sophisticated parser, and a domain-dependent knowlege base/lexicon. FUNES attempts to fill in frame roles (e.g., name, age, origin, position, works-for) by processing newswire text. This system is similar to the work described here in that it recognizes some features of the context in which the proper noun occurs in order to identify some relevant semantic attributes. For instance, Coates-Stephens mentions that *known as* can explicitly introduce meanings for terms, as can appositives. However, this is one small component in a complex, knowledge-intensive system.

Two more acquisition techniques that make use of extensive domain knowledge are those of Velardi and Pazienza (1989), who use hand-coded selectional restriction and conceptual relation rules in order to assign case roles to lexical items, and Jacobs and Zernik (1988), who use extensive domain knowledge to fill in missing category information for unknown words.

5.7.2 Automatic Acquisition from Machine-Readable Dictionaries

Researchers have attempted several approaches to acquisition of lexical and syntactic information from machine-readable dictionaries. As mentioned earlier, dictionaries are extremely rich resources for lexicosemantic relations, but are inherently limited in their scope.

Much of the dictionary extraction work (e.g., Boguraev et al. 1987) focuses on acquisition of part-of-speech and syntactic information such as subcategorization frames for verbs. Several of these projects also involve extracting different types of lexical relations. The two main approaches to extraction are (1) using patterns tailored to dictionary definitions and (2) syntactically parsing the definitions.

Several research groups use patterns to acquire lexical relation information from machine-readable dictionaries. In interpreting definitions from the *Longman Dictionary of Contemporary English*, Alshawi (1987) uses a hierarchy of patterns that consist mainly of part-of-speech indicators and wildcard characters. Markowitz, Ahlswede, and Evens (1986) and

Chodorow, Byrd, and Heidorn (1985) have created a taxonomic hierarchy based on information extracted from patterns, as have Wilks et al. (1990) and Guthrie et al. (1990). Nakamura and Nagao (1988) also run pattern recognizers over LDOCE to extract relations such as taxonomy, meronymy, action, state, degree, and form.

Ahlswede and Evens (1988) compared an approach based on parsing with one based on pattern recognition for interpreting definitions from *Webster's Seventh New Collegiate Dictionary*. The pattern matcher was more accurate and much faster than the parser, although the authors speculate that if they had been extracting more complex relations, the parser would probably have produced the better results. Montemagni and Vanderwende (1992), however, demonstrate why structural information is crucial to successful extraction of semantic relations such as location, color, and purpose. Jensen and Binot (1987) and Ravin (1990) explored the extraction of detailed semantic information using careful analysis of the possible semantic and syntactic configurations that appear in dictionary definitions. These analyses are somewhat brittle because they require many of the words in the definitions to have already been unambiguously identified. Vanderwende (1995) improves this procedure by bootstrapping with unambiguous words and iterating through the contents of the dictionary, each time disambiguating new words on the basis of those identified in the previous iteration and some straightforward similarity information.

5.7.3   Automatic Acquisition from Corpora

There is a growing body of work on acquisition of semantic information from unrestricted text. In early work Church and Hanks (1990) used frequency of co-occurrence of content words to create clusters of semantically similar words, and Hindle (1990) used both simple syntactic frames and frequency of occurrence of content words to determine similarity among nouns. For example, the nouns most similar to *legislator* in a 6-million-word sample of AP newswire text were found to be *Senate, committee, organization, commission, legislature, delegate,* and *lawmaker.* As can be seen from this example, these nouns represent a wide variety of relations to the target word *legislator*, including meronymy, synonymy, and general relatedness. Grefenstette (1994) takes this approach a bit further by using shallow syntactic analysis on local text contexts to determine semantic relatedness information.

More recent examples of algorithms that derive lexical co-occurrence information from large text collections include the work of Schütze (1993) and Resnik (1993). In Word Space (Schütze 1993), statistics are collected about the contexts in which words co-occur, and the results are placed in a term-by-term co-occurrence matrix that is reduced using a variant of multidimensional scaling. The resulting matrix can be used to make inferences about the closeness of words in a multidimensional semantic space. Hearst and Schütze (1996) show how the distributional association information of Word Space can be combined with word similarity information from WordNet to classify frequently occurring proper nouns. A different approach is taken by Resnik (1993, 1995), who develops an information-theoretic model of word similarity based on frequency of occurrence in a corpus combined with the structural information available in WordNet.

Although the focus in this chapter has been on automatic acquisition of lexicosemantic information, it is appropriate to mention as well some recent work on automatically deriving syntactic association information. For example, the acquisition algorithm of Smadja and McKeown (1990; Smadja 1993) uses statistical techniques to derive well-formed collocation information from large text collections. Calzolari and Bindi (1990) use corpus-based statistical association ratios to determine lexical relations such as prepositional complementation and modification. More recent work by Basili, Pazienza, and Velardi (1992) uses a shallow syntactic analyzer to find binary and ternary syntactically defined collocations (e.g., subject-verb, noun-preposition-noun, verb-adverb).

Brent (1990, 1993) describes methods for finding verb subcategorization frames by searching for simple syntactic patterns across large collections. The patterns all reflect well-known linguistic phenomena; for example, English has a class of verbs that can take an infinitive argument, so one of Brent's algorithms tries to find instances of the verb of interest followed by the pattern to *INF-VERB*. Brent employs statistical filtering techniques in order to reduce the already small error rates. The fact that only unambiguous distinguishers are allowed to supply positive information ensures that this method is very accurate; however, its conservativeness inherently limits its scope and coverage. For example, it cannot discover all kinds of verb frames.

Manning (1993) describes an algorithm that is able to find a much larger dictionary of subcategorization frames than Brent's algorithms by filtering the results statistically, rather than requiring that every relation detected be unambiguously correct. Manning's algorithm makes use of a finite-state parser run on the output of a stochastic part-of-speech tagger.

Like Brent's approach, LSPE is able to distinguish clear pieces of evidence from ambiguous ones. Unlike Brent's approach, however, it is at least potentially extensible, using the procedure for discovery of new patterns described above, and perhaps culling out ambiguous results using a statistical filtering pattern like that suggested by Manning.

5.8 SUMMARY

This chapter has described LSPE, a low-cost approach for augmenting the structure and contents of WordNet. LSPE uses lexicosyntactic patterns to automatically extract lexicosemantic relations from unrestricted text collections. Since LSPE requires only a single specially expressed instance of a relation, it is complementary to those methods that infer semantic relations based on word co-occurrence or other statistical measures. However, there is a trade-off between the simplicity of the knowledge-free text interpretation and the sparseness of coverage that it offers.

The LSPE approach also suggests a linguistic insight: some semantic relations in English are indicated unambiguously by simple lexicosyntactic patterns. This idea merits further exploration, in at least two directions. First, are other relations besides hyponymy unambiguously indicated by lexicosyntactic patterns in English, or is the IS-A relation a special case? Second, do other languages exhibit similar behavior for hyponymy or other lexical relations? The answers to these questions may lead to further advances in automated lexical acquisition.

Notes

This work was performed while I was a member of the research staff at Xerox Palo Alto Research Center. I would like to thank Geoff Nunberg for very helpful comments on the analysis of the results of the algorithm, Julian Kupiec for getting the noun phrase recognition software into a form that I could use, Jan Pedersen for helpful comments on the chapter, Robert Wilensky for earlier support of this work, and Christiane Fellbaum for unflagging enthusiasm, very helpful suggestions for the chapter, and very gentle deadline reminders.

1. All code described in this chapter is written in Common LISP and run on Sun SparcStations.

2. In earlier work (Hearst 1992) a more general constituent analyzer was used.

References

Academic American encyclopedia. (1990). Danbury, CT: Grolier Electronic Publishing.

Ahlswede, T., and Evens, M. (1988). Parsing vs. text processing in the analysis of dictionary definitions. In *Proceedings of the 26th Annual Meeting of the Association for Computational Linguistics,* 217–224. Association for Computational Linguistics.

Alshawi, H. (1987). Processing dictionary definitions with phrasal pattern hierarchies. *American Journal of Computational Linguistics, 13,* 195–202.

Basili, R., Pazienza, M., and Velardi, P. (1992). A shallow syntactic analyser to extract word associations from corpora. *Literary and Linguistic Computing, 7,* 113–123.

Boguraev, B., Briscoe, T., Carroll, J., Carter, D., and Grover, C. (1987). The derivation of a grammatically indexed lexicon from LDOCE. In *Proceedings of the 25th Annual Meeting of the Association for Computational Linguistics,* 193–200. Association for Computational Linguistics.

Brent, M. R. (1990). Semantic classification of verbs from their syntactic contexts: Automated lexicography with implications for child language acquisition. In *Proceedings of the 12th Annual Conference of the Cognitive Science Society,* 428–437. Hillsdale, NJ: Erlbaum.

Brent, M. R. (1993). From grammar to lexicon: Unsupervised learning of lexical syntax. *Computational Linguistics, 19,* 243–262.

Brill, E. (1995). Unsupervised learning of disambiguation rules for part of speech tagging. In *Proceedings of the Third Workshop on Very Large Corpora.* Association for Computational Linguistics.

Calzolari, N., and Bindi, R. (1990). Acquisition of lexical information from a large textual Italian corpus. In *Proceedings of the Thirteenth International Conference on Computational Linguistics (COLING-90).* Association for Computational Linguistics.

Chodorow, M. S., Byrd, R. J., and Heidorn, G. E. (1985). Extracting semantic hierarchies from a large on-line dictionary. In *Proceedings of the 23rd Annual Meeting of the Association for Computational Linguistics,* 299–304. Association for Computational Linguistics.

Church, K. W., and Hanks, P. (1990). Word association norms, mutual information, and lexicography. *American Journal of Computational Linguistics, 16,* 22–29.

Coates-Stephens, S. (1991). Coping with lexical inadequacy: The automatic acquisition of proper nouns from news text. In *Proceedings of the Seventh Annual Conference of the UW Centre for the New OED and Text Research: Using Corpora,* 154–169. Waterloo, Ontario, Canada: UW Centre for the New OED and Text Research.

Coates-Stephens, S. (1992). The analysis and acquisition of proper names for the understanding of free text. *Computers and the Humanities, 26,* 441–456.

Cutting, D. R., Kupiec, J., Pedersen, J. O., and Sibun, P. (1991). A practical part-of-speech tagger. In *Proceedings of the Third Conference on Applied Natural Language Processing*. Association for Computational Linguistics.

Cutting, D. R., Pedersen, J. O., and Halvorsen, P.-K. (1991). An object-oriented architecture for text retrieval. In *Intelligent text and image handling: Proceedings of a conference on intelligent text and image handling "RIAO 91,"* 285–298. New York: Elsevier. Also available as Tech. Rep. No. SSL-90-83, Xerox PARC.

Fayyad, U. M., and Uthurusamy, R. (Eds.). (1996). *The First International Conference on Knowledge Discovery and Data Mining*. Menlo Park, CA: AAAI Press.

Grefenstette, G. (1994). *Explorations in automatic thesaurus discovery*. Boston: Kluwer.

Guthrie, L., Slator, B. M., Wilks, Y., and Bruce, R. (1990). Is there content in empty heads? In *Proceedings of the Thirteenth International Conference on Computational Linguistics (COLING-90)*. Association for Computational Linguistics.

Hearst, M. A. (1992). Automatic acquisition of hyponyms from large text corpora. In *Proceedings of the Fourteenth International Conference on Computational Linguistics (COLING-92)*, 539–545. Association for Computational Linguistics.

Hearst, M. A., and Schütze, H. (1996). Customizing a lexicon to better suit a computational task. In B. Boguraev and J. Pustejovsky (Eds.), *Corpus processing for lexical acquisition*. Cambridge, MA: MIT Press.

Hindle, D. (1990). Noun classification from predicate-argument structures. In *Proceedings of the 28th Annual Meeting of the Association for Computational Linguistics*, 268–275. Association for Computational Linguistics.

Hobbs, J. R. (1984). *Sublanguage and knowledge*. Paper presented at the Workshop on Sublanguage Description and Processing, New York University, January.

Jacobs, P., and Rau, L. (1990). SCISOR: Extracting information from on-line news. *Communications of the ACM, 33*(11), 88–97.

Jacobs, P., and Zernik, U. (1988). Acquiring lexical knowledge from text: A case study. In *Proceedings of the Seventh National Conference on Artificial Intelligence (AAAI-88)*, 739–744. Menlo Park, CA: AAAI Press, and Cambridge, MA: MIT Press.

Jensen, K., and Binot, J.-L. (1987). Disambiguating prepositional phrase attachments by using on-line dictionary definitions. *American Journal of Computational Linguistics, 13*(3), 251–260.

Kupiec, J. (1993). MURAX: A robust linguistic approach for question answering using an on-line encyclopedia. In *Proceedings of the Sixteenth Annual International ACM SIGIR Conference on Research and Development in Information Retrieval*, 181–190. New York: ACM Press.

Manning, C. D. (1993). Automatic acquisition of a large subcategorization dictionary from corpora. In *Proceedings of the 31st Annual Meeting of the Association for Computational Linguistics*, 235–242. Association for Computational Linguistics.

Markowitz, J., Ahlswede, T., and Evens, M. (1986). Semantically significant patterns in dictionary definitions. In *Proceedings of the 24th Annual Meeting of the Association for Computational Linguistics*, 112–119. Association for Computational Linguistics.

Montemagni, S., and Vanderwende, L. (1992). Structural patterns vs. string patterns for extracting semantic information from dictionaries. In *Proceedings of the Fourteenth International Conference on Computational Linguistics (COLING-92)*, 546–552. Association for Computational Linguistics.

Nakamura, J., and Nagao, M. (1988). Extraction of semantic information from an ordinary English dictionary and its evaluation. In *Proceedings of the Twelfth International Conference on Computational Linguistics*, 459–464. Association for Computational Linguistics.

Quinlan, J. R. (1986). Induction of decision trees. *Machine Learning, 1*, 81–106. Reprinted in J. W. Shavlik and T. G. Dietterich (Eds.), *Readings in machine learning*. San Mateo, CA: Morgan Kaufmann.

Ravin, Y. (1990). Disambiguating and interpreting verb definitions. In *Proceedings of the 28th Annual Meeting of the Association for Computational Linguistics*, 260–267. Association for Computational Linguistics.

Resnik, P. (1993). *Selection and information: A class-based approach to lexical relationships.* Unpublished doctoral dissertation, University of Pennsylvania, Philadelphia. (Rep. No. IRCS-93-42, Institute for Research in Cognitive Science.)

Resnik, P. (1995). Using information content to evaluate semantic similarity in a taxonomy. In *Proceedings of the 14th International Joint Conference on Artificial Intelligence (IJCAI-95)*, 448–453. San Francisco: Morgan Kaufmann.

Schütze, H. (1993). Word Space. In S. J. Hanson, J. D. Cowan, and C. L. Giles (Eds.), *Advances in neural information processing systems 5*. San Mateo, CA: Morgan Kaufmann.

Smadja, F. A. (1993). Retrieving collocations from text: Xtract. *Computational Linguistics, 19*, 143–177.

Smadja, F. A., and McKeown, K. R. (1990). Automatically extracting and representing collocations for language generation. In *Proceedings of the 28th Annual Meeting of the Association for Computational Linguistics*, 252–259. Association for Computational Linguistics.

Vanderwende, L. (1995). Ambiguity in the acquisition of lexical information. In *Working Notes of the 1995 AAAI Spring Symposium on Representation and Acquisition of Lexical Knowledge*, 174–179. American Association for Artificial Intelligence.

Velardi, P., and Pazienza, M. T. (1989). Computer aided interpretation of lexical cooccurrences. In *Proceedings of the 27th Annual Meeting of the Association for Computational Linguistics*, 185–192. Association for Computational Linguistics.

Wilks, Y. A., Fass, D. C., Guo, C. M., McDonald, J. E., Plate, T., and Slator, B. M. (1990). Providing machine tractable dictionary tools. *Machine Translation, 5*(2), 99–151.

Chapter 6

Representing Verb Alternations in WordNet

Karen T. Kohl, Douglas A. Jones, Robert C. Berwick, and Naoyuki Nomura

6.1 INTRODUCTION

The WordNet enterprise, as George Miller (1993) has so aptly put it, forges "the passage from computing with numbers to computing with words."[1] In this chapter we show how the largely semantic information in WordNet can be extended to further the marriage of lexicography—traditional dictionary making—with linguistic science. Although conventional dictionaries often give very good descriptions of the kind of *explicit* word knowledge that speakers possess, they do not usually provide the *tacit* information shared by speakers of a language. In this chapter we focus on just one sort of tacit knowledge: the fact that verbs that are close in meaning tend to occur in the same syntactic patterns. For example, many verbs that express some kind of transfer, like *give* and *send*, can be used in the two syntactic patterns illustrated in (1):

(1) a. Max gave Ida the roses.
    b. Max gave the roses to Ida.
    c. Ida sent Max a letter.
    d. Ida sent a letter to Max.

However, the semantic similarity is not always reflected in syntactic parallelism. For example, even though the verbs *circle* and *revolve* are near synonyms, they cannot occur in the same contexts. Compare (2a) and (2b) with (2c) and (2d):

(2) a. The planet circles around the sun.
    b. The planet revolves around the sun.
    c. The planet circles the sun.
    d. *The planet revolves the sun.

Although we will draw attention to theoretical work that explores why such alternations occur, our main concern here will be simply to describe how we have added such data to WorldNet. As Miller (1993) points out, traditional dictionaries usually do not include this kind of information in their verb entries:

> But they [people] have a persistent problem. When they look up a word, especially a commonly used word, they often find a dozen or more different meanings. What the dictionary does not make clear are the contexts in which each of these different meanings would be understood. So we know what kind of information is required, but we have not yet learned how to provide it to a computer.

We not only provide the actually occurring alternation patterns, but we do so in a form that we hope will be easily understandable for WordNet users. We include a system that can generate simple example sentences for grammatical and ungrammatical contexts. The next publicly released version of WordNet, 1.6, will most likely include alternation information for over 2,600 verbs (3,034 word senses) along with our simple generation component to make these alternation patterns accessible.

6.2   ENHANCEMENT OF THE VERB COMPONENT OF WORDNET

We first turn to the enhancement of the WordNet verbs developed by Karen Kohl. These verbs are encoded in Douglas Jones's on-line database of part I of *English Verb Classes and Alternations* (Levin 1993; hereafter *EVCA*). We will refer to the on-line version as "EVCA-I." EVCA-I contains a list of the 2,600 verbs of part I, grouped into classes and illustrated by example sentences.

Two steps were required:

1. the annotation of the 2,600 EVCA-I verbs with WordNet word senses, and

2. the development of resources for generating sample sentences for verbs in WordNet.

Kohl's system generates 10,153 example sentences, which are read by a modified version of WordNet containing much of the material from EVCA-I.

6.2.1   Overview

The 2,600 verbs in part I of *EVCA* can be reduced to 226 sentence patterns. Our goal was to add information about these patterns to WordNet,

```
evca_datset (2,
     [coil-3, revolve-2, rotate-1, spin-1, turn-2,
          twirl-1, twist-5, whirl-1, wind-3],
     [pattern(7:ii, 'Motion around an Axis',
          [
          eg (12:a, s, 1,
               'Janet turned the cup.',
               [np, v, np]),
          eg (12:b, s, 1,
               'The cup turned.',
               [v,np])]),
     [pattern(105:ii, 'Verbs of Motion around an Axis',
          [
          eg(106:a,s,1,
               'The spaceship revolves around the
               earth.',
               [v,np, [p(around,1),np]]),
          eg(106:b,s,0,
               'The spaceship revolves the earth.',
               [v,np,[p(around 0,1),np]])])]).
```

Example number in Levin 1993.
Means this example is grammatical.

Means this example is a sentence.
The example sentence in Levin 1993.

Abstract underlying pattern for the example sentence.

Means this sentence is NOT grammatical

Incorporated preposition, does not appear in the surface form of a sentence, but its meaning is implicitly understood.

Figure 6.1
EVCA-I Prolog notation for one *EVCA* verb class, the causative/inchoative class

both to improve the sample sentences for verbs given in current versions of WordNet and to boost the total number of sentence patterns, since WordNet uses only the 34 listed in appendix A. Many of the verbs and alternation patterns in part I of *EVCA* were used to build a Prolog system for generating new example sentences, which were then added to Word-Net. In addition to fine-tuning the coverage in WordNet, we added a "negative example" component, as shown below. Both of these enhancements are intended to make WordNet more closely model speakers' knowledge of verb syntax.

The EVCA-I Prolog notation for one *EVCA* verb class, the causative/inchoative class, is displayed in figure 6.1.

Since *EVCA* itself gives only one example sentence per verb class, significant effort was required to reach our goal of producing natural-sounding example sentences for all of the verbs. For instance, the class of verbs "Motion around an Axis" includes *coil, revolve, rotate, spin, turn, twirl, twist, whirl, wind*. The example sentences given in *EVCA* use only the verb *turn*, in two variants: *Janet turned the cup* and *The cup turned*. But when other verbs in the class are mechanically substituted for *turn* in the example sentences, some of them sound odd: for example, *Janet wound the cup*.

The difficulty arises from the fact that not all the verbs that are grouped together in *EVCA* share the same constraints to the other relevant elements in the sentence, such as the noun phrases. That is, the verbs vary in terms of their selectional restrictions. If we had adopted the *EVCA* example sentences for all verbs in the same class without modifying the noun phrases, some semantically deviant sentences would have resulted. For instance, consider again the *EVCA* alternation type 12, the causative/ inchoative alternation, illustrated in (3):

(3) a. Janet turned the cup.
     b. The cup turned.

The verbs *bend, crease, crinkle, crumple, fold, rumple,* and *wrinkle* share the causative/inchoative alternation with *fold*. However, substituting these verbs in sentence (3a) would allow Janet to fold/crease/crumple/etc. the cup, which are not possible actions (unless one is dealing with a paper cup). The distinction between verbs like *turn* and *fold* stems from a difference in the verbs' selectional restrictions rather than the shared alternation pattern. To generate natural-sounding sentences for all the verbs in the class, then, we needed to add relevant constraints to EVCA-I.

To generate acceptable example sentences, we therefore included both alternation patterns and selectional restrictions grounded on a miniature semantic specification that we called "Toyworld." We annotated verbs with minimal information about the nouns that naturally go with them (the selectional restrictions), and in turn, we marked those nouns with that information in our database. For example, we marked the verb *roll* as requiring something AXIAL. We then added a typical noun to the database that would normally be understood to be "axial": namely, the noun *log*. Now, when we generate an example sentence with *roll*, the program inserts the noun *log* into the sentence pattern.

6.2.2 Enhancing WordNet with *EVCA* Syntactic Classes

To add the syntactic classification of *EVCA* verbs to WordNet, our goal was to generate one sentence per word sense per alternation pattern.

To do this, we first parsed the *EVCA* example sentences by hand. Next, we assigned each verb the corresponding WordNet sense number. (See appendix B for examples of EVCA-I datasets, or verb classes, containing the verbs with sense numbers, the example sentences, and the parses of the example sentences.) Finally, we studied all the verbs and the noun phrases that these verbs co-occurred with in the sentences, to determine the semantic properties of each noun phrase that a particular verb subcategorizes for. Using a finite set of semantic properties, we selected specific nouns, which comprised a "toy world" from which we generated the final, natural-sounding sentences. Properties were represented by features such as THING, SOLID, and ANIMATE. Consider again the verb *rotate*. Not all things can rotate. For something to rotate, it must be solid and axial. Thus, the property list for the direct object of *rotate* is [thing, solid, axial], and one instance of a solid, axial thing is a top.

When the verbs that appear in WordNet are compared with those that appear in EVCA-I, it is clear that although WordNet makes very fine-grained distinctions for some polysemous verbs, some semantic classes are missing. For example, the morphologically relatively productive classes made up of verbs prefixed with *de-* and *un-* (e.g., *declaw* and *unzip*) are largely missing from WordNet.

We now review the enhancement procedure step by step.

6.2.2.1   Parsing Verb Class Alternations: From Sentences to Schemas

We first hand-parsed the *EVCA* example sentences, replacing the lexical items in each sentence with annotated part-of-speech labels.[2] These parses, or *schemas*, include labels for constituents such as noun phrases, verbs, prepositions, pronouns, and adverbs. These parses correspond to underlying representations, encoding relations among verbs, nouns, and so on, at an abstract level. That is, the schemas were regularized to abstract away from a strict adherence to surface word order in order to allow us to keep them maximally simple. We used the linear order of the schemas to encode a canonical form, which typically did in fact correspond to the surface order of the sentence. The parses were refined further to specify the particular preposition for each alternation in a class of verbs.

In order to collapse these verb alternation classes into larger groups, we assigned semantic or thematic roles to the noun phrases in the sentences. We used a small inventory of roles that seemed the most useful to us, for example, AGENT and THEME. These labels indicate what role the noun phrase plays, at a very abstract level. For example, in *John broke the vase*, John is responsible for the breaking. In *The vase broke*, the subject has a different role. Both subjects are related to the verb *break*, but they are related to it in different ways. *John* is said to be an AGENT (the person who causes some event to happen), whereas *the vase* is a THEME (the person or thing that is affected by the event). It is not easy to give a precise definition of what constitutes a theme or an agent in every case, but these rough intuitions are what we used to build the encodings for generating natural-sounding sentences. Mechanically, we encoded thematic roles by saying that the underlying subject is always and AGENT and the underlying object is always a THEME.

6.2.2.2 Abstract Lexical Forms   To help us encode abstract patterns, we drew on ideas from generative grammar. Two of these ideas, which we will introduce briefly here, are the *Unaccusativity Hypothesis* and *Preposition Incorporation*. Both make reference to overt patterns in syntax that have covert counterparts. These ideas allowed us to keep the lexical entries simple; all we needed to do was mark whether the pattern was overt or whether it held at a more abstract level.

The key insight of the Unaccusativity Hypothesis, originally formulated by Perlmutter (1978), is that the subjects of certain intransitive verbs are very much like the objects of ordinary transitive verbs. Consider, for instance, the verb *break*. In both *The vase broke* and *John broke the vase*, we understand the vase to have undergone the same process. Either way, the vase is broken, and most importantly, in the intransitive case of *The vase broke* we do not infer that the vase did anything by itself. According to the Unaccusativity Hypothesis, then, *break* is an unaccusative verb. In other words, the verb has a direct object underlyingly, but not a subject; and since the subject position is vacant, the underlying direct object appears in the same surface position as an ordinary subject. The mechanics of this process are spelled out in detail by Burzio (1986), who formulates Perlmutter's original insights in terms of the Government-Binding framework of Chomsky (1981).

But not every intransitive verb is unaccusative: some have a "real" subject, and no object. These are the *unergative* verbs (one example being *talk*). The two kinds of intransitive verbs can be distinguished by means of a simple diagnostic, the adjectival passive: unaccusative verbs typically allow an adjectival form, and unergatives do not. Thus, one can say that the vase is *broken*, or refer to a *broker vase*; but one cannot say that a man is *talked,* or refer to a *talked man.* (A comprehensive treatment of these points, which are somewhat simplified here, can be found in Levin and Rappaport Hovav 1995 and the extensive references cited there.)

The key insight of Preposition Incorporation, a notion introduced by Gruber (1965), is that in some cases a sentence is interpreted as if it contains a preposition, even though the preposition does not appear overtly. For example, in (4) the verb *climb* appears with a variety of prepositions:

(4) a. John climbed down the ladder.
     b. John climbed up the mountain.
     c. John climbed into the tent.
     d. John climbed along the grass.

It can also appear without a preposition:

(5) John climbed the ladder.

Without a preposition, though, the only interpretation is that John climbed *up* the ladder, not *down* it. This is true even though one can say *John climbed down the ladder,* where the preposition *down* is explicitly included. Gruber suggests that the actual preposition *up* is "incorporated" into the verb *climb.* Although it does not appear overtly, its meaning is nonetheless implicit. We found it simpler to encode the basic relations using ordinary prepositions and to refer to these relations as being the same semantically, even though the preposition does not appear in the sentence. Thus, we did not need to create new abstract semantic relations with a different set of properties.

We combined the key ideas of the Unaccusativity Hypothesis and Preposition Incorporation in formulating lexical entries that encode the grammatical roles in the sentence. For example, we used the Unaccusativity Hypothesis as follows: The sentence *The glass broke* is derived from ____ *broke the glass.* Therefore, when we encountered a similar sentence with *break,* we assigned the subject the THEME role. We also combined the Unaccusativity Hypothesis with Preposition Incorporation: in a single sentence it can be the case that a preposition is incorporated (i.e., it is covert) *and* that the preposition's noun phrase object appears as the subject of the sentence. Such a sentence is *This knife cut the bread,* which is derived from ____ *cut the bread with_0 this knife. With_0* in *This knife cut the bread* is an incorporated preposition; therefore, *this knife* is the object of the preposition *with,* rather than an AGENT, although it appears in subject position.

The three cases in which a surface subject is derived by movement into subject position, and where it should consequently not be labeled as an AGENT, can thus be summed up as follows:

1. If the verb phrase has a subject, it becomes the subject of the sentence.

2. If the verb phrase does not have a subject and there is no incorporated preposition (except *around*), then the object of the verb phrase becomes the subject of the sentence.

3. Otherwise, the object of an incorporated preposition becomes the subject of the sentence.

A sentence pair illustrating the causative/inchoative alternation is shown in (6) (= (12) in *EVCA*):[3]

(6) *Sentence*   *Argument structure matrix*
    a. Janet broke the cup.   vp (v,np,np)
    b. The cup broke.   vp (v,e,np)

Most of the alternations in EVCA-I hinge on the placement of prepositions and their objects. For most prepositions, alternations imply binary relations between noun phrases, such as figure and ground or material and artifact. These relations can be counted and numbered, so a preposition is given a reading number that identifies the thematic or semantic label of the object. Because there are a limited number of prepositions and few reading numbers for each preposition, the preposition is a good place to store information about noun phrases and relations. Encoding semantic information with the prepositions has the effect of reducing the number of schema elements. For example, the preposition *to* in (7a) indicates that its object is an indirect object. In (7b) the indirect object has moved to the position before the direct object and has lost the preposition *to*.

(7) a. Bill sold a car to Tom.
    b. Bill sold Tom a car.

The preposition *to* actually appeared in the underlying representation we used for generating sentence (7b), but it was marked as being incorporated, so it did not appear in the sentence itself. Nonetheless, it was used to select an appropriate noun phrase for the sentence, namely, *a car*.

Another case that demonstrates our motivation for using incorporated prepositions is the "*spray/load*" alternation (*x sprayed/loaded y with z*; *x sprayed/loaded z on y*), illustrated in (8). These prepositions, like overt prepositions, can have reading numbers indicating the kinds of noun phrases they can appear with:

(8) a. Jack sprayed paint on the wall.
```
[np,v,np(figure),[p(on),np(ground)]]
[np,v,[p(with_0,4),np],[p(on,5),np]]
```
  b. Jack sprayed the wall with paint.
```
[np,v,np(ground),[p(with),np(figure)]]
[np,v,[p(on_0,1),np],[p(with,7),np]]
```

Notice that we generate a sentence that has *wall* and *paint*, regardless of whether the noun appears as object of the verb or object of the preposition in the surface form. In the case where the noun phrase is the object of the verb, the underlying representation had an incorporated preposition.

When there is an incorporated preposition *with, to, in, for, from, into,* or *of* in a sentence with no underlying subject, it is the object of the incorporated preposition, not the direct object (if one exists), that is moved to subject position (see rules 1–3). Only when the incorporated preposition is *around* does the direct object, rather than the object of the incorporated preposition, move into subject position.

Examples illustrating when objects can be moved to subject position are given in (9):

(9) a. The top rotates.
  b. The top rotates around its axis.
  c. *The top rotates its axis.
  d. This knife cut the bread.
  e. This knife doesn't cut.

The EVCA-I schema of (9d), for instance, is `[v,np,[p(with_0),` `np(instrument)]]`, which gives the underlying form _____ *cut the bread with_0 the knife*. Since no subject is available, the phrase *the knife*— being the object of an incorporated preposition—moves to subject position. This movement produces the surface form *The knife cut the bread*.

6.2.2.3 Toyworld: A Model World for Sentence Generation   In order to create felicitous sentences, we needed a small set of noun phrases that could be used with the verbs. We called this set a "toy world." In several cases the same noun phrase can be used in all the sentences illustrating a given syntactic alternation. Almost all verbs can take a human subject (i.e., *Mary*). Some cannot; we listed subjects for these verbs in a separate set. Still other verbs can take both human and nonhuman subjects. WordNet gives two sample sentences for these verbs, using *somebody* and *something* as subject. In adding real sentences to WordNet, we created only one sentence per schema per sense, so we chose only the human sub-ject if that was appropriate. See figure 6.5 in appendix C for an example.

In order to generate suitable noun phrases for the sentences whose verb does not select for a human referent, we reexamined the properties a noun phrase needs to satisfy the restrictions of particular verbs—the traditional notion of selectional restrictions, but now grounded in the EVCA-I alter-nations. In our database we associated with a verb certain properties for each noun phrase in its alternation. These properties include such general descriptions as *thing, animal, person, solid, liquid,* and *abstract,* as well as some more specific qualities like *texture:springy, shape:axial, feathered,* and *physical_property:flammable.* (For verbs that select nouns from a very small class, however, we included a specific noun.) In non-subject positions many verbs can take nouns referring either to a human being or to an inanimate entity.[4] Since we were creating only one schema per sense, for each verb we chose the form, (human or inanimate) that is most commonly used with that verb. The main point is that we marked both the noun and the verb with the relevant properties, so that when the system generated a sentence, filling in the blanks for noun phrases for a given verb, the resulting sentence sounded natural. See figure 6.5 in appendix C for an example.

In most cases, verbs that cluster semantically select the same kind of noun for a particular noun phrase slot. For example, in most of their uses many verbs select solid direct objects. Thus, *move* (in one of its senses) takes a solid direct object, as do *drop, hit, put,* and *shellac.* Moving is a fairly general action that can be performed on a solid object. Noticing that *drop, hit, put, shellac,* and many other verbs share the properties of the verb *move,* we devised an experimental system whereby the properties of a verb are inherited from other verbs semantically related to it.

6.2.2.4 The Sentence Generator Karen Kohl wrote the program to generate, in Prolog, the example sentences for EVCA-I verbs. With this program it is possible to create four levels of sentence description for WordNet to read. The simplest level simply generates the sentence, as shown in figure 6.2 in appendix C. The second generates the sentence plus semantic or thematic roles for many noun phrases. The third generates the sentence, the role labels, and the property lists used for selectional restrictions for many noun phrases (see figure 6.3, appendix C). The fourth generates all of the above, plus a few paraphrases for verbs like *spray* (e.g., *Mary caused the paint to go on the wall by spraying the paint is a paraphrase of Mary sprayed the paint on the wall*) (see figure 6.4, appendix C). On a Sparc 10, it takes about 8 minutes to create a Prolog file of such sentences with the thematic role labels and property lists and another 15 minutes to read this file into Prolog and create three other files for EVCA WordNet to read. Examples of EVCA WordNet sessions are given in appendix C.

6.3   A SURVEY OF THE WORD SENSES IN WORDNET AND *EVCA*

An important addition to our enhanced WordNet was word sense differentiation. Quite a few verbs listed in *EVCA* appear in more than one verb class. Often, but not always, the appearance of a verb in more than one class means that the verb is polysemous. Whether a verb is polysemous is not determined mechanically, but the process is nonetheless simple: one looks at the syntactic alternations in which the verb can appear, its WordNet synonyms and sample sentences, and the other verbs that occur in the same verb class, or dataset. To each polysemous verb, we appended a hyphen and its WordNet sense number: for instance, sense 2 of *bake* became *bake-2*. Although WordNet separates the causative/inchoative verbs into two senses, we used only the causative sense number in displaying EVCA-I sentences, as can be seen in figure 6.7 of appendix C.

WordNet 1.5 contains 14,726 verb forms, corresponding to 25,761 verbs across all synsets; so the ratio of verbs to verb forms is 1.75. EVCA-I contains 2,600 verb forms with 3,034 senses, giving a ratio of 1.17. Of these verb senses, 156 (e.g., *bail* as in 'bailing water out of a boat') do not appear in WordNet. (For a graphical display of this information, see figures 6.9 and 6.10 in appendix D.)

Sometimes more than one word sense of a verb exhibits a given alternation. Instead of creating sentences for all the possible senses that could fit into the alternation, we chose only the most familiar or most general one. Other possible senses were taken to have similar or figurative meanings. See figure 6.8 in appendix C for an example, which is taken from WordNet 1.3. In this example, senses other than sense 2 of the verb *burn* fit the alternation illustrated in (10). Sense 3 is derived from sense 2, as is sense 6 from sense 5 and sense 9 from sense 8. Example sentences created for EVCA WordNet in sense 2 are shown in (11). Example sentences for this alternation could also be made from the senses numbered 5, 7, 8, and 10, as shown in (12)–(15).

(10) burn: `[np,v,np];[v,np]`

(11) *Sense 2*

   a. Mary burns the leaves.

   b. The leaves burn.

(12) *Sense 5*

   a. The pepper is burning my eye.

   b. My eye is burning.

(13) *Sense 7*

   a. Mary is burning the building.

   b. The building is burning.

(14) *Sense 8*

   a. Mary is burning the log.

   b. The log is burning.

(15) *Sense 10*

   a. The acid is burning my skin.

   b. My skin is burning.

6.4 FUTURE WORK ON EVCA WORDNET

If more verbs are to be added to an existing verb class in EVCA Word-Net, then the necessary properties for the noun phrases selected by these verbs will need to be determined. If the class already contains a verb V_1 whose complements have the same properties as the complements of the new verb V_2, then V_2 will have to be added as a child of V_1. If no such verb V_1 exists, then it will be necessary to find a representative noun phrase having the appropriate property list.

In generating the example sentences, we added only the tense/aspect markers $+s$, $+ed$, $+en$, $+ing$ to the verb stems. We are considering writing a morphological analyzer that will generate strong verb forms like *gave*. Thus, correct verb forms will be generated after the sentences are produced.

Appendix A: WordNet Verb Frames

```
1   Something ----s
2   Somebody ----s
3   It is ----ing
4   Something is ----ing PP
5   Something ----s something Adjective/Noun
```

```
 6 Something ----s Adjective/Noun
 7 Somebody ----s Adjective
 8 Somebody ----s something
 9 Somebody ----s somebody
10 Something ----s somebody
11 Something ----s something
12 Something ----s to somebody
13 Somebody ----s on something
14 Somebody ----s somebody something
15 Somebody ----s something to somebody
16 Somebody ----s something from somebody
17 Somebody ----s somebody with something
18 Somebody ----s somebody of something
19 Somebody ----s something on somebody
20 Somebody ----s somebody PP
21 Somebody ----s something PP
22 Somebody ----s PP
23 Somebody's (body part) ----s
24 Somebody ----s somebody to INFINITIVE
25 Somebody ----s somebody INFINITIVE
26 Somebody ----s that CLAUSE
27 Somebody ----s to somebody
28 Somebody ----s to INFINITIVE
29 Somebody ----s whether INFINITIVE
30 Somebody ----s somebody into V-ing something
31 Somebody ----s something with something
32 Somebody ----s INFINITIVE
33 Somebody ----s VERB-ing
34 It ----s that CLAUSE
```

Appendix B: EVCA Verb Classes (Datasets) in Prolog

In this Prolog representation, *12:a* and *12:b* refer to examples (12a) and (12b) in *EVCA*. The letter *s* means 'sentence'; *0* means that this pattern is ungrammatical for this particular verb class; and *1* means that it is grammatical. The example sentences and their parses follow this notation.

```
evca_dataset(2,
    [coil-3, revolve-2, rotate-1, spin-1, turn-2, twirl-1,
    twist-5, whirl-1, wind-3],
    [pattern(7:ii, 'Motion around an Axis',
        [
        eg(12:a,s,1,
            'Janet turned the cup.',
            [np,v,np]),
```

```
        eg(12:b,s,1,
           'The cup turned.',
           [v,np])]),
     pattern(105:ii,'Verbs of Motion around an Axis',
        [
        eg(106:a,s,1,
           'The spaceship revolves around the earth.',
           [v,np,[p(around,1),np]]),
        eg(106:b,s,0,
           'The spaceship revolves the earth.',
           [v,np,[p(around_0,1),np]])])]).

evca_dataset(101,
     [brush-3, cram-1, crowd-1, cultivate-2, dab-1, daub-1,
     drape-2, drizzle-2, dust-1, hang-4, heap-1, inject-6,
     jam-3, load-2, mound, pack-4, pile-2, plant-3,
     plaster-3, pump-2, rub-3, scatter-3, seed, settle-3,
     sew-2, shower-2, slather, smear-3, smudge-1, sow,
     spatter-3, splash-1, splatter-1, spray-1, spread-3,
     sprinkle-2, spritz, squirt-1, stack-2, stick-1,
     stock-1, strew-1, string-7, stuff-1, swab-2, wrap-1],
     [pattern(124,'Spray/Load Verbs',
        [
        eg(125:a,s,1,
           'Jack sprayed paint on the wall.',
           [np,v,[p(with_0,4),np],[p(on,5),np]]),
        eg(125:b,s,1,
           'Jack sprayed the wall with paint.',
           [np,v,[p(on_0,1),np],[p(with,7),np]])])]]).

evca_dataset(126,
     [alter-4, change-4, convert-3, metamorphose-1,
     transform-1, transmute-1, turn-10],
     [pattern(156,'Turn Verbs',
        [
        eg(157:a,s,0,
           'He turned from a prince.',
           [v,np,[p(from,6),np]]),
        eg(157:b,s,1,
           'He turned into a frog.',
           [v,np,[p(into,2),np]])]),
     pattern(158,'Turn Verbs',
        [
        eg(159:a,s,1,
           'The witch turned him into a frog.',
           [np,v,np,[p(into,2),np]]),
```

```
       eg(159:b,s,1,
          'The witch turned him from a prince into a
          frog.',
          [np,v,np,[p(from,6),np],[p(into,2),np]])]),
     pattern(150:b,'Turn Verbs',
          [
          eg(151:a,s,1,
             'I kneaded the dough into a loaf.',
             [np,v,np,[p(into,2),np]]),
          eg(151:b,s,0,
             'I kneaded a loaf from the dough.',
             [np,v,[p(into_0,2),np],[p(from,1),np]]),
          eg(152:a,s,1,
             'The witch turned him into a frog.',
             [np,v,np,[p(into,2),np]]),
          eg(152:b,s,0,
             'The witch turned him from a prince.',
             [np,v,np,[p(from,6),np]])])]).
```

Appendix C: Sample WordNet Computer Sessions

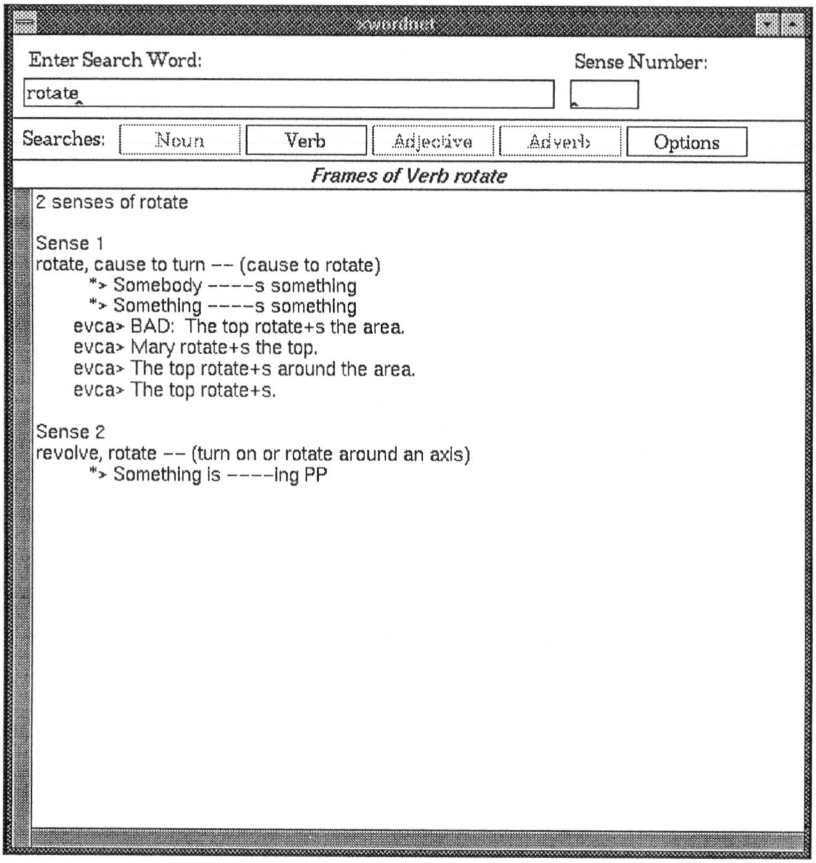

```
┌─────────────────────────────── xwordnet ─────────────────────────┐
│  Enter Search Word:                              Sense Number:     │
│  ┌──────────────────────────────────────────┐   ┌──────────────┐  │
│  │ rotate_                                   │   │              │  │
│  └──────────────────────────────────────────┘   └──────────────┘  │
│  Searches:  ┌ Noun ┐ ┌ Verb ┐ ┌ Adjective ┐ ┌ Adverb ┐ ┌ Options ┐│
│  ─────────────────── Frames of Verb rotate ───────────────────     │
│  2 senses of rotate                                               │
│                                                                   │
│  Sense 1                                                          │
│  rotate, cause to turn -- (cause to rotate)                       │
│        *> Somebody ----s something                                │
│        *> Something ----s something                               │
│     evca> BAD:  The top rotate+s the area.                        │
│     evca> Mary rotate+s the top.                                  │
│     evca> The top rotate+s around the area.                       │
│     evca> The top rotate+s.                                       │
│                                                                   │
│  Sense 2                                                          │
│  revolve, rotate -- (turn on or rotate around an axis)            │
│        *> Something is ----ing PP                                 │
│                                                                   │
└───────────────────────────────────────────────────────────────────┘
```

Figure 6.2
EVCA WordNet session for *rotate*, showing *EVCA* sample sentences and sentences generated by EVCA-I (marked *evca*). The example marked *BAD* is important because verbs like *rotate* do not allow this pattern whereas ones like *circle* do.

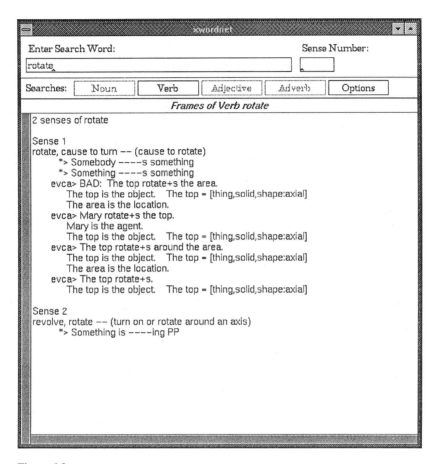

Figure 6.3
EVCA WordNet session for *rotate*, showing *EVCA* sample sentences, sentences
generated by EVCA-I (marked *evca*), the thematic roles of the noun phrases, and
the property lists for the noun *top*.

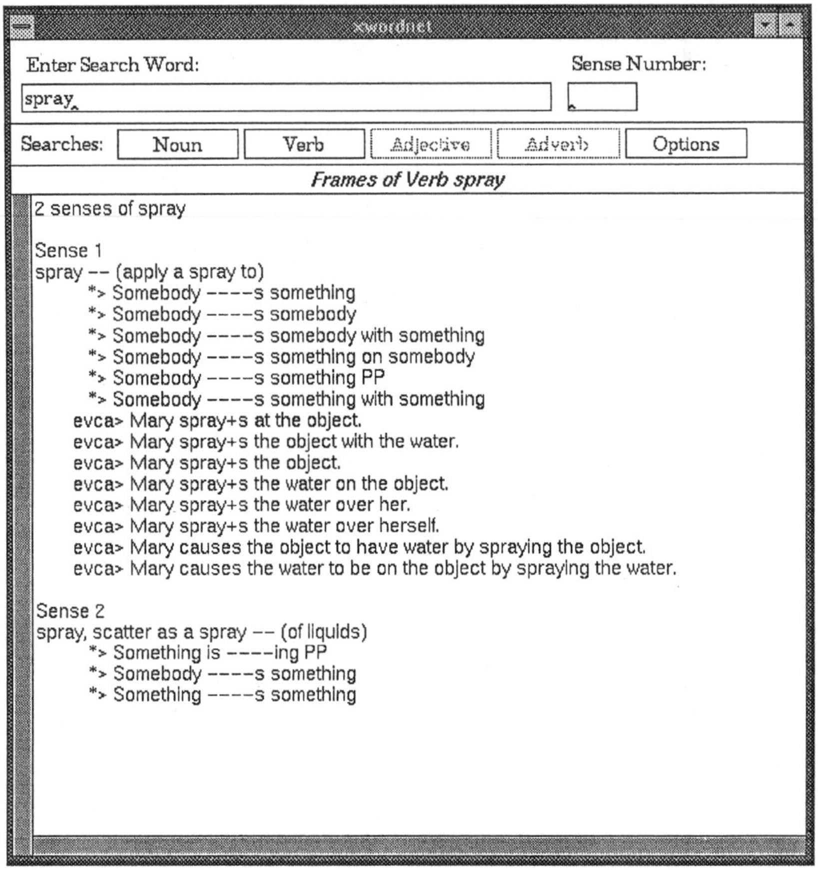

```
┌────────────────────────────────────────────────────────────────────┐
│ ▬                            xwordnet                          ▾ ▪   │
├────────────────────────────────────────────────────────────────────┤
│  Enter Search Word:                          Sense Number:          │
│  ┌──────────────────────────────────────┐    ┌──────────┐           │
│  │ spray                                │    │          │           │
│  └──────────────────────────────────────┘    └──────────┘           │
│  Searches: ┌────────┐┌────────┐┌───────────┐┌────────┐┌──────────┐  │
│            │  Noun  ││  Verb  ││ Adjective ││ Adverb ││ Options  │  │
│            └────────┘└────────┘└───────────┘└────────┘└──────────┘  │
├────────────────────────────────────────────────────────────────────┤
│                        Frames of Verb spray                         │
```

2 senses of spray

Sense 1
spray -- (apply a spray to)
  *> Somebody ----s something
  *> Somebody ----s somebody
  *> Somebody ----s somebody with something
  *> Somebody ----s something on somebody
  *> Somebody ----s something PP
  *> Somebody ----s something with something
evca> Mary spray+s at the object.
evca> Mary spray+s the object with the water.
evca> Mary spray+s the object.
evca> Mary spray+s the water on the object.
evca> Mary spray+s the water over her.
evca> Mary spray+s the water over herself.
evca> Mary causes the object to have water by spraying the object.
evca> Mary causes the water to be on the object by spraying the water.

Sense 2
spray, scatter as a spray -- (of liquids)
  *> Something is ----ing PP
  *> Somebody ----s something
  *> Something ----s something

Figure 6.4
EVCA WordNet session for *spray*, showing *EVCA* sample sentences and sentences generated by EVCA-I. The EVCA-I sentences *Mary causes the object ...* and *Mary causes the water ...* are paraphrases of the EVCA-I sentences *Mary sprays the object with the water* and *Mary sprays the water on the object*.

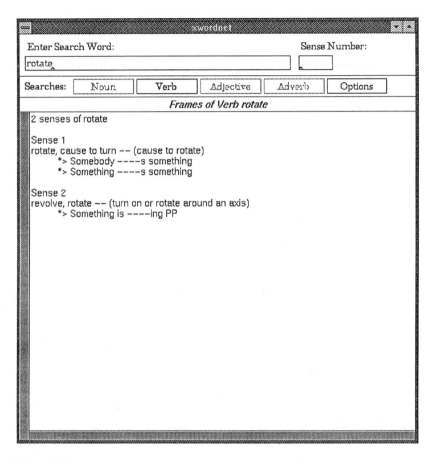

Figure 6.5
This standard session of WordNet 1.3 shows that some verbs can take more than
one kind of object. When EVCA-I sample sentences were created, a human subject was chosen whenever possible.

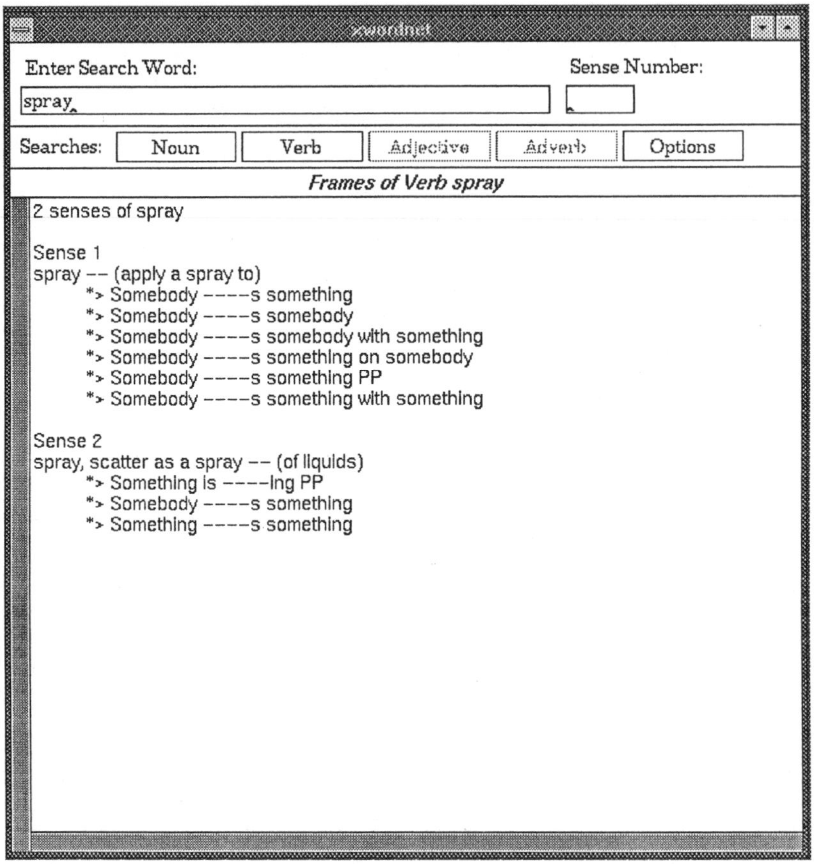

Figure 6.6
This standard session of WordNet 1.3 shows that some verbs can take more than one kind of object or other noun phrase. When EVCA-I sample sentences were created, only the most intuitively common noun phrase was chosen.

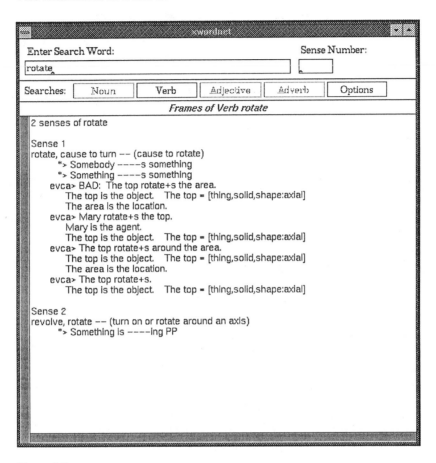

Figure 6.7
The EVCA-I sentences *The top rotates the area, The top rotates around the area,* and *The top rotates,* shown under sense 1, actually belong with sense 2. However, if they had been separated from *Mary rotates the top* under sense 1, the alternation would not have been clear.

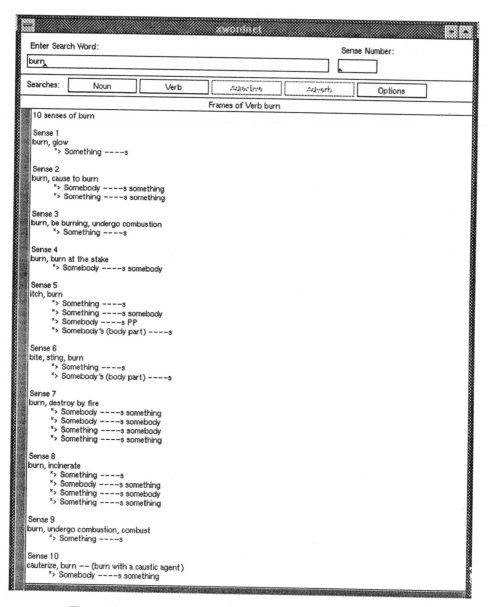

Figure 6.8
Ten senses of the verb *burn* from *EVCA*. When sample sentences were generated for EVCA-I, sense 2 was chosen because it was considered the core sense of the word. However, senses 5, 7, 8, and 10 could also fit the same alternation.

Appendix D: A Survey of the Word Senses in WordNet and *EVCA*

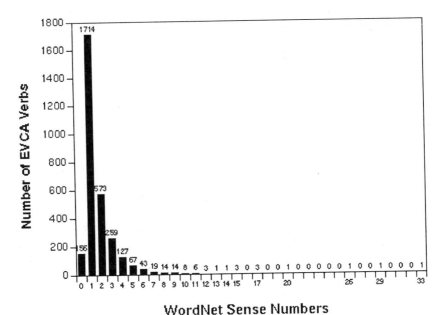

Figure 6.9
Frequency of WordNet sense numbers (0–24) in EVCA-I. Sense 0 means that
either the verb itself or the correct sense of the verb did not appear in WordNet.

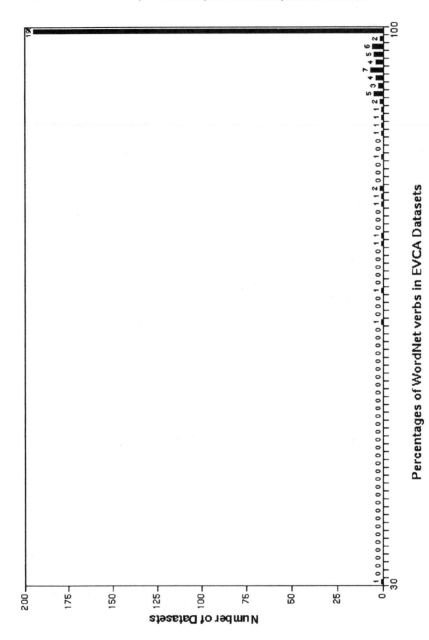

Percentages of WordNet verbs in EVCA Datasets

Figure 6.10

Correspondence between WordNet verbs and *EVCA* verb classes. For example, 196 of the *EVCA* datasets were 100% covered by WordNet verbs, whereas 1 *EVCA* dataset was only 30% covered by WordNet verbs.

Notes

1. This research was greatly aided by the "EVCA summer working group," consisting of the authors, Frank Cho, Zeeshan Khan, Anand Radhakrishnan, Uli Sauerland, and Brian Ulicny. This project examined the relationship between the semantic and syntactic properties of verbs in several languages. Cho and Khan also investigated ways to enhance WordNet by making it multilingual. A description of this work can be found in Jones et al. 1994.

We would especially like to thank Christiane Fellbaum for her invaluable editorial work with this chapter. All residual errors are our own. The work described here was supported by NSF grant 9217041-ASC, by ARPA under the HPCC program, and by a generous grant from the NEC Corporation.

2. Douglas Jones did the initial hand parse, and we modified the parses as the project progressed to suit our needs. See Jones 1995 for a continuation of this work in which schemas were automatically extracted from Levin's example sentences by means of a simple grammar, and see Dorr and Jones 1996 for further applications of this work.

3. In this representation of argument structure, vp means 'verb phrase', and e denotes an empty element. Our current representation of (6a) is [np,v,np], which is parsed as vp(v,np,np), on the basis of which thematic roles are assigned. The verb phrase subject (the first np) becomes the sentence AGENT, and the verb phrase object (the second np) becomes the sentence THEME.

4. In some case we were also able to find the relevant information in WordNet itself. WordNet reflects this by specifying *somebody* and *something* in its verb frames.

References

Burzio, L. (1986). *Italian syntax: A government-binding approach*. Dordrecht: Reidel.

Chomsky, N. (1981). *Lectures on government and binding*. Dordrecht: Foris.

Dorr, B. J., and Jones, D. A. (1996). Role of word sense disambiguation in lexical acquisition: Predicting semantics from syntactic cues. In *Proceedings of the Sixteenth International Conference on Computational Linguistics*, 322–327. Association for Computational Linguistics.

Gruber, J. (1965). *Studies in lexical relations*. Unpublished doctoral dissertation, MIT, Cambridge, MA.

Jones, D. A. (1995). *Predicting semantics from syntactic cues: An evaluation of Levin's* English Verb Classes and Alternations (Tech. Rep. No. UMIACS-TR-95-121). College Park: University of Maryland, Institute for Advanced Computer Studies.

Jones, D. A., et al. (1994). *Verb classes and alternations in Bangla, German, English, and Korean* (Memo No. 1517). Cambridge, MA: MIT, Artificial Intelligence Laboratory. Available: http://www.ai.mit.edu/

Levin, B. (1993). *English verb classes and alternations.* Chicago: University of Chicago Press.

Levin, B. and Rappaport Hovav, M. (1995). *Unaccusativity: At the syntax–lexical semantics interface.* Cambridge, MA: MIT Press.

Miller, G. A. (1993). Keynote speech. U.S./Japan Joint Workshop on Electronic Dictionaries and Language Technologies. University of Pennsylvania, January 23–25.

Perlmutter, D. (1978). Impersonal passives and the Unaccusative Hypothesis. In *Proceedings of the Fourth Annual Meeting of the Berkeley Linguistics Society,* 157–189. Berkeley: University of California, Berkeley Linguistics Society.

Chapter 7

The Formalization of WordNet by Methods of Relational Concept Analysis

Uta E. Priss

7.1 INTRODUCTION

In this chapter a mathematical formalization of WordNet that relies on WordNet's hierarchical and relational structure is described.[1] Conceptual hierarchies are formalized in formal concept analysis (Ganter and Wille 1996), a theory developed at the Technische Hochschule Darmstadt over the last 16 years (section 7.2). This theory can be extended to relational concept analysis by adding further relations (section 7.4). In a linguistic application the conceptual hierarchies can be interpreted as hypernymy orderings, and other semantic relations such as meronymy and antonymy can be taken as additional relations. The theoretical analysis shows dependencies among semantic relations such as inheritance of relations from subconcepts to superconcepts. It does not provide a complete system of axioms for semantic relations, but it can facilitate the investigation of the logical properties of those relations. For example, it does not answer the question of whether meronymy is transitive in general, but it defines sufficient transitivity conditions to identify those properties that intransitive meronymy relations cannot have.

Conceptual structures are modeled as a hierarchical network in the form of a mathematical lattice. This enables a graphical representation that would be difficult to obtain without using mathematical structures. Some of the concepts of the lattice are lexicalized, because they are denominated by words. (In what follows, all lexical units that could appear as dictionary entries are called "word.") Other concepts constitute lexical gaps; they exist in the conceptual structure and can be described by their hypernyms, attributes, and other relations, but they are not denominated by words. Two formal contexts are needed for the study of semantic relations: a *denotative context*, which contains the denotational meanings of word forms (denotata) and their conceptual ordering, and a *lexical context*, which has the words as constitutive elements. The words are always assumed to be disambiguated (for example, by WordNet sense numbers) to avoid problems of polysemy and homonymy. A denotative context is usually incomplete because it is not possible to write a list of all denotata of a language. But, as semantic relations refer to relations among denotata, they cannot be defined on words without studying the denotata in a denotative context. Examples for lexical contexts are lexical fields (Kipke and Wille 1987). Furthermore, every dictionary or thesaurus can be interpreted as a lexical context. Words are names for concepts in a denotative context and formal objects in a lexical context. Therefore, it has to be investigated whether semantic relations have the same properties in both contexts. WordNet is formalized as such a lexical context, but only the noun synsets (synonym sets) are investigated in this chapter (section 7.3). The other parts of speech and more details can be found elsewhere (Priss 1996). The semantic relations meronymy, hyponymy, and synonymy are formally defined in terms of relational concept analysis in sections 7.5 and 7.6, respectively. In section 7.7 three examples of the meronymy relation in WordNet show how this theoretical framework can be used to find irregularities among the semantic relations in WordNet 1.5.

7.2   FORMAL CONCEPT ANALYSIS

Formal concept analysis (Ganter and Wille 1996) starts with the definition of a *formal context* $\mathcal{K}$ as a triple (G, M, I) consisting of two sets G and M and a relation I between G and M (i.e., $I \subseteq G \times M$). The elements of G and M are called *formal objects* (Gegenstände) and *formal attributes* (Merkmale), respectively. The relationship is written as gIm or $(g, m) \in I$ and is read as 'the formal object g has the formal attribute m'. A formal context can be represented by a cross table that has a row for each formal object g, a column for each formal attribute m, and a cross in the row of g and the column of m if gIm. The upper half of figure 7.1 shows an example of a formal context. It has "person," "adult," and so on, as formal objects, and "young," "old," "female," and "male" as formal attributes. It should be noted that this use of *context* must be distinguished from the linguistic use of *context*. In a context (G, M, I) the set of all common formal attributes of a set $A \subseteq G$ of formal objects is denoted by $\iota A := \{m \in M | gIm \text{ for all } g \in A\}$ and, analogously, the set of all common formal objects of a set $B \subseteq M$ of formal attributes is $\varepsilon B :=$

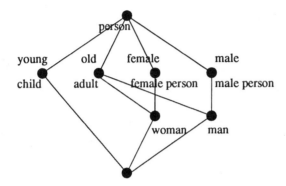

	young	old	female	male
person				
adult		×		
female person			×	
male person				×
child	×			
woman		×	×	
man		×		×

Figure 7.1
A formal context and a line diagram of its concept lattice

$\{g \in G | gIm$ for all $m \in B\}$. For example, in the formal context in figure 7.1, $\iota\{\text{man}\} = \{\text{old, male}\}$ and $\varepsilon\{\text{old}\} = \{\text{adult, woman, man}\}$ hold.

A pair (A, B) is said to be a *formal concept* of the formal context (G, M, I) if $A \subseteq G$, $B \subseteq M$, $A = \varepsilon B$, and $B = \iota A$. In this chapter formal concepts are denoted by c, c_1, c_i, and so on. For a formal concept $c := (A, B)$, A is called the *extent* (denoted by $Ext(c)$) and B is called the *intent* (denoted by $Int(c)$) of the formal concept. In the example of figure 7.1, $(\{\text{adult, woman, man}\}, \{\text{old}\})$ is a formal concept, because $\iota\{\text{adult, woman, man}\} = \{\text{old}\}$ and $\varepsilon\{\text{old}\} = \{\text{adult, woman, man}\}$. The set of all formal concepts of (G, M, I) is denoted by $\mathscr{B}(G, M, I)$. The most important structure on $\mathscr{B}(G, M, I)$ is given by the formal subconcept-superconcept relation that is defined as follows: the formal concept c_1 is a *formal subconcept* of the formal concept c_2 (denoted by $c_1 \leq c_2$) if $Ext(c_1) \subseteq Ext(c_2)$, which is equivalent to $Int(c_2) \subseteq Int(c_1)$; c_2 is then a *formal superconcept* of c_1 (denoted by $c_1 \geq c_2$). For example, $(\{\text{adult, woman, man}\}, \{\text{old}\})$ as a formal superconcept of $(\{\text{woman}\}, \{\text{old, female}\})$ has more formal objects but fewer formal attributes than ({woman}, {old, female}). It follows from this definition that each formal concept is a formal subconcept of itself, in contrast to the natural language use of *subconcept*, which precludes a concept from being a subconcept of itself. The relation $\leq$ is a mathematical order relation called *formal conceptual ordering* on $\mathscr{B}(G, M, I)$ with which the set of all formal concepts forms a mathematical lattice denoted by $\underline{\mathscr{B}}(G, M, I)$.

Graphically, mathematical lattices can be depicted as line diagrams that represent a formal concept by a small circle. For each formal object g, the smallest formal concept to whose extent g belongs is denoted by γg; and for each formal attribute m, the largest formal concept to whose intent m belongs is denoted by μm. The concepts γg and μm are called *object concept* and *attribute concept*, respectively. In the line diagram it is not necessary to write the full extent and intent for each concept; instead, the name (verbal form) of each formal object g is written slightly below the circle of γg and the name of each formal attribute m is written slightly above the circle of μm. The lower half of figure 7.1 shows the line diagram of the concept lattice of the formal context in the upper half of the figure. In a line diagram the extent of a formal concept consists of all formal objects that are retrieved by starting with the formal concept and then collecting all formal objects that are written at formal subconcepts of that formal concepts. Analogously, the intent is retrieved by collecting all formal attributes that are written at formal superconcepts of the formal concept. More details on formal concept analysis can be found in Ganter and Wille 1996.

7.3   WORDNET AS A FORMAL CONTEXT

As mentioned in section 7.1, it is necessary for the formalization of WordNet to define two contexts. In a *denotative context* $\mathscr{K}_D := (D, A_D, I_D)$, denotata $d \in D$ are the formal objects. The set A_D of formal attributes consists of attributes of the denotata. The concepts can additionally be denominated by disambiguated words $w \in W$ via the function $dnt : W \to \mathscr{B}(\mathscr{K}_D)$. Because the words are disambiguated, dnt is really a function. A relational structure consisting of a denotative context $\mathscr{K}_D$, a set W of words, the function dnt, and further optional relations on the denotata, attributes, or concepts is called *denotative structure* and is denoted by $\mathscr{S}_D$. A *lexical context* $\mathscr{K}_L := (W, A_L, I_L)$ consists of a set W of disambiguated words as formal objects, a set A_L of attributes, and a relation I_L. The attributes in A_L can be attributes of the denotata of the words, connotative attributes, or formal attributes, such as "has four letters." In many applications the attributes of a word in $\mathscr{K}_L$ are the attributes of its denotata in an underlying $\mathscr{K}_D$; this means that I_L is defined by $w I_L m :\Leftrightarrow (dnt(w) \leq \mu m \text{ in } \underline{\mathscr{B}}(\mathscr{K}_D))$ and therefore $A_L = A_D$. In other applications, especially in componential analysis, which uses a combination of denotational and connotational attributes, the lexical context would not have A_D as the set of attributes. An equivalent representation of $\underline{\mathscr{B}}(\mathscr{K}_D)$ is $\underline{\mathscr{B}}(\mathscr{K}_D^*)$ with $\mathscr{K}_D^* := (D \cup W, A_D, I_D^*)$, where the words are interpreted as a second set of objects joined with the set of denotata. The relation I_D^* is then defined as $I_D \cup I_L$. As $\mathscr{K}_L$ (with set A_D of attributes) is obviously contained in $\mathscr{K}_D^*$, $\underline{\mathscr{B}}(\mathscr{K}_L)$ is isomorphic to a join-preserving sublattice of $\underline{\mathscr{B}}(\mathscr{K}_D^*)$ ($\cong \underline{\mathscr{B}}(\mathscr{K}_D)$).

WordNet is a lexical context $\mathscr{K}_{WN} := (W, S, I_{WN})$ with disambiguated words $w \in W$ as objects. As there is no set A_D of attributes given in Word-Net that discriminates the words explicitly, the following construction is needed. An equivalence relation, synonymy (SYN), is defined on the set W of disambiguated words via $w_1 \text{ SYN } w_2 :\Leftrightarrow syn(w_1) = syn(w_2)$, where the synset of a word w is denoted by $syn(w)$. Then an order relation, hyponymy (HYP), is defined on the set S of synsets and the concept lattice is computed as the Dedekind closure of this ordered set. Therefore, formally each synset is interpreted as an attribute; for example, the synset $\{dog\}$ is interpreted as the attribute TO-BE-A-DOG. The relation I_{WN} is defined by $w I_{WN} syn(w_1) :\Leftrightarrow syn(w) \text{ HYP } syn(w_1)$. It follows that the extent of a concept consists of all words that belong to the synsets of that concept or lower concepts. The intent of a concept consists of the synsets of that concept or higher concepts. Each concept can be an object concept for at most one synset. An open question concerning WordNet is whether the set S of formal attributes could be replaced by a set A_D of attributes of the denotata or whether that would change the hypernymy ordering of the synsets. Prototypical attributes cannot be used as A_D, because they are not inherited by all subconcepts; for example, not all birds fly. Obviously, the underlying context $\mathscr{K}_D$ is not considered at all for the construction of $\mathscr{K}_{WN}$. But it can be shown (Priss 1996) that, assuming some axioms hold, $\mathscr{K}_{WN}$ reveals information about a possibly corresponding $\mathscr{K}_D$.

7.4 RELATIONAL CONCEPT ANALYSIS

Relational concept analysis is the extension of formal concept analysis—which provides a conceptual hierarchy—to a more general theory that includes other relations among objects or attributes. It is also an extension of Woods's (1991) quantificational tags and inheritances. In what follows, only binary relations $r \subseteq G \times G$ are considered. These relations are transferred to relations among concepts (i.e., $R \subseteq \mathscr{B}(G, M, I) \times \mathscr{B}(G, M, I)$), according to the following definitions. The quantifiers that are used in the definitions can be natural language quantifiers or mathematical expressions, such as $\|\text{all}\|$, $\|\text{at least } 1\| =: \|\geq 1\|$, or $\|\text{exactly } 1\| =: \|1\|$ (for more details on natural language quantifiers, see Westerstahl 1989).

DEFINITION 7.1   For a context (G, M, I), concepts $c_1, c_2 \in \mathscr{B}(G, M, I)$, a relation $r \subseteq G \times G$, and quantifiers Q^i, $1 \leq i \leq 4$, we define

$$c_1 R^r[Q^1, Q^2;]c_2 :\Leftrightarrow Q^1_{g_1 \in Ext(c_1)} Q^2_{g_2 \in Ext(c_2)} : g_1 r g_2 \tag{1}$$

$$c_1 R^r[; Q^3, Q^4]c_2 :\Leftrightarrow Q^3_{g_2 \in Ext(c_2)} Q^4_{g_1 \in Ext(c_1)} : g_1 r g_2 \tag{2}$$

$$c_1 R^r[Q^1, Q^2; Q^3, Q^4]c_2 :\Leftrightarrow c_1 R^r[Q^1, Q^2;]c_2 \text{ and } c_1 R^r[; Q^3, Q^4]c_2 \tag{3}$$

r is called the *relational component*, and $[Q^1, Q^2;]$, $[; Q^3, Q^4]$, or $[Q^1, Q^2; Q^3, Q^4]$ is called the *quantificational tag* of a relation. If no ambiguities are possible, relational component and quantificational tag can be omitted in the notation of the relation.

Depending on the quantifiers, each relation r therefore leads to several different relations R^r among concepts. The terms *quantificational tag* and *relational component* are taken from Woods's terminology. The formalization can best be understood through an example: *All door-handles are parts of doors* states a meronymy relation between door-handles and doors. More precisely, it means that all objects that belong to the extent of the concept "door-handle" have an object in the extent of the concept "door" so that the meronymy relation holds between them. The variables in equivalence (1) are for this example $Q^1 := \|\text{all}\|$, $Q^2 := \|\geq 1\|$; c_1 is the concept "door-handle"; c_2 is the concept "door"; and r is the relation IS-PART-OF. Equivalence (2) could be *There is at least one door which has a handle*, because *All doors have to have handles* is not true. Equivalence (3) is the combination of the first two. For the door-handle example the quantifiers are $Q^1 := \|\text{all}\|$, $Q^2 := \|\geq 1\|$, $Q^3 := \|\geq 1\|$, and $Q^4 := \|\geq 1\|$. Abbreviations are used for the more frequently used types of relations:

DEFINITION 7.2 $R^r[\|\geq 1\|, \|\geq 1\|; \|\geq 1\|, \|\geq 1\|]$ is abbreviated as R^r_0.
$R^r[\|\text{all}\|, Q^2; \|\text{all}\|, Q^4]$ is abbreviated as $R^r_{(Q^4; Q^2)}$. The vertical lines $\|$ can be left out for Q^4 and Q^2 in the subscript of $R^r_{(Q^4; Q^2)}$.

Table 7.1
Examples of quantifiers in equivalence (4)

Q^1	Q^2	Q^5	Q^6
$\|\text{all}\|$	$\|\text{all}\|$	$\|\text{all}\|$	$\|\text{all}\|$
$\|\geq 1\|$	$\|\geq 1\|$	$\|\geq 1\|$	$\|\geq 1\|$
$\|\text{all}\|$	$\|\geq n\|$	$\|\text{all}\|$	$\|\geq 1\|$
$\|\geq n\|$	$\|\text{all}\|$	$\|\geq 1\|$	$\|\text{all}\|$

Besides its applications to the modeling of lexical databases, this formalization can be used to describe functions $R^r_{(\geq 0;1)}$, bijections $R^r_{(1;1)}$, or Cartesian products $R^r_{(\text{all;all})}$. It is useful to characterize a conceptual relation by considering the concepts only and not the objects. This leads to a classification of certain relations R^r into different types.

DEFINITION 7.3   A relation $R \subseteq \mathscr{B}(G, M, I) \times \mathscr{B}(G, M, I)$ for which there exist quantifiers Q^5, Q^6 so that for all $c_1, c_2 \in \mathscr{B}(G, M, I)$

$$c_1 R c_2 \Leftrightarrow Q^5_{c_{11} \leq c_1} Q^6_{c_{21} \leq c_2} : c_{11} R c_{21} \tag{4}$$

holds is called *of type* $[Q^5, Q^6;]$. Relations of type $[; Q^5, Q^6]$ are defined analogously.

It seems to be impossible to find such quantifiers Q^5 and Q^6 for all $R^r[Q^1, Q^2;]$, but it can be proved (Priss 1996) that the quantifiers Q^5 and Q^6 fulfill equivalence (4) for the quantifiers Q^1 and Q^2 in table 7.1 (n is always larger than or equal to 1). Furthermore, if $Q^1, Q^2 \in \{\|> (\text{all} - n)\|,$ $\|\geq n\|, \|\leq (\text{all} - n)\|, \|< n\|\}$ ($n \geq 1$), then Q^5, $Q^6 \in \{\|\text{all}\|, \|\geq 1\|\}$. An interpretation of table 7.1 is that if a specific number occurs on the object level (e.g., all hands have five fingers), it does not occur on the conceptual level. For a concept "hand" there is one concept "finger" so that each object of "hand" has five parts among the objects of "finger"; and not: for a concept "hand" there exist five concepts "finger" with that property. A linguistic example where this is even reflected in the language is that *having two shoes* can also be expressed as *having a pair of shoes*. From equivalence (4) follows equivalence (5):

$$\gamma g_1 R^r[Q^1, Q^2;] \gamma g_2 \Leftrightarrow Q^5_{g_{11} \in Ext(\gamma g_1)} Q^6_{g_{21} \in Ext(\gamma g_2)} : \gamma g_{11} R^r[Q^1, Q^2;] \gamma g_{21} \tag{5}$$

It is therefore enough to consider object concepts in order to determine the type of relation.

Additional properties of the relation r have consequences for the relations R^r. For example, if r is irreflexive and transitive (and thus, by implication, antisymmetric) and all sets of objects are finite, then $R^r_{(\geq 0; \geq 1)}$, $R^r_{(\geq 1; \geq 0)}$, and $R^r_{(\geq 1; \geq 1)}$ are also irreflexive, antisymmetric, and transitive. If r is the equality relation $=$, then $R^=_{(\geq 0; \geq 1)}$ is an order relation, $R^=_{(\geq 1; \geq 0)}$ is the dual order, and $R^=_{(\geq 1; \geq 1)}$ is an equivalence relation, and the following equivalences hold:

$$c_1 R^=_{(\geq 0; \geq 1)} c_2 \Leftrightarrow c_1 \leq c_2 \tag{6}$$

$$c_1 R^=_{(\geq 1; \geq 0)} c_2 \Leftrightarrow c_1 \geq c_2 \tag{7}$$

$$c_1 R^=_0 c_2 \Leftrightarrow Ext(c_1) \cap Ext(c_2) \neq \emptyset \tag{8}$$

$$c_1 R^=_{(\geq 1; \geq 1)} c_2 \Leftrightarrow c_1 = c_2 \tag{9}$$

Therefore, the conceptual ordering itself results from a relation between objects. For further details and the proofs of the statements above, see Priss 1996.

7.5 MERONYMY

Semantic relations, such as meronymy, synonymy, and hyponymy, are according to WordNet terminology relations that are defined among synsets. They are distinguished from lexical relations, such as antonymy, which are defined among words and not among synsets. In the terminology used here, a relation $s \subseteq W \times W$ among disambiguated words is called a *semantic relation* if

$$dnt(w_1) = dnt(w_2) \Rightarrow \forall_{w \in W}(w_1 s w \Leftrightarrow w_2 s w) \text{ and } (w s w_1 \Leftrightarrow w s w_2) \tag{10}$$

is fulfilled. Relations $s \subseteq W \times W$ that do not fulfill condition (10) are called *lexical relations*. In this section meronymy is formally defined as a semantic relation according to this terminology. In the next section hyponymy and synonymy are defined. Although antonymy is a lexical relation, *indirect antonymy* is a semantic relation that holds among "antonymous" concepts.

Although meronymy is a hierarchical relation, it should not be modeled as a mathematical lattice. One obvious reason for not modeling meronymy as a concept lattice using denotata as formal objects and attributes and meronymy as the relation between them is that, for example, the formal attributes "ketchup" and "pizza" share the formal objects "sugar" and "salt" as parts. Therefore, a formal concept "salt, sugar" would evolve, but "salt, sugar" is usually only a mixture and not a denotative word concept itself in the English language. Such a concept lattice would therefore provide an embedding of meronymy, but not all concepts would have useful interpretations. A better solution is therefore to use part-whole relations as attributes, such as HAS-HANDLE-AS-PART, which would, for example, differentiate a cup from a glass. A third option is to interpret meronymy as an additional relation besides the conceptual ordering. This is done in the following definition:

DEFINITION 7.4 In a denotative structure $\mathscr{S}_D$ the semantic relation meronymy is defined as follows: Two disambiguated words are in *meronymy relation* if their denotative word concepts are in relation $R^m_{(Q^4;Q^2)}$ where m is a meronymy relation among denotata, that is,

$$w_1 \ \mathit{MER}^m_{(Q^4;Q^2)} w_2 :\Leftrightarrow dnt(w_1) R^m_{(Q^4;Q^2)} dnt(w_2) \tag{11}$$

and the meronymy relation m is irreflexive, antisymmetric, and acyclic.

In contrast to indirect antonymy, whose types are distinguished by the relational components, many types of meronymy differ in their quantificational tags, which can therefore be used for a rough classification of meronymy. For example, the four kinds of meronymy relations described by Cruse (1986) consist of combinations of the basic quantifiers $\|\geq 1\|$, $\|\geq 0\|$, and $\|\text{all}\|$:

1. MER^m_0: facultative-facultative;[2] for example, a child can be a member of a tennis club, but not all children are members of tennis clubs, nor do all tennis clubs have children as members.
2. $\mathit{MER}^m_{(\geq 0;\geq 1)}$: canonical-facultative; for example, all door-handles are parts of doors, but not all doors have to have handles.
3. $\mathit{MER}^m_{(\geq 1;\geq 0)}$: facultative-canonical; for example, all ice cubes consist of water, but not all water is frozen.
4. $\mathit{MER}^m_{(\geq 1;\geq 1)}$: canonical-canonical; for example, each bird feather is part of a bird, and each bird has feathers.

The question of transitivity of meronymy, which has been widely discussed (Winston, Chaffin, and Hermann 1987), is not answered here in general. But it can be shown (Priss 1996) that if m is defined (according to definition 7.4) to be irreflexive, antisymmetric, and acyclic, then it follows that $\mathit{MER}^m_{(\geq 0;\geq 1)}$, $\mathit{MER}^m_{(\geq 1;\geq 0)}$, and $\mathit{MER}^m_{(\geq 1;\geq 1)}$ are also irreflexive, antisymmetric, and acyclic. And if m is transitive, then $\mathit{MER}^m_{(\geq 0;\geq 1)}$, $\mathit{MER}^m_{(\geq 1;\geq 0)}$, and $\mathit{MER}^m_{(\geq 1;\geq 1)}$ are also transitive. This means that if the relation m is transitive on the denotative level, then meronymy is also transitive on the conceptual level for these kinds of meronymy relations. As the pure spatial inclusion on the object level seems to be always transitive (a particular door-handle is part of a particular door that is part of a particular house), it follows that meronymy is often not a conceptual extension of the spatial inclusion, but that it has other features, such as functional dependencies, which are not transitive. (The concept of "door-handle" does not include "in general having a function for a house.") Relational concept analysis facilitates a more detailed analysis of where features occur (on the denotative or on the conceptual level) and can help to show inconsistencies in a linguistic model (e.g., to assume that m is the spatial inclusion for an intransitive relation $MER^m_{(\geq 0; \geq 1)}$ would be contradictory).

Most classifications of semantic relations are based on qualitatively different attributes of the relations. Relational concept analysis shows, however, that there may even be differences in the quantificational conditions. These can be discovered in a formalization of the four models described by Iris, Litowitz, and Evens (1988):

1. Functional component: m can be described as 'part of and functional dependency between part and whole'; $MER^m_{(\geq 0;1)}$ seems to be the dominant form, because each object is part of exactly one whole. For example, a door-handle belongs to exactly one door. $MER^m_{(\geq 0;n)}$, for $n > 1$, is also possible. For example, for any section, a border belongs to exactly two countries.

2. Segmented whole/mass nouns/IS-SUBSTANCE-OF relation: $MER^m_{(\text{some}; \leq 1)}$ is a typical form, because, for example, each pile of paper consists of several sheets, and each sheet belongs to at most one pile. Using the $\|\text{some}\|$ quantifier leaves open the actual number of pieces needed to form the whole.

3. Membership relation: $MER^m_{(\geq 0; > 1)}$ is possible, because, for example, a human is usually a member of different sets (clubs, family, cultures) at the same time.

4. Individual concepts: $MER^m_{(1;1)}$ holds, because, for example, all objects that are "Princeton (NJ)" are part of the only existing state "New Jersey." (There is no possible confusion with other towns called "Princeton," because of the disambiguation of the words.) This also holds for some abstract nouns: each day has one morning, and each morning is part of one day.

This analysis of the differences in the quantificational conditions is missing in WordNet, which distinguishes only among PART-OF, SUBSTANCE-OF, and MEMBER-OF meronymy relations.

7.6 HYPONYMY AND SYNONYMY

If a relation r is the equality relation, then equivalences (6)–(9) show that the corresponding conceptual relations $R^=$ coincide with the conceptual ordering of the lattice. In the linguistic application these relations are given special names.

DEFINITION 7.5   In a denotative structure $\mathscr{S}_D$ the following semantic relations are defined:

A disambiguated word is a *hyponym* of another word if the concept it denotes is a subconcept of the concept the other word denotes; that is,

$$w_1 \; HYP \; w_2 :\Leftrightarrow dnt(w_1) \leq dnt(w_2)(\Leftrightarrow dnt(w_1)R^=_{(\geq 0;\geq 1)}dnt(w_2)) \tag{12}$$

The inverse relation of hyponymy is called *hypernymy*.

Two disambiguated words are *not disjoint* if they have a common object in their extents; that is,

$$w_1 \neg DISJ \; w_2 :\Leftrightarrow dnt(w_1)R^=_0 dnt(w_2) \tag{13}$$

Two disambiguated words are called *synonyms* if they denote the same concept; that is,

$$w_1 \; SYN \; w_2 :\Leftrightarrow dnt(w_1) = dnt(w_2)(\Leftrightarrow dnt(w_1)R^=_{(\geq 1;\geq 1)}dnt(w_2)) \tag{14}$$

These definitions are consistent with the formalization of WordNet in section 7.3. If an underlying denotative context for WordNet is assumed, then a word is a hyponym of another word if its denotata are a subset of the denotata of the other word. Synonymy is defined between two words if their concepts have the same extent (and therefore also the same intent) in $\mathscr{K}_D$. It should be noted that these definitions of synonymy and hypernymy depend on the context $\mathscr{K}_D$. It is possible to apply these definitions to any other kind of context, but then, if the underlying context is not a $\mathscr{K}_D$, these definitions can have a completely different meaning.

Concerning the combination of hyponymy and meronymy, it follows from equivalence (4) that some quantifiers cause inheritance of relations: $MER^m_{(\geq 0;\geq 1)}$ is inherited by hypernyms of the whole and hyponyms of the part; $MER^m_{(\geq 1;\geq 0)}$ is inherited by hyponyms of the whole and hypernyms of the part; MER_0^m is inherited by hypernyms of part and whole. (This contradicts the statement about transitivity in Winston, Chaffin, and Hermann 1987, 435.) It is possible to have both a meronymy and a hyponymy relation between two concepts. For example, "ice" is a kind of "water" and consists of "water," and "musical strings" are "musical supplies" and part of "musical supplies" at the same time. However, usually it is possible to add additional concepts with single relations. In the examples, "water molecules" and "musical instruments" can be added because "ice" consists of "water molecules" and is a kind of "water" and "musical strings" are part of "musical instruments," which are a kind of "musical supplies."

7.7   IDENTIFYING IRREGULARITIES IN WORDNET

Properties of semantic relations can be used to identify irregularities in the relations of a lexical database or thesaurus. Rules can be implemented as a computer program and then be automatically tested. Fischer (1991) has written Smalltalk software to check some mathematical properties of semantic relations, such as inverse relations, circularity, and implicit relations. It would be possible to implement the rules that are implied by relational concept analysis in a similar way, but this has not been undertaken so far. Some irregularities can be corrected automatically. For example, if Fischer's software detects a relation that should be symmetric, but is implemented as a unidirectional pointer, the other direction can simply be added. In many cases, however, it is not possible to correct the irregularities automatically. Irregularities can be detected, but then lexicographers are needed to decide which concepts or relations have to be added or changed to solve the problems. Three examples of the meronymy relation in WordNet are chosen to demonstrate the possibilities of relational concept analysis. WordNet distinguishes only PART-OF, SUBSTANCE-OF, and MEMBER-OF meronymy, but not the quantificational tags, such as MER_0^m and $MER_{(\geq 1; \geq 1)}^m$. But because comparatively few meronymy relations are implemented in WordNet, a first approach assumes all of them to be of the strongest kind, $MER_{(\geq 1; \geq 1)}^m$. If irregularities are found, they can be changed to weaker kinds such as $MER_{(\geq 1; \geq 0)}^m$ or be otherwise repaired.

Figures 7.2, 7.4, and 7.6 show parts of the WordNet 1.5 lattice; figures 7.3, 7.5, and 7.7 demonstrate how they could be improved. The examples

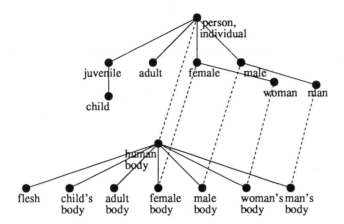

Figure 7.2
An example of the PART-OF meronymy in WordNet 1.5

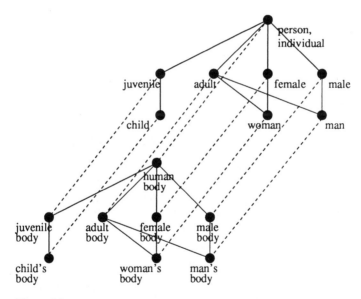

Figure 7.3
A modified version of the example in figure 7.2

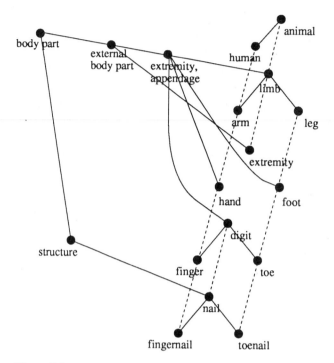

Figure 7.4
Another example of the PART-OF meronymy in WordNet 1.5

from WordNet are not complete, because some relations are omitted and only one or two representative words are selected for each synset. The dashed lines represent meronymy, the others hyponymy. In the first example in figure 7.2 "human body $MER^m_{(\geq 1; \geq 1)}$ person" holds; therefore, a child's body and an adult body must also be part of a person. "Flesh," which does not follow that pattern, seems to be misplaced as a subconcept to "human body." If, furthermore, "female body $MER^m_{(\geq 1; \geq 1)}$ female" holds, then, likewise, a woman has to have a female body; therefore, "woman's body" should be a subconcept of "female body." It should be noted, though, that not all of the changes from figure 7.2 to figure 7.3 can be derived from the theoretical properties of the relations only. In most cases additional semantic knowledge is needed that can be provided only by lexicographers.

The reason for the irregularities in figure 7.4 is probably the polysemy of "extremity," because "hand" and "foot" are subconcepts of the wrong

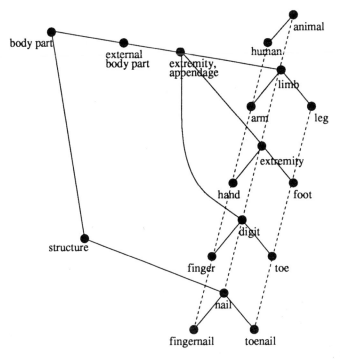

Figure 7.5
A modified version of the example in figure 7.4

"extremity" concept. The "extremity" concept with the meaning 'hand and foot' should be a subconcept of "extremity, appendage." The meronymy relation is irregular in this example, because, if there are no digits other than fingers or toes, and if all fingers or toes are part of some concepts that have a common hypernym "extremity," then digits should be part of extremities. The corrected version in figure 7.5 shows a more regular pattern than figure 7.4.

The last example of the SUBSTANCE-OF meronymy in figure 7.6 probably needs improvement, too, as all those fluids should have a common substance—water molecules (see figure 7.7). Similarly, a distinction should be made between ice crystals and ice. This example does not contain further irregularities, but it shows a certain pattern that can be discovered by comparing the hypernyms at different levels. It seems to be a property of the SUBSTANCE-OF meronymy that shapeless and shaped forms alternate. Drops and crystals are small shapes. On the next level, "tear," "dew,"

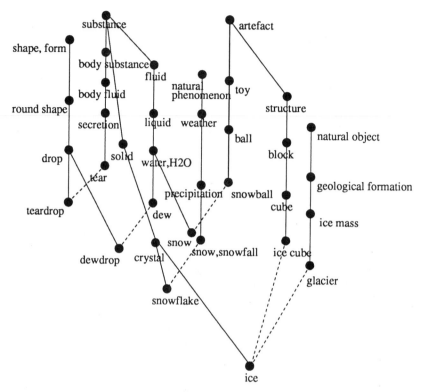

Figure 7.6
An example of the SUBSTANCE-OF meronymy in WordNet 1.5

"snow," and "ice" are shapeless nouns with the hypernym "substance."
On the last level, objects are shaped again, but this time the shape is
formed by humans ("artefact") or nature ("geological formation"). This
last example shows how meronymy and hyponymy may form a regular
pattern in some areas of the vocabulary. A more complete analysis of all
the relations in WordNet will probably reveal more patterns, which can
ultimately be formalized as properties of special relations.

Notes

1. The research for this chapter was partially supported by the Zentrum für
Interdisziplinäre Technikforschung, Technische Hochschule Darmstadt.

2. Cruse uses *facultative* and *canonical* instead of Lyons's (1977) *contingent* and
necessary.

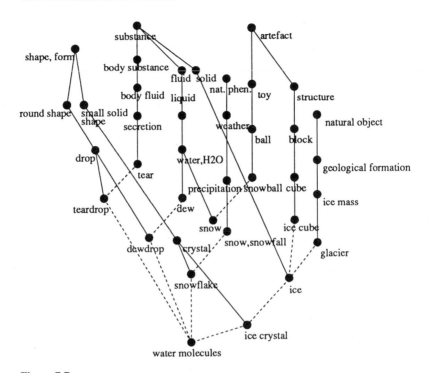

Figure 7.7
A modified version of the example in figure 7.6

References

Cruse, D. A. (1986). *Lexical semantics.* New York: Cambridge University Press.

Fischer, D. H. (1991). Consistency rules and triggers for thesauri. *International Classification, 18,* 212–225.

Ganter, B., and Wille, R. (1996). *Formale Begriffsanalyse: Mathematische Grundlagen.* Berlin: Springer-Verlag.

Iris, M., Litowitz, B., and Evens, M. (1988). Problems of the part-whole relation. In M. Evens (Ed.), *Relational models of the lexicon,* 261–288. Cambridge, England: Cambridge University Press.

Kipke, U., and Wille, R. (1987). Formale Begriffsanalyse erläutert an einem Wortfeld. In *LDV-Forum 5,* 31–36. Fachhochschule Darmstadt, Germany.

Lyons, J. (1977). *Semantics.* 2 vols. Cambridge, England: Cambridge University Press.

Priss, U. E. (1996). *Relational concept analysis: Semantic structures in dictionaries and lexical databases.* Unpublished doctoral dissertation, Technische Hochschule Darmstadt, Germany.

Westerstahl, D. (1989). Quantifiers in formal and natural languages. In D. Gabbay and F. Guenther (Eds.), *Handbook of philosophical logic*, vol. 4, 1–131. Dordrecht: Kluwer.

Winston, M. E., Chaffin, R., and Hermann, D. (1987). A taxonomy of part-whole relations. *Cognitive Science, 11*, 417–444.

Woods, W. A. (1991). Understanding subsumption and taxonomy: A framework for progress. In J. Sowa (Ed.), *Principles of semantic networks: Explorations in the representation of knowledge*, 45–94. San Mateo, CA: Morgan Kaufmann.

PART III

APPLICATIONS OF WORDNET

Chapter 8

Building Semantic Concordances

Shari Landes, Claudia Leacock, and Randee I. Tengi

8.1 INTRODUCTION

Miller et al. (1993, 303) define a *semantic concordance* as "a textual corpus and a lexicon so combined that every substantive word in the text is linked to its appropriate sense in the lexicon." We have built semantic concordances from two textual corpora: 103 passages from the Standard Corpus of Present-Day Edited American English (the Brown Corpus) and the complete text of Stephen Crane's novella *The Red Badge of Courage*. The lexicon used in the semantic concordances is WordNet (version 1.5). The Brown Corpus contains 1 million words of written American English assembled by W. Nelson Francis and Henry Kučera in the early 1960s (Kučera and Francis 1967). It consists of 500 passages excerpted from edited, contemporary American English documents, each about 2,000 words long. It was designed to be balanced across literary styles and genres—ranging from popular print media to scientific reports to literary criticism. The second textural corpus is Stephen Crane's 1895 novella about the American Civil War, *The Red Badge of Courage* (hereafter *RBC*).[1] It consists of 24 short chapters, totaling 45,600 words of text. About half of the words in these corpora are open-class words that are linked to WordNet senses and the other half are closed-class or function words that are not.[2]

The semantic concordances were manually constructed with the aid of a software tool designed specifically for this purpose. ConText is a semantic tagging program that is used to annotate English prose with WordNet senses. It displays the text, highlighting each target word (the word to be tagged) in turn. Below the text, the set of WordNet senses for the highlighted word is displayed. A person tagging the text, hereafter called a *tagger*, reads the text and selects an appropriate WordNet sense (or senses) for the target word. The selected senses are stored with the text representing links between it and the WordNet database. These links are called *semantic tags*.

When a word has only one sense (i.e., when it is monosemous), a tagger's job is fairly straightforward—to make sure that the sense is appropriate and, if it is, to use ConText to assign the semantic tag. However, although only 18% of the word forms in WordNet are polysemous, about 83% of the open-class words in the Brown semantic concordance are polysemous. This is due to the simple fact that frequently used words tend to have many different senses. Therefore, a tagger's primary job is to choose the correct sense or senses of a polysemous word from among its set of WordNet senses.

In addition to creating semantic concordances, the tagging process was used as a vehicle for improving WordNet coverage. As the texts are tagged, missing words, missing senses, and senses that are indistinguishable from one another are discovered, and the lexicographers adjust WordNet accordingly.

This chapter describes the two semantic concordances: their components, how they were built, some of the problems encountered along the way, and some ways to view them. In the following sections we describe how corpora are prepared for semantic tagging, the format of the semantic concordance files, and the procedure for building a semantic concordance. Next we attempt to give the reader a feel for what the ConText interface looks like and how it is used. We describe the procedures for training the taggers who assign senses to the text and for checking the results of their work, and we discuss potential sources of error. Finally, we describe some tools that have been developed for viewing semantic concordance files, and an educational application, Reader, for viewing a semantically tagged text and obtaining contextually appropriate definitions.

8.2　PREPROCESSING

The text that is to be semantically tagged can come from a variety of sources and in many different formats. In some cases the text may have to be reorganized into files of a reasonable size. For example, *RBC* had to be divided into separate files, one for each chapter. Each corpus must be converted from the format it is distributed in to one that is accepted by ConText. This conversion is called *preprocessing* (see figure 8.1).

The first step in preprocessing is to mark up the text in a standard SGML text file format in which sentences and paragraphs are delineated

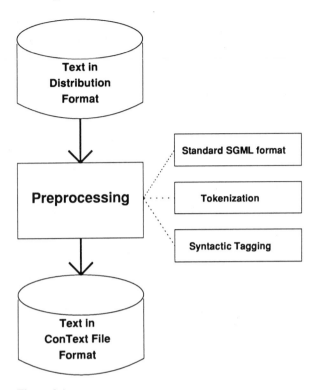

Figure 8.1
Preparing text for semantic tagging

and sentences are numbered. A small example from a Brown Corpus file is shown in appendix A. Files in this format are passed through a filter program that inserts spaces around punctuation marks in preparation for the next preprocessing step, *tokenization*. Tokenization is an attempt to automatically identify those collocations found in WordNet that are also in the text. This is of particular advantage for the task of sense identification, since collocations tend to be monosemous. The *tokenizer* joins independent words to form a collocation by replacing intervening spaces with underscore characters, then appending a syntactic tag. Adjacent proper nouns (e.g., *Mr. John Smith*) are also joined and assigned a syntactic tag (e.g., *Mr_John_Smith/NNP*).

Next, a part-of-speech tagger (Brill 1994) is used to automatically assign syntactic tags to the remainder of the text. It has been trained on the Brown Corpus, and it was modified by Brill to use the tokenized and syntactically tagged collocations to help drive it. The output is a syntactically tagged file. Although the accuracy of the syntactic tags is not perfect, their presence speeds up sense assignment by enabling ConText to display the set of WordNet senses for a word with the assigned part of speech. The final preprocessing step is to convert the files into the ConText file format. During this step, syntactic tags are examined. Open-class words (i.e., those to be semantically tagged) are identified in the resulting file; closed-class words are marked as words to be skipped during semantic tagging.

8.3   CONTEXT FILES

The ConText file format follows SGML guidelines, using elements and attribute-value pairs to record information about the file, paragraph, and sentence boundaries, and syntactic and semantic information. SGML elements give a file its structure; attribute-value pairs provide additional information (van Herwijnen 1990). A ConText file is composed of one or more *context* elements (represented as `<context>`), which in turn are composed of *sentence* elements (`<s>`) embedded in optional *paragraph* elements (`<p>`). Sentences contain only *word form* (`<wf>`) and *punctuation* (`<p>`) elements. The format of untagged and tagged files is the same—additional attributes are used to represent a semantic tag. Examples of both can be found in appendix B. This structure is convenient in that ConText can deal with untagged, partially tagged, and fully tagged files.

A word form element contains attribute-value pairs indicating the state of semantic tagging with respect to the word form, the syntactic category, and semantic tag information. When a sense is assigned, several attribute-value pairs representing the semantic tag are added to a word form element (see appendix B for a list of attribute-value pairs). The `lemma` attribute indicates the base form of the word (its value is the form of the word as stored in the WordNet database); the `lexsn` attribute is an encoding of the location of the sense in the database; the `wnsn` attribute specifies the WordNet sense number. When more than one sense is assigned to a word form, the values for these attributes are concatenated and separated by semicolons.

The values of the `lemma` and `lexsn` attributes together represent a semantic tag pointing to a sense in the WordNet database. They can be concatenated, using `%` to join them, to form a *sense key* suitable for searching the WordNet database sense index file. The sense index, described by Tengi (this volume), provides a mapping between semantic tags and the WordNet database. The `wnsn` attribute provides another way to map the semantic tag to the database, using either the WordNet interface or the database index files.

8.4   PROCEDURE FOR DEVELOPING A SEMANTIC CONCORDANCE

Using ConText, taggers make several passes through a file to assign WordNet senses to word forms in the text (see figure 8.2). Initially, the tagger moves sequentially through the text, stopping at each open-class word or collocation to assign a semantic tag to it. When more than one sense is applicable for a usage, the tagger assigns all appropriate WordNet senses. Multiple tags are clearly required in the case of punning. They are also required when two senses of a word are closely related and the context is not sufficient to distinguish between them. If a sense is missing from WordNet, ConText allows the tagger to add a note to this file. The results of the initial tagging are verified by a different tagger, who uses ConText to review all of the semantic tags and notes in a file. Then ConText is used to make any necessary corrections.

After a file is tagged and verified, notes regarding missing or duplicate senses are sent to the appropriate lexicographers, who modify WordNet as necessary. The lexicographers do not always comply with the taggers' requests and may decide that a tagger is drawing sense distinctions too finely or that the particular usage is metaphoric and should not be tagged. Ultimately it is the lexicographers who decide what senses are added to WordNet so that a word can be tagged. Once all the changes to WordNet are incorporated into the database, a tagger again uses ConText to assign senses whenever possible to the words that were not tagged earlier. Thus, tagging is an iterative process that continues until taggers and lexicographers agree on which senses should be included in WordNet so that a word can be tagged.

As the WordNet database evolves, *tagged senses* (those pointed to from the semantic concordance files) may be altered or deleted by the lexicographers. An updating system has been developed for keeping semantic concordance files synchronized with the WordNet database. Each time a new database is built, a program is run to locate semantic tags that point to a sense that has been removed from the database. These invalid semantic tags are automatically removed from the semantic concordance files, and a tagger then uses ConText to assign senses from the current WordNet database.

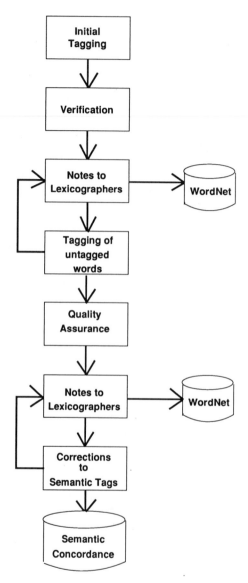

Figure 8.2
The semantic tagging process

To help ensure that similar but distinct usages of a polysemous word are tagged consistently within a Brown Corpus passage, each file is tagged by only one person. Many taggers have worked on the Brown semantic concordance and many authors are represented in the Brown Corpus, so consistency between files is harder to obtain. *RBC* has a single author and is generally accessed as one document. Therefore, consistency of the semantic tags throughout the text is a priority, especially when multiple senses are selected. In an attempt to achieve this consistency, only two people tagged the entire novella. They tagged alternating chapters, and each verified the chapters tagged by the other. In this manner both taggers became familiar with all the chapters and all the sense assignments that were made. Finally, all of the chapters were verified by a third tagger.

8.5   THE CONTEXT INTERFACE

The ConText interface (see figure 8.3) was designed to give taggers all the tools needed for assigning semantic tags to text.[3] It displays about 10 lines of the text, with the currently selected word highlighted. Synonym sets for each sense of the word (in the indicated syntactic category), along with glosses and sample sentences, are displayed below the text. A sense selection window contains numbered boxes that correspond to the WordNet senses. The tagger clicks on the appropriate box(es) to assign a sense or senses to the target word.

When a tagger is unable to select a WordNet sense, a `tagnote` is used to classify the problem. The appropriate sense of the word may be missing, the word may be missing from WordNet, or there may by two or more senses that are indistinguishable. After a file is tagged, these notes are forwarded to the lexicographers for review and subsequent changes to WordNet.

ConText does enable the tagger to manipulate the text to some extent. For example, two or more words can be joined to create new collocations (e.g., *kidney_bean*) that a tagger thinks should be added to WordNet. Similarly, when the tokenizer has identified a collocation in error, it can be split so that the component words can be tagged. Finally, to handle discontinuous constituents, colloquial dialogue, and typographical errors, words can be redefined to the appropriate WordNet search string.

Although WordNet contains *only* open-class words, it does not contain *all* open-class words. Open-class words not usually found in WordNet include nonconventional metaphoric usages, idioms, foreign words, and

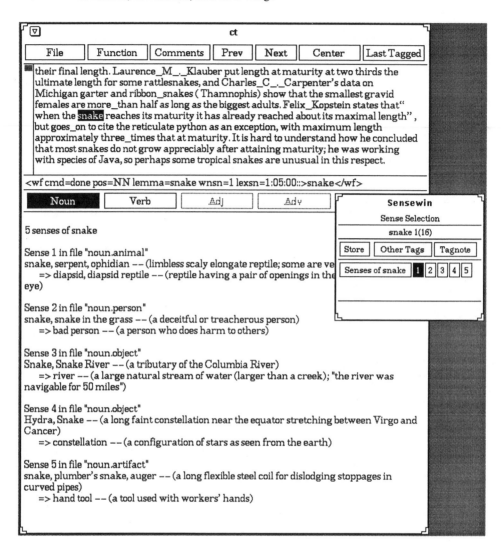

Figure 8.3
ConText window

nonsense words. Although these words are not semantically tagged, Con-Text enables the tagger to assign a label indicating their category.[4] Function words of one type, complex prepositions, are also labeled after their elements are joined (e.g., *in_lieu_of*).

Proper nouns are treated somewhat differently. They are labeled with one of four categories *person*, *location*, *institution*, and *other*. Words labeled with one of the first three categories are also automatically assigned predetermined semantic tags. A proper noun labeled *person* points to the appropriate person sense in WordNet. Similarly, *location* points to 'location', and *institution* to 'group'.

Originally, ConText provided only one *tagging method* for selecting and assigning WordNet senses: a tagger was presented with all senses for the selected word from which to choose one or more appropriate senses. This can be cumbersome when tagging highly polysemous words, since a tagger must scroll through the WordNet Window to compare all the senses, without being able to see, at one time, only those senses that are close to one another in meaning. The number of senses for polysemous words in WordNet 1.5 can be as high as 41, making it difficult for taggers to keep track of the meaning of each as they scroll through the WordNet Window.

In order to help the taggers differentiate senses of highly polysemous words and more easily assign multiple senses when appropriate, two additional tagging methods were implemented: *Elimination* and *SaveAll*. The Elimination method allows a tagger to *remove* senses from the WordNet Window by selecting those sense numbers that are not appropriate in the given context. Senses can be eliminated until only those that are closely related are displayed, enabling the tagger to compare them more easily. When using the SaveAll method, a tagger selects all the senses that are to *remain* in the WordNet Window; the other senses are removed. Both methods allow the tagger to reduce the list of senses being compared until the correct choice or choices can be made.

To semantically tag a file, the tagger works through the text, from beginning to end, assigning senses to open-class words. The tagger reads the text, studies the senses for the selected word, identifies the appropriate sense (or senses), clicks on the corresponding sense number box(es), and stores the selection. The next target word is automatically highlighted, its senses are displayed, and the process is repeated until the entire file is tagged.

8.6 TRAINING

Taggers receive extensive training to ensure proficiency in determining and assigning senses, using the ConText interface, identifying parts of speech, and understanding WordNet's structure. Trainees are first introduced to word sense identification using a system they are already familiar with—looking words up in a dictionary. They are given a booklet containing a printed text[5] and dictionary of WordNet senses and are asked to look up the polysemous open-class words from the first half of the text in this dictionary and to choose the appropriate sense. Once this sense assignment task is completed, their answers are compared with those of the researchers who prepared the training text (Christiane Fellbaum and Shari Landes).

After completing the dictionary task, the trainees use ConText to assign semantic tags to the same training passage. As they work through the file, the trainer explains the functions and features of ConText. To ensure that they focus all their attention on learning how to use ConText, the trainees assign senses from the corrected training booklet. Next, the trainees use ConText to assign semantic tags to the second half of the training passage (which they have not previously seen). At regular intervals, the trainer reviews and discusses the assigned semantic tags. During this phase, the trainees are introduced to various tools that facilitate the tagging process. Finally, each trainee reviews and assesses a file that has been tagged by an experienced tagger before being assigned a new file for semantic tagging.

8.7 QUALITY CONTROL

In preparation for the release of a semantic concordance, a series of quality control steps are performed. The first step is to confirm that all words that should be semantically tagged are, in fact, tagged. All remaining notes and words marked as *metaphor*, *idiom*, or *foreign word* are retrieved and sent to the lexicographers for review.

Every 11th semantically tagged word in the Brown semantic concordance is checked to determine whether the correct sense(s) and part of speech were assigned. All errors are recorded to help locate problem areas and are then corrected. A list of difficult words is identified from the tabulated errors, and all sentences containing them are retrieved from the semantic concordance. For each difficult word, a tagger who has studied all of its senses examines all the semantic tags for it in the retrieved sentences, looking for incorrect sense assignments. In addition, it was found that many nouns and adjectives were syntactically tagged as verbs. (The reason for this is discussed in the next section.) To identify and correct syntactic and semantic tagging errors, searches are made to find unlikely sequences of syntactic tags (e.g., a verb in a noun phrase, DET VERB NOUN). At this point the error margin is calculated for each file and the semantic tag verification procedure previously described is repeated on all files with an error margin above the mean. Next, every 12th tagged word is examined to determine the new error margin, and any errors found are also corrected.

To ensure the consistent use of multiple sense assignments within *RBC*, words having more than one semantic tag are reviewed. All uses of each word assigned multiple senses, in the same syntactic category, are retrieved and examined to make sure that the senses were assigned consistently throughout the text.

8.8 SOURCES OF ERROR AND INCONSISTENCY

Potential tagging errors are introduced into a semantic concordance during two phases of preprocessing: tokenization and syntactic tagging. When the tokenizer joins words that are not used as a collocation in that text, or when a word is assigned the wrong part of speech, a tagger must recognize and correct the error. For example, the tokenizer always joins a verb to an adjacent preposition when the result matches a phrasal verb in WordNet. When the sense distinction between a verb with a preposition and a phrasal verb is subtle (e.g, *come up* in *He came up the stairs*), the error may go unrecognized. As a result, a verb followed by a preposition may be incorrectly semantically tagged to a phrasal verb.

The tokenizer cannot recognize collocations or phrases that are discontinuous in a sentence, so it is up to the taggers to identify them during semantic tagging. For example, taggers must spot the phrasal verb *look up* in *John looked the name up* and change the WordNet Window display to show the corresponding set of senses. To make it easier for taggers to know which discontinuous phrases to look for, ConText displays, along with the senses for the verb *look*, a list of all phrasal verbs containing *look*. Nevertheless, especially in the case of discontinuous phrasal verbs, these can be overlooked.

The part-of-speech tagger often identifies syntactically ambiguous open-class words as being closed-class. For example, the adverb *beyond* in the phrase *rich beyond her wildest dreams* can be tagged as being a preposition. Although the taggers read the entire text during semantic tagging with ConText, not all of the mistagged open-class words are discovered. As a result, words that should be semantically tagged may be missed. Conversely, closed-class words are sometimes identified as being open-class (e.g., the pronoun *one* may be tagged as a noun) and may be semantically tagged in error. Finally, adjectives are sometimes identified as verbs, verbs as nouns, and so on. These errors are not always caught.

The part-of-speech tagger uses a subset of the original Brown Corpus syntactic tags that includes two ambiguous syntactic tags: VBN and VBG. The VBN tag indicates that a word is either a past tense verb or an adjective, for example, *exposed*. The VBG tag is even more ambiguous, indicating that a word is a verb, is being used adjectivally, or is a noun (a gerund), for example, *cheating*. When a word is syntactically tagged as VBN or VBG, ConText displays the corresponding set of verb senses. Although taggers try to validate every syntactic tag, some gerunds and adjectival participles end up semantically tagged to verb senses.

Another problem is introduced because the part-of-speech tagger is not very good at identifying the syntactic category of a prenominal modifier. Prenominal nouns are often identified as adjectives and prenominal adjectives as nouns, potentially introducing semantic tagging errors as well as a source of semantic tag inconsistency. Inconsistent tagging may occur with a word like *American* that appears in WordNet (and in most dictionaries) as both a noun and an adjective. When such a word is used prenominally, taggers tend to accept the syntactic category assigned by the part-of-speech tagger. Thus, it is possible for *American* in *American citizen* to be semantically tagged sometimes to a noun sense and sometimes to an adjective sense.

Collocations may be inconsistently tagged within a semantic concordance because taggers do not always agree on the identification of new collocations. They are taught that if a phrase is compositional (e.g., *ink pen* where *ink* is some kind of attribute of *pen*), the individual words are semantically tagged; if it is noncompositional (e.g., *fountain pen*), the collocation is added to WordNet. But noncompositionality is not the only way to identify collocations—frequency of occurrence also plays an important role. For example, *ballpoint pen* is as compositional as *ink pen*, but because of its high frequency it has found its way into many dictionaries. Inconsistency may be introduced when a new collocation is identified and added to WordNet, since we do not determine if that same collocation has already occurred in previously tagged files with its constituent words individually tagged. However, once the new collocation is put into the WordNet database, the tokenizer will find it when pre-processing subsequent files.

Many words belong to more than one syntactic category—*right*, for example, can be a noun, a verb, an adjective, or an adverb. This is problematic when a word can be a preposition or an adverbial (e.g., *before*) or a preposition or an adjective (e.g., *over*). The decision to not semantically tag prepositions and the part-of-speech tagger's tendency to identify these as being prepositions conspire to cause these adverbials and adjectives to be often overlooked during semantic tagging.

Inconsistent tagging within the Brown semantic concordance occurs especially often in the case of adverbs. They were introduced into Word-Net shortly after we began semantically tagging the Brown Corpus. Since many adverbs were not yet in WordNet, the tokenizer could not find them. As a result, files that were tagged early in this project have fewer adverbs semantically tagged than do the files that were tagged more recently. Now that more of these adverbs are in WordNet, the tokenizer identifies them, and fewer semantic tags are omitted.

8.9   VIEWING A SEMANTIC CONCORDANCE

Once a semantic concordance has been created, methods for viewing the tagged text are obviously needed. Different areas of interest and research naturally lead to different examination tools. A semantic concordance can be viewed as a concordance of senses for which semantic tags are search keys, as a text annotated with information on the meanings of the words in the text, and as a large database of contexts and word senses that lends itself to statistical analyses.

Escort (**E**xamine **S**emantic **C**oncordance **o**f **W**ritten **T**ext) is an X Windows application for viewing a semantic concordance as a concordance of word senses. WordNet senses are the search keys; sentences in the Brown semantic concordance containing semantic tags to them can be retrieved and displayed. The user has a wide range of search criteria and display options available including the specification of co-occurring senses, the choice of KWIC (**k**ey **w**ord **i**n **c**ontext) output display format, and parameters for designating the distance between primary and co-occurring keys in a sentence.

Miller and Gildea (1987, 99) made the following proposal: "[S]uppose reading material was presented to the student by a computer that had been programmed to answer questions about the meaning of all the words in the material.... [T]he computer would know in advance which particular sense of a word was appropriate in the context." The Reader interface does just this. A semantic concordance constructed from a literary or instructional text, such as *RBC*, can be read on-line with Reader. The Reader interface displays the text in a format resembling a book. Students reading the text can move through the on-line version much as they would through a book: by page, by chapter, or by looking for the uses of a particular word. While reading, the student uses the mouse to select any unfamiliar word or usage, and the meaning of the word (i.e., its WordNet sense or senses) is displayed. Additionally, literature may be annotated with notes about the text, and drawings or figures may be included in instructional manuals.

A significant benefit of formatting ConText files in SGML is that they can easily be examined using standard text-processing tools. A useful utility for examining tagged files is one of the most useful Unix tools of all: grep (**get r**egular **exp**ression). Lines corresponding to a word or collocation, matching many different criteria, may be culled from any number of files in a semantic concordance with one simple command. Many of the statistics that appear in appendix C were generated using grep.

8.10   CONCLUSION

We have described procedures for building semantic concordances that are currently in place. When we started building the Brown semantic concordance, two part-time taggers worked with a very fragile version of ConText. Over time, some features have been added, others have been removed, and ConText has been completely rewritten. The original version of ConText automatically highlighted the previously selected senses of a word that had already been semantically tagged earlier in the passage. This feature was removed because taggers tended to select the highlighted sense—regardless of whether the sense was appropriate. Similarly, the original output files were not in an SGML format and had to be converted. Another late introduction is the verification procedure, whereby all tagged files are checked by a second tagger. We hope that with the introduction of verification, checking every nth tagged word will need to be done only once in the quality control phase of a semantic concordance's development.

A semantic concordance can be approached from a number of directions (Miller et al. 1993). It can be used as a corpus of syntactically and semantically disambiguated text, as the Reader application does with the *RBC* semantic concordance. Conversely, a semantic concordance can be used as a lexicon where many of the word senses are accompanied by example sentences. This is the approach used in the Escort interface. Finally, a semantic concordance such as the Brown semantic concordance provides data for linguistic research. It can be used to find information on the relative frequency of word senses in written text (Miller et al. 1994), or context surrounding different senses of a polysemous word can be extracted from the concordance and used to train word sense identification systems. No doubt people will find uses for these semantic concordances that have not yet occurred to us.

Appendix A: SGML File Examples

File in SGML Text File Format
```
<doc>
<docno>br-a02</docno>
<txt>
<h1>AUSTIN,TEXAS</h1>
<p>
<s snum=1>Committee approval of Gov. Price Daniel's
"abandoned property" act seemed certain Thursday despite
the adamant protests of Texas bankers.</s></p>
</txt>
</doc>
```

Preprocessed File before Semantic Tagging
```
<contextfile concordance=brownl>
<context filename=br-a02 paras=yes>
<p pnum=1>
<s snum=1>
<wf cmd=tag pos=NNP>Committee</wf>
<wf cmd=tag pos=NN>approval</wf>
<wf cmd=ignore pos=IN>of</wf>
<wf cmd=tag pos=NNP>Gov._Price_Daniel</wf>
<wf cmd=ignore pos=POS>'s</wf>
<punc>"</punc>
<wf cmd=tag pos=VBN>abandoned</wf>
<wf cmd=tag pos=NN>property</wf>
<punc>"</punc>
<wf cmd=tag pos=NN>act</wf>
<wf cmd=tag pos=VBD>seemed</wf>
<wf cmd=tag pos=JJ>certain</wf>
<wf cmd=tag pos=NNP>Thursday</wf>
<wf cmd=ignore pos=IN>despite</wf>
<wf cmd=ignore pos=DT>the</wf>
```

```
<wf cmd=tag pos=JJ>adamant</wf>
<wf cmd=tag pos=NNS>protests</wf>
<wf cmd=ignore pos=IN>of</wf>
<wf cmd=tag pos=NNP>Texas</wf>
<wf cmd=tag pos=NNS>bankers</wf>
<punc>.</punc>
</s>
</p>
</context>
</contextfile>
```

Semantically Tagged ConText File

```
<contextfile concordance=brown>
<context filename=br-a02 paras=yes>
<p pnum=1>
<s snum=1>
<wf cmd=done pos=NN lemma=committee wnsn=1 lexsn=1:14:00::>
Committee</wf>
<wf cmd=done pos=NN lemma=approval wnsn=1 lexsn=1:04:00::>
approval</wf>
<wf cmd=ignore pos=IN>of</wf>
<wf cmd=done rdf=person pos=NNP lemma=person wnsn=1
lexsn=1:03:00::pn=person>Gov._Price_Daniel</wf>
<wf cmd=ignore pos=POS>'s</wf>
<punc>"</punc>
<wf cmd=done pos=JJ lemma=abandoned wnsn=1 lexsn=5:00:00:
unoccupied:00>abandoned</wf>
<wf cmd=done pos=NN lemma=property wnsn=1 lexsn=1:21:00::>
property</wf>
<punc>"</punc>
<wf cmd=done pos=NN lemma=act wnsn=1 lexsn=1:10:01::>act
</wf>
<wf cmd=done pos=VB lemma=seem wnsn=1 lexsn=2:39:00::>
seemed</wf>
<wf cmd=done pos=JJ lemma=certain wnsn=4 lexsn=3:00:03::>
certain</wf>
<wf cmd=done pos=NN lemma=thursday wnsn=1 lexsn=1:28:00::>
Thursday</wf>
<wf cmd=ignore pos=IN>despite</wf>
<wf cmd=ignore pos=DT>the</wf>
<wf cmd=done pos=JJ lemma=adamant wnsn=1 lexsn=5:00:00:
inflexible:02>adamant</wf>
<wf cmd=done pos=NN lemma=protest wnsn=1 lexsn=1:10:00::>
protests</wf>
<wf cmd=ignore pos=IN>of</wf>
<wf cmd=done pos=NN lemma=texas wnsn=1 lexsn=1:15:00::>
Texas</wf>
```

```
<wf cmd=done pos=NN lemma=banker wnsn=1 lexsn=1:18:00::>
bankers</wf>
<punc>.</punc>
</s>
</p>
</context>
</contextfile>
```

Appendix B: Word Form Element Attribute-Value Pairs

Attribute name	Attribute values
cmd	tag, done, ignore, retag, update, verify, verify_done, verify_ignore
pos	*syntactic tags from Brill tag set*
lemma	*base form of word*
lexsn	*sense key(s) for semantic tag(s)*
wnsn	*WordNet sense number(s) corresponding to sense key(s)*
rdf	*redefinition of word*
ot	*other tags:* notag, metaphor, idiom, complexprep, foreignword, nonceword
pn	*proper noun:* person, location, group, other
tagnote	sns_miss, indist_sns, wd_miss, insuffctxt, sense_lost, misc, none
note	*comment string*

Appendix C: Semantic Concordance Statistics

	Brown	*RBC*
Number of files in concordance	103	27
Number of words including nonalphanumerics	198,160	45,679
Number of words with semantic pointers to WordNet	106,584	22,898
Number of words with multiple senses	108	896
Number of semantic tags including multiple senses	10,666	23,582
Number of sentences	11,182	3,502
Tags by part of speech (POS)		
Number of semantic pointers to POS noun	48,643	9,053
Number of WordNet senses pointed to by POS noun	11,407	2,821
Number of semantic pointers to POS verb	26,690	6,951
Number of WordNet senses pointed to by POS verb	5,597	2,097
Number of semantic pointers to POS adjective	19,768	4,155
Number of WordNet senses pointed to by POS adjective	5,221	1,958
Number of semantic pointers to POS adverb	11,455	2,524
Number of WordNet senses pointed to by POS adverb	1,489	656

Notes

1. The text was obtained from the on-line Gutenberg Project.

2. Since WordNet contains only open-class words, only open-class words are tagged in the semantic concordances.

3. The original version of the X Windows interface ConText was developed by Brian Gustafson, Claudia Leacock, and Randee Tengi. Subsequent additions and modifications were developed by Ross Bunker, Shari Landes, Randee Tengi, Daniel Markham, and Paul Bagyenda.

4. Because the goal of tagging *RBC* is to create a concordance for educational use, metaphor and figurative language must be addressed. The locations of phrases that require subsequent annotation are recorded by ConText.

5. This training text is the first half of a Brown Corpus fictional passage. To prepare the passage, Christiane Fellbaum and Shari Landes verified that all syntactic tags were correct, eliminated problematic words, and determined which WordNet senses were appropriate for each word in the passage. The resulting training passage contains about 250 polysemous open-class words to be semantically tagged.

References

Brill, E. (1994). Some advances in rule-based part of speech tagging. In *Proceedings of the Twelfth National Conference on Artificial Intelligence (AAAI-94)*, 256–261. Menlo Park, CA: AAAI Press, and Cambridge MA: MIT Press.

Kučera, H., and Francis, W. N. (1967). *The standard corpus of present-day edited American English* [the Brown Corpus]. (Electronic database.) Providence, RI: Brown University.

Leacock, C. (1993). *ConText: A tool for semantic tagging of text: User's guide* (CSL Rep. No. 54). Princeton, NJ: Princeton University, Cognitive Science Laboratory.

Miller, G. A., Chodorow, M., Landes, S., Leacock, C., and Thomas, R. G. (1994). Using a semantic concordance for sense identification. In *Proceedings of the ARPA Human Language Technology Workshop*, 240–243. San Francisco: Morgan Kaufmann.

Miller, G. A., and Gildea, P. M. (1987). How children learn words. *Scientific American, 255*(9), 94–99.

Miller, G. A., Leacock, C., Tengi, R., and Bunker, R. T. (1993). A semantic concordance. In *Proceedings of the ARPA Human Language Technology Workshop*, 303–308. San Francisco: Morgan Kaufmann.

van Herwijnen, E. (1990). *Practical SGML.* Dordrecht: Kluwer.

Chapter 9

Performance and Confidence in a Semantic Annotation Task

Christiane Fellbaum, Joachim Grabowski, and Shari Landes

9.1 INTRODUCTION

The work described in this chapter grew out of the semantic concordance project (Landes, Leacock, and Tengi, this volume), in which each content word in a text is linked ("tagged") to a corresponding synset (synonym set) in WordNet.[1] Human taggers are instructed to select, from among the available senses in WordNet, the one that best fits the given context. In Fellbaum, Grabowski, and Landes 1995 (hereafter the *agreement analysis*) we analyzed the taggers' performance by comparing their sense selections with those of experienced taggers with respect to several lexicosemantic properties of the tagged words and their position on the list of available senses. Here we analyze the taggers' choices of word senses in light of the confidence with which they made their selections.

Each time they matched a word usage to a corresponding WordNet sense, the taggers were asked to rate the degree of confidence with which they selected a sense. Our assumption was that the taggers' confidence ratings reflected the ease with which they could discriminate among the senses in WordNet and identify one and only one sense that appeared to match the usage in the text. The text had been carefully examined by two of the authors, who ascertained that each content word that the participants were asked to tag had a matching entry in WordNet with at least two distinct senses; the lexicographers had independently identified a sense as the most appropriate one in each case. (Throughout this chapter the sense deemed the best match by the lexicographers will be called the *expert* sense.) Thus, the available senses always included one that matched the given usage; however, in some cases the taggers had to choose from among several semantically close senses that were difficult to discriminate, whereas in other cases the different senses were sufficiently distinct that the matching one could easily be identified. The less clear the choice seemed to the taggers, the less likely it was that they either agreed on a sense selection among themselves or chose the expert sense, and the lower a confidence rating we expected.

In the agreement analysis we found that tagger-expert matches were rather high overall (74%) and that intertagger agreement was even higher (78.6%). We attributed this result to a difference in the representation of word meanings between naive taggers and experienced lexicographers; we explored the possibility of different approaches to dictionary representations of meanings and different strategies for mapping dictionary entries onto the corresponding representations in speakers' mental lexicons. In the analysis reported here (the *confidence analysis*) we expected confidence ratings to reflect the extent to which taggers agreed among themselves and with the expert selections. We assume that the senses chosen most often by the taggers were the ones most easily identifiable as the best matches; we also believe that these choices were made with relatively high certainty. If the taggers were uncertain about their choice and hesitated among several options, it seems unlikely that their choice coincided with that of most of the other taggers.

In the agreement analysis we found that taggers agreed significantly more often among themselves and with the experts when they tagged nouns than when they tagged words from other word classes. To explain this part-of-speech effect, we argued that nouns may be easier to tag because they tend to denote persons and objects, which are often imageable and concrete (Schwanenfluegel 1991). Noun meanings tend to be relatively stable. By contrast, modifiers like adjectives and adverbs tend to change their meanings depending on the meaning of the constituent that they modify. For example, Katz (1964) showed that the central meaning of the adjective *good* varies with that of the head noun and is thus infinitely polysemous. The meanings of adverbs often depend on their scope or their position in the sentence (see, e.g., Vendler 1984). The meanings of verbs can differ to some extent depending on their head nouns. By contrast, the meanings of nouns tend to be more stable in the presence of different verbs. Gentner and France (1988) demonstrated what they call the high mutability of verbs, showing people's willingness to assign highly flexible meanings to verbs, whereas they held the meanings of nouns constant. Gentner and France argue that verb meanings are more easily altered because they are less cohesive than those of nouns. In the agreement analysis we speculated that the representation of verb meanings (and derived adverb meanings) may be less stable than that of noun meanings. The results we obtained in that analysis led us to expect higher confidence ratings for noun tags than for tags on words from other word classes.

In the agreement analysis we found that, with increasing polysemy, both intertagger and tagger-expert matches decreased significantly. This is not particularly surprising if one considers that the more polysemous a word is, the more difficult it is to select the most appropriate sense, especially in cases where several of the senses in WordNet are fairly close in meaning. Thus, for highly polysemous words, we expected taggers in the confidence analysis to make their choices with less confidence than for words that had only two or three senses in WordNet.

There is an interaction between polysemy and syntactic class membership. Verbs and adjectives, whose semantics make them inherently harder to tag, have on average more senses than nouns in WordNet. We believe that both number of senses and syntactic class membership accounted for fewer intertagger and expert-tagger matches in the case of verbs and modifiers, and we expected that these words would be tagged with less confidence than nouns for the same reason.

When the dictionary booklet from which taggers selected the WordNet senses of the words they were tagging listed those senses in the order of frequency of occurrence, the taggers agreed with the lexicographers' choice 75.2% of the time, and they agreed among themselves 79.7% of the time. When the booklet listed the senses in random order, the taggers chose the same sense as the lexicographers only 72.8% of the time, and they agreed among themselves 79.9% of the time. We believe that the taggers were less often "correct" in the random order condition because the choices were more difficult here. In the frequency order condition, the first (most frequent) sense tends to be the most general and salient one, given a reasonably balanced corpus. In the agreement analysis, we argued that this sense, which is most frequently encountered, is also the one that is most clearly represented in the mental lexicon of both naive speakers and lexicographers. In the frequency order condition, this sense had a greater chance of being the "correct" one; since we believe that its centrality makes it easy to identify, we were not surprised at the high tagger-expert agreement rates in this condition.

However, in the random order condition, the taggers could not rely on the first sense being the "correct" one, since all senses were equally likely to be the best match. The fact that the agreement rate here was higher than in the frequency order condition for both tagger-expert and inter-tagger matches shows that the taggers must have examined all senses rather carefully before making a selection; the high agreement could not have arisen by chance. We expected the confidence ratings to reflect the agreement results and to show that in the random order condition, the taggers were more certain of their choices because they were forced to carefully examine the entire lexical entry without being able to rely on the chance that the first, core sense was likely to be the best choice.

In both conditions, taggers agreed significantly more often with the experts and among themselves when the chosen sense was listed at the top of the available choices in the dictionary booklet than when it was in a subsequent position. In the frequency order condition, the high agreement was probably due to the fact that the first, core sense was most easily identifiable; when it seemed like a good match, the choice was easy. We expected confidence ratings to be particularly high for tagger-expert matches when the sense that was selected was in the first position.

In the agreement analysis, we explained the high agreement rates for senses that occurred in first position in the random order condition by hypothesizing that taggers may have followed a dictionary lookup strategy. Kilgarriff (1993) notes that when dictionary users encounter the first sense that seems to match a given word usage reasonably well, they stop reading and comparing other senses. Having found a sense that satisfies their need, dictionary users are not generally bothered by the existence of subsequent, possibly overlapping or duplicate senses. Thus, in the random order condition, taggers may often have chosen the sense at the top of the list when they were not able to discriminate among the available senses. We argued that the dictionary lookup strategy might be particularly characteristic for novice taggers, who have not yet developed skills to discriminate among a large number of often subtly differing senses.

In the confidence analysis we expected the taggers to be more confident about the words they selected when they were at the top of the list of available senses. We predicted this effect in particular for those cases where the senses were ordered by the frequency with which they had previously been tagged to text. Given that the most frequent sense tends to be the most salient or core sense, we reasoned that taggers would feel rather confident about identifying it and differentiating it from the other available senses.

9.2   THE TASK

The analyses presented here are based on data from the training session that the taggers underwent before they began to work on the semantic concordance. We investigated data from the training sessions of 17 undergraduate and graduate students (6 male, 11 female).

The taggers were given a booklet containing a 660-word fiction passage from the Standard Corpus of Present-Day Edited American English (the Brown Corpus; Kučera and Francis 1967), of which large parts are semantically tagged to WordNet (see Landes, Leacock, and Tengi, this volume). The section we chose (reproduced in full in the appendix) contained 336 function words and proper nouns. The remaining 324 words were all open-class words. Of these, 70 were monosemous and 254 had two or more senses. Of these polysemous words, 88 were nouns, 100 were verbs, 39 were adjectives, and 27 were adverbs. The ratio of the different parts of speech reflects that found in a typical prose text. The task of the taggers was to select appropriate senses from WordNet for these 254 words.[2]

The number of different senses per word ranged from 2 to 41. The mean number of senses across all four parts of speech was 6.62. Verbs were the most polysemous category (mean number of senses = 8.63), followed by adjectives (mean number of senses = 7.95), nouns (mean number of senses = 4.74), and adverbs (mean number of senses = 3.37). The low polysemy of adverbs in the text may not be indicative of their actual polysemy in the language, but may be due to the fact that adverbs were added relatively late to WordNet; those that were included at the time the data for this study were collected were entered for the most part because they were tagged in the Brown Corpus. Therefore, although the most frequently occurring senses were represented, some less frequent senses might not yet have been encountered in the corpus and would not have been included in WordNet.

The taggers were given a booklet containing the typed text that was specially created for the analyses. The text was typed onto the page in such a way that each line contained one word. The line containing the word to be tagged further listed its part of speech, a box in which the taggers marked the sense number they chose for the usage, and a box in which they indicated the degree of confidence with which they made their choice in each case. Confidence was rated on a semantically labeled 5-point Likert scale (Matell and Jacoby 1971) from "highly certain" to "highly uncertain." In our analyses we will refer to the values on this scale with the digits 1 to 5, where 1 indicates "highly certain" and 5 indicates "highly uncertain."

Each tagger was also given a dictionary booklet, in which the senses for the words in the text were shown as they are represented in WordNet.[3]

The dictionary booklet listed all the senses of the words that the trainees were instructed to tag, along with their hyponyms. No other semantically related words or synsets were provided. Two versions of the dictionary booklet were prepared, one for each training condition.

In the first condition (the *frequency order condition*), 8 taggers were given a dictionary booklet that listed the WordNet senses as they appear in the WordNet interface (see Tengi, this volume), that is, in the order of frequency with which they appear in the tagged Brown Corpus. In the second condition (the *random order condition*), the remaining 9 taggers were given a dictionary booklet in which the same WordNet senses were arranged in random order. The random order, produced by means of a random number generator, was the same for all 9 taggers. In this order, the first sense was no longer necessarily the most inclusive or central one.

9.3 PROCEDURE

The participants were being trained as taggers for the semantic concordance project. The tagging project was explained to them. They were instructed to match the content words in the text booklet to senses in the dictionary booklet and to indicate clearly for each word both the sense number they had chosen and the degree of confidence with which they had made their choice. The participants, who worked independently of each other, finished the task within 4 to 6 hours. The trainees were not aware of having been assigned to one of two groups of taggers.

9.4 RESULTS

9.4.1 Overall Results

Figure 9.1 shows the overall results (both conditions) for all parts of speech and polysemy groups. The overall mean confidence rating was 1.8. This shows that taggers were fairly sure of their choices. Overall, nouns were tagged with more confidence than adverbs, which in turn were tagged with more confidence than adjectives. Taggers were least certain about their choice of senses for verbs. Conforming to our expectations,

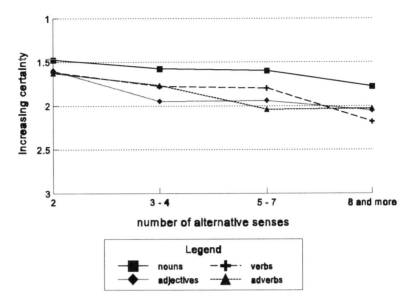

Figure 9.1
Overall mean confidence ratings

the more polysemous words were tagged with the least confidence. This
was true for all parts of speech.

9.4.2 Tagger-Expert Matches

Figure 9.2 and 9.3 show the confidence ratings for all parts of speech and
all polysemy groups in the two conditions for the tagger-expert matches.
Figures 9.4 and 9.5 show the corresponding percentages of tagger-expert
matches. As the figures indicate, the taggers' confidence generally matches
the extent to which they chose the same senses as the lexicographers.

In both conditions, we found that nouns were tagged with the highest
degree of confidence; the taggers were significantly less certain about their
choices of senses for adverbs and, especially, adjectives and verbs. The
more polysemous the word was, the less confident the taggers were about
their choice, although in the random order condition, there was not much
difference between words with 3–4 senses and words with 5–7 senses. In
the frequency order condition, words with 3–4 senses were tagged with
about the same degree of confidence as words with only 2 senses. And the
taggers were no less confident about choosing from 8 or more adjective
senses than they were when they had 3–7 senses to choose from. For

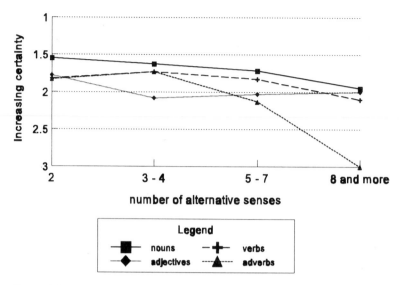

Figure 9.2
Mean confidence ratings, tagger-expert matches, frequency order

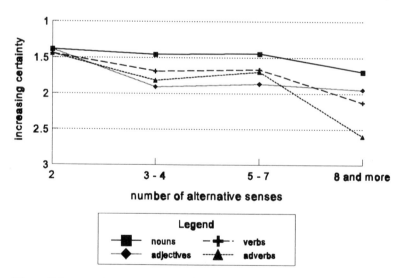

Figure 9.3
Mean confidence ratings, tagger-expert matches, random order

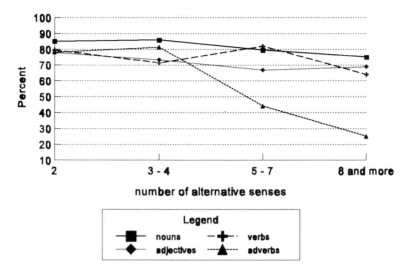

Figure 9.4
Percentage agreement, tagger-expert matches, frequency order

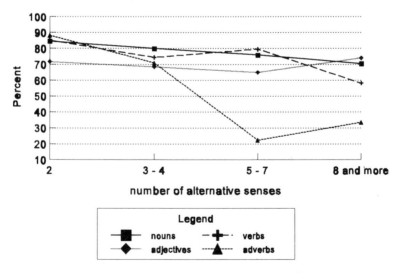

Figure 9.5
Percentage agreement, tagger-expert matches, random order

adverbs with more than 8 senses, confidence dropped sharply in both orders, although overall, senses for adverbs were chosen with more certainty than senses for adjectives and, especially, verbs. Although these patterns were the same for both conditions, confidence was higher for choices made in the random order condition, although fewer tagger-expert matches were made in this condition.

9.4.3   Intertagger Agreement

In the agreement analysis we found that taggers agreed most often among themselves in the case of nouns, and least frequently when they tagged verbs and adverbs. Taggers agreed on words with only 2 senses almost 90% of the time, whereas they agreed on the most polysemous words (8 or more senses) only about 70% of the time. The latter finding follows the general pattern for those tagger choices that matched the lexicographers' choices. However, in the confidence analysis the confidence ratings for the choices most often made by the taggers revealed a slightly different pattern. In the random order condition, noun senses were still chosen with the highest degree of certainty, but adverb senses were chosen with more confidence than verb and adjective senses (this effect is also found in the frequency order condition, but it is not significant here). As in the cases where they chose the same senses as the lexicographers, the taggers made their choices with significantly more confidence in the random order condition than when the senses were ordered by frequency. Figures 9.6 and 9.7 show the percentages of agreement for the frequency and random order conditions; figures 9.8 and 9.9 show the corresponding confidence ratings.

9.4.4   First versus Subsequent Position on the List of Senses

In the agreement analysis we found higher rates of tagger-expert and intertagger matches for choices that were at the top of the list of available WordNet senses. Our results from the confidence analysis show that confidence ratings were higher for these senses as well. Tables 9.1 and 9.2 show, for both conditions, the confidence ratings for the tagger-expert matches when the choices were at the top of the list of senses and when they were listed in a subsequent position.

For the choices agreed on by most taggers, the picture was very similar. Confidence was higher when the agreed-upon sense was the first on the list, in both conditions. Again, confidence was higher overall when the senses were presented in random order. Tables 9.3 and 9.4 show, for both

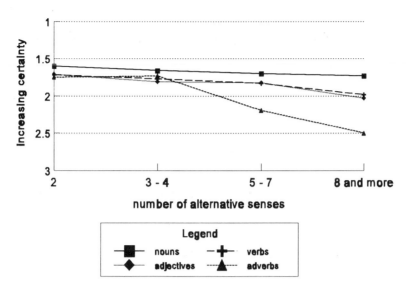

Figure 9.6
Mean confidence ratings, intertagger matches, frequency order

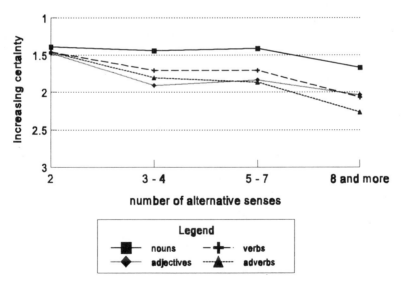

Figure 9.7
Mean confidence ratings, intertagger matches, random order

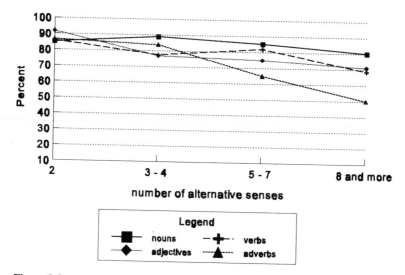

Figure 9.8
Percentage agreement, intertagger matches, frequency order

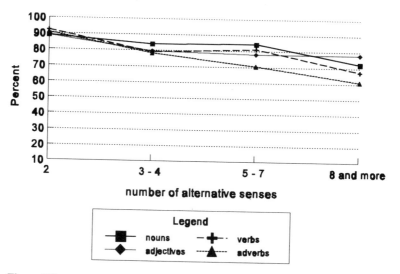

Figure 9.9
Percentage agreement, intertagger matches, random order

Table 9.1
Confidence rating means for tagger-expert matches, expert choice in first position, frequency order

Part of speech	Position of expert choice	Number of alternative senses				
		2	3–4	5–7	>7	Mean
Nouns	First	1.42	1.63	1.55	1.95	1.64
	Subsequent	1.71	1.62	1.80	1.94	1.73
Verbs	First	1.82	1.59	1.65	2.19	1.85
	Subsequent	1.81	1.93	2.11	2.04	2.01
Adjectives	First	1.53	1.71	1.43	1.88	1.69
	Subsequent	1.97	2.36	2.33	2.07	2.14
Adverbs	First	1.92	1.60	2.40	*	1.84
	Subsequent	1.75	1.82	2.00	3.00	1.90
Mean	First	1.68	1.62	1.63	2.07	1.75
	Subsequent	1.80	1.82	1.97	2.07	1.93

Table 9.2
Confidence rating means for tagger-expert matches, choice in first position, random order

Part of speech	Position of agreed-upon choice	Number of alternative senses				
		2	3–4	5–7	>7	Mean
Nouns	First	1.35	1.35	1.59	*	1.37
	Subsequent	1.49	1.54	1.43	1.70	1.53
Verbs	First	1.48	1.49	1.73	2.69	1.67
	Subsequent	1.38	1.83	1.67	2.09	1.91
Adjectives	First	1.31	1.61	1.89	2.50	1.51
	Subsequent	2.00	2.03	1.87	1.92	1.93
Adverbs	First	1.54	1.76	*	2.60	1.74
	Subsequent	1.16	1.85	1.70	*	1.64
Mean	First	1.42	1.46	1.68	2.63	1.55
	Subsequent	1.42	1.54	1.59	1.98	1.76

Table 9.3
Confidence rating means for intertagger matches, choice in first position, frequency order

Part of speech	Position of agreed-upon choice	Number of alternative senses				
		2	3–4	5–7	>7	Mean
Nouns	First	1.48	1.63	1.56	1.66	1.60
	Subsequent	1.71	1.70	1.79	1.94	1.75
Verbs	First	1.65	1.68	1.64	2.06	1.80
	Subsequent	1.80	1.89	2.12	1.93	1.93
Adjectives	First	1.53	1.56	1.69	1.61	1.60
	Subsequent	1.85	1.94	1.94	2.17	2.03
Adverbs	First	1.82	1.46	2.28	*	1.80
	Subsequent	1.68	1.85	2.00	2.50	1.87
Mean	First	1.63	1.63	1.67	1.87	1.70
	Subsequent	1.75	1.80	1.92	2.03	1.89

Table 9.4
Confidence rating means for intertagger matches, choice in first position, random order

Part of speech	Position of agreed-upon choice	Number of alternative senses				
		2	3–4	5–7	>7	Mean
Nouns	First	1.28	1.36	1.38	*	1.33
	Subsequent	1.62	1.49	1.41	1.67	1.51
Verbs	First	1.48	1.57	1.75	2.11	1.67
	Subsequent	1.44	1.81	1.70	2.07	1.90
Adjectives	First	1.34	1.57	1.75	*	1.51
	Subsequent	2.50	2.02	1.61	2.04	2.00
Adverbs	First	1.57	1.85	*	2.20	1.69
	Subsequent	1.25	1.79	1.87	2.33	1.69
Mean	First	1.41	1.47	1.78	2.13	1.53
	Subsequent	1.52	1.68	1.57	2.00	1.76

conditions, the confidence ratings for the intertagger matches when the choices were at the top of the list of senses and and when they were listed in a subsequent position.

9.5 DISCUSSION

Overall, confidence ratings were rather high. We interpret this to mean that the taggers, who were complete novices, found the annotation task doable and not overwhelmingly difficult. Our expectation that the confidence ratings would reflect the taggers' sense of the difficulty of the task was confirmed by the fact that the ratings generally went in tandem with the taggers' performance as measured by tagger-expert and intertagger matches (Fellbaum, Grabowski, and Landes 1995). We also believe that the high overall certainty means that the WordNet senses were reasonably clearly represented and distinguishable. The high ratings may further indicate that the taggers worked conscientiously and considered all sense alternatives before making a choice, a conclusion that is supported by the high confidence ratings in the random order condition.

In the agreement analysis we found that the taggers agreed among themselves more often than they agreed with the lexicographers, and the present results show that the confidence ratings followed this pattern. We found slightly lower confidence ratings in those cases where the taggers' choices were also those of the lexicographers (overall confidence rating: 1.77) than in the cases where the taggers agreed among themselves (overall confidence rating: 1.74). This supports the hypothesis in the agreement analysis that lexicographers, who are experienced at creating and interpreting dictionary entries, approach a semantic annotation task differently than naive speakers, who are not as skilled at discriminating a large number of subtly differing senses. The large overlap in the taggers' choices points to the reality of such a "naive" lexicon, as distinguished from the lexicographers' mental representation of polysemous words.

Our results in the confidence analysis show the same main effects for degree of polysemy and part of speech that we found in the agreement analysis when comparing the taggers' choices with those of the experts and with those of other taggers. Taggers were most certain of their choices when the word to be tagged had few senses (2–4) in WordNet; for highly polysemous words (8 and more senses), the taggers' confidence about their choices dropped significantly. This result is not surprising considering that a large number of alternatives made the choice more difficult, because it entailed that the taggers had to weigh and compare more options.

The taggers were consistently more certain of their choices when they tagged nouns than when they tagged words from other syntactic categories. Overall, adjectives and especially verbs were tagged with the least confidence. (For highly polysemous adverbs, confidence dropped most dramatically, but there were too few adverbs among the words to be tagged to permit any confident conclusions about the meaning of this result. In any case, confidence here mirrors the taggers' performance in terms of their agreement among themselves and with the lexicographers.) The high confidence ratings for nouns, which shows that they were perceived as "easier" to tag, may be due to the particular semantic properties of nouns, as opposed to words that function as modifiers. Nouns usually denote referents that are delimited in space and time, and people have been shown to be less flexible in their interpretation of nouns than other parts of speech (Gentner and France 1988). Verb and adjective meanings, on the other hand, depend more on context, in particular on the meanings of the nouns with which they co-occur. People's mental representation of noun concepts may be more fixed and stable and less vague than their representation of verbs and adjectives (Fellbaum, Grabowski, and Landes 1995). Nouns not only have more distinguishable senses, but also are less polysemous.

Contrary to our prediction, we found that in the random order condition, confidence was significantly higher for both tagger-expert and inter-tagger matches, although the taggers performed "worse" in that they chose the expert sense less often than the taggers in the frequency order condition did. We believe that these results may be due to the fact that the taggers who had to choose the best sense from a randomly ordered list of senses did have a more difficult task to perform than the taggers who worked with the list of senses that were ordered by the frequency with which they appeared in the already tagged text. In the frequency order condition, the first sense was most often the most salient, central sense, and in many cases it represented the best choice for the words that were to be tagged. We assume that in the course of carrying out their task, the taggers realized that the first sense was the core sense and that it tended to be the "safe" choice in many cases. Many standard dictionaries similarly list the most prevalent, central sense of a polysemous word before other senses, so this order may have appeared quite natural to the taggers.

In the random order condition, the taggers had to examine all senses before making their choice without relying on a strategy that told them that the first sense had a good chance of being the best match. When the word had many senses (and some words had 30 or more), this task was quite difficult. The relatively greater difficulty of this task may be reflected in the fact that in this condition, taggers agreed less often among themselves on the best choice, and they also chose the sense that had been selected by the lexicographers less often. We suggest that the taggers who performed this challenging task worked harder at examining and comparing all available senses and that this may have been why they felt more certain about their choices than the taggers whose choice was facilitated by the fact that the most frequent and salient sense was listed first.

Additional evidence for this explanation comes from the agreement analysis of the tagger-expert matches for words that were at the top of the list of available senses. There, we found that overall, the taggers chose the first sense on the list of available choices significantly more often than a sense that was further down on the list, both when it was the experts' choice and when the taggers agreed among themselves. This was generally true for words from all polysemy groups and part-of-speech classes. We argued that in the frequency order condition, where the first sense is usually the most central and salient one, the taggers tended to choose this sense when it was at all appropriate because it was most easily identifiable. Selecting it meant that the taggers did not have to examine and compare the remaining senses in search of an even better choice. Weighing all available senses against each other and against the given usage can be a difficult task especially for novice taggers, and a general tendency to gravitate toward the first, core sense is not surprising. Not reading further after encountering the first sense that seems appropriate resembles the dictionary lookup strategy of not reading the entry further after finding a sense that seems to match the given usage.

Overall, confidence was higher each time that the taggers' choice was first on the list of available senses in the WordNet dictionary than when it was in a subsequent position. This was true for both tagger-expert matches and intertagger matches, and for both the frequency and random order conditions. These results are parallel to those showing the rate of tagger-expert and intertagger agreement, and they confirm our conclusion in the agreement analysis that the first sense listed in the dictionary is a big attractor and tends to be perceived as the "correct" one. In the frequency order condition, this follows from the particular properties of the most frequent, core sense. In the random order condition, the higher confidence ratings for first choices may be due to the taggers' following a dictionary lookup strategy when they could not clearly discriminate among a large number of semantically similar, randomly ordered senses, choosing the first sense that seemed to qualify at all as a match for the given usage.

Confidence ratings were higher in the random order condition than in the frequency order condition. This was true both when the chosen sense was in first position and when it was in a subsequent position. In the former case, this result puts in doubt an explanation whereby in the random order condition, the first sense was chosen more often and with more confidence than subsequent senses because taggers chose the first sense when they could not discriminate among a large number of similar senses and the first one seemed like a reasonably good candidate. A closer look at the results suggests another explanation.

In the random order condition, more tagger-expert matches were made when the expert sense was not the first on the list in the case of highly polysemous words (8 or more senses). This suggests that taggers in the random order condition did not pick the first sense when they failed to discriminate among a large number of similar senses, instead making a careful choice based on an examination of all senses. This result agrees with those showing high tagger-expert matches in the random order condition, and the fact that the confidence ratings were higher for the random order condition not only when the chosen sense was at the top of the list of available senses, but also when it appeared further down. We believe that the results suggest that the taggers examined and compared all alternative senses, and that they could not and did not adopt the "dictionary lookup strategy" that was an option for the taggers working in the frequency order condition. The careful work of the taggers working in this condition is reflected in the high percentage of tagger-expert and intertagger matches, their excellent performance in the case of the most polysemous words, and their confidence ratings.

In sum, we found that the taggers' confidence ratings reflected their performance as measured by the number of tagger-expert and intertagger matches. When the choice of appropriate word senses was more difficult, the taggers' certainty about their choice decreased. This was generally the case for highly polysemous words, as well as for modifiers and, especially, verbs. Taggers working in the random order condition, where the chances that the first sense was the best match were no greater than for the other available senses, showed that they carefully examined all available senses and were consequently rather certain of their choices. In the frequency order condition, where the first sense tended to be the central, most salient sense, taggers showed a preference for this sense when making their selection (Fellbaum, Grabowski, and Landes 1995), but this preference also resulted in less confident choices.

More fine-grained analyses of the confidence ratings in conjunction with the taggers' performance need to be undertaken. In particular, the confidence ratings for words with specific semantic properties need to be more closely examined to see which kinds of words posed the greatest difficulties for taggers and resulted in decreased certainty.

APPENDIX

For three days, their stolid oxen had plodded up a blazing valley as flat and featureless as a dead sea. Molten glare singed their eyelids an angry crimson; suffocating air sapped their strength and strained their nerves to snapping; dust choked their throats. And the valley stretched out endlessly ahead, scorched and baked and writhing in its heat, until it vanished into the throbbing wall of fiery haze.

Ben Prime extended his high-stepped stride until he could lay his goad across the noses of the oxen. "Hoa-whup!" he commanded from his raw throat, and felt the pain of movement in his cracked, black burned lips. He spat. The dust-thick saliva came from his mouth like balled cotton. He moved back to the wheel and stood there blowing, grasping the top of a spoke to still the trembling of his played-out limbs. He cleared his throat. As cheerfully as possible, he said, "Well, I guess we could all do with a little drink."

He unlashed the dipper and drew water from a barrel. They could no longer afford the luxury of the canvas sweat bag that cooled it by evaporation. The water was warm and stale and had a brackish taste. He cleansed his mouth with a small quantity. He took a long but carefully controlled draught. His wife drank too, and set the dipper on the edge of the deck, leaving it for him to stretch after it.

"What happens when there's no more water?" she asked. Her thick hair was the color and texture of charcoal. Her temper sparked like charcoal when it first lights up. And all the time, she had the heat of hatred in her, like charcoal that is burning. A ripple ran through the muscles of his jaws, but he kept control upon his voice. "We can get water if we dig," he said patiently. "And add fever to our troubles?" she scoffed. "Or do you want to see if I can stand fever, too?"

Her chin sharpened: "We're lost. The tires are rattling on the wheels now. They'll roll off in another day." Ben said, "Somewhere, we'll hit a trail." "Somewhere!" she repeated. "Maybe in time to make a cross and dig our graves." His wide mouth compressed. In a way, he couldn't blame her.

He had picked out this pathless trail, instead of the common one, in a moment of romantic fancy, to give them privacy on their honeymoon. It wasn't the roughness and crudity and discomfort of the trip that had frightened her. She had hated him before she ever saw him. It had been five days too late before he learned that she'd gone through the wedding ceremony in a semitrance of laudanum, administered by her mother. The bitterness of their wedding night still ripped within him like an open wound. She had jumped away from his shy touch like a cat confronted by a sidewinder. He had left her inviolate, thinking familiarity would gentle her in time. "I suppose," he muttered, "I can sell the outfit for enough to send you home to your folks, once we find a settlement." "Don't try to be noble!" Her laugh was hard. "They wouldn't have sold me in the first place if there'd been food enough to go around."

He winced. "They thought it would be a chance for us to make a life out where nobody will be thought any better than the next except for just what's inside of them. Without money or property, what would you have had at Baton Rouge?"

Hettie said, "I might have starved, but at least I wouldn't be fried to a crisp and soaked with dirt!"

He darkened under his heavy burn. To his puzzlement, the valley lay clear and open to the eye, right up to the sharp line of gaunt, scoured hills that formed the horizon. Then he noticed clouds forming and racing upon them—heavy, ominous, leaden clouds. He had the primitive feel of danger that gripped a man before a hurricane.

Notes

1. We thank Martin Chodorow, Adam Kilgarriff, Joel Lachter, and Philip Resnik for valuable comments that shaped the present version of this chapter, and Anna Poplawski for technical assistance.

2. We had made a few minor alterations to the text; for example, we omitted short passages that repeated words/senses that had previously occurred in the text.

3. Since WordNet changes daily, and an in-house version is updated every week (see Tengi, this volume), we reproduced in the dictionary booklet the WordNet version that existed at the time of the training sessions.

References

Fellbaum, C., Grabowski, J., and Landes, S. (1995). *Matching words to senses: Naive vs. expert differentiation of senses* (Tech. Rep. No. 60). Mannheim, Germany: University of Mannheim, Psychology Department.

Gentner, D., and France, I. (1988). The verb mutability effect: Studies of the combinatorial semantics of nouns and verbs. In S. Small, G. Cottrell, and M. Tanenhaus (Eds.), *Lexical ambiguity resolution*, 343–382. Los Altos, CA: Morgan Kaufmann.

Katz, J. J. (1964). Semantic theory and the meaning of "good." *Journal of Philosophy, 61*, 739–766.

Kilgarriff, A. (1993). Dictionary word sense distinctions: An enquiry into their nature. *Computers and the Humanities, 26*, 365–387.

Kučera, H., and Francis, W. N. (1967). *The standard corpus of present-day edited American English* [the Brown Corpus]. (Electronic database.) Providence, RI: Brown University.

Matell, M. S., and Jacoby, J. (1971). Is there an optimal number of alternatives for Likert scale items? *Educational and Psychological Measurements, 31*, 657–674.

Schwanenfluegel, P. (1991). Why are abstract concepts hard to understand? In P. Schwanenfluegel (Ed.), *The psychology of word meaning*, 223–250. Hillsdale, NJ: Erlbaum.

Vendler, Z. (1984). Adverbs of action. In: *CLS 20.* Vol. 2, *Parasession on the Lexicon*, 297–307. Chicago: University of Chicago, Chicago Linguistic Society.

Chapter 10

WordNet and Class-Based Probabilities

Philip Resnik

10.1 INTRODUCTION

The availability of on-line information is changing the way researchers study and work with language.[1] It has changed the focus of applications, as information access to full text on the World Wide Web overtakes database interfaces as a priority (Foley and Pitkow 1994). It has changed research methodology, as large on-line corpora yield empirical data on every topic from child language acquisition (MacWhinney 1991) to on-line sentence processing (Merlo 1994). It has changed the definition of what constitutes a research result, as quantitative measures using common training and test sets become the standard for evaluation (e.g., Sundheim and Chinchor 1993; Hoffman 1995; Black 1991).

At the same time, it is clear that prior knowledge of language—the lexicons, grammars, and domain models of traditional natural language research in the artificial intelligence paradigm—still has an important role to play, even as it changes form to meet the demands of large scale and broad coverage. Attempts to acquire such knowledge automatically, though promising, are still in their infancy, and most successful methods still require a healthy amount of manual data annotation in order to get started. (As examples, consider manual bracketing in grammatical inference (Pereira and Schabes 1992), bootstrapping from sense-tagged material in word sense disambiguation (Yarowsky 1993), and training on disambiguated text for part-of-speech tagging (Brill 1993), though this is beginning to change (Brill 1995; Yarowsky 1995).)

More to the point, although some corpus-based methods are described as "purely statistical," there really is no such thing. Even the purest statistical methods embody prior knowledge: the algebraic structure of the underlying probability model captures, in nonquantitative terms, what assumptions are being made a priori about the nature of the data. Markov models, as used in part-of-speech tagging, demonstrate this nicely. These days they are the paradigm case of statistical methods in language processing, yet the assumptions they embody—about capturing dependencies in a finite-state setting—go straight to the heart of long-standing debates about the *grammatical* character of language (Chomsky 1957; Miller and Chomsky 1963; also see Abney 1996).

In this chapter I discuss one particular kind of prior knowledge, taxonomic lexical knowledge. My ultimate focus is a basic question about language: what combinations of words make sense, semantically? But exploring that question using WordNet and text corpora requires answering a more general question: how does one work with corpus-based statistical methods in the context of a taxonomy?

10.2 WORD CLASSES AND TAXONOMIES

10.2.1 Distributionally Derived Word Classes

Before getting involved in how taxonomies can be used in a corpus-based setting, it is worth asking whether a knowledge-based lexical taxonomy is actually necessary. There is, after all, a great deal of current work on deriving word classes directly from text. In this section I briefly review some of the issues, pointing out certain limitations of the more knowledge-free distributional approaches.[2] I then explore the ways in which distributional analysis and taxonomic knowledge can be combined.

Word classes, whether knowledge based or distributionally derived, are important in corpus-based language work because no collection of text is large enough to provide enough information about the usage of very infrequent words. This problem of sparse data persists as text collections grow larger and larger: even in a corpus on the order of tens or hundreds of millions of words, many words appear so infrequently that it is impossible to conclude anything statistically reliable about them.

One way to solve this problem is to make inferences about the behavior of a word, on the basis of words that are similar to it. This is analogous to making inferences about things in the world, on the basis of things that are similar to them. You may not know what witloof is, but if it is light colored and leafy and found in salads, this will probably lead you to infer other facts about it, such as the fact that it is edible, based on your experience with other things that have similar properties.

Table 10.1
General configuration for representing words in terms of distributional contexts. The representation of a word w_i is its row in the table (i.e., the vector $\langle f_{i1}, \ldots, f_{iM} \rangle$).

Word	Contextual feature				
	a_1	$\cdots$	a_j	$\cdots$	a_M
w_1					
$\vdots$					
w_i			f_{ij}		
$\vdots$					
w_N					

A great deal of recent work addresses the creation and use of classes of similar words, using lexical distributions in text corpora. The premise behind all such approaches is that the relatedness of words is reflected by similarities in their distributional contexts, as observed in large collections of naturally occurring text. This idea has a long history, often described in terms of Firth's (1957) pithy pronouncement that "You shall know a word by the company it keeps" and with Harris's (1968) distributional hypothesis, which suggests that "the meaning of entities, and the meaning of grammatical relations among them, is related to the restriction of combinations of these entities relative to other entities." These intuitions are often realized in implemented systems by creating a representation for each word that encodes the kinds of distributional contexts in which it appears and then calculating similarity or class membership on the basis of those representations.

Table 10.1 gives an overall picture of how words tend to be represented for distributional analyses of this kind. The w_i are the words that one is interested in representing. The a_j are things that can be observed in the context of a word when it is used in text (e.g., the word that appears immediately to its left). And each cell f_{ij} in the table typically contains the frequency with which word w_i is observed to appear in the context of a_j, or some number based on that frequency. A table of this kind can be thought of as defining an M-dimensional feature space, so that the row for each word, the vector $\langle f_{i1}, \ldots, f_{iM} \rangle$, can be interpreted as the coordinates for a point in that space. The analogy then extends to the notion of proximity in that space: the "semantic distance" between two words is measured as the distance between their corresponding points in the semantic space.

Most often the features of the space are themselves words. For example, Pereira, Tishby, and Lee (1993) define contexts in terms of verb-object constructions: w_i is a noun, and a_j a verb, and f_{ij} is computed as $p(a_j|w_i)$. That is, the representation of a noun consists in the distribution of verbs it is likely to be the direct object of. By hypothesis, nouns for which those *distributions* are similar will have *meanings* that are similar. Pereira, Tishby, and Lee explore this in a variety of experiments, using similarity between the distributional representations of nouns as the basis for hierarchical clustering, and in many cases the resulting clusters are satisfyingly coherent. For example, clustering of the 1,000 most frequent nouns in Grolier's encyclopedia on the basis of their distributional representations leads to such groupings as {*essay comedy poem treatise*} and {*recognition acclaim renown nomination*}.

Although results of this kind are encouraging, distributional approaches also tend to have a number of drawbacks. First, in general, the classes that emerge via distributional techniques are not identified with symbolic labels of any kind. For some applications this is not a problem, particularly in applications where measures of word similarity are used for improving quantitative estimates by smoothing together information about similar words (Brown et al. 1992; Grishman and Sterling 1993). When a symbolic component is involved, however, some method is needed for relating clusters to other information. For example, Schütze (1993) computes syntactically coherent word clusters automatically, but must manually identify which part-of-speech categories are to be associated with which clusters. Similarly, methods like the one proposed by Pereira, Tishby, and Lee show the promise of automatically identifying regions in semantic space corresponding to word senses, but if those senses are to be used in semantic interpretation, some mapping to discrete symbolic categories is likely to be necessary. Consider using natural language as an interface to a relational database: in order to produce a result, ultimately the system must be able to map from symbols within the semantic interpretation of the utterance to discrete relations within the database.

A second difficulty common in distributional approaches is the focus on word tokens rather than word senses. Consider, for example, the work of

Brown et al. (1992), who use distributional clustering techniques to derive word classes like those shown in (1).

(1) a. question questions asking answer answers answering
    b. write writes writing written wrote pen
    c. school classroom teaching grade math
    d. attorney counsel trial court judge

Distributional groupings of this kind are perceived as semantically coherent because readers assign an appropriate interpretation to each word on the basis of the other words in the group. However, most distributional clustering methods, including the one used by Brown et al., allow each word to appear in only one word class. As a result, it is difficult to see how their classification could succeed in grouping together *school* and *grade*, as shown in (1), yet also manage to encode the relationship between, say, *slope* and *grade*, without putting words that do not belong together into the same class. More generally, if each word is associated with a single point in semantic space, then the coordinates for a polysemous word will be determined by conflating the behavior of the individual senses, with the high-frequency senses having the greatest influence. Sometimes conflating word senses is not a problem, since distinct senses do share relevant properties—for example, the 'newspaper' and 'term paper' senses of *paper*. However, in other instances a single point in semantic space will represent a hodgepodge of distributional properties, not doing a good job of representing any of the word's senses.

A third, related problem arises when one tries to establish a semantics for the word classes that result from distributional methods. Although the representations or classes discovered are sometimes described as "semantic," the information captured by means of statistical analysis often defies simple description. For example, clusters hand-selected by Brown et al. as particularly "interesting" include the following (they list just the 10 most frequent items in each group):

(2) a. feet miles pounds degrees inches barrels tons acres meters bytes ...
    b. asking telling wondering instructing informing kidding reminding bothering thanking deposing ...

These groups are encouragingly coherent and even "semantic" in some sense—but notice that other information is encoded, as well, such as number (plural units of measurement) and inflection (verbs of communication in the progressive).

Furthermore, when one looks at arbitrarily chosen clusters, rather than handpicked examples, it is not clear exactly what information is being captured even in the more coherent cases. For example, Brown et al. present the following two groups among a set of clusters chosen at random for inspection:

(3) a. rise focus depend rely concentrate dwell capitalize embark intrude typewriting . . .
   b. aware unaware unsure cognizant apprised mindful partakers . . .

With the exception of *rise* and *typewriting*, the clustering in (3a) seems primarily to capture a set of verbs that tend to be followed by *on*. Similarly, although the group in (3b) seems more coherent, the presence of *partakers* is incongruous and strongly suggests that the clustering method has a hard time separating the semantic commonality underlying the class from the distributional property of being followed by the word *of*. Other clusters show even less semantic commonality. Beyond a connecting link among the first few items, they become increasingly opaque:

(4) a. cost expense risk profitability deferral earmarks capstone cardinality mintage reseller . . .
   b. force ethic stoppage force's conditioner stoppages conditioners waybill forwarder Atonabee . . .
   c. industry producers makers fishery Arabia growers addition medalist inhalation addict . . .

It would seem that the information captured using distributional techniques is often not precisely syntactic, nor purely semantic. And even among the more semantically coherent classes produced by distributional methods, such as those in (1), it is not clear what connects the members of these classes. *Pen* and *writing* are undoubtedly associated, as are *judge* and *trial* or *math* and *classroom*, but it is difficult to go beyond that to a discussion of what general properties hold of classes discovered by this procedure. The best description seems to be "words that tend to appear in similar contexts," which is no more than a restatement of the method by which the classes were derived.

Finally, the sensitivity of distributional methods to observable evidence in a corpus is both a blessing and a curse. Deriving linguistic knowledge from lexical behavior in a corpus has the advantage of tuning that knowledge to the kind of language found in that corpus, a clear benefit if language use there reflects the facts that one is interested in. On the other hand, overtuning can be a problem: relying heavily on a corpus means that the resulting model will inherit the idiosyncrasies of the material on which it has been trained. Church and Mercer (1993) argue that this problem is unavoidable and suggest that it is best mitigated by aiming for diversity, so that "quirks [are] uncorrelated across a range of different corpora" (p. 19).

10.2.2   Probabilistic Models Involving a Taxonomy

The four problems just described—absence of symbolic labels, failure to respect word sense distinctions, absence of a semantics, and oversensitivity to specific observed data—are all addressed by WordNet. First, symbolic labels are available for automatic processing, in the form of unique synset (synonym set) identifiers, and it is also not difficult to establish a reasonable convention for human-readable symbolic descriptions of synsets.[3] Second, word sense distinctions are, of course, the basis for the taxonomy. Third, the network's basic taxonomic relationships, synonymy and hyponymy, can be given a reasonable semantic description in terms of a differential theory of semantics and the inheritance of plausible entailments (Miller 1990; Resnik 1993a, chap. 2). And fourth, like most dictionaries and thesauruses, WordNet was designed to reflect general knowledge and not the idiosyncrasies of any particular domain.

However, WordNet, also like most dictionaries and thesauruses, is a repository of knowledge about linguistic relationships, not language use, which means that it has limitations of its own. Ultimately, understanding word meaning—and using lexical knowledge in practical systems— requires attention to words in context. This is not the kind of information that one can expect to find in a lexicon. But it is, of course, just the sort of information that distributional analysis provides.

The most natural first step in using WordNet with distributional methods is to define a probability model—and from this point on, I will restrict myself to considering models involving just WordNet's noun taxonomy, though some of the principles may hold true for the other parts of speech, as well.[4] Taking a distributional approach does not absolutely require that a probabilistic framework be adopted (e.g., see Brill 1993), but doing so has a number of advantages. In terms of characterizing the kind of information being used, a probabilistic framework makes explicit what aspects of the taxonomy will play a role in the model, and it identifies what observable information is to be considered relevant. In terms of theoretical foundations, a well-defined underlying probability model is a prerequisite if one is to use statistical and information-theoretic methods.

Working with WordNet in a probabilistic setting is actually more difficult than it appears at first, compared to working with many other probabilistic models. The difficulty is that, although the most straight-forward sample space for the model would consist of words, the taxonomy is organized in terms of word senses. Consider, by way of contrast, a coin-flipping experiment, where the sample space consists of the set {HEADS, TAILS}. When you observe a coin flip, it is easy to identify which element of the sample space represents the outcome of the experiment. The same is true of many word-based probabilistic models. In the case of Word-Net, however, this is not true: each word belongs to many classes in the taxonomy, so it is not immediately clear which taxonomic class should receive the "credit" when a word is observed. Relating observable tokens to unobservable word senses is the central problem in formalizing a probabilistic model involving the taxonomy.

There are really two different dimensions to this problem. The first is *sense ambiguity*: a given instance of a word might represent any of the synsets to which the word belongs. The second is *level of abstraction*: even when an intended sense is known, that sense can be described in succes-sively more abstract terms as one moves up the hierarchy, and it is not clear how to determine which level of description is the appropriate one. I think of these two dimensions as *horizontal* and *vertical* ambiguity, respectively, since sense distinctions tend not to involve hierarchical rela-tionships, and questions about level of abstraction always do.

Having described the problem in those terms, I will consider a number of possible solutions.

• *Fixing levels of abstraction*: One possibility is to select a single level of abstraction in advance and to consider categorization in WordNet, for probabilistic purposes, only in terms of classes at that level. This elimi-nates the problem of vertical ambiguity. Yarowsky (1992) adopts this approach in his work with Roget's thesaurus, using the thousand or so numbered categories in that thesaurus as the chosen level of abstraction. Unfortunately, however, WordNet lacks any meaningful notion of levels as found in Roget's. For the same reason, it is not possible to define a probabilistic model in terms of multiple levels of abstraction, the proba-bilities at each level summing to 1.

• *Flattening the taxonomy*: In the absence of well-defined levels of abstraction, another approach is to adapt WordNet by partitioning the full collection of synsets into a set of flat categories, as done by Hearst and Schütze (1996). Their approach treats the full set of synsets as a collection to be broken into "buckets" of roughly equal size, with each synset going into only one bucket, and each synset in a bucket bearing some semantic or conceptual relationship to the others (e.g., ⟨football⟩ and ⟨referee⟩ might end up grouped together). This eliminates the problem of vertical ambiguity, effectively creating a cut through the taxonomy that is parameterized by the desired size of the categories in the partition. Because Hearst and Schütze assign each synset to only one category, however, multiple inheritance can lead to some arbitrary choices in assigning synsets to categories. More generally, fixing a single level of abstraction in WordNet in advance, as would be done on the model of Yarowsky (1992) or Hearst and Schütze (1996), precludes the possibility of letting the particular application, or the distributional properties of the language sample in question, automatically determine what levels of abstraction are appropriate.

• *Bayesian networks*: Bayesian networks (or belief networks) can be used to formalize dependencies in a probabilistic setting (for an excellent introduction, see Russell and Norvig 1995), and WordNet's structure lends itself to a network representation. One could, for example, imagine creating a Bayesian network based on WordNet in which the nodes (random variables) corresponded to synsets, and dependencies corresponded to IS-A links. This would provide a way to work with the existing structure of the network, addressing both horizontal and vertical ambiguity within a well-understood framework. However, algorithms for Bayesian inference, particularly in multiply-connected networks, have not been applied on the scale that WordNet would require: the WordNet taxonomy would give rise to a network one to two orders of magnitude larger than the largest Bayesian networks researchers have worked with (on the order of 1,000 to 2,000 nodes, except for special limited-topology cases). In addition, the most natural way of formalizing WordNet as a Bayesian network would associate a separate probability distribution with each node in the taxonomy, and for some purposes—for example, computing information-theoretic quantities such as entropy—such a model is not appropriate, since they require defining a single random variable ranging over Word-Net classes.

• *Hidden models and reestimation*: In some ways, the problem of working with WordNet in a probabilistic setting resembles the problem of formalizing models for stochastic part-of-speech tagging, when supervised training data are not assumed to be available. In the case of models for tagging parts of speech, what is observable (the sequence of words) is treated as arising from an underlying source that is unobservable (the sequence of tags), in much the same way that observable word tokens reflect underlying word senses in WordNet. In an unsupervised setting, probabilistic taggers are typically trained using an expectation-maximization (EM) algorithm (Dempster, Laird, and Rubin 1977), a process often called *reestimation* because it involves iteratively improving initial probability estimates by making use of observable data. Although reestimation is a way to improve probability estimates, regardless of the model, simply adapting the hidden models and reestimation algorithms of part-of-speech tagging is probably not a solution in and of itself, again because of issues of scale. Given the granularity of WordNet, the number of possible word sense sequences is vastly larger than the corresponding number of possible tag sequences, so the number of parameters to estimate in a hidden model would be correspondingly, and prohibitively, larger.

Considering different approaches to augmenting WordNet with probabilities has brought out a number of issues. Fist, scale is clearly important, since WordNet's size and fine-grainedness mean that any probabilistic model preserving the information in the taxonomy will have a great many parameters. Second, vertical ambiguity introduces a dimension not found in other probabilistic models such as those used in part-of-speech tagging or language modeling for speech recognition; I would argue that it is preferable to keep vertical ambiguity as part of the probabilistic framework, to be resolved on an application- or corpus-dependent basis, rather than restricting the model in advance to particular levels of abstraction. Third, not all probabilistic adaptations of WordNet provide the same foundation for computing information-theoretic quantities such as entropy. Since information-theoretic constructs play an important role in models involving words, the choice of model should make it possible to make use of them in class-based setting, as well.

These considerations have led me to adopt the following probabilistic formalization of the WordNet noun taxonomy. Define a probability space $\langle \Omega, \mathscr{F}, p \rangle$ consisting of

$$\Omega = \{c_1, c_2, \ldots, c_k\}$$

$$\mathscr{F} = \mathscr{P}(\Omega)$$

$$p : \mathscr{F} \to [0, 1],$$

where Ω is the complete set of unique synset identifiers in the taxonomy, $\mathscr{F}$, the power set of Ω, is simply the maximally fine-grained event space based on such a sample space, and p is a probability function. Thus, the probability space here is just like the space for rolling a die; in this case it just happens that the die has k sides.

The structure of the taxonomy is captured by the following constraint on the probability function p: if c_1 IS-A c_2, then $p(c_2) \geq p(c_1)$. This requirement reflects the intuition that as the level of abstraction increases, so does the probability. It does not, however, mean that the probability of a node in the taxonomy must be the *sum* of the probabilities of its child nodes. If that were the case, then one could not have a model in which $\{c_1, c_2, \ldots, c_k\}$ included all the nodes at all levels within the taxonomy, and still have

$$\sum_{i=1}^{k} p(c_i) = 1.$$

Yet just such a model is what one needs in order to define a random variable over the entire space of classes in WordNet, and information-theoretic functions of that variable such as entropy.

This formalization can be interpreted as saying that, when a noun is realized in text or speech, it reflects an underlying intent to communicate semantic content associated with a taxonomic category. Exactly *which* taxonomic category is often not clear, owing to both horizontal and vertical ambiguity. The sentences in (5) illustrate this for a familiar case of horizontal, or sense, ambiguity: *bank* can refer to a building, to a river-bank, or to an organization, among other things.[5] The sentences in (6) illustrate the less often considered, and perhaps less clear cut, question of what level of description is relevant in a particular utterance. In (6a) the entailments associated with *wine* as an alcoholic beverage are relevant; in (6b) drinkability, not alcohol content, is primary; and in (6c) what is most relevant is that *wine* describes a liquid.

(5) a. I walked into the *bank* and deposited my paycheck.
    b. Bill walked along the east *bank* of the river.
    c. Mary is president of a *bank* with six thousand employees.

(6) a. I decided not to drive because I'd had too much *wine*.
    b. Bill was thirsty so he decided to have some *wine*.
    c. Mary cleaned up the spilled *wine* with a sponge.

The monotonicity requirement—that probability increase monotonically as one moves up the hierarchy—reflects the interpretation of the IS-A relationship in terms of inheritance of entailments. In (6a) and (6b) liquidness may not be of primary concern, but it is nonetheless entailed by the use of this sense of *wine* in the sentence. One should note that logical entailment is probably too restrictive a notion to form the basis for a semantics of the WordNet taxonomy—I have proposed elsewhere (Resnik 1993a) that the semantics of synonymy and inheritance in WordNet be understood in terms of a relationship called *plausible entailment*.[6]

Though not perfect, this model has a number of attractive properties. Placing all the concepts in the taxonomy within the same probability model means that there need be no single, predefined level of abstraction; rather, vertical ambiguity can be resolved by statistical means on the basis of distributional information in much the same fashion as horizontal, or sense, ambiguity. It also makes it possible to define a random variable ranging over all the classes in the taxonomy. Finally, by reflecting the structure of the taxonomy as a constraint on the probability function p, rather than in the algebraic structure of the probability model, the model is simplified, and disambiguation issues become a part of the parameter estimation problem.

At present, estimating the parameters of the probability model on the basis of corpus data is quite straightforward, the credit for an observed noun being distributed equally among all the concepts subsuming any sense of that noun. That is,

$$\text{freq}(c) = \sum_{w \in words(c)} \frac{1}{|classes(w)|} \text{freq}(w), \tag{1}$$

where $words(c)$ is the set of words in any synset subsumed by c, and where $classes(w)$ is the set $\{c | w \in words(c)\}$. (This estimation scheme could easily be modified to take into account a priori or contextually determined word sense probabilities, or used as the first step in iterative re-estimation.) There are many ways to estimate class probabilities p(c) on the basis of such a frequency distribution; in the work reported here I use maximum likelihood estimates (MLE). Although there are known problems with maximum likelihood estimates of probability, this method seems a reasonable starting point, especially since one of its main draw-backs—the assignment of zero probability to all unseen data—is in fact one of the problems that work with word classes is attempting to resolve (cf. Pereira, Tishby, and Lee 1993).

The maximum likelihood estimation of probabilities is straightforward:

$$\hat{p}(c) = \frac{\text{freq}(c)}{N}, \tag{2}$$

where $N = \sum_{c'} \text{freq}(c')$, for c' ranging over all classes in WordNet. The calculation of joint probabilities is similarly straightforward: if the observed sample contains co-occurrences (x, w), where x is an element of some set $\mathcal{X}$ of tokens, one need only replace equation (1) with

$$\text{freq}(x, c) = \sum_{w \in words(c)} \frac{1}{|classes(w)|} \text{freq}(x, w). \tag{3}$$

For example, a training sample derived from corpus data might contain pairs consisting of a verb and its direct object.

Note that, in the absence of sense disambiguation, it is not unreasonable to distribute the credit for an observed noun equally among all the classes subsuming it, as a first approximation. This works because related words tend to be ambiguous in different ways. For example, consider the observation of two verb-object combinations, *drink wine* and *drink water*. On the basis of these observations, the joint frequency will be incremented for each class containing *wine* in any sense—including, for example, ⟨chromatic_color⟩. Similarly, the second pair will be recorded as a co-occurrence between *drink* and inappropriate categorizations of *water* such as ⟨body_of_water⟩. However, evidence for co-occurrence will *accumulate* only for classes containing both *water* and *wine*, such as ⟨beverage⟩. The cumulative evidence of co-occurrence with *drink* will thus tend to support appropriate interpretations, and counts with inappropriate senses will appear only as low frequencies dispersed throughout the taxonomy. A similar point is made by Yarowsky (1992), commenting on the calculation of statistics using the numbered categories in Roget's thesaurus:

While the level of noise introduced through polysemy is substantial, it can usually be tolerated because the spurious senses are distributed through the 1041 other categories, whereas the signal is concentrated in just one. (p. 455)

Given the much larger set of categories in WordNet, the dispersal of inappropriate senses should be even more effective. However, using classes at all levels of the WordNet taxonomy has its disadvantages, relative to the flat set of Roget's categories used by Yarowsky: classes low in the taxonomy accumulate less evidence than classes higher up. For example, the co-occurrence of *break* with various body parts (arm, leg, etc.) provides ample evidence for an association between that verb and the class

⟨body_part⟩, even though each of the co-occurring lexical items is multiply ambiguous. However, the frequent co-occurrence of *blow* and *nose* provides little evidence to distinguish between the sense of *nose* as a body part and, say, its sense as the front part of an airplane. Examples such as this one make it clear that one danger of working with multiple levels in a taxonomy, in the absence of reliable word sense disambiguation, is that among small classes it can be more difficult to distinguish which correlations are signal and which are noise.

10.3   MODELING SELECTIONAL PREFERENCES

Many aspects of the probabilistic framework described in the previous section were motivated by the particular question of how verbs and their arguments can be combined. My interest in WordNet began with the question of how easily one can predict the kind of direct object that will appear, given a particular choice of verb. The context was a discussion of verbs in English for which an indefinite direct object can sometimes be omitted, such as *eat* (see, e.g., Lehrer 1970; Fellbaum and Kegl 1989; Cote 1992; Levin 1993). This problem clearly bore a similarity to word prediction in stochastic language modeling for speech recognition, where predicting the next word given prior context is the primary goal. However, in this case the problem involved not predicting a word *token*, but predicting some aspects of *meaning*—the *kind* of direct object that will appear (e.g., some kind of food), not necessarily the direct object itself.

The problem at first appears to be one that is already well understood. Selectional preferences, formalized in traditional terms as Boolean selectional restrictions (Katz and Fodor 1964), characterize the potential arguments of verbs in terms of their semantic properties. On closer inspection, however, the mechanism of selectional restrictions falls short of what is needed for this task. In addition to well-known criticisms of the definitional semantics underlying the Katz-Fodor approach (see, e.g., McCawley 1968; Fodor 1977; Armstrong, Gleitman, and Gleitman 1983; Resnik 1993a), little attention has been paid to the problem of automatically acquiring such constraints. Doing so requires a characterization of the semantic space on a far larger scale than is found in traditional settings— McCawley (1968) argues convincingly that the representational vocabulary of selectional restrictions cannot be limited to a small set of semantic primitives, as suggested by Katz and Fodor. In addition, the statement of the problem in terms of how *easily* one can predict argument properties

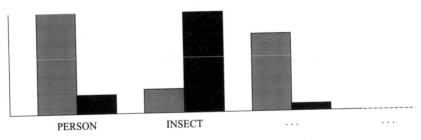

Figure 10.1
Prior and posterior distributions over argument classes. (▧ = prior, $p_R(c)$; ■ = posterior, $p_R(c \mid buzz)$)

strongly suggests the need for a quantitative characterization, which traditional Boolean selectional restrictions do not provide.

WordNet is well suited to this problem in theoretical terms, because its underlying semantics is nondefinitional, and in practical terms, because it is machine readable and covers a large subset of English. The probabilistic adaptation of WordNet described in the previous section allows for continuous-valued constraints on semantic combination; the remainder of this section is devoted to formalizing those constraints and illustrating their properties (also see Resnik 1996).

The intuition behind the statistical model of selectional preference is illustrated in figure 10.1. The *prior* distribution $p_R(c)$ captures the probability that a class will occur as the argument in verb-argument relation R, regardless of the identity of the verb.[7] For example, given that R is the verb-subject relationship, the prior probability for ⟨person⟩ tends to be significantly higher than the prior probability for ⟨insect⟩. However, once the identity of the verb is taken into account, the probabilities can change: if the verb is *buzz*, then the probability for ⟨insect⟩ as subject can be expected to the higher than its prior, and ⟨person⟩ will likely be lower. In probabilistic terms, it is the difference between this conditional or *posterior* distribution and the prior distribution that determines selectional preference.

Information theory provides an appropriate way to quantify the difference between the prior and posterior distributions, in the form of relative entropy (Kullback and Leibler 1951). The relative entropy between two probability distributions, $D(d_1 \| d_2)$, can be viewed as a measure of how much information is lost by using d_2 to approximate d_1, with lower values representing better approximations and a value of zero if and only if $d_2 = d_1$. For example, the average mutual information $I(X; Y)$ is equivalent to $D(p(x, y)\|p(x)p(y))$, that is, a measure of how well the independence distribution $p(x)p(y)$ approximates the actual joint distribution $p(x,y)$. Similarly, the *selectional preference strength* of a verb is defined as

$$S_R(v) = D(p(c|v)\|p(c)) = \sum_c p(c|v) \log \frac{p(c|v)}{p(c)}. \tag{4}$$

Intuitively, $S_R(v)$ measures how much information, in bits, verb v provides about the conceptual class of its argument. The better $p(c)$ approximates $p(c|v)$, the less influence v is having on its argument, and therefore the less strong its selectional preference.

Given this definition, a natural way to characterize the "semantic fit" of a particular class as the argument to a verb is by its relative contribution to the overall selectional preference strength. In particular, classes that fit very well can be expected to have higher posterior probabilities, compared to their priors, as is the case for ⟨insect⟩ in figure 10.1. Formally, *selectional association* is defined as

$$A_R(v, c) = \frac{1}{S_R(v)} p(c|v) \log \frac{p(c|v)}{p(c)}. \tag{5}$$

Since $I(v; c) = \log \frac{p(c|v)}{p(c)}$, this is closely related to mutual information.

There are several things to notice about these measures. First, the prior and posterior distributions range over all the classes in the taxonomy; thus, the characterization of selectional preference described here takes into account all levels of abstraction in a way that might be described as holistic. Figure 10.2 provides an illustration: it shows the selectional behavior of two verbs, *eat* (above) and *find* (below), as computed using the brown Corpus of American English (Francis and Kučera 1982) to provide probability estimates. WordNet classes are lined up along the x-axis, and the vertical bar for each indicates its selectional association as direct object of the verb. As one might expect, the selectional profile for *eat* has a greater overall magnitude than the profile for *find*, as measured by selectional preference strength. Moreover, the profile is more specific: the class with the highest value (far left) describes the conceptual category of foods, and some other classes with particularly high values include substances and meals. In contrast, the selectional profile for *find* shows a far weaker and less specific pattern of preference. Notably, however, this is *not* equivalent to saying that *find* places no constraints at all on its direct object.

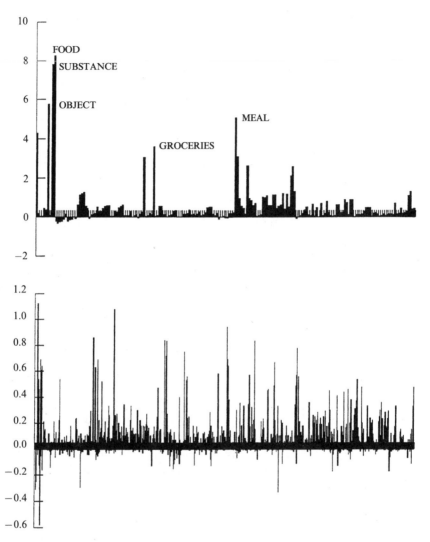

Figure 10.2
Top, the selectional behavior of *eat*; *bottom*, the selectional behavior of *find*.

Table 10.2
Strength of selectional preference for direct objects

Verb	Preference strength	Verb	Preference strength
bring	1.33	pack	4.12
call	1.52	play	2.51
catch	2.47	pour	4.80
do	1.84	pull	2.77
drink	4.38	push	2.87
eat	3.51	put	1.24
explain	2.39	read	2.35
find	0.96	say	2.82
get	0.82	see	1.06
give	0.79	show	1.39
hang	3.35	sing	3.58
have	0.43	steal	3.52
hear	1.70	take	0.93
hit	2.49	want	1.52
like	2.59	watch	1.97
make	0.72	wear	3.13
open	2.93	write	2.54

Although no clear pattern is evident among classes with positive values of selectional association, the two WordNet classes most *dispreferred* as objects of *find* are those describing actions and states.

The second thing to note is that selectional preference strength, as defined in equation (4), collapses the entire selectional profile for a verb into a single number that represents how strongly the verb selects for the argument in question. Table 10.2 shows a set of verbs that occur frequently in a collection of parent-child interactions (Anne Lederer, personal communication), each with the strength of its selectional preference for the direct object (as measured using probability estimates acquired from the Standard Corpus of Present-Day Edited American English (the Brown Corpus; see Francis and Kučera 1982)). Qualitatively, verbs that constrain their objects strongly (e.g., *drink*, *eat*, *open*) show a greater selectional preference strength than verbs for which the object is intuitively less constrained (e.g., *find*, *get*, *give*, *take*).

Third, when selectional association is used to assess the semantic fit of an argument with a verb, both horizontal and vertical ambiguity are addressed in interesting ways. Table 10.3 presents a selected sample of

Table 10.3
Selectional association for plausible objects

Verb	Object	A(*Verb, Object*)	Class
write	letter	7.26	⟨writing⟩
read	article	6.80	⟨writing⟩
warn	driver	4.73	⟨person⟩
hear	story	1.89	⟨communication⟩
remember	reply	1.31	⟨statement⟩
expect	visit	0.59	⟨act⟩

plausible verb-object pairs, taken from a study by Holmes, Stowe, and Cupples (1989); the values for selectional association in the table were obtained according to equation (5), using verb-object probability estimates from the Brown Corpus. I used a larger sample of the data from the study by Holmes, Stowe, and Cupples in an experiment to assess how well the computational model predicts human judgments of argument plausibility (Resnik 1996), and the experiment did confirm that the model generally assigns higher values of selectional association for plausible arguments than it does for implausible arguments. However, what is most interesting here is the way in which strongly selecting verbs "choose" the sense of their arguments. For example, *letter* has three senses in WordNet ('written message', 'varsity letter', 'alphabetic character') and belongs to 19 classes in all, when all levels of abstraction are considered. In order to approximate its plausibility as the object of *write*, the selectional association with *write* was computed for all 19 classes, and the highest value returned—in this case, ⟨writing⟩ ('anything expressed in letters; reading matter'). Since only one sense of *letter* has this class as an ancestor, this method of determining argument plausibility has, in essence, performed sense disambiguation as a side effect. I have begun to explore the application of this idea to sense disambiguation in unrestricted text (Resnik 1997).

Fourth, the selectional association measure deals with vertical ambiguity in an interesting way. Consider the verb-object combination *drink wine*. Table 10.4 shows the WordNet classes that subsume *wine* in its sense as a beverage, together with the selectional association of each class considered as the object of *drink*. As the table shows, describing *wine* at a higher level of abstraction than its immediate synset—⟨alcoholic beverage⟩ rather than ⟨wine, vino⟩—leads to a higher value for selectional association

Table 10.4
Selectional association of classes of *wine* as direct object of *drink* (in the sense of *wine* as a beverage)

A (drink, c)	c
0.38	⟨wine/vino⟩
5.04	⟨alcoholic_beverage⟩
7.65	⟨beverage/drink⟩
5.70	⟨food/nutrient⟩
5.61	⟨substance/matter⟩
2.45	⟨inanimate_object⟩
1.13	⟨entity⟩

(equation (5)), because the posterior probability p(c|drink) increases as one moves to classes c higher in the taxonomy. (This is guaranteed by the monotonicity constraint.) However, as one moves to "too high" a level of abstraction (e.g., ⟨substance⟩), the association score actually goes down again, as the posterior distribution stops increasing and the prior probability p(c) in the denominator begins to dominate.

The verb-object pairs in table 10.3 illustrate this, as well. As the object of *write*, the word *letter* is characterized by the class ⟨writing⟩, which is a level or two more general than ⟨letter⟩, ('a written message addressed to a person or organization'), but a level or two more specific than ⟨communication⟩ ('something that is communicated between people or groups'). But ⟨communication⟩ is just the right level of description for *story*, appearing as the object of *hear*, since it subsumes the sense of *story* as a lie or fib, as a news report, as a chronicle or narrative description, or as a work of fiction. As the object of *read*, the most strongly associated class subsuming *story* is naturally ⟨writing⟩.

10.4 CONCLUSIONS

Combining taxonomic lexical knowledge with probabilistic models requires further exploration. In this chapter I have outlined some of the issues, in particular the following:

• why one would wish to use a knowledge-based taxonomy rather than induce lexical knowledge directly from text corpora using statistical methods,

- what properties a probabilistic taxonomic framework should have, and
- how a computational model based on such a framework can be used to characterize selectional constraints.

Ambiguity turns out to be a recurring theme, including both simple word sense ambiguity and the question of what level of abstraction to use in formulating a conceptual description of a word in context. The probability space used here takes a minimalist approach, affording all classes in the noun taxonomy equal status and thus allowing maximum freedom in the design of algorithms to distinguish among senses and among levels of abstraction. The model of selectional constraints takes advantage of that flexibility by allowing observed corpus data to determine the probability estimates and therefore, by way of the selectional association measure, to determine which senses and levels of abstraction are most appropriate given a particular combination of verb and argument.[8] The model turns out to make reasonable predictions about human judgments of argument plausibility obtained by psycholinguistic methods and about the omissibility of direct objects (Resnik 1996; Olsen and Resnik 1997); in addition, closely related proposals have been applied in syntactic disambiguation (Resnik 1993b; Lauer 1994) and to automatic acquisition of somewhat more traditional selectional restrictions in the form of weighted disjunctions (Ribas 1994). In recent work I have been exploring the use of a closely related probabilistic framework to characterize semantic similarity in the WordNet noun taxonomy (Resnik 1995b) and to use semantic similarity as the basis for word sense disambiguation (Resnik 1995a).

Notes

1. Much of this work was conducted as part of my doctoral dissertation at the University of Pennsylvania. I gratefully acknowledge the discussions and criticism of Steve Abney, Michael Brent, Henry Gleitman, Lila Gleitman, Ellen Hays, Aravind Joshi, Judith Klavans, Mark Liberman, Mitch Marcus, Peter Norvig, Jeff Siskind, and an anonymous reviewer, as well as the financial support of grants ARO DAAL 03-89-C-0031, DARPA N00014-90-J-1863, and Ben Franklin 91S.3078C-1, and an IBM Graduate Fellowship.

2. For a more comprehensive review, see Resnik 1993a.

3. For example, Peter Norvig (personal communication) has explored augmenting a singleton synset with terms from its immediate superclass, among others (e.g., distinguishing *file/record* from *file/hand_tool*).

4. I also assume throughout that (at most) the IS-A links in the taxonomy are relevant—that is, there is no attempt to model other relationships encoded in WordNet such as meronymy (PART-OF).

5. Notice that sense ambiguity in WordNet is finer grained than homonymy: typically the senses of *bank* found in (5a) and in (5c) would be considered instances of the same homonym.

6. Plausible entailment is based on a notion of implication found in work in lexical semantics by Lyons (1961) and discussed by Sparck Jones (1964): the plausible entailments associated with membership in a class are those properties that any reasonable speaker would infer of something by virtue of its membership in that class. For example, the synset {*board, plank*}, viewed as a taxonomic class, has associated with it such plausible entailments as "*x* is flat" and "*x* can be used for building things."

7. Although verbs are the focus of attention here, the model is equally applicable to any predicate taking a noun as its argument, such as adjectives and prepositions.

8. Li and Abe (1995), motivated by many of the same considerations, have recently proposed an alternative model to the one presented here of using probabilities with WordNet, based on the use of the minimum description length principle to select relevant subsets of the taxonomy on the basis of corpus data. They have applied their model to the problem of prepositional phrase attachment and the approach strikes me as both elegant and promising. Velardi and colleagues have also recently proposed interesting techniques to tune taxonomic knowledge on the basis of corpus data (Velardi and Cucchiarelli 1997).

References

Abney, S. (1996). Statistical methods and linguistics. In J. Klavans and P. Resnik (Eds.), *The balancing act: Combining symbolic and statistical approaches to language*, 1–26. Cambridge, MA: MIT Press.

Armstrong, S., Gleitman, L., and Gleitman, H. (1983). What some concepts might not be. *Cognition, 13*, 263–308.

Black, E. (1991). A procedure for quantitatively comparing the syntactic coverage of English grammars. In *Proceedings of the February 1991 DARPA Speech and Natural Language Workshop*, 306–311. San Francisco: Morgan Kaufmann.

Brill, E. (1993). *A corpus-based approach to language learning.* Unpublished doctoral dissertation, University of Pennsylvania, Philadelphia.

Brill, E. (1995). Unsupervised learning of disambiguation rules for part of speech tagging. In *Proceedings of the Third Workshop on Very Large Corpora*. Association for Computational Linguistics. [To appear in *Natural language processing using very large corpora*. Dordrecht: Kluwer.]

Brown, P. F., Della Pietra, V. J., deSouza, P. V., Lai, J. C., and Mercer, R. L. (1992). Class-based n-gram models of natural language. *Computational Linguistics, 18*, 467–480.

Chomsky, N. (1957). *Syntactic structures.* The Hague: Mouton.

Church, K. W., and Mercer, R. (1993). Introduction to the special issue on computational linguistics using large corpora. *Computational Linguistics, 19*, 1–24.

Cote, S. (1992). *Discourse functions of two types of null objects in English.* Paper presented at the 66th Annual Meeting of the Linguistic Society of America, Philadelphia, PA.

Dempster, A., Laird, N., and Rubin, D. (1977). Maximum likelihood from incomplete data via the EM algorithm. *Journal of the Royal Statistical Society, 39*(B), 1–38.

Fellbaum, C., and Kegl, J. (1989). Taxonomic structures and cross-category linking in the lexicon. In *Proceedings of the Sixth Eastern States Conference on Linguistics,* 93–104. Columbus: Ohio State University, Department of Linguistics.

Firth, J. R. (1957). *A synopsis of linguistic theory 1930–1955.* London: Longman.

Fodor, J. D. (1977). *Semantics: Theories of meaning of generative grammar.* Cambridge, MA: Harvard University Press.

Foley, J., and Pitkow, J. (Eds.). (1994). *Research priorities for the World-Wide Web: Report of the NSF workshop sponsored by the Information, Robotics, and Intelligent Systems Division.* National Science Foundation. Available: http://www.cc.gatech.edu/gvu/nsf-ws/report/Report.html

Francis, W. N., and Kučera, H. (1982). *Frequency analysis of English usage: Lexicon and grammar.* Boston: Houghton Mifflin.

Grishman, R., and Sterling, J. (1993). Smoothing of automatically generated selectional constraints. In *Proceedings of the ARPA Human Language Technology Workshop,* 254–259. San Francisco: Morgan Kaufmann.

Harris, Z. (1968). *Mathematical structures of language.* New York: Wiley.

Hearst, M., and Schütze, H. (1996). Customizing a lexicon to better suit a computational task. In B. Boguraev and J. Pustejovsky (Eds.), *Corpus processing for lexical acquisition,* 77–96. Cambridge, MA: MIT Press.

Hoffman, D. (1995). Text REtrieval (TREC) home page [on-line]. Available: http://potomac.ncsl.nist.gov/TREC/

Holmes, V. M., Stowe, L., and Cupples, L. (1989). Lexical expectations in parsing complement-verb sentences. *Journal of Memory and Language, 28,* 668–689.

Katz, J. J., and Fodor, J. A. (1964). The structure of a semantic theory. In J. A. Fodor and J. J. Katz (Eds.), *The structure of language,* 479–518. Englewood Cliffs, NJ: Prentice-Hall.

Kullback, S., and Leibler, R. A. (1951). On information and sufficiency. *Annals of Mathematical Statistics, 22,* 79–86.

Lauer, M. (1994). Conceptual association for compound noun analysis. In *Proceedings of the 32nd Annual Meeting of the Association for Computational Linguistics,* 337–339. Student Session. Association for Computational Linguistics. Available: http://xxx.lanl.gov/abs/cmp-lg/, number 9409002

Lehrer, A. (1970). Verbs and deletable objects. *Lingua, 25,* 227–254.

Levin, B. (1993). *English verb classes and alternations.* Chicago: University of Chicago Press.

Li, H., and Abe, N. (1995). Generalizing case frames using a thesaurus and the MDL principle. In *Proceedings of the International Conference on Recent Advances in Natural Language Processing*, Velingrad, Bulgaria, September 1995, 239–248. Available: http://xxx.lanl.gov/abs/comp-lg/, number 9507011

Lyons, J. (1961). *A structural theory of semantics and its application to lexical subsystems in the vocabulary of Plato*. Doctoral dissertation, University of Cambridge, England. Published as *Structural semantics*, No. 20 of the Publications of the Philological Society, Oxford, 1963.

MacWhinney, B. (1991). *The CHILDES project: Tools for analyzing talk*. Hillsdale, NJ: Erlbaum.

McCawley, J. (1968). The role of semantics in a grammar. In E. Bach and R. Harms (Eds.), *Universals in linguistic theory*, 124–169. New York: Holt, Rinehart and Winston.

Merlo, P. (1994). A corpus-based analysis of verb continuation frequencies for syntactic processing. *Journal of Psycholinguistic Research, 23*, 435–457.

Miller, G. A. (Ed.). (1990). *WordNet: An on-line lexical database*. Special issue of *International Journal of Lexicography, 3*(4).

Miller, G. A., and Chomsky, N. (1963). Finitary models of language users. In R. Luce, R. Bush, and E. Galanter (Eds.), *Handbook of mathematical psychology*, vol. 2. New York: Wiley.

Olsen, M. B., and Resnik, P. (1997). Implicit object constructions and the (in)transitivity continuum. In *Papers from the 33rd Regional Meeting of the Chicago Linguistic Society*. Chicago: University of Chicago, Chicago Linguistic Society. Available: ftp://ftp.umiacs.umd.edu/pub/resnik/papers/cls1997_paper.ps.gz

Pereira, F., and Schabes, Y. (1992). Inside-outside reestimation from partially bracketed corpora. In *Proceedings of the February 1992 DARPA Speech and Natural Language Workshop*, 122–127. San Francisco: Morgan Kaufmann.

Pereira, F., Tishby, N., and Lee, L. (1993). Distributional clustering of English words. In *Proceedings of the 31st Annual Meeting of the Association for Computational Linguistics*, 183–190. Association for Computational Linguistics.

Resnik, P. (1993a). *Selection and information: A class-based approach to lexical relationships*. Unpublished doctoral dissertation, University of Pennsylvania, Philadelphia. Available: ftp://ftp.cis.upenn.edu/pub/ircs/tr/93–42.ps.Z

Resnik, P. (1993b). Semantic classes and syntactic ambiguity. In *Proceedings of the ARPA Human Language Technology Workshop*, 278–283. San Francisco: Morgan Kaufmann.

Resnik, P. (1995a). Disambiguating noun groupings with respect to WordNet senses. In *Proceedings of the Third Workshop on Very Large Corpora*. Association for Computational Linguistics. Available: http://xxx.lanl.gov/abs/cmp-lg/, number 9511006

Resnik, P. (1995b). Using information content to evaluate semantic similarity in a taxonomy. In *Proceedings of the 14th International Joint Conference on Artificial*

Intelligence (IJCAI-95), 448–453. San Francisco: Morgan Kaufmann. Available: http://xxx.lanl.gov/abs/cmp-lg/, number 951107

Resnik, P. (1996). Selectional constraints: An information-theoretic model and its computational realization. *Cognition, 61*, 127–159.

Resnik, P. (1997). Selectional preference and sense disambiguation. In *Proceedings of the ACL SIGLEX Workshop on Tagging Text with Lexical Semantics: What, Why, and How?*, 52–57. Association for Computational Linguistics.

Ribas, F. (1994). An experiment on learning appropriate selectional restrictions from a parsed corpus. In *Proceedings of the Fifteenth International Conference on Computational Linguistics (COLING-94)*, 769–774. Association for Computational Linguistics. Available: http://xxx.lanl.gov/abs/cmp-lg/, number 9409004

Russell, S., and Norvig, P. (1995). *Artificial intelligence: A modern approach.* Englewood Cliffs, NJ: Prentice-Hall.

Schütze, H. (1993). Part-of-speech induction from scratch. In *Proceedings of the 31st Annual Meeting of the Association for Computational Linguistics.* Association for Computational Linguisitics.

Sparck Jones, K. (1964). *Synonymy and semantic classification.* Doctoral dissertation, University of Cambridge, England. Published 1986, Edinburgh: Edinburgh University Press.

Sundheim, B., and Chinchor, N. (1993). Survey of the message understanding conferences. In *Proceedings of the ARPA Human Language Technology Workshop*, 56–60. San Francisco: Morgan Kaufmann.

Velardi, P., and Cucchiarelli, A. (1997). Automatic selection of class labels from a thesaurus for an effective semantic tagging of corpora. In *Proceedings of the Fifth Conference on Applied Natural Language Processing.* Association for Computational Linguistics.

Yarowsky, D. (1992). Word-sense disambiguation using statistical models of Roget's categories trained on large corpora. In *Proceedings of the Fourteenth International Conference on Computational Linguistics (COLING-92)*, 454–460. Association for Computational Linguistics.

Yarowsky, D. (1993). One sense per collocation. In *Proceedings of the ARPA Human Language Technology Workshop*, 266–271. San Francisco: Morgan Kaufmann.

Yarowsky, D. (1995). Unsupervised word sense disambiguation rivaling supervised methods. In *Proceedings of the 33rd Annual Meeting of the Association for Computational Linguistics*, 189–196. Association for Computational Linguistics. Available: http://www.cs.jhu.edu/ ~ yarowsky/acl95.ps.gz

Chapter 11

Combining Local Context and WordNet Similarity for Word Sense Identification

Claudia Leacock and Martin Chodorow

11.1 INTRODUCTION

Word sense identification is the mapping between words in a text and their appropriate senses in a lexicon.[1] Some level of word sense identification is required for virtually all natural-language-processing applications. Text must be disambiguated before it can be translated into another language, before documents appropriate to a search query can be retrieved reliably, or before a question can be answered appropriately.

Recently much of the research on automatic word sense identification has been *corpus based*. Corpus-based approaches typically train a statistical classifier on contexts containing a polysemous word in a known sense. Based on what it has found in the training, the classifier assigns a sense to novel occurrences of the polysemous word. A fundamental problem with such corpus-based approaches is sparseness of the training data. In order to ensure that the training data are reliable, the training contexts for each polysemous word have to be assigned their appropriate senses by hand.[2] This phase of the project is tedious and slow. (For a description of such a project, see Landes, Leacock, and Tengi, this volume.) It might not seem like such a big task, considering that only about 12% of the word forms in WordNet are polysemous. However, 12% still represents approximately 15,400 polysemous word forms. The task of collecting large training sets for each sense of each polysemous word is simply not feasible. At best, the training sets will be small, resulting in sparse training data. One of the goals of this research is to use the semantic relations in WordNet to increase the effective size of the training data.

Corpus-based research on word sense identification has focused on either topical context or local context, and some work has been done on combining the two. *Topical context* is made up of the substantive words that are likely to co-occur with a given sense of a polysemous word. For example, co-occurrence of the noun *stock* in a text with *cattle* or *breed* suggests a different sense of *stock* than does co-occurrence with *Microsoft* or *Chrysler*. *Local context* consists of syntactic and semantic cues in the immediate vicinity of a polysemous word. For example, *in stock* or *out of stock* suggests one sense of the noun *stock*, whereas *stock split* or *stock soars* suggests another.

Topical context has been found to be very effective for identifying senses of homonyms that are not semantically related, such as *bank* (the land formation) and *bank* (the financial institution). Since topical contextual clues occur throughout a text, statistical approaches that use topical context fill in the sparse training space by increasing the size of the context window. Gale, Church, and Yarowsky (1992) found that their Bayesian classifier works most effectively with a ± 50-word window (including punctuation) from the target. Topical classifiers can perform almost perfectly on homonyms such as *bass* (the fish) and *bass* (having anything to do with music). However, performance drops on semantically related polysemous words. Voorhees, Leacock, and Towell (1995) tested three statistical classifiers on six senses of the polysemous noun *line* with a two-sentence window[3] and found that, with 200 training contexts for each of the six senses of *line*, the methods converged at about 73% overall accuracy. In the case of *line*, where chance would yield below 17% accuracy, the topical classifiers are still very effective, but there is room for improvement. The experiment has been repeated on four senses of the verb *serve* using two of the three original topical classifiers. The topical classifiers achieved an average of 74% overall accuracy when trained on 200 contexts for each of four senses of *serve*.

Similarly, topical information is unlikely to be strongly indicative of the distinction between *bass* (the voice) and *bass* (a musical instrument) since the topic is *music* in both cases. Here, local information should be a more reliable indicator of sense. Two examples where local information resolves these senses in the Standard Corpus of Present-Day Edited American English (the Brown Corpus; Kučera and Francis 1967) are " ... female to sing *bass*, baritone ... " and " ... to play *bass* because he ... "; here, *sing* and *play* appear to be highly reliable discriminators.

Local information also provides valuable evidence for word sense identification. Kaplan (1955) reported that people can assign a sense to a polysemous word when given a window of ± 2 words from the polysemous target. Choueka and Lusignan (1985) replicated these results. Hearst (1991), Resnik (1993b), Yarowsky (1993), Leacock, Towell, and Voorhees (1996), and Bruce and Wiebe (1994a), among others, have also found local information to be highly reliable for automatic sense identification. However, the sparse data problem is particularly acute when one tries to capture local context. Whereas topical context looks at a large window around the target, local context is contained in a much smaller window. As a result, there is often little or no statistical information available from training with which to classify novel contexts.

In this chapter we first describe a classifier that trains on local context, and we test the classifier on four senses of the verb *serve*. We then describe an experiment that uses similarity measures on the WordNet noun hierarchy to identify the same four senses of *serve*. Finally, we propose and test a method for combining the local classifier with WordNet similarity measures.

11.2   TRAINING AND TESTING DATA

We use the approach of training on a set of contexts where the sense is known for each instance of the polysemous target, and testing on a set of novel contexts. The same training and testing sets were used in all of the experiments described here. Sentence-length contexts for the verb *serve* and its inflections were extracted from the APHB corpus and from the 1987 edition *Wall Street Journal*.[4] Two Princeton University students tagged each word form of *serve* with a WordNet sense. The taggers' outputs were compared, and only sentences where the two taggers agreed were used. The resulting corpus contained at least 350 sentences for each of four senses of the verb *serve*, and these were used to build training and testing sets in the experiment. Three sets of training and testing data were created by putting the sentences for each sense in random order. The first 200 sentences were used for training. The next 150 were used for testing. Smaller training sets were formed by taking the first 10, 25, 50, and 100 sentences from the training set of 200 sentences. Examples of the four senses of *serve* used in the experiment are shown in figure 11.1.

11.3   EXPERIMENT 1: THE LOCAL CONTEXT CLASSIFIER

Before the local context representations of each sense were constructed, all of the training and testing sentences were tagged with Brill's (1994)

1. 'serve a function or purpose'

*Paine saw no objection to being paid for writing in this vein, but the affair of the Indiana Company had **served** as a warning that his motives might not be understood.*

2. 'provide a service'

*Wometco Cable operates cable systems **serving** about 362,000 subscribers, primarily in North and South Carolina, Georgia, and Louisiana.*

3. 'supply with food or drink'

*If you insist on **serving** fruit as a salad, don't cut it into cubes and mix it up.*

4. 'hold an office'

*Mr. Farley will continue to **serve** as a director.*

Figure 11.1
Definitions and example contexts for the four senses of *serve* used in the experiments

part-of-speech tagger. Special tags were also inserted for the beginning and end of each sentence. Next each noun found in WordNet was replaced with its base form. For example, if the noun *years* appeared in a sentence, it was replaced with *year*. This was done to normalize across morphological variants without resorting to the more drastic measure of stemming. Morphological information is not lost in this process since the syntactic tag still indicates number.[5] Thus, the original sentence (1a) was presented to the classifier as the string shown in (1b):

(1) a. In the years 1847–49 Lincoln served one term in Congress, where he had the distinction of being the only Whig from Illinois.
     b. In/IN the/DT year/NNS 1847–49/JJ lincoln/NNP serve/VBD one/CD term/NN in/IN congress/NNP ,/, where/WRB he/PRP had/VBD the/DT distinction/NN of/IN being/VBG the/DT only/JJ whig/NN from/IN illinois/NNP ./.

For each sense *i* of *serve*, the local context in the training corpus was represented by three distributions: one for part-of-speech tags, one for closed-class items, and one for open-class items. The part-of-speech distribution was constructed in the following way: For each occurrence of *serve* in sense *i*, a window was marked off beginning two positions to the left and ending two positions to the right of *serve* (i.e., covering five positions in all). A preliminary study used the semantically tagged Brown Corpus[6] and a version of the local classifier that looked only at the part-of-speech distribution. It performed best with a window of ± 2 positions when tested on a large number of nouns, verbs, and adjectives. Therefore, this value was chosen for the current experiments.

For each position p in the window, a list was constructed of all part-of-speech tags that appeared at p across all occurrences of sense i in the training corpus. The list actually consisted of pairs, with each pair composed of a tag and its frequency of occurrence at position p in sense i. The closed-class distribution was constructed in a similar fashion and a window of ± 2 positions was also found to be optimal. Closed-class items are words and symbols (e.g., punctuation marks) that are *not* tagged as a noun, verb, adjective, or adverb by the syntactic tagger. Prominent among these are prepositions, pronouns, determiners, and numbers.

The open-class distribution for sense i was constructed in a slightly different way. Here the window was wider, encompassing k positions to the left and k positions to the right of *serve*, but the positional coding was less specific. A single position, LEFT, was used for all open-class words in the window to the left of *serve*, and RIGHT was used for all open-class words in the window to the right. For each sense i, the open-class distribution consisted of the LEFT and RIGHT lists of open-class items with their associated frequencies of occurrence.

Tables 11.1 and 11.2 show the three representations of local context for two senses of *serve* based on a 50-sentence training corpus. The number of occurrences of the verb *serve* is greater than 50 because it appears twice in some of the contexts.

Testing was carried out as follows. For each occurrence of *serve* in the test corpus, the part-of-speech representation of the occurrence was constructed. Then, for each sense i, a part-of-speech score was computed by taking the product of 1 plus the conditional probability of sense i given the part-of-speech tag found at each position p in the window:

$$pos\_score_i = \prod_{p=-2}^{2} (P(sense_i|pos\_tag_p) + 1).$$

This formula allows us to combine evidence for a sense even though some of the conditional probabilities are zero (as suggested in Hearst 1991). In a similar manner, a closed-class score and an open-class score were produced for each sense, but the open-class score was computed over only two positions LEFT and RIGHT and these contained all of the open-class words that appeared in the window. The overall score for sense i was the product of its part-of-speech score, closed-class score, and open-class score. The sense with the largest overall score was selected, and perfor-

Table 11.1
Local context for sense 6 of *serve*, 'fulfill a role or need' (54 occurrences)

Position	Item
	CLOSED-CLASS ITEMS
−2	of sentence_beginning to(2) its which(3) what the , " a will in who it
−1	to(6) that(3) at(2) can ,(2) which of(2) in it will
+1	about by(5) a the(11) 5.5 29 both .(3) 220,000 itself its in(2) 460,000 some
+2	362,000 the(2) and(2) 's than million .(3) us of to ,(2) who our 1971, 300,000
	OPEN-CLASS ITEMS
LEFT	operates cable(3) system(4) needs student college Eastern flight management subsidiary immunity airline(2) says zoning Raytheon unit already(3) is(3) aimed best business publication carrier fast-food format San Diego are(2) abstract market(2) Rico
RIGHT	subscriber mission local student atlanta arrived corporate public(2) chicago O'Hare military operation more(2) long-distance route consumer aviation london clientele better airport primarily USAir group self-proclaimed customer(2) same area most N
	PART-OF-SPEECH TAGS
−2	NN(13) IN(2) NNP(3) NNS(7) TO(2) PRP$ WDT(3) VBN(2) WP(2) RB DT(2) , " JJ(7) JJR VBZ MD VB(2) PRP
−1	NNS(8) NNP(4) TO(6) NN(9) WDT(4) RB(6) IN(5) JJS MD(2) ,(2) VBP(2) JJ VB(2) VBZ PRP
0	VBZ(33) VBN(8) VB(11) VBD VBP
+1	IN(8) DT(14) NNP(5) JJ(6) JJR(3) CD(4) NNS(2) .(3) JJS RB(5) PRP NN PRP$
+2	CD(4) DT(2) JJ(8) VBD CC(2) POS NN(6) NNS(9) IN(2) .(3) NNP(5) PRP VBN TO ,(2) WP PRP$ VBG

mance was evaluated by comparing this selection with the sense that had been assigned by human judges.

11.3.1   Local Context Results

Table 11.3 shows the results obtained by varying the width of the window for open-class words and the size of the training set. Since we had no prior knowledge of the optimal window for open-class words, we used the open-class word window as a variable. Local classifier performance on the *serve* data consistently improved as the open-class window was increased from a ± 3- to a ± 6-item window, after which performance began to

Table 11.2
Local context for sense 10 of *serve*, 'supply with food or drink' (51 occurrences)

Position	Item
	CLOSED-CLASS ITEMS
−2	,(3) It(2) his While they We sentence_beginning may
−1	on(2) sentence_beginning(17) and(9) which between she , from She or
+1	with(8) 6(6) 4(5) ,(2) at from me the(3) a an to him of in(2) . on over
+2	as to(5) with on and(3) .(6) both , or(2) a(2) in(2) the(3) my their
	OPEN-CLASS ITEMS
LEFT	insist(2) most likely be(2) split pea Treehouses Brewster liquor were(3) have been are often coffee shop fruit whipped cream(2) prepared temporarily blocked fritter cooking dinner(2) fork su
RIGHT	fruit pan-fried potato(2) topped crumbled pie(2) elevated food(2) ale so often coffee dessert mount melted butter aluminum trolley catsup heat cherry hot(2) cold(2) barley existed New same complimentary apple juice were game aspic boiled slice coo
	PART-OF-SPEECH TAGS
−2	VBP(3) JJ(3) NNS ,(3) PRP(4) NN(12) PRP$ IN VB NNP VBN(2) MD
−1	IN(4) VB(2) CC(10) WDT VBZ(3) VBD(6) NN PRP(2) , VBN RB NNP NNS
0	VBZ(17) VBN(13) VB(13) VBD(8)
+1	NN(6) IN(15) CD(11) VBN RB(2) ,(2) PRP(2) JJ(3) VBD(2) DT(5) TO .
+2	IN(5) JJ(6) TO(5) CC(5) .(6) RB DT(6) NN(8) , NNS(2) VBN(2) PRP$(2) JJS

Table 11.3
Results of the local context classifier (average percentage correct, ± 2 closed-class items)

	Open-class window size						
Training size	± 3	± 4	± 5	± 6	± 7	± 8	± 9
10	54	54	55	**56**	56	57	56
25	66	67	68	**68**	69	70	69
50	72	74	75	**75**	75	76	75
100	76	78	79	**79**	78	78	78
200	79	81	82	**83**	83	82	82

drop off. Performance steadily improved with increases in set size. When the optimal window of ± 6 items was used, the classifier performed an average of 75% correct when trained on 50 sentences, which increased to 79% when training was doubled to 100 sentences, and finally to 83% when it was doubled again to 200 sentences.

Although the results appear very encouraging, they probably over-estimate classifier performance when all senses of a word, including low-frequency ones, appear in the training and test corpora. Unless the low-frequency senses are extremely distinctive in their local context features, they will almost always be misclassified because it will be difficult to amass a sufficient training corpus for them. For example, the semantic concordance contains 167 occurrences of the verb *serve* representing 11 different WordNet senses. Four of these are very low frequency (2–3% each), but together they account for more than 10% of all occurrences. If the rare senses of *serve* are consistently missed owing to inadequate training, then the upper bound on the classifier's performance will be less than 90% accuracy. One important area for future research is to determine if rare senses are more distinctive in their local contexts. Another possibility is that these senses will be related to identifiable topical contexts, as when a common word has a special use in a sublanguage.

11.3.2   Related Work

Recent studies by Hearst, Yarowsky, and Bruce and Wiebe have also explored the use of local context in sense identification. They differ from the work described here, and from one another, in three general respects: the type of sense distinction tested, the form of representation used for local context, and the means of combining multiple pieces of evidence.

Hearst (1991) tested noun homographs and semantically related noun senses with her CatchWord program. Local context was represented by an automatically generated shallow syntactic parse in which words that had been stochastically tagged for part of speech were segmented into prepositional phrases, noun phrases, and verb groups. The target noun was coded for the word it modified, the word that modified it, and the prepositions that preceded and followed it. Open-class items within ± 5 phrase segments of the target were coded in terms of their relationship to the target (modifier or head) or their role in a construct that was adjacent to the target. In training, all senses were represented by equal numbers of examples, and no prior probabilities were used in selecting a sense during testing. For each test example, the local context was coded as in training and the resulting properties were used as evidence for the various senses. Evidence was combined in a manner similar to that described in experiment 1 above. With training of up to 70 sentences per sense, performance on three homographs was quite good (88–100% correct); with fewer training examples and semantically related senses, performance on two additional words was less dramatic (73–77% correct).

Bruce and Wiebe (1994a,b) report work on identification of senses for three nouns, two verbs, and one adjective. The degree of semantic relatedness varied among the senses from homography to close semantic proximity. Between 800 and 1,700 training examples were used for the different words, but the frequencies of senses varied so that very rare senses may have had fewer than 10 examples. Local context was represented by morphology (the inflection on the target word), the part of speech of words within a window of ± 2 words from the target (obtained from the Penn Treebank), and collocation-specific items found in the sentence. The collocation-specific items were those determined to be the most informative, where an item was considered informative if the model for independence between it and a sense tag provided a poor fit to the training data. The relative probabilities of senses, available from the training corpus, were used in the decision process as prior probabilities. For each test example, the evidence in its local context was combined in a Bayesian-type model of the probability of each sense, and the most probable sense was selected. Performance ranged from 77% to 84% correct on the test words, where the lower bound for performance based on selecting the most frequent sense (i.e., the sense with the greatest prior probability) would have yielded 53% to 80% correct.

Yarowsky (1994), building on his earlier work (1993), used local context to disambiguate the homographs that result from accent removal in Spanish and French (e.g., *seria*, *sería*). For words within $\pm k$ positions of the target, lemma forms were obtained through morphological analysis, and a coarse part-of-speech assignment was performed by dictionary lookup. Context was represented by collocations based on words or parts of speech at specific positions within the window or, less specifically, in any position. Also coded were some special classes of words, such as WEEKDAY, that might serve to distinguish among word senses. For each type of local context evidence found in the corpus, a log likelihood ratio was constructed, indicating the strength of the evidence for one form of the homograph versus the other. These ratios were then arranged in a sorted decision list with the largest values (strongest evidence) first. A decision was made for a test sentence by scanning down the decision list until a match was found. Thus, only the single best evidence was used. In tests with the number of training examples ranging from a few hundred to several thousands, overall accuracy was quite high, above 90%.

The different classifiers have varied in so many different ways that it is difficult to compare their performance. However, we can draw a few general conclusions from the overall patterns: As expected, disambiguation of homographs is easier than that of semantically related senses. The amount of automated preprocessing of the data varies across the systems, but the results do not seem to differ dramatically as a consequence. Another trend that is evident in all of these systems is that the more data the local context classifier trains on, the better it is at classifying novel occurrences of the target. However, the time and expense involved in obtaining hundreds or thousands (as some systems used) of training examples is prohibitive. What is required, then, is a means of generalizing from a limited amount of training.

11.4   EXPERIMENT 2: MEASURING WORD SIMILARITY IN WORDNET

The idea of augmenting a local context classifier with semantic information is a logical next step (Hearst 1991; Leacock, Towell, and Voorhees 1996; Bruce and Wiebe 1994b). In this experiment we try to fill in gaps in a sparse training space by exploiting similarity measures based on Word-Net. Our reasoning is as follows: Semantically similar words should provide similar contextual clues. For example, if *baseball* is a good discriminator for a particular sense of the verb *play*, then words similar in meaning to *baseball*, such as *hockey* or *football* or *soccer*, should also discriminate the same sense even though they did not happen to occur in the training space. In other words, can the semantic structure in the WordNet lexical database (Miller 1990) be exploited to increase effective size of the training data?

In WordNet, nouns are organized into taxonomies where each node is a set of synonyms (a synset) representing a single sense. If a word has multiple senses, it will appear in multiple synsets at various locations in the taxonomy. These synsets contain bidirectional pointers to other synsets to express a variety of semantic relations. The semantic relation among synsets in WordNet that we use in this experiment is that of hyponymy/hypernymy, or the IS-A-KIND-OF relation, which relates more general and more specific senses.

One obvious way to measure the semantic similarity between two words a and b is to measure the distance between them in WordNet. This can be done by finding the paths from each sense of a to each sense of b and then selecting the shortest such path. We compute path length similarity between a and b using the formula

$$sim_{ab} = max[-\log(Np/2D)],$$

where Np is the number of nodes in path p from a to b and D is the maximum depth of the taxonomy. Note that path length is measured in nodes rather than links, so the length of the path between sister nodes is 3 (one for each sister and one for the parent); the length of the path between members of the same synset is 1. In addition, we have joined together all 11 top nodes of the noun taxonomy as daughters of a single topmost node so that a path can always be found between any two nouns.

Resnik (1992) points out that measures based on path length will suffer from the great differences in depth found in various parts of the WordNet taxonomy. He suggests using an information-based measure, the most informative class, instead of path length when computing similarity. A class consists of the synonyms found at a node and the synonyms at all the nodes that it dominates (all of its hyponyms). The frequency of a class is the frequency of all the words in the class, as determined by the analysis of a corpus. (Actually, the corpus frequencies are adjusted to take into account the number of classes to which each word belongs, as described in Resnik 1993a, 136.) From these frequencies it is possible to compute the probability of a class. The similarity between words a and b is determined by the least probable (most informative) class they belong to, as shown here,

$$sim_{ab} = max[-\log(Pr(c))],$$

where $Pr(c)$ is the probability of class c, a class containing a sense of a and a sense of b. We shall refer to this as the *most informative class measure* of similarity. To obtain word frequencies for estimating class probabilities, we used a corpus consisting of newspaper, newswire, and prose selections from the ACL Data Collection Initiative database. Words were tagged for part of speech with Brill's (1994) tagger, and base forms of nouns were obtained via an interface to WordNet. In this corpus the total frequency of nouns found in WordNet is 12.5 million.

Just how good are these measures of semantic similarity; that is, how closely do they mirror human judgments? Resnik (1993a) has compared the most informative class measure with data reported by Miller and

Charles (1991) for human subjects' ratings of 28 word pairs. The correlation is quite high ($r = .77$), especially when one considers that the correlation between individual human subjects and Miller and Charles's data was only $r = .88$. The correlation between the path length measure and the human data was somewhat lower ($r = .74$).[7]

Before combining the local context classifier with measures of similarity, we needed to determine how much generalization they provide. Accordingly, we used similarity measures for word sense identification as follows. The first noun to the left and the first noun to the right of each verbal instance of *serve* were extracted. When the syntactic tagger identified a compound noun (i.e., tagged two or more words in a row as nouns), all members of the string of nouns were used, for example, *bacon bits* and *hard sauce* (where *hard* was incorrectly tagged as a noun). An interface to WordNet returned the base forms of the nouns that were found in WordNet. When a noun was not in WordNet, the original string was kept. Separate left and right context sets, corresponding very roughly to the subject and complement of *serve*, were used for training and testing. A simple rule switched nouns in passive constructions.

The similarity measures were run on the training sets and testing sets for the left context and for the right context. The maximum similarity between each context word and all of the training sets was computed for the path length similarity measure and for the most informative class measure. The sense chosen by a similarity measure is the one whose training set contained the word most similar to the test word. In the event that two senses were tied for most similar with a given measure, the system returned *don't know* for that metric.

Preliminary comparisons of the predictive value of nouns to the left of a verb (its subject) with the predictive value of those to the right (its complement) confirmed our expectation that, in the case of a verb, the complement is a more reliable indicator of the sense than the subject. Accordingly, we weighted right context over left context in the following manner: If the classifier could choose a sense on the basis of right context, that sense was chosen. When there was no right context, or if two or more senses were tied based on right context, then selection was made on the basis of left context. If there was no left context, or two or more senses were tied for first place, the classifier returned *don't know*.

As an example of this expansion, the following base forms were not in the training sets: *tart, refrigerator, chill, truffle, madeira, claret, dumpling, caviar, stew, mayonnaise, tarragon*, and *pepper*. However, they occurred in test contexts and were found to be similar to the training context for the

Table 11.4

Average results of path length, most informative class and combined similarity measures over three trials in each training size

Similarity measure	Average percentage	Training size				
		10	25	50	100	200
Path length	Correct	40	47	52	56	52
	Wrong	26	29	27	20	18
	Don't know	24	24	22	23	30
Most informative class	Correct	35	44	49	54	54
	Wrong	28	24	23	20	18
	Don't know	37	32	27	27	28
Combined	Correct	25	34	40	44	44
	Wrong	12	10	9	8	8
	Don't know	64	57	51	48	48

sense of *serve food*, and *serve* was correctly classified by both similarity measures.

As can be seen in table 11.4, both of the similarity measures performed above chance (25%), even when trained on 10 contexts, but the percentage of wrong answers was high. In terms of percentage correct, the path length measure outperformed the most informative class measure slightly for smaller training sets, but the most informative class measure had fewer errors. With training sets of size 200, there was a small advantage for the most informative class measure. In order to reduce the number of wrong answers, we required that the two sources of information agree; otherwise, a *don't know* was returned. As can be seen in the "Combined" row of table 11.4, this resulted in greater precision (fewer wrong answers) and lower recall (more *don't know*s).

Local context was found to be highly reliable when an exact match is found (Hearst 1991; Leacock, Towell, and Voorhees 1996; Yarowsky 1993). Therefore, we took an exact match between testing input and training examples to be the strongest form of evidence, even if it occurred only once in a training set. When a test sentence had exactly the same noun to the right (in the object position) as had occurred in training sentences, a sense of *serve* could be selected on that basis; when no selection could be made on the basis of right context, the left context was used;[8] when neither right nor left noun matched the training material, the system returned *don't know*. With this procedure, the system correctly identified

Table 11.5
Growth of effective training space

Classifier	Average percentage	Training size				
		10	25	50	100	200
Base form match	Correct	**17**	**29**	**39**	**46**	**47**
	Wrong	3	5	8	10	11
	No match	80	66	53	44	42
Base form match +	Correct	**30**	**43**	**48**	**54**	**56**
similarity measures	Wrong	12	12	12	13	14
	Don't know	58	46	40	33	30

the sense of *serve* 47% of the time after training on 200 instances, with 42% returning no exact match. These results provide a basis for evaluating the use of WordNet to generalize the match. When no exact match was found, the similarity measures were used. As before, they were used only when the two metrics agreed. Now, performance improved to 56% correct with only 30% *don't know*, as shown in table 11.5.

The exact-match-plus-semantic-similarity approach more than doubled the effective size of the training set. That is to say, when the classifier combined exact match with the similarity metrics, it consistently performed better than the classifier that relied exclusively on base form matches with twice the training data. For example, the exact match algorithm correctly predicted the sense of *serve* 46% of the time when trained on 100 sentences. When the training space was increased using a combination of similarity measures and WordNet, the resulting classifier achieved 48% accuracy with half of the training (50 sentences).

Interesting though this may be, an inevitable conclusion to be reached from these results is that expansion using WordNet is inadequate as a stand-alone classifier. This is hardly surprising, as the local context needed for disambiguating verbs includes more than just its arguments. The next step is to incorporate the expansion gained from the WordNet similarity measures with the local context classifier.

11.5   EXPERIMENT 3: COMBINING LOCAL CONTEXT AND WORDNET SIMILARITY MEASURES

The metrics discussed in the previous experiment compute the maximum similarity between a noun in each test example and one found in the

By/IN 1973/CD it/PRP will/MD have/VB 70/CD earth/NN station/NNS
and/CC be/VB **serve**/VBZ every/DT heavily/RB populated/VBN **area**/NN of/IN
the/DT free/JJ world/NN ./.

Bending/VBG the/DT elbow/NN slightly/RB as/IN the/DT arm/NN is/VBZ
lifted/VBN out/IN of/IN the/DT water/NN **serve**/VBZ the/DT three/CD
following/VBG essential/JJ **purpose**/NNS :/: first/NNP ,/, it/PRP release/VBZ
the/DT tension/NN of/IN the/DT arm/NN flexor/NN muscle/NNS and/CC
permit/VBZ them /PRP to /TO rest/VB ./.

Figure 11.2
Example training sentences for *serve*

training set. We have combined the local context classifier and WordNet
similarity measures by substituting the most similar nouns found in
training for the novel nouns found in testing. For example, one of the test
sentences is *Sauerbraten is usually served with dumplings*, where neither
sauerbraten nor *dumpling* appears in any training sentence. In one of the
sets, the similarity measures found that *sauerbraten* was most similar to
dinner in the training, and *dumpling* to *bacon*. These nouns were substituted for the novel ones in the test sets. Thus, the sentence *Dinner is usually
served with bacon* was substituted for the original sentence. Substitutions
were made only when both similarity measures predicted the same sense.
If the classifiers did not agree, the context remained unchanged. The
revised test sentences were then submitted to the local classifier.

Since a ± 6-item window was optimal for the local context classifier,
we used the same window size for this experiment. This seems to be a
reasonable choice because it is common in written text to have several
modifiers between a verb and its object, as shown figure 11.2 for
serve...area and *serve...purpose*.

Augmentation of the local context classifier with WordNet similarity
measures showed a small but consistent improvement in the classifier's
performance. There was less than 1% improvement when the local context
classifier was trained on 200 sentences for each of the four senses of *serve*.
However, such large training sets are unrealistic. It took months to com-
pile the *serve* corpus, and doing the same for 15,400 different polysemous
words is impractical. Of greater interest to us is how the classifier fares
on the smaller training sets. If the training sets can be kept small, then it
will be feasible to collect training data for a large number of words. As
shown in table 11.6, augmentation of the local classifier with WordNet
similarity information made the biggest difference on the smaller sets.
When the classifier was trained on 10 contexts for each sense, the average

Table 11.6

Results of the local context classifier looking at open-class words at a ±6-item window, and the same classifier augmented with WordNet similarity measures, averaged across three training and test sets

Training size	Local context classifier (% correct)	Augmented with WordNet (% correct)
10	55.9	59.4
25	68.4	70.7
50	75.4	77.7
100	78.5	80.1
200	82.5	83.1

improvement was 3.5%; when it was trained on 25 and 50 contexts for each sense, average improvement was 2.3%.

The local classifier averaged 75.4% accuracy when trained on 50 sentences for each sense of *serve*. When the WordNet similarity measures are added to the local classifier, performance rose to 77.7%. We can compare these results with those of the topical classifiers. The *serve* sentences were trained and tested on two of the topical classifiers used by Leacock, Towell, and Voorhees (1993). Ellen Voorhees ran a content vector classifier as used in information retrieval and Geoffrey Towel ran a neural network. When trained on 200 contexts, each two sentences long, these topical classifiers averaged 74% accuracy.[9]

The upper boundary of performance, how well people perform this task, could be determined by having subjects assign senses to test examples of *serve* in a ±6-word window. It would be interesting to see how far the upper level of performance is from the 83.1% accuracy that the augmented classifiers achieved when trained on 200 sentences for each sense.

The results reported here are preliminary, and methods for decreasing the sources of error remain to be explored. For example, we have kept the cost of preprocessing to a minimum by using a rule-based part-of-speech tagger and some simple heuristics for finding a verb's arguments. Both of these processes introduce errors.

Another source of error is that the similarity measures sometimes find inappropriate links between low-frequency WordNet senses. For example, one test sentence contained *serve* in the 'serving food' sense and the first noun to its right was *salt* as in *serve with salt*. The similarity measures found the shortest path was between *salt* and *seaman,* which is in the training set for a different sense of *serve* ('serve as a seaman'). In WordNet 1.5 *salt* 'a mariner' is in the same synset as *seaman.*

Finally, the local classifier did not take advantage of prior knowledge of word sense frequencies. Miller et al. (1994) report that in the semantically tagged Brown Corpus, on average, the most frequent sense of a polysemous word accounts for 58% of its occurrences. However, in the experiments reported here, the prior probabilities of the senses did not differ, as equal numbers of training examples were used for each sense. This can be overcome by constructing training sets through random sampling, so that the distribution of senses is in proportion to their frequency of occurrence in the corpus.

11.6   CONCLUSIONS

Local context classifiers are especially sensitive to the sparse data problem. As one possible method for increasing the local training space, we have identified a method for combining local syntactic information with semantic information from WordNet. Augmenting the local classifier in this way produces a modest improvement in performance, especially when training on small sets.

The local context classifier that we have implemented performs better on *serve* than the topical classifiers that were tested. Clearly, we need to learn whether this difference in performance generalizes to other verbs and to other parts of speech. In addition, we have worked exclusively with the hypernomy/hyponymy relation. Several other semantic relations have been encoded in WordNet. The usefulness of these semantic relations for sense identification remains to be evaluated.

Notes

1. This work was supported in part by grant N00014-91-1634 from the Defense Advanced Research Projects Agency, Information and Technology Office, and the Office of Naval Research, and by the James S. McDonnell Foundation. We are indebted to Scott Wayland and Tim Allison for manually tagging the *serve* corpus, and to Shari Landes for overseeing their work. We are also indebted to George A. Miller, Ben Johnson-Laird, Randee Tengi, Robert G. Thomas, Geoffrey Towell, and Ellen Voorhees for assistance and advice.

2. Some researchers have tried to generate the training data automatically; see Schütze 1992 and Gale, Church, and Yarowsky 1992. However, it is unclear whether they will ever be able to generate data for semantically related polysemous words (as opposed to semantically unrelated homonyms).

3. This is a smaller window than the ± 50-word window found to be optimal by Gale, Church, and Yarowsky (1992).

4. The 25-million-word APHB corpus, obtained from the American Printing House for the Blind, is archived at the IBM Thomas J. Watson Research Center; it consists of stories and articles from books and general circulation magazines. The *Wall Street Journal* corpus is from the ACL Data Collection Initiative compact disc.

5. We did not retrieve the base forms of verbs, adverbs, or adjectives, though we will in the future.

6. For a description of the semantic concordance, see Landes, Leacock, and Tengi, this volume.

7. See Resnik 1995 for other comparisons of the two measures with human judgments of similarity.

8. Some of the exact matches were in the left context while the similarity measures' decision was based on right context. In these cases, exact matches were overridden by the similarity measure.

9. Both experiments were conducted at Siemens Corporate Research in Princeton, New Jersey.

References

Brill, E. (1994). Some advances in rule-based part of speech tagging. In *Proceedings of the Twelfth National Conference on Artificial Intelligence (AAAI-94)*, 256–261. Menlo Park, CA: AAAI Press, and Cambridge, MA: MIT Press.

Bruce, R., and Wiebe, J. (1994a). A new approach to word sense disambiguation. In *Proceedings of the ARPA Human Language Technology Workshop*, 244–249. San Francisco: Morgan Kaufmann.

Bruce, R., and Wiebe, J. (1994b). Word-sense disambiguation using decomposable models. In *Proceedings of the 32nd Annual Meeting of the Association for Computational Linguistics*, 139–146. Association for Computational Linguistics.

Choueka, Y., and Lusignan, S. (1985). Disambiguation by short contexts. *Computers and the Humanities, 19*, 147–157.

Gale, W., Church, K. W., and Yarowsky, D. (1992). *A method for disambiguating word senses in a large corpus. Computers and the Humanities, 26.*

Hearst, M. A. (1991). Noun homograph disambiguation using local context in large text corpora. In *Proceedings of the Seventh Annual Conference of the UW Centre for the New OED and Text Research: Using Corpora*, 1–22. Waterloo, Ontario, Canada: UW Centre for the New OED and Text Research.

Kaplan, A. (1955). An experimental study of ambiguity and context. *Mechanical Translation, 2*, 39–46.

Kučera, H., and Francis, W. N. (1967). *The standard corpus of present-day edited American English* [the Brown Corpus]. (Electronic database.) Providence, RI: Brown University.

Leacock, C., Towell, G., and Voorhees, E. M. (1993). Corpus-based statistical sense resolution. In *Proceedings of the ARPA Human Language Technology Workshop*, 260–265. San Francisco: Morgan Kaufmann.

Leacock, C., Towell, G., and Voorhees, E. M. (1996). Towards building contextual representations of word senses using statistical models. In B. Boguraev and J. Pustejovsky (Eds.), *Corpus processing for lexical acquisition*, 97–113. Cambridge, MA: MIT Press.

Miller, G. A. (Ed.). (1990). *WordNet: An on-line lexical database.* Special issue of *International Journal of Lexicography*, 3(4).

Miller, G. A., and Charles, W. G. (1991). Contextual correlates of semantic similarity. *Language and Cognitive Processes*, 6, 1–28.

Miller, G. A., Chodorow, M., Landes, S., Leacock, C., and Thomas, R. G. (1994). Using a semantic concordance for sense identification. In *Proceedings of the ARPA Human Language Technology Workshop*, 240–243. San Francisco: Morgan Kaufmann.

Resnik, P. (1992). WordNet and distributional analysis: A class-based approach to lexical discovery. In *Statistically-Based Natural-Language-Processing Techniques: Papers from the 1992 AAAI Workshop.* Menlo Park, CA: AAAI Press.

Resnik, P. (1993a). *Selection and information: A class-based approach to lexical relationships.* Unpublished doctoral dissertation, University of Pennsylvania, Philadelphia.

Resnik, P. (1993b). Semantic classes and syntactic ambiguity. In *Proceedings of the ARPA Human Language Technology Workshop*, 278–283. San Francisco: Morgan Kaufmann.

Resnik, P. (1995). Using information content to evaluate semantic similarity in a taxonomy. In *Proceedings of the 14th International Joint Conference on Artificial Intelligence (IJCAI-95)*, 448–453. San Francisco: Morgan Kaufmann.

Schütze, H. (1992). Dimensions in meaning. In *Proceedings of Supercomputing '92*, 787–796. Los Alamitos, CA: IEEE Computer Society Press.

Voorhees, E. M., Leacock, C., and Towell, G. (1995). Learning context to disambiguate word senses. In T. Petsche, S. J. Hanson, and J. Shavlik (Eds.), *Computational learning theory and natural learning systems*, 279–305. Cambridge, MA: MIT Press.

Yarowsky, D. (1993). One sense per collocation. In *Proceedings of the ARPA Human Language Technology Workshop*, 266–271. San Francisco: Morgan Kaufmann.

Yarowsky, D. (1994). Decision lists for lexical ambiguity resolution: Application to accent restoration in Spanish and French. In *Proceedings of the 32nd Annual Meeting of the Association for Computational Linguistics*, 88–95. Association for Computational Linguistics.

Chapter 12

Using WordNet for Text Retrieval

Ellen M. Voorhees

12.1 INTRODUCTION

Text retrieval, also known as document or information retrieval, is concerned with locating natural language documents whose contents satisfy a user's information need (Salton and McGill 1983; Salton 1991). Historically, an information need is represented as a statement in a query language that is matched against document surrogates, such as the document's title or abstract or a set of keywords selected to represent the document's content. Since large quantities of full-text documents are now available electronically—and many of these documents don't have abstracts or even titles—there is considerable interest in developing techniques that provide access to heterogeneous collections of full-text documents. Indeed, the explosive growth of documents of all types that are available electronically makes tools that assist users in finding documents of interest indispensable.

This chapter describes two investigations into using WordNet to enhance access to collections of text. The particular focus of the work is to exploit the knowledge encoded in WordNet to ameliorate the effects synonyms and homographs have on text retrieval systems that use word matching. To provide the background necessary to discuss the work, section 12.2 reviews the particular retrieval model used in the experiments and defines the measures commonly used to evaluate retrieval performance. Sections 12.3 and 12.4 provide the details of the investigations. In the first investigation, WordNet synsets (synonym sets), as opposed to words, are used to represent documents' content. In the second investigation, WordNet is the source of words that are added to the user's query. In both investigations, the inability to automatically resolve the intended sense of polysemous words limits the benefits of using WordNet.

Future work addressed at the sense resolution problem is described in section 12.5.

12.2   TEXT RETRIEVAL BACKGROUND

12.2.1   The Vector Space Model

All the experiments reported in this chapter use the vector space model (Salton, Wong, and Yang 1975) as implemented in the SMART (Buckley 1985) text retrieval system. In this model, documents and queries are represented by vectors in T-dimensional space, where T is the number of distinct terms in the document collection. The terms assigned to a piece of text are generated by a process known as *automatic indexing*. A basic automatic indexing procedure treats character strings delimited by white space as "words," removes very frequent words (called *stop words*) such as prepositions and pronouns, and conflates related word forms to a common stem by removing suffixes. The resulting word stems are the terms for the given text. These terms are usually weighted to reflect the relative importance of a term in the text (Salton and Buckley 1988). A common scheme is to make the weight of a term in a text proportional to the number of times the term occurs in the text and inversely proportional to the number of documents in which the term occurs.

Given a query, a vector system produces a ranked list of documents ordered by similarity to the query. The similarity between a query and a document is computed using a similarity metric on the respective vectors. A common similarity measure, and the one used in the experiments below, is the cosine of the angle formed between the two vectors. That is, if d_i is the weight of term i in the document vector D and q_i is the weight of the corresponding term in the query vector Q, then the cosine similarity between the document and query is

$$\text{sim}(Q, D) = \cos(Q, D) = \frac{\sum_{i=1}^{T} q_i d_i}{(\sum_{i=1}^{T} q_i^2 \sum_{i=1}^{T} d_i^2)^{1/2}}.$$

The similarity between a document and a query is thus heavily dependent on the number of terms they have in common (i.e., the number of terms that have a positive weight in both vectors).

The experiments below use an extended vector space model that was introduced by Fox (1983). In this model a vector may actually be a collection of subvectors. The subvectors are used to represent different aspects of the documents in the collection. For example, one subvector may include single terms extracted from the text, a second subvector may include phrases, and a third may include bibliographic information such as author and date of publication. The overall similarity between two extended vectors is computed as the weighted sum of the similarities of corresponding subvectors:

$$\mathrm{sim}(Q, D) = \sum_{\text{subvector } i} \alpha_i \, \mathrm{sim}_i(Q_i, D_i),$$

where α_i reflects the importance of subvector i in the overall similarity between texts. For all experiments reported here, the individual subvector similarity is always the cosine measure given above.

12.2.2 Evaluating Retrieval System Effectiveness

The effectiveness of a particular retrieval scheme can be judged by comparing its performance with that of other schemes on a *test collection*. A test collection consists of a set of documents, a set of queries, and, for each query, a list of the documents that are relevant to that query (called the *relevance assessments*). Relevance assessments are generally binary (a document is either relevant or not) and assumed to be exhaustive (if a document is not listed as being relevant, it is irrelevant).

A number of different effectiveness measures can be computed using the relevance assessments of a test collection. A very common method of evaluating a retrieval run is to plot *precision* against *recall*. Precision is the proportion of retrieved documents that are relevant, and recall is the proportion of relevant documents that are retrieved. Whereas a perfect retrieval run will have a value of 1.0 for both recall and precision, in practice precision and recall are inversely related. The best general-purpose retrieval systems (those systems that are not limited to documents in a single domain) generally achieve a precision of 50% at 50% recall on average.

The effectiveness of individual queries varies greatly, so the average precision and recall over a set of queries is used to compare different schemes. The precision of an individual query can be interpolated to obtain the precision at a standard set of recall values (for example, 0.0 to 1.0 in increments of .1). The precision at these recall points is then averaged over the set of queries in the test collection. The "3-point" average precision is used below as a single measure of retrieval effectiveness for some experiments; this average is the mean of the average precision values at each of 3 recall values (.2, .5, and .8). Similarly, the

"11-point average" is the mean of the average precision values at the 11 recall points equally spaced from 0.0 to 1.0 inclusive.

12.3   CONCEPT MATCHING

One of the problems of using word-matching techniques for text retrieval is that the mapping between words and the concepts the words represent is not a function. In the case of homographs, words that appear to be the same represent two distinct concepts, such as *bank* meaning both the sides of a river and a financial institution. With synonyms, two distinct words represent the same concept, as when both *board* and *plank* mean a piece of wood. Homographs depress precision because false matches are made, and synonyms depress recall because true matches are missed. Retrieval effectiveness should improve if matching is performed not on the words themselves, but on the concepts the words represent.

Such concept matching can be performed in a variety of ways. Controlled vocabularies, which are frequently used with systems that rely on manual indexing, generally have a canonical descriptor term that is to be used for a given concept. Concept matching is also at the heart of automatic retrieval systems such as SCISOR (Rau 1987) that attempt to understand the texts; in these systems, meaning structures are used to represent the concepts and sophisticated matching algorithms operate on the structures. Less knowledge-intensive approaches to concept matching have also been developed. For example, abstracting away from the particular words that happen to be used in a given text is the motivation behind latent semantic indexing (Deerwester et al. 1990).

WordNet provides another way of defining a concept: a synset. Once again, there are several different ways synsets as concepts can be used for text retrieval. Sussna (1993) and Richardson (1994) treat the structure created by WordNet's relational pointers as a semantic network and define metrics for computing the similarity between two synsets. The similarity between a query and a document is then computed from the similarities between the set of synsets in the query and the set of synsets in the documents. This approach is very computation intensive owing to its combinatorial nature—there are many pairs of synsets and there may be many paths in WordNet between a pair of synsets.

Chakravarthy and Haase (1995) and Chakravarthy (1994) use WordNet to find matches when both queries and documents are short and structurally predictable. For example, one application of their system matches queries to picture captions. The representations of both the queries and the captions are automatically derived and identify the roles (such as agent and action) the words play in the text. A query word matches a caption word if the two words are semantically related in WordNet and they play the same role in their respective texts.

A third approach to synset concept matching is motivated by a desire to improve retrieval effectiveness while maintaining the robustness and efficiency afforded by the vector space model (Voorhees 1993). The focus of the approach is a completely automatic indexing procedure designed to select a single WordNet synset as the meaning of each noun in a text. The result of the indexing procedure is a vector in which some of the terms represent word senses (the synsets) instead of word stems. Once created, the synset-based vectors can be processed exactly like word-based vectors.

12.3.1   Word Sense Resolution

The heart of the indexing procedure is a word sense resolution module based on the idea that a set of words occurring together in context will determine appropriate senses for one another even though each individual word is multiply ambiguous. A common example of this effect is the set of nouns *base*, *bat*, *glove*, and *hit* (Salton and Lesk 1971b). Although most of these words have several senses, when taken together they clearly refer to the game of baseball. To exploit this idea automatically, a set of categories representing the different senses of words needs to be defined. Once such categories are defined, the number of words in the text that have senses that belong to a given category is counted. The senses that correspond to the categories with the largest counts are selected to be the intended senses of the ambiguous words.

A new WordNet construct called a *hood* is used to define the required sense categories. A hood, as suggested by George Miller, is an area in WordNet in which a string is unambiguous. More precisely, to define the hood of a given synset, *s*, consider the set of synsets and the hyponymy links in WordNet as the set of vertices and directed edges of a graph. Then the hood of *s* is the largest connected subgraph that contains *s*, contains only descendants of an ancestor of *s*, and contains no synset that has a descendant that includes another instance of a member of *s* as a member. A hood is represented by the synset that is the root of the hood.

As an example, consider the piece of WordNet shown in figure 12.1. In the figure, synsets are represented as boxes, and arrows connect synsets to

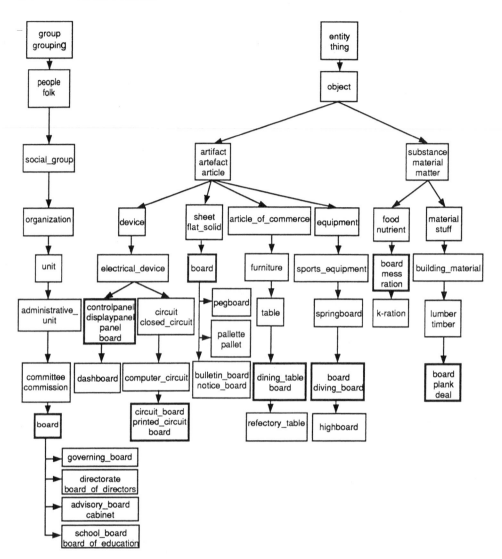

Figure 12.1
The WordNet hierarchy for eight different senses of the noun *board*

their hyponyms. Boxes with bold outlines are synsets containing the word form *board*. The hood of the synset for the 'committee' sense of *board* is rooted at the synset {*group, grouping*} (and thus the hood for that sense is the entire hierarchy in which it occurs). The hood for the 'computer circuit' sense of *board* is rooted at {*circuit, closed_circuit*}. The hood for the 'panel' sense of *board* is rooted at the synset itself. Because some synsets have more than one parent, synsets can have more than one hood. A synset has no hood if the same word is a member of both the synset and one of its descendants.

We use the hoods of the synsets containing an ambiguous word w to define the categories that represent the different senses of w. Another word that occurs in a text with w and is a member of a synset in the hood of one of the senses of w is evidence for that sense of w. The sense of w in a particular text can be selected by counting the number of other words in the text that occur in each of w's hoods and choosing the hood with the greatest count. We use the two-stage disambiguation process described below to efficiently resolve the senses of the many ambiguous words that occur in a collection of text. The idea behind the process is to first form a baseline for the collection as a whole of how many times words occur in each others' hoods, and to then look for significant deviation from this baseline within the individual texts of the collection.

A marking procedure that visits synsets and maintains a count of the number of times each synset is visited is fundamental to both stages of the disambiguation process. Given a word w, the marking procedure finds all instances of w in (the noun portion of) WordNet. For each identified synset, the procedure follows the hypernymy pointers up to the root of the hierarchy, incrementing a counter at each synset it visits. In the first stage the marking procedure is called once for each occurrence of a content word (i.e., a word that is not a stop word) in all of the documents in the collection. The total number of times the procedure was called and found the word it was invoked with in WordNet is also maintained. This produces a set of *global counts* (relative to this particular collection) at each synset. In the second stage the marking procedure is called once for each occurrence of a content word in an individual text (document or query). Again the total number of times the procedure was called and found the word in WordNet for the individual text is maintained. This produces a set of *local counts* at the synsets. Given the local and global counts, a sense for a particular ambiguous word w contained within the text that generated the local counts is selected as follows:

• The difference

$$\frac{\# \text{ local visits}}{\text{total } \# \text{ of calls in stage 2}} - \frac{\# \text{ global visits}}{\text{total } \# \text{ of calls in stage 1}}$$

is computed at the root of the hood for each sense of w. If a sense does not have a hood or if the local count at its hood root is less than 2 (i.e., no other word provided evidence for this sense), that difference is set to 0. If a sense has multiple hoods, that difference is set to the largest difference over the set of hoods.

• The sense corresponding to the hood root with the largest positive difference is selected as the sense of w in the text. If no sense has a positive difference, no WordNet sense is chosen for w.

12.3.2   Retrieval Experiments

To judge the effectiveness of the disambiguation in retrieval, the performance of sense vectors is compared with the performance of a standard run. In the standard run, both document and query vectors consist of one subvector containing word stems for all content words. In the sense-based runs, document and query vectors contain three subvectors: stems of words not found in WordNet or not disambiguated, synset IDs of disambiguated nouns, and stems of the disambiguated nouns. The second and third subvectors are alternative representations of the text in that the same text word causes an entry in both subvectors. The noun word stems are kept to act as a control group in the experiments. If the weight of the synset ID subvector is set to 0 in the overall similarity measure, document and query texts are matched solely on the basis of word stems.

Table 12.1 compares the effectiveness of the baseline standard run (one subvector, all word stems) and three different sense-based vector runs for five standard test collections. The five test collections are

CACM   3,204 documents on computer science and 50 queries,
CISI   1,460 documents on information science and 35 queries,
CRAN   1,400 documents on engineering and 225 queries,
MED   1,033 documents on medicine and 30 queries, and
TIME   423 documents extracted from *Time* magazine and 83 queries.

Each row in the table gives the 3-point average precision value obtained by the four different retrieval runs for a particular collection, where the average is over the number of queries in that collection. For each of the sense-based vector runs, the percentage change in average precision over

Table 12.1
3-point average precision for sense-based vector runs

	Standard	110		211		101	
Collection	3-pt.	3-pt.	%	3-pt.	%	3-pt.	%
CACM	.3291	.1994	−39.4	.2594	−21.2	.2998	−8.9
CISI	.2426	.1401	−42.3	.1980	−18.4	.2225	−8.3
CRAN	.4246	.2729	−35.7	.3261	−23.2	.3538	−16.7
MED	.5527	.4405	−20.3	.4777	−13.6	.4735	−14.3
TIME	.6891	.6044	−12.3	.6462	−6.2	.6577	−4.6

the standard run is also given. Thus, the entry in row "MED," column "211" of the table indicates that the average precision for the MED collection when searched using sense-based vectors 211 (explained below) is .4777, which is a 13.6% degradation in effectiveness as compared with the average precision of .5527 obtained when standard stem-based vectors were used. Put another way, the sense-based vectors will, on average, retrieve slightly less than one fewer relevant document per query than the stem-based vectors will for the MED collection.

The three sense-based vector runs differ in the way the subvectors are weighted when computing the overall similarity between documents and queries, and these weights are used to label the runs. The run labeled "110" gives equal weight to the nonnoun word stems and the synset IDs and ignores the noun word stems. This run is as close to a pure sense-based run as we can get. The run labeled "211" gives the nonnoun word stems twice the weight given to each of the synset IDs and the noun word stems. This run weights the nonnoun stems twice to counterbalance the fact that both the noun stems and the noun senses are included. The final run ("101") is a control run. All of the word stems are given equal weight and the synset IDs are ignored. This is not equivalent to the standard run since the overall similarity measure only counts a term match if the term occurs in the same subvector in both the query and the document.

Unfortunately, the effectiveness of the sense-based vectors is worse than that of the stem-based vectors, sometimes much worse. Examination of the individual query results shows that most of this degradation is caused by term matches between documents and queries that are made in the standard run but missed in the sense-based runs (recall that the cosine similarity measure is heavily dependent on the number of terms two vectors have in common). As an example of how this occurs, consider query 16 of the MED collection. The query, requesting documents on separation anxiety in infants and preschool children, retrieves 7 relevant documents in the top 15 for the standard run and only 1 relevant document in the top 15 for the "110" run. The problem is selecting the sense of *separation* in the query. WordNet contains eight senses of the noun *separation*. With so few other words to use in the disambiguation processing of the query, the process selects a sense of *separation* that is never selected for any document. The separation concept can, therefore, never match any document, and retrieval performance suffers accordingly.

The importance of finding matches between document and query terms is underscored by the degradation in performance of the control run "101" compared with the standard run. The only major difference between the "101" run, which ignores the senses and just uses the word stems, and the standard run, which also uses only word stems, is the introduction of subvectors in the "101" run. In the sense-based vectors, stems of words that are not nouns or nouns that are not in WordNet are in one subvector and stems of WordNet nouns are in the other subvector. The extended vector similarity measure matches a word stem in the document vector only if that word stem appears in the same subvector in the query. Therefore, adjectives and verbs that conflate to the same stem as a noun are counted as a match in the standard run but not in the "101" run.

Since this problem of missing some good matches remains even if the sense resolution procedure works perfectly, these results do not imply anything about how accurately word senses were resolved. However, a subjective evaluation of the procedure obtained while looking at the individual query retrieval results suggests that the procedure is not a reliable method for choosing among the fine sense distinctions WordNet makes. As an example of why this is true, consider the *board* example of figure 12.1. The nouns *nail, hammer,* and *carpenter* are all good hints that the intended sense of *board* is the 'lumber' sense. However, within WordNet a nail is a fastener, which in turn is a device, so *nail* would help select the 'control panel' sense of *board*. Similarly, a hammer is a tool, which is an implement, which is an article of commerce, so *hammer* would help select the 'dining table' sense of *board*. Finally, a carpenter is a worker, which is a person, which is both an agent and a life form, which are both things. Thus, *carpenter* would not help select any sense of *board*. This analysis indicates that specialization/generalization relations are unlikely to contain sufficient information to choose among fine sense distinctions.

12.4   QUERY EXPANSION

In practice, the problem of homographs depressing precision is not severe unless the query is very short or the searcher is interested in very high recall (Krovetz and Croft 1992): if a document has enough terms in common with a query to have a high similarity to the query, then the contexts in the two texts are similar and polysemous words tend to refer to the same sense. Furthermore, as the experimental results above indicate, it is much more deleterious to retrieval performance to miss a good match than it is to make a few spurious matches.

These considerations suggest another approach to using WordNet during indexing. Instead of trying to select a single synset to represent a concept—an error-prone process where a single error can severely degrade retrieval effectiveness—use WordNet as a source of additional words to supplement the user's query. The goal is to add to a query all the different words that can be used to express the query's concepts. Whichever word is used to express a concept in a relevant document will then find a match in the query, and the remaining additional words will have little impact on the overall similarity. This process, known as *query expansion*, has improved retrieval effectiveness in small, homogenous collections (Salton and Lesk 1971a; Wang, Vandendorpe, and Evens 1985). Using WordNet as a word source tests whether similar improvements can be realized when querying a large collection that spans several domains.

Two sets of experiments were performed to investigate the effectiveness of using WordNet for query expansion (Voorhees 1994). The first set explores the expansion strategy itself, using handpicked synsets as the starting points of the expansion. Starting with handpicked synsets removes the confounding effects of expanding a poor selection of words, and thus provides an upper bound on the performance to be expected from a completely automatic procedure that uses this expansion technique. The second set of experiments extends the expansion strategy to include automatically selecting the starting synsets.

The query expansion experiments were run using the TREC test collection (Harman 1993). The TREC documents consist of English prose obtained from a variety of sources including newspapers, abstracts of technical papers, and the *Federal Register*. The text of a TREC query statement (called a *topic statement* in TREC parlance) is a complex natural language statement of need as shown in figure 12.2. Each topic statement has a set of fields flagged by special markers (the words

```
<dom> Domain: Medical & Biological

<title> Topic: RDT&E of New Cancer Fighting Drugs

<desc> Description:

Document will report on the research, development, testing,
and evaluation (RDT&E) of a new anti-cancer drug developed
anywhere in the world.

<narr> Narrative:

A relevant document will report on any phase in the
worldwide process of bringing new cancer fighting drugs to
market, from conceptualization of government marketing
approval. The laboratory or company responsible for the
drug project, the specific type of cancer(s) which the drug
is designed to counter, and the chemical/medical properties
of the drug must be identified.

<con> Concept(s):

1. cancer, leukemia

2. drug, chemotherapy
```

Figure 12.2
Detailed query statement of TREC query 122

enclosed in angle brackets). The Narrative field provides a particularly detailed description of what constitutes a relevant document; the Concepts field usually lists words and phrases that the creator of the statement thinks are related to the topic. A shorter version of each topic statement is also available. This shorter version, the Summary Statement, is usually a single sentence describing the search request. The Summary Statement for the topic shown in figure 12.2 is the sentence given in the Description field. (The Summary Statement is frequently, but not always, identical to the Description field.) The indexing process extracts the words from the various fields to produce a query vector.

A new query field consisting of synsets handpicked by the author as containing nouns germane to the subject was added to the query statements. Since one of the goals of the experiments is to examine the efficacy of expansion assuming good starting concepts, the selection of synsets was governed by both subject matter and the fact that the synsets would be used to expand the query. As an example, the synsets added to the query statement shown in figure 12.2 were {*cancer*}, {*skin_cancer*}, and {*pharmaceutical*}.

12.4.1 Expanding by Manually Selected Synsets

Once the text of a query is hand-annotated with synsets, the indexing and processing of the query are automatic. The words from the main query fields are extracted and stemmed using the standard indexing procedures. This produces a set of "original query terms." The expansion procedure is invoked when the synset section of the query text is reached.

Given a synset, there is a wide choice of words to add to a query vector: one can add only the synonyms within the synset, or all descendants in the specialization/generalization hierarchy, or all words in synsets one link (relational pointer) away from the original synset regardless of pointer type, and so on. The expansion procedure is parameterized to facilitate comparing the effectiveness of a variety of these schemes. The parameter set for a given run specifies for each relation type included in WordNet the maximum length of a chain of that type of link that may be followed. A chain begins at each synset listed in the synset section of the query text and may contain only links of a single type. All synonyms contained within a synset of the chain are added to the query. Collocations such as *article_of_commerce* are broken into their component words, stop words such as *of* are removed, and the remaining words are stemmed. The word stems plus a tag indicating the lexical relation through which the stems are related to the original synset are then appended to the original query terms.

As an example of the expansion process, consider the {*furniture*} synset in figure 12.1, and assume there is a substance meronymy pointer from that synset to the {*lumber*, *timber*} synset. If the parameters to the expansion procedure indicate that only hyponym pointers should be followed, but they can be followed to any length, an occurrence of *furniture* in the original query will cause the stems for *table*, *dining*, *board*, and *refectory* to be added to the query vector. If instead the expansion procedure allows any link to be followed to a depth of 1, an occurrence of *furniture* would cause the stems of *table*, *article*, *commerce*, *lumber*, and *timber* to be added to the query vector.

Stems added through different lexical relations are kept separate using different subvectors in the query. Each query vector is composed of 11 subvectors: 1 for original query terms, 1 for synonyms, and 1 for each of the other relational pointers contained within the noun portion of Word-Net. Since the document vectors contain only one subvector, the overall similarity measure computed for these queries is the weighted sum of the similarities of each subvector in the query with the document's one subvector. That is,

$$\text{sim}(Q, D) = \sum_{\text{subvector } i} \alpha_i \, \text{sim}(Q_i, D),$$

where α_i reflects the importance of lexical relation i.

Starting with the set of synsets that were selected for a query text, a variety of different expanded runs are possible. The effectiveness of an expanded run is dependent on the link types followed during expansion and the relative weight given to each link type (the α_i's in the overall similarity measure above). Four different expansion strategies with a variety of different link-weighting schemes were tested on queries derived from the full query statement and queries derived from only the Summary Statement (Voorhees 1994). The expansion strategies included expanding by synonyms only, expanding by synonyms plus all descendants in the hierarchy, expanding by synonyms plus parents and all descendants in the hierarchy, and expanding by synonyms plus any synset directly related to the given synset (i.e., a chain of length 1 for all link types). For query vectors derived from the full query statement, none of the expansion methods produced an improvement greater than 2% in the 11-point average precision as compared with an unexpanded run. However, some of the expansion methods materially improved query vectors derived from the Summary Statement.

The graph in figure 12.3 demonstrates how the expanded Summary Statement queries compare with both unexpanded Summary Statement queries and unexpanded Full Query Statement queries (expanding Full Query Statement queries did not materially affect retrieval performance). The graph plots average recall versus average precision for each of the three runs where the averages are taken over 50 queries. The two unexpanded runs use only the word stems that occur in either the full text of the query ("full unexpanded") or the Summary Statement ("smry unexpanded") to compute the document rankings. The expanded run ("smry expanded") uses the original query terms from the Summary Statement and then expands by following any link type to a length of 1. Terms that are added to the query are weighted at .5 the weight given to original

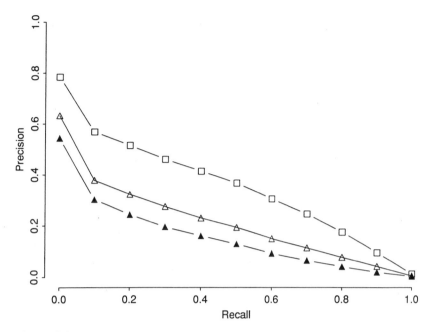

Figure 12.3
Effectiveness of queries derived from Summary Statement. (□ = full unexpanded; ▲ = smry unexpanded; △ = smry expanded)

query terms (i.e., $\alpha_{\text{original}} = 1$ and all other α's = .5 in the similarity computation). The 11-point average precision values for the three runs plotted in the figure are .3586 (full unexpanded), .1634 (smry unexpanded), and .2205 (smry expanded). This is a 35% improvement in the 11-point average for the expanded run as compared with its unexpanded counterpart, but still a 39% degradation in effectiveness as compared with unexpanded full topic queries. Clearly, retrieval performance is enhanced if users can specify detailed statements of need.

12.4.2   Expanding by Automatically Selected Synsets

Given that short queries have the potential to be significantly improved by expansion, it is necessary to see if the potential can be realized by a completely automatic procedure. Although it is possible to present users with a list of candidate synsets and have them select the ones to expand, choosing correct synsets is a tedious process, and a poor choice can be worse than not expanding.

```
for (each query word w) {
    if (w not already expanded and
                document frequency of w ≤ N) {
        expand all synsets containing w producing kin
        list of w
    }
}
for (each relative in the set of kin lists) {
    if (relative occurs in more than 1 list)
        add relative to query vector
}
```

Figure 12.4
Procedure to automatically select synsets to expand

Figure 12.4 provides a high-level description of the algorithm developed to automatically select the synsets that are the seeds of the expansion process. The algorithm is based on the observation that the synsets need to represent the correct sense of *important* concepts of the query (Voorhees and You 1993). Importance is approximated by the number of documents in which a query term occurs—a term occurring in more than N documents is not expanded. Sense resolution is approximated by requiring a new term to be related to at least two original query terms before it is included in the expanded query.

A series of retrieval runs using the above procedure on the Summary Statements tested the procedure's effectiveness. The experiments tested different values of N: 70,000, approximately 10% of the collection, and 35,000, approximately 5% of the collection; different limits on the lengths of chains to follow when expanding (all link types were treated identically): 1 and 2; and different link weights (α's): .3, .5, and .8. The results of these runs are summarized in table 12.2. Each row in the table gives the 11-point average precision values obtained by the run and, for the expanded runs, the percentage difference between the run and the unexpanded query run. As can be seen, none of the runs materially improves the performance of the unexpanded Summary Statement queries.

Inspection of the queries that resulted from the automatic selection procedure suggests that the requirement that a term appear in two lists is not a good approximation to sense resolution. The correct senses of words contained in a short query seldom have common relatives. Instead, the words that appear in more than one list are likely to be fairly general terms with more than one sense themselves. For example, since colloca-

Table 12.2
Effectiveness of expansion strategies on Summary Statement queries when expanding automatically selected synsets

	11-point average precision	% change
Unexpanded queries	.1634	—
$N = 70,000$; max chain length $= 1$		
$\alpha = .3$	.1627	−0.5
$\alpha = .5$	.1603	−1.9
$\alpha = .8$	.1543	−5.6
$N = 70,000$; max chain length $= 2$		
$\alpha = .3$	.1633	−0.1
$\alpha = .5$	.1557	−4.7
$\alpha = .8$	.1402	−14.2
$N = 35,000$; max chain length $= 1$		
$\alpha = .3$	.1636	+0.1
$\alpha = .5$	.1635	+0.1
$\alpha = .8$	.1639	+0.3
$N = 35,000$; max chain length $= 2$		
$\alpha = .3$	.1645	+0.7
$\alpha = .5$	.1642	+0.5
$\alpha = .8$	.1617	−1.0

tions are split into their components during the expansion process, general nouns such as *system* tend to appear in multiple lists.

12.5 CONCLUSION

This chapter has presented two attempts to exploit the knowledge encoded in WordNet to improve text retrieval effectiveness. In both cases the inability to automatically resolve word senses prevented any improvement from being realized. When word sense resolution was not an issue (e.g., when synsets were manually chosen), significant effectiveness improvements resulted.

These findings provide strong motivation for developing automatic word sense resolution techniques. However, the experiments above suggest that the paradigmatic relations contained within WordNet together with the text to be disambiguated do not supply the information required for this sense resolution task. Although the paradigmatic relations can be exploited once the correct sense of a term is known, syntagmatic information is needed to automatically determine which sense is of interest (Leacock, Towell, and Voorhees 1996). The feasibility of annotating WordNet synsets with concise representations of the contexts in which words are used is currently under investigation. If such annotation proves feasible, the contexts can be used to locate the most likely sense(s) of text words, with the synsets so identified used as the seeds for the expansion process.

References

Buckley, C. (1985). *Implementation of the SMART information retrieval system* (Tech. Rep. No. 85-686). Ithaca, NY: Cornell University, Computer Science Department.

Chakravarthy, A. S. (1994). Toward semantic retrieval of pictures and video clip captions. In *RIAO 94 Conference Proceedings: Intelligent multimedia information retrieval systems and management*, vol. 1, 676–686. Paris: C.I.D.-C.A.S.I.S.

Chakravarthy, A. S., and Haase, K. B. (1995). NetSerf: Using semantic knowledge to find Internet information archives. In *Proceedings of the Eighteenth Annual International ACM SIGIR Conference on Research and Development in Information Retrieval*, 4–11. New York: ACM Press.

Deerwester, S., Dumais, S. T., Furnas, G. W., Landauer, T. K., and Harshman, R. (1990). Indexing by latent semantic analysis. *Journal of the American Society for Information Science, 41*, 391–407.

Fox, E. A. (1983). *Extending the Boolean and vector space models of information retrieval with p-norm queries and multiple concept types.* Unpublished doctoral dissertation, Cornell University, Ithaca, NY. University Microfilms, Ann Arbor, MI.

Harman, D. K. (1993). The first Text REtrieval Conference (TREC-1), Rockville, MD, U.S.A., 4–6 November, 1992. *Information Processing and Management, 29*, 411–414.

Krovetz, R., and Croft, W. B. (1992). Lexical ambiguity in information retrieval. *ACM Transactions on Information Systems, 10*, 115–141.

Leacock, C., Towell, G., and Voorhees, E. M. (1996). Towards building contextual representations of word senses using statistical models. In B. Boguraev and J. Pustejovsky (Eds.), *Corpus processing for lexical acquisition*, 97–113. Cambridge, MA: MIT Press.

Rau, L. F. (1987). Knowledge organization and access in a conceptual information system. *Information Processing and Management, 23*, 269–283.

Richardson, R. (1994). *A semantic-based approach to information processing.* Unpublished doctoral dissertation, Dublin City University.

Salton, G. (1991). Developments in automatic text retrieval. *Science, 253,* 974–980.

Salton, G., and Buckley, C. (1988). Term weighting approaches in automatic text retrieval. *Information Processing and Management, 24,* 513–523.

Salton, G., and Lesk, M. E. (1971a). Computer evaluation of indexing and text processing. In G. Salton (Ed.), *The SMART retrieval system: Experiments in automatic document processing,* 143–180. Englewood Cliffs, NJ: Prentice-Hall.

Salton, G., and Lesk, M. E. (1971b). Information analysis and dictionary construction. In G. Salton (Ed.), *The SMART retrieval system: Experiments in automatic document processing,* 115–142. Englewood Cliffs, NJ: Prentice-Hall.

Salton, G., and McGill, M. J. (1983). *Introduction to modern information retrieval.* New York: McGraw-Hill.

Salton, G., Wong, A., and Yang, C. S. (1975). A vector space model for automatic indexing. *Communications of the ACM, 18,* 613–620.

Sussna, M. (1993). Word sense disambiguation for free-text indexing using a massive semantic network. In *Proceedings of the Second International Conference on Information and Knowledge Management (CIKM 93),* 67–74. New York: ACM Press.

Voorhees. E. M. (1993). Using WordNet to disambiguate word senses for text retrieval. In *Proceedings of the Sixteenth Annual International ACM SIGIR Conference on Research and Development in Information Retrieval,* 171–180. New York: ACM Press.

Voorhees, E. M. (1994). Query expansion using lexical-semantic relations. In *Proceedings of the Seventeenth Annual International ACM SIGIR Conference on Research and Development in Information Retrieval,* 61–69. London: Springer-Verlag.

Voorhees, E. M., and Hou, Y.-W. (1993). Vector expansion in a large collection. In *Proceedings of the First Text REtrieval Conference (TREC-1),* 343–351. NIST Special Publication 500-207. Gaithersburg, MD: US Department of Commerce, National Institute of Standards and Technology.

Wang, Y.-C., Vandendorpe, J., and Evens, M. (1985). Relational thesauri in information retrieval. *Journal of the American Society for Information Science, 36,* 15–27.

Chapter 13

Lexical Chains as Representations of Context for the Detection and Correction of Malapropisms

Graeme Hirst and David St-Onge

13.1 INTRODUCTION

Natural language utterances are, in general, highly ambiguous, and a unique interpretation can usually be determined only by taking into account the constraining influence of the context in which the utterance occurred.[1] Much of the research in natural language understanding in the last 20 years can be thought of as attempts to characterize and represent context and then derive interpretations that fit best with that context. Typically, this research was heavy with artificial intelligence, taking context to be nothing less than a complete conceptual understanding of the preceding utterances. This was reasonable, as such an understanding of a text was often the main task anyway. However, there are many text-processing tasks that require only a partial understanding of the text, and hence a "lighter" representation of context is sufficient. In this chapter we examine the idea of *lexical chains* as such a representation. We show how they can be constructed by means of WordNet and how they can be applied in one particular linguistic task: the detection and correction of *malapropisms*.

A malapropism is the confounding of an intended word with another word of similar sound or similar spelling that has a quite different and malapropos meaning, for example, *an ingenuous* [for *ingenious*] *machine for peeling oranges*. In this example there is a one-letter difference between the malapropism and the correct word. Ignorance, or a simple typing mistake, might cause such errors. However, since *ingenuous* is a correctly spelled word, traditional spelling checkers cannot detect this error. In section 13.4 we propose an algorithm for detecting and correcting malapropisms that is based on the construction of lexical chains.

13.2   LEXICAL CHAINS

If a text is cohesive and coherent, successive sentences are likely to refer to concepts that were previously mentioned and to other concepts that are related to them. Halliday and Hasan (1976) suggested that the words of the text that make such references can be thought of as forming *cohesive chains* in the text. Each word in the chain is related to its predecessors by a particular *cohesive relation* such as identity of reference. For example, in (1) the italicized words form a chain with this relation:

(1) The major potential complication of total joint replacement is *infection*. *It* may occur just in the area of the wound or deep around the prosthesis. *It* may occur during the hospital stay or after the patient goes home.... *Infections* in the wound area are generally treated with antibiotics.

But the relation need not be identity; there are also cohesive chains of words whose meanings (in the text) are related to one another in more general ways such as hyponymy or meronymy or even just general association of ideas. Example (2) shows a chain in which the relation is hyponymy (an infection is a kind of complication), and (3) shows a chain in which the relation is general association:

(2) The major potential *complication* of total joint replacement is *infection*.

(3) The evening prior to admission, take a *shower* or *bath*, *scrubbing* yourself well. Rinse off all the *soap*.

Morris and Hirst (1991; Morris 1988) suggested that the discourse structure of a text may be determined by finding *lexical chains* in the text, where a lexical chain is, in essence, a cohesive chain in which the criterion for inclusion of a word is that it bear a cohesive relation of one kind or another (not necessarily one specific relation) to a word that is already in the chain. To make this idea precise, it is necessary to specify exactly what counts as a cohesive relation between words—and in particular, what counts as "general association of ideas." Morris and Hirst's suggestion was that a thesaurus, such as *Roget's* (e.g., Chapman 1992), could be used to define this. Two words could be considered to be related if they are "connected" in the thesaurus in one (or more) of five possible ways:

1. Their index entries point to the same thesaurus category or to adjacent categories.

2. The index entry of one contains the other.

3. The index entry of one points to a thesaurus category that contains the other.

4. The index entry of one points to a thesaurus category that in turn contains a pointer to a category pointed to by the index entry of the other.

5. The index entries of each point to thesaurus categories that in turn contain a pointer to the same category.

Morris and Hirst showed that the distribution through a text of lexical chains defined in this manner was indicative of the intentional structure of the text, in the sense of Grosz and Sidner (1986). They also suggested that lexical chains often provided enough context to resolve lexical ambiguities, an idea subsequently developed by Okumura and Honda (1994).

Unfortunately, however, Morris and Hirst were never able to implement their algorithm for finding lexical chains with *Roget's* because no on-line copy of the thesaurus was available to them.[2] However, the subsequent development of WordNet raises the possibility that, with a suitable modification of the algorithm, WordNet could be used in place of *Roget's*.

13.3   WORDNET AS A KNOWLEDGE SOURCE FOR A LEXICAL CHAINER

13.3.1   Relations between Words

Because the structure of WordNet is quite different from that of *Roget's Thesaurus*, if we are to replace *Roget's* with WordNet in Morris and Hirst's algorithm, we must replace their *Roget's*-based definition of semantic relatedness with one based on WordNet, while retaining the algorithm's essential properties.

Our new definition centers upon the synset (synonym set). In WordNet a word may be associated with many synsets, each corresponding to a different sense of the word. When we look for a relation between two different words, we consider all the synsets associated with each word that have not already been ruled out as inapplicable (by methods that will be described below), looking for a possible connection between some synset of the first word and some synset of the second. Three kinds of relation are defined: extra-strong, strong, and medium-strong. (If a relation is not any of these, it is said to be *weak* and is not used in the creation of lexical chains.) The definitions of these relations use a classification of WordNet synset relations into the directions *upward*, *downward*, and *horizontal*, as shown in table 13.1.

Table 13.1
Classification of WordNet relations into directions

Relation	Direction
Also see	Horizontal
Antonymy	Horizontal
Attribute	Horizontal
Cause	Down
Entailment	Down
Holonymy	Down
Hypernymy	Up
Hyponymy	Down
Meronymy	Up
Pertinence	Horizontal
Similarity	Horizontal

An *extra-strong* relation holds only between a word and its literal repetition; such relations have the highest *weight* of all relations. There are three kinds of *strong* relations, illustrated in figure 13.1. The first occurs when there is a synset common to two different words, such as *human* and *person* in figure 13.1(a). The second occurs when there is a horizontal link (e.g., ANTONYMY, SIMILARITY, SEE-ALSO) between synsets associated with two different words, such as *precursor* and *successor* in figure 13.1(b). The third occurs when there is any kind of link at all between a synset associated with each word if one word is a compound word or a phrase that includes the other, such as *school* and *private school* in figure 13.1(c). A strong relation has a lower weight than an extra-strong relation and a higher weight than a medium-strong relation.

A *medium-strong* relation between two words occurs when there is an *allowable path* connecting a synset associated with each word. A path is a sequence of between two and five links between synsets; it is allowable if it corresponds to one of the patterns shown in figure 13.2(a) (where each vector represents a sequence of one or more links in the same direction). Paths whose patterns are not allowed are shown in figure 13.2(b). Figure 13.3 shows an example of a medium-strong relation between two words, *apple* and *carrot*. Unlike extra-strong and strong relations, medium-strong relations have different weights. The weight of a path is given by

$$weight = C - path\ length - k * number\ of\ changes\ of\ direction$$

(where C and k are constants). Thus, the longer the path and the more changes of direction, the lower the weight.

The rationale for the allowable patterns of figure 13.2 is as follows: If a multilink path between two synsets is to be indicative of some reasonable semantic proximity, the semantics of each lexical relation must be taken into consideration. Now, an upward direction corresponds to generalization. For instance, an upward link from {*apple*} to {*fruit*} means that {*fruit*} is a semantically more general synset than {*apple*}. Similarly, a downward link corresponds to specialization. Horizontal links are less frequent than upward and downward links; a synset rarely has more than one. Such links are usually highly indicative of meaning. (In figure 13.1(b) the horizontal link between {*successor*} and {*predecessor, precursor, antecedent*} is a very accurate indication of that meaning of the word *successor*.) So, to ensure that a path corresponds to a reasonable relation between the source and the target word, two rules have been stated to define which patterns are allowable:

(R1) No other direction may precede an upward link.

Once a link that narrows down that context (downward or horizontal) has been used, it is not permitted to enlarge the context again by using an upward link.

(R2) At most one change of direction is allowed.

Changes of direction constitute large semantic steps. Therefore, they must be limited. However, this second rule has the following exception:

(R2′) It is permitted to use a horizontal link to make a transition from an upward to a downward direction.

Horizontal links correspond to small semantic distance for words such as *height* and *high*, which are linked by an attribute relation. In this case, this exception to (R2) enables connections between subordinates of *height* and subordinates of *high*. Thus, it has been assumed that enabling such a connection between two superordinates does not imply too large a semantic step.

13.3.2   Creating and Managing Chains

Although a lexical chain may be thought of as a sequence of words, its internal structure is more complex. Figure 13.4 gives an example of the construction of a chain. First, an empty chain is created (see figure

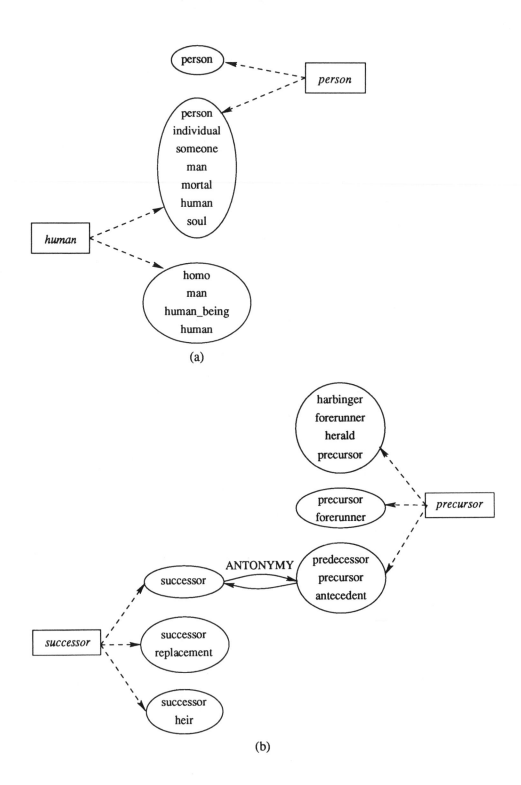

(a)

(b)

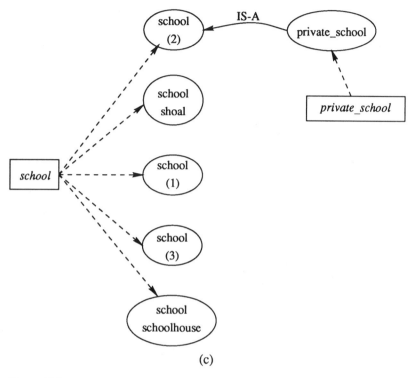

(c)

Figure 13.1
Examples of the three kinds of strong relation between words: (*a*) a synset in common; (*b*) a horizontal link between two synsets; (*c*) any link between two synsets if one word is a compound word or phrase that includes the other word. (Rectangles indicate words and ellipses indicate synsets; dashed arrows connect words with their associated synsets.)

13.4(a)). Then, a chain word record is allocated, initialized with the word *economy*, and inserted into the new chain (figure 13.4(b)). Next, to insert *sectors*, another word record is constructed and inserted into the chain. The kind of relation (extra-strong, strong, or medium-strong) between the new word and its related word (or words) in the chain is also stored in the word record. In figure 13.4(c) *sectors* precedes *economy* in the chain and another connection denotes its relation with *economy*. In figure 13.4(d) *economic system* is inserted into the chain, not from a relation with *sectors*, its immediate successor in the chain, but from a relation with *economy*, with which it shares a synset and hence has a strong relation. Thus, the word order in a chain corresponds only to insertion order, not necessarily to relations between words.

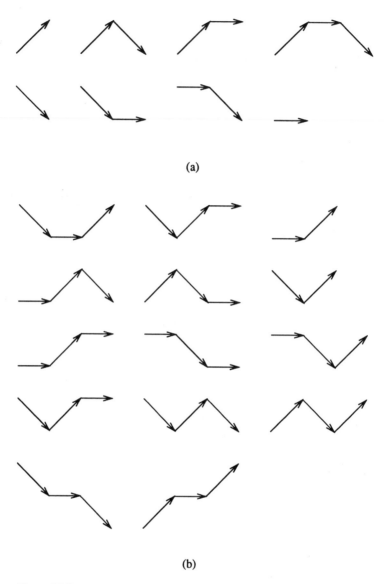

Figure 13.2
(*a*) Patterns of paths between synsets that are allowable in medium-strong relations and (*b*) patterns of paths that are not allowable. (Each arrow denotes one or
more synset relations in the same direction: upward, downward, or horizontal.)

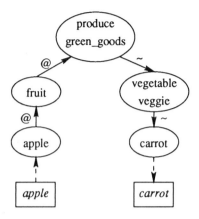

Figure 13.3
Example of a medium-strong relation between two words. (@ = hypernymy,
~ = hyponymy)

Because a word form may be associated with more than one synset, when a new word record is constructed, a list of pointers to every synset of the word is created and attached to it. When a word starts a new chain, all its synsets are kept, since, at this point, no contextual information is available to discriminate among them (see figure 13.5). Inserting another word into the chain results in a connection between the words by linking the synsets involved in the relation. When a word is inserted into a chain because of an extra-strong relation, all corresponding synsets are connected; when the relation involved is strong, all the strongly related synsets are connected; and when the relation involved is medium-strong, the pair (or pairs) of synsets whose weight is greatest are connected (see figure 13.6).

After the connection between words is made, any unconnected synsets of the new word are deleted and the chain is scanned to remove other synsets wherever possible. Synsets that are not involved in the current word connection are removed. Removing synsets while inserting words in a chain progressively disambiguates each word of the chain by removing unchained, and presumably inapplicable, interpretations, thereby narrowing down the context. This idea comes from Hirst's Polaroid Words (1987). Figure 13.7 illustrates the word sense disambiguation process resulting from the situation illustrated in figure 13.6. When *sector* in figure 13.4(c) is added to the chain, both its synset lists and those of *economy* are updated.

(a)   [ ]

chain

(b)   [economy]

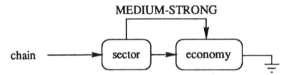
chain

(c)   [sector, economy]

MEDIUM-STRONG

chain ──────►│ sector │─►│ economy │

(d)   [economic system, sector, economy]

MEDIUM-STRONG

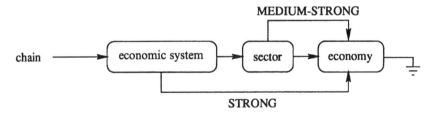
chain

STRONG

Figure 13.4
Building a chain: (*a*) an empty chain; (*b*) insertion of the first word; (*c*) insertion of a second word related to the first; (*d*) insertion of another word related to the first. (Round-cornered rectangles indicate chain records, which include words and their associated synsets (not shown); unlabeled arrows indicate chain pointers; labeled arrows indicate relationships between the words in the records; the ground symbol indicates the null pointer.)

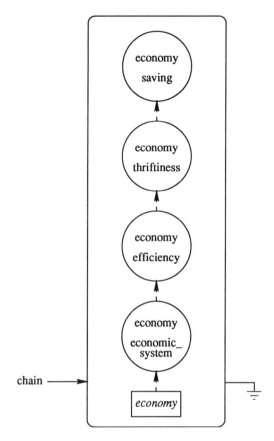

Figure 13.5
A word starting a new chain. (The word *economy* has four synsets.)

13.3.3   Identifying Words and Relations

Because the verb file of WordNet has no relation with the three other files and the adverb file has only unidirectional relations with the adjective file, we limited the chaining process to nouns in the present version of our software. (We hope that future versions of WordNet will allow us to remove this limitation.) However, we have not used any parsing or part-of-speech tagging in our program, because of the slowdown and the error that would have resulted. Instead, we decided to consider as a noun any word that could be found in the noun index as is or could be morphologically transformed to such a word. This decision is based on the assumption that most words in other grammatical categories that

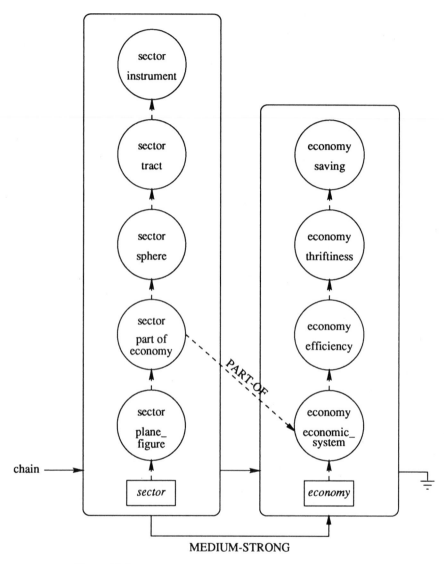

Figure 13.6
Adding a related word

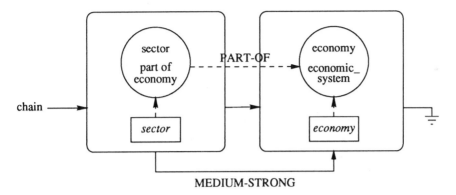

Figure 13.7
Updated chain after insertion

have a nominal form are semantically close to that form (e.g., *to walk* and *a walk*), and our experimentation has shown that this assumption was valid.

Wherever possible, we try to identify in the input text any compound words and phrases that are included in WordNet, because they are much better indicators of the meaning of the text than the words that compose them, taken separately. For instance, *private school*, which is listed in the noun index as *private_school*, is more indicative than *private* and *school* taken separately. During this phrase identification process, each word must also pass a validity test to ensure its suitability for lexical chaining: as explained above, it must be a WordNet noun or transformable to a noun, and it must not appear in the stop-word list. The stop-word list contains closed-class words and many vague high-frequency words that tend to weaken chains by having little content (e.g., *one, two, dozen, little, relative, right*).

If a word is potentially chainable, an extra-strong relation is sought throughout all chains, and if one is found, the word is added to the appropriate chain. If not, strong relations are sought, but for these, the search scope is limited to the words in any chain that are no more than seven sentences back in the text; the search ends as soon as a strong relation is found. Finally, if no relation has yet been found, medium-strong relations are sought; here, the search scope is limited to words in chains that are no more than three sentences back. Since the weight of medium-strong connections varies, all medium-strong connections within the search scope must be found, in order to retain the one with the highest weight.[3] If no relation can be found at all, a new chain is created for the word.

A formal algorithmic specification of the chaining algorithm and details of the software implementation of the chainer—the LexC program—are given by St-Onge (1995).

13.3.4 Testing the Lexical Chainer

Testing the lexical chainer is difficult, because what counts as a reasonable chain depends upon linguistic intuition, and what counts as a useful chain depends upon the particular application to which it is being put, where one can see whether it does or doesn't serve the task. Consequently, much of our evaluation is postponed to section 13.4.3.2, where we describe our results in real-word spelling correction. Here we briefly outline some of our observations from trying the chainer out on various texts, examining the chains that it builds, and seeing how they accord with intuition. We found that many chains did indeed match our expectations, and many words were correctly disambiguated. More details and many examples are given by St-Onge (1995).

Two kinds of disappointment were possible: words not included in chains in which they clearly belonged, and words included in chains in which they did not belong. These situations arise from several problems:

1. limitations in the set of relations in WordNet, or a missing connection;
2. inconsistency in the measure of semantic proximity that is implicit in links in WordNet; and
3. incorrect or incomplete disambiguation.

The following sentence gives an example of the first problem, missing connections:

(4) Nasdaq volume has been burgeoning daily, and yesterday hit 146.1 million shares.

Here, one would want *Nasdaq* to be connected to *shares*. However, WordNet does not have a sufficient set of relations to connect these two words. In fact, relations such as antonymy, holonymy, or meronymy are not appropriate to link the two. Rather, the relation that exists between these two words is a *situational relation*: shares are the subject of the processing that Nasdaq performs. Many such relations are hard to classify (e.g., the situational relation between *physician* and *hospital*), and it was a strength of Morris and Hirst's original *Roget's*-based algorithm that it was able to make such connections nonetheless.

Similarly, WordNet has a paucity of links between words of different syntactic categories. In (5), for example, the adjective *over-the-counter* cannot be connected to the noun *stock*:

(5) Prices of over-the-counter stocks surged yesterday ...

(Consequently, as described in section 13.3.3, we did not even attempt to include in chains any words that could not be construed as nouns.)

The following sentence illustrates the second problem, inconsistencies in the semantic distance or proximity implicit in a link.

(6) The cost means no holiday trips and more *stew* than *steak*, but she is satisfied that her children, now in grades 3 and 4, are being properly taught.

Here, *stew* and *steak* are obviously somehow related. However, these two words were not linked to each other. Here is their mutual relation in WordNet:

(7) {*stew*} IS-A {*dish*} IS-A {*aliment*} INCLUDES {*meat*} INCLUDES {*cut*, *cut_of_meat*} INCLUDES {*piece, slice*} INCLUDES {*steak*}

The intersynset distance between {*stew*} and {*steak*} is six synsets, which is greater than the limit that is set in the lexical chainer. In general, the greater the distance limit, the greater the number of weak connections. However, links in WordNet do not all reflect the same semantic distance. In other words, there are situations, as with *stew* and *steak*, where words have an obvious semantic proximity but are distant in WordNet.

There are also situations where words are close to each other in Word-Net while being quite distant semantically. This introduces the problem of overchaining. For example, in one chain we found *public* linked to *professionals* by the following relationship:

(8) {*public*} IS-A {*people*} HAS-MEMBER {*person*} INCLUDES {*adult*} INCLUDES {*professional*}

The third problem, incorrect or incomplete disambiguation, often follows from under- and overchaining, as the following example demonstrates:

(9) We suppose a very long *train* traveling along the *rails* with the constant *velocity v* and in the direction indicated ...

Here, a chain is created with the word *train*, which has six senses in WordNet. But the word *rails* is not associated with it, the distance between these two words being too great in WordNet. The word *velocity* is then connected to *train* with the undesired effect of wrongly disambiguating it, as the following sense is selected:

(10) {*sequence, succession, sequel, train*}—events that are ordered in time.

13.4 AUTOMATICALLY DETECTING MALAPROPISMS

We now propose an algorithm for detecting and correcting malapropisms that is based on the construction of lexical chains.

13.4.1 Spelling Checkers

Traditional spelling checkers can detect only nonword errors. The two main techniques that they use are lexicon lookup and *n*-gram analysis. In the former case, each word of the input text is sought in a lexicon and considered to be an error if not found. The size of the lexicon is an important issue: a too-small lexicon will result in too many false rejections, whereas a too-large lexicon (with rare or unusual words) will result in too many false acceptances (Peterson 1986). False rejections might also be caused by the use of a lexicon that is not adapted to a specific area of application. The second detection method, *n*-gram analysis, is based on the probability of a given sequence of letters of length *n*, where usually $n = 2$ (digram) or $n = 3$ (trigram). Under a certain threshold, an error is signaled. In either method, an attempt may then be made to find candidates for the word that was intended. Techniques for doing this typically generate strings that are similar to the erroneous word, by means of transformations such as adding, deleting, or transposing characters and then filtering out nonwords by checking the lexicon. (See Kukich 1992 or Vosse 1994 for a survey of techniques.)

Real-word errors are much more difficult to detect than nonword errors and even more difficult to correct. Kukich (1992) classifies real-word errors into four categories:

1. syntactic errors (e.g., *The students are doing there homework*);
2. semantic errors or malapropisms (e.g., *He spent his summer traveling around the word*);
3. structural errors (e.g., *I need three ingredients: red wine, sugar, cinnamon, and cloves*); and

4. pragmatic errors (e.g., *He studied at the University of Toronto in England*).

Errors that belong to the first category (which are, strictly speaking, also malapropisms) can be detected by using a natural language parser or by performing a word-level *n*-gram analysis to detect words that have a low probability of succession. The same tools could be used to suggest replacements. However, errors that belong to the other three categories are much harder to detect and even harder to correct.

Few studies have been made on the frequency of real-word errors. Mitton (1987) studied 925 essays written by high-school students and found that 40% of all errors were real-word errors. He noticed that most of these real-word errors belonged to the first category. Atwell and Elliot (1987) analyzed three different kinds of text that had not been automatically proofread: published texts, 11- and 12-year-old students' essays, and text written by nonnative speakers of English. They found that the corresponding amounts of real-word errors were 48%, 64%, and 96%, respectively. Among the real-word errors, 25%, 16%, and 38%, respectively, belonged to the semantic category.

13.4.2   An Algorithm for Detecting Probable Malapropisms

As discussed above, each discourse unit of a text tends to use related words. Our hypothesis is that the more distant a word is semantically from all the other words of a text, the higher the probability is that it is a malapropism. But lexical chains can be thought of as sets of words that are semantically close. Hence, a word in a text that cannot be fitted into a lexical chain, but is close in spelling to a word that *could* be fitted, is likely to be a malapropism. More formally, a spelling checker can detect likely malapropisms, and suggest corrections, by the following method:

Assume that (as in all but the simplest spelling checkers) the program already includes a mechanism that, given a character string *w*, can produce a set $P(w)$ of all words in the program's lexicon for which *w* is a plausible mistyping.

1. The program first looks for nonword errors in the text and solicits corrections from the user (or chooses a correction automatically).
2. The program next constructs lexical chains between the high-content words in the text. (Stop words are not considered; the erroneous occurrence of these words cannot be detected by this method.)

3. The program then hypothesizes that a word w is in error, even though it is a correctly spelled word, if w is not a member of any lexical chain, but there is a word $w' \in P(w)$ that would be in a lexical chain had it appeared in the text instead of w. It is then likely enough that w' was intended where w appears that the user should be alerted to the possibility of the error.

We have implemented this algorithm with the lexical chainer described in section 13.3. (The implementation covers only the detection of malapropisms in steps 2–3; it does not check for nonword spelling errors.) Any *atomic chain*—a chain that contains only one word[4]—is extracted and considered to be a potential malapropism.[5] A set of possible corrections is then sought for each potential malapropism, using the spelling correction procedure of a spelling checker. For each possible correction, an attempt is made to find a relation with a word that is in one of the lexical chains. This chaining process is done with the normal chaining mechanism, except that the word chain search scope is both backward and forward and is limited to the same word chain distance in both directions. All possible corrections that have a relation with a word in a chain are retained. If a potential malapropism has a chainable possible correction, an alarm is raised, suggesting to the user the possibility that the potential malapropism is an error and that one of the chainable corrections was the word that was intended.

13.4.3 An Experiment

It is difficult to test the algorithm on naturally occurring text, because large on-line corpora that are available consist mostly of edited, published texts by professional writers and hence may be assumed to contain an extremely small number of malapropisms. Ideally, we would test the algorithm on a large supply of the kinds of texts that are submitted to spelling checkers—unedited first drafts written by typical users of word processors, including students and others who are not professional writers—in which all the malapropisms have been identified by a human judge, so that the algorithm's performance may be compared to the human's. Such texts are not available, but we can simulate them by inserting deliberate malapropisms into a published text.

So, to test our algorithm, we took 500 articles on many different topics selected randomly from the *Wall Street Journal* from 1987 to 1989, replacing roughly each 200th word with a malapropism. We then ran our algorithm on the modified text, seeing what proportion of the malapropisms could be identified as such.

13.4.3.1 Creating the Experimental Text   To create malapropisms, we used the code that generates error replacement suggestions in Ispell 1.123, a spelling checker for nonword errors.[6] This code returns "near misses"— words found in the lexicon that differ only slightly (usually by a single letter or a transposition) from the input string. When it is given a real word as input instead of a nonword error, it becomes, in effect, a malapropism generator. It tries the following transformations:

1. restore a missing letter (e.g., *girder* → *girdler*);
2. delete an extra letter (e.g., *beast* → *best*, *lumpfish* → *lumpish*);
3. transpose a pair of adjacent letters (e.g., *elan* → *lean*);
4. replace one letter (e.g., *recuse* → *refuse*);
5. restore a missing space, (e.g., *weeknight* → *wee knight*, *Superbowl* → *Superb owl*);
6. restore a missing hyphen (e.g., *relay* → *re-lay*).

A string transformed in this way is accepted as a malapropism if it meets three conditions: it must not be in the stop-word list; it must be in the noun database of WordNet; and it must not be a morphological variation upon the original word.[7]

We replaced one word in every 200 in our sample texts with a malapropism that was generated in this way. If a malapropism could not be found for a target word, subsequent words were considered one by one until a suitable one was found.

Some of the sample texts did not have any malapropisms because they were less than 200 words long. However, whenever a text is too small to provide enough context, the algorithm used to identify lexical chains is not valid. For this experiment, a text was considered too small if it did not get at least one malapropism (though some small articles *did* get one). Eighteen such articles were found and removed.

Here is a sample of the malapropisms inserted in one article. The original words are shown in brackets:

(11) Much of that data, he notes, is available *toady* [*today*] electronically.

(12) Among the largest OTC issues, Farmers Group, which expects B.A.T. Industries to launch a hostile *tenter* [*tender*] offer for it, jumped $2\frac{3}{8}$ to 62 yesterday.

(13) But most of yesterday's popular issues were small out-of-the-limelight technology companies that slipped in price a bit last year after the *crush* [*crash*], although their earnings are on the rise.

13.4.3.2 Results

We will give examples of successes and failures in the experiment and then quantify the results.

First, we show examples of the algorithm's performance on genuine malapropisms. The malapropism *toady* shown in (11) is an example of a malapropism that was detected as such and for which the correct replacement was found; that is, *toady* was placed in a chain by itself, and the spelling variant *today* was found to fit in a chain with other words such as *yesterday* and *month* from the same article.[8] The malapropism *tenter* shown in (12) was not detected, as it did not appear in an atomic chain, having been connected to *stock* by the following chain:

(14) {*tenter*} IS-A {*framework, frame*} INCLUDES {*handbarrow*} HAS-PART {*handle, grip, hold*} INCLUDES {*stock*}

This happened because although the article contained many references to *stock* in the financial sense, there was no other noun in the article to disambiguate it—except, ironically, the word that was transformed into a malapropism! The malapropism *crush* shown in (13) was also detected, but the correct replacement, *crash*, was not suggested, as it did not fit into any chain; rather, *brush* was suggested, as that too fitted with *stock* (because brushes have handles).

Now we show examples of the algorithm's performance on non-malapropisms. In the following sentence on new stock issues, the word *television* was placed in an atomic chain (despite the presence of *network*, which was wrongly disambiguated) and hence regarded as suspicious:

(15) QVC Network, a 24-hour home *television* shopping issue, said yesterday it expects fiscal 1989 sales of $170 million to $200 million, ...

However, no spelling variants were found for *television*, so no alarm was raised. In the following sentence, the word *souring* was placed in an atomic chain and hence regarded as suspicious:

(16) It is suffering huge loan losses from *souring* real estate loans, and is the focus of increased monitoring by federal regulators who have braced themselves for a possible rescue.

Table 13.2
Results of testing the algorithm for detecting malapropisms

Total number of words in corpus	322,645
Number of words in chains	109,407
—malapropisms	1,409
—nonmalapropisms	107,998
Number of atomic chains	8,014
—containing malapropisms	442
—not containing malapropisms	7,572
Performance factor	4.47
Number of alarms	3,167
—true alarms	397
—false alarms	2,770
Performance factor	2.46
Performance factor overall	11.0
Number of perfectly detected and corrected malapropisms	349

It has three spelling variants—*pouring, scouring,* and *soaring*—but none of them was chainable, and so no alarm was raised. In the following sentence, the word *fear* was placed in an atomic chain:

(17) And while institutions until the past month or so stayed away from the smallest issues for *fear* they would get stuck in an illiquid stock, . . .

Moreover, chains were found for three of its many spelling variants—*gear, pear,* and *year*—and so the word was flagged as a possible error and an alarm raised. (*Pear* was chained to *Lotus,* the name of a company mentioned in the article, because both are plants.)

Table 13.2 displays the results of the experiment quantitatively. The 482 articles retained for the experiment included a total of 322,645 words, of which 1,409 were malapropisms. Of all the words, 33.9% were inserted into lexical chains. Of the malapropisms, 442 (31.4%) were placed in atomic chains. Of the nonmalapropisms, 7,572 (7.01%) were also inserted in atomic chains. Thus, actual malapropisms were 4.47 times more likely to be inserted in an atomic chain.

Alarms resulted from 89.8% of the malapropisms in atomic chains and from 36.6% of the nonmalapropisms (the latter being false alarms). Thus, malapropisms were 2.46 times more likely to result in alarms than non-malapropisms. The proportion of alarms that were false was 87.5%. The average number of replacement suggestions per alarm was 2.66.

Overall, an alarm was generated for 28.2% of the malapropisms. Furthermore, an alarm in which the original word (the word for which a malapropism was substituted) was one of the replacement suggestions was generated for 24.8% of the malapropisms. Malapropisms were 11 times more likely to result in an alarm than other words. However, this was at the cost of 25.3 false alarms per 1,000 words eligible for chaining, or 8.59 false alarms per 1,000 words of text.

13.5 CONCLUSION

13.5.1 Review

In this chapter we have adapted Morris and Hirst's (1991) *Roget's*-based algorithm for lexical chains to WordNet and used the result in an experiment in the detection and correction of malapropisms. Although concessions had to be made to the structure and content of WordNet, the results are nonetheless encouraging. The further development of WordNet will surely permit better lexical chaining, which in turn will lead to more acceptable performance by the algorithm for malapropism detection and correction.

Two important ways in which WordNet is limited compared to *Roget's* are its restriction to formal relations rather than connections by general association, which the *Roget's*-based algorithm exploits, and its varying conceptual density. The reasons for the first restriction are understandable: if "fuzzy" relationships such as *secretary–typewriter* are admitted, it is hard to know where to stop; unlike *Roget's*, WordNet is not intended as a "memory-jogger." Nonetheless, the addition of relations based on required or typical role-fillers, such as *bath–soap*, would surely be helpful. The density problem is not just a problem with WordNet; one would naturally expect to find more concepts in some subjects than others and therefore a higher density of synsets. But the formal structure of WordNet exacerbates the problem compared to *Roget's*.

In addition, like many others who have worked with WordNet (e.g., Agirre and Rigau 1995; Al-Halimi and Kazman, this volume; Resnik 1995; Sussna 1993; Voorhees, this volume), we were obliged to limit our investigations to nouns, because of WordNet's division into syntactic categories with limited cross-category connections. But the relations of lexical chaining stand above syntactic category; for our purposes, the relation between *scholar* and *teach* (noun and verb) is no different than that between *scholar* and *teacher* (noun and noun); stronger cross-category connections in WordNet would be helpful.

Our method for detecting and correcting malapropisms with lexical chains is, of course, limited by the accuracy of the lexical chainer, which can never be perfect. However, it is in the nature of the task that although occasional errors in chaining and disambiguation will sometimes lead to false alarms or undetected malapropisms, they are not fatal to the overall process. This contrasts with information retrieval, a task in which erroneous disambiguation will send matters seriously awry (Sanderson 1994; Voorhees, this volume).

A more deep-seated limitation of the method lies in its assumption that a malapropism will almost always be unique in the text and unrelated semantically to the text in which it occurs. This is probably untrue. Lexical substitution errors in speech show a bias toward concepts that are active in the current discourse (see the papers in Fromkin 1980, especially Hotopf 1980), and it is reasonable to expect analogous errors in typing to follow a similar pattern (as is implicit in, for example, Rumelhart and Norman's (1982) model of typing).[9] For similar reasons, there is probably a bias to repetition of the same malapropism in a text, which would make it no longer suspicious to our algorithm.

13.5.2   Lexical Chains as Context

The use of lexical chains as a context for tasks such as disambiguation, discourse segmentation, and finding malapropisms can be thought of as a lite form of methods based on spreading activation or marker passing in knowledge bases (Hirst 1987). The ideas that all such methods have in common are that semantic distance is the primary cue that context provides, and that measures of semantic distance are inherent in a network structure (Rada et al. 1989). In the case of spreading activation or marker passing, the network in question is assumed to be a fully articulated network of concepts; in lexical chaining, it is assumed to be a network of word senses with conceptual relations. The former, of course, is a richer representation and (at least in principle) can perform the task more accurately; but its use assumes the ability to determine fairly precisely the concepts that are explicit and implicit in the text, and it is easily led completely astray by errors. The latter, on the other hand, is a relatively impoverished representation that could not be the basis for any kind of conceptual "understanding" of a text; but it is more flexible and forgiving of errors and hence can be used in tasks that, although semantic, do not require a complete analysis of meaning.

13.5.3 Related Research

Stairmand (1994) has also developed a lexical chainer based on WordNet. Unlike the one described here, Stairmand's is intended primarily for use in information retrieval, taking into account the idea of the *density* of a chain in different places in the text. Stairmand's chainer works by a method somewhat different from ours. First, it collects all the content words in the text; it then generates the set of all word senses in WordNet that are close to the words of the text, the set of so-called expanded terms; and finally it looks for links that expanded terms form between words in the text. Disambiguation, to the extent that it occurs, is apparently an implicit side effect. It is unclear whether or not this batch-oriented approach, which has a more limited notion of semantic relatedness, leads to chains that differ significantly from ours. However, as it seems to discard the necessary information regarding position in the text, the method could not be used for tasks such as discourse segmentation, which was one of Morris and Hirst's original motivations for lexical chains.

Al-Halimi and Kazman (this volume) have adapted the idea of lexical chaining in their LexTree system for real-time indexing of video by topic rather than keyword. The lexical chains represent clusters of concepts in segments of the video that a query, represented similarly, can be matched against in order to find a particular segment. Al-Halimi and Kazman do not retain the textual linear sequence of words in their chains, but only the tree of lexical relationships, and hence refer to their structures as *lexical trees*. In addition, they have modified some of the criteria for word relatedness.

Word sense disambiguation is, of course, a problem that requires knowledge from many sources, and possibly arbitrary inference, for a complete solution (Hirst 1987; McRoy 1992). A large number of researchers have described thesaurus- or WordNet-based algorithms for the problem (Ginsberg 1993; Sussna 1993; Okumura and Honda 1994; Agirre and Rigau 1995; Li, Szpakowicz, and Matwin 1995; Resnik 1995; Richardson and Smeaton 1995a,b; Leacock and Chodorow, this volume; Voorhees 1993, this volume). Generally speaking, these algorithms are all based on some form of the notion of minimizing *semantic distance* (or maximizing *similarity*) between the senses of a set of words (Hirst 1987;

the central point of debate is how this notion is best conceived. For example, Sussna (1993) observes that nearby words that are deep in the WordNet hierarchy are more likely to be closely related than words that are the same graph distance apart but higher up, and he factors this into his formula for semantic distance. Leacock and Chodorow (this volume) take this one step further by using a logarithmic measure of path length that takes into account the depth of the path in the hierarchy. Likewise, Resnik (1995) proposes a logarithmic measure of the information content in a WordNet node, deeper nodes being more informative; the similarity between two nodes is given by their most informative subsumer. Richardson and Smeaton (1995a,b) combine Resnik's and Sussna's methods. Li, Szpakowicz, and Matwin (1995) use simple graph distance to measure similarity in WordNet, but add a number of context-dependent heuristics for its use. Voorhees (1993, this volume) and Agirre and Rigau (1995) both propose measures of the similarity of one word to others in the same text that are based on the density of words in that text that fall within some particular area of the WordNet hierarchy. It is as yet unclear which of these measures is most effective; but the basic concept of lexical chains is independent of any particular measure of semantic distance, and one may plug in whichever measure one likes best.

Given a measure of semantic distance or similarity, one must then supply some representation of context within which the senses of an ambiguous word can be considered. In this chapter, this is the set of lexical chains, each representing a cluster of active concepts. In Sussna's method, it is the *n*-word window of (disambiguated) text that precedes the target word. In batch-oriented methods, such as that of Voorhees, it is in effect the entire text. The advantage of lexical chains, as we have used them, is that they provide a representation of context that is used both for the final task itself, searching for malapropisms, and for the disambiguation that helps "sharpen" that context; in other words, the chains are the means of their own improvement.

Notes

1. We are grateful to Jane Morris, Marti Hearst, Christiane Fellbaum, Stephen Green, Daniel Marcu, Philip Edmonds, Rick Kazman, Jeffrey Mark Siskind, and Chrysanne DiMarco for discussions, help, feedback, and comments on earlier drafts of this chapter. This research was supported by a grant to the first author from the Natural Sciences and Engineering Research Council of Canada, and a scholarship to the second author from Fonds pour la Formation de Chercheurs et l'Aide à la Recherche.

2. Recent editions of *Roget's* could not be licensed. The on-line version of the 1911 edition was available, but it does not include the index that is crucial to the algorithm. Moreover, because of its age, it lacks much of the vocabulary that is necessary for processing many contemporary texts, especially newspaper and magazine articles and technical papers. Stairmand (1994) nonetheless tried to implement a lexical chainer with this edition, but concluded that it was not possible.

3. The searches for both extra-strong and strong relations are very fast processes. However, the search for medium-strong relations is the most expensive operation of the whole lexical chaining process in terms of CPU time.

4. Since a chain is, by definition, a sequence, the term *atomic chain* may seem awkward. However, it provides a convenient way to speak of a word that, although potentially chainable, has not been related to any other words in the text.

5. Atomic chains that contain a compound word (e.g., *black-and-white*) or a phrase (e.g., *elementary_ school*) in WordNet are not considered to be potential malapropisms. The probability that two adjacent words form a known compound and yet are malapropos is extremely low; indeed, such compounds can be thought of as a special kind of chain in and of themselves.

6. Ispell is a program that has evolved in PDP-10, Unix, and Usenet circles for more than 20 years, with contributions from many authors. Principal contributors to the current version include Pace Willisson and Geoff Kuenning.

7. This technique has the disadvantage of sometimes generating a new word that is very close semantically to the original one (e.g., *billion → million*). These new words are not actual malapropisms in the sense of being malapropos in the text, and hence are not candidates for detection by our algorithm. Nonetheless, they were counted as malapropisms in the computation of the results of the experiment. Fortunately, such situations were rare.

8. The success of the algorithm here is surprising, as these surely are all such common words in newspaper articles that we should really have made them stop words.

9. For example, one of our colleagues observed the following malapropism:

(i) In this model, auxin-enhanced excytotic vesicle transport and insertion of a rapidly turning-over H^+-ATPase into the plasma membrane are envisioned to stimulate hydrogen ion excretion into the apoplast and initiate wall loosening. In this model, fusicoccin stimulates *protein* excretion via a separate independent mechanism.

The word *protein* (which does not occur elsewhere in the paper) should be *proton* (which has many related words in the context); but the previous sentence does contain the name of a particular protein, H^+-ATPase, and this is surely the cause of the malapropism. Similarly, our algorithm would connect *protein* back to H^+-*ATPase* (were the latter to find its way into WordNet) and would find nothing to worry about. (We are grateful to Nadia Talent for pointing this example out to us. It appeared in Rayle, D. L., and Cleland, R. E. (1992). The acid growth theory of auxin-induced cell elongation is alive and well. *Plant Physiology, 99,* 1274.)

References

Agirre, E., and Rigau, G. (1995). *A proposal for word sense disambiguation using conceptual distance.* Paper presented at the International Conference on Recent Advances in Natural Language Processing, Velingrad, Bulgaria, September 1995. Available: http://xxx.lanl.gov/ps/cmp-lg/9510003

Atwell, E., and Elliot, S. (1987). Dealing with ill-formed English text. In R. Garside, G. Leech, and G. Sampson (Eds.), *The computational analysis of English: A corpus-based approach*, 120–138. London: Longman.

Chapman, R. L. (Ed.). (1992). *Roget's international thesaurus.* 5th ed. New York: HarperCollins.

Fromkin, V. A. (Ed.). (1980). *Errors in linguistic performance: Slips of the tongue, ear, pen, and hand.* New York: Academic Press.

Ginsberg, A. (1993). A unified approach to automatic indexing and information retrieval. *IEEE Expert, 8*(5), 46–56.

Grosz, B. J., and Sidner, C. L. (1986). Attention, intentions, and the structure of discourse. *Computational Linguistics, 12*, 175–204.

Halliday, M. A. K., and Hasan, R. (1976). *Cohesion in English.* London: Longman.

Hirst, G. (1987). *Semantic interpretation and the resolution of ambiguity.* Cambridge, England: Cambridge University Press.

Hotopf, W. H. N. (1980). Semantic similarity as a factor in whole-word slips of the tongue. In V. A. Fromkin (Ed.), *Errors in linguistic performance: Slips of the tongue, ear, pen, and hand*, 97–109. New York: Academic Press.

Kukich, K. (1992). Techniques for automatically correcting words in text. *ACM Computing Surveys, 24*, 377–439.

Li, X., Szpakowicz, S., and Matwin, S. (1995). A WordNet-based algorithm for word sense disambiguation. In *Proceedings of the 14th International Joint Conference on Artificial Intelligence*, 1368–1374. San Francisco: Morgan Kaufmann.

McRoy, S. W. (1992). Using multiple knowledge sources for word sense discrimination. *Computational Linguistics, 18*, 1–30.

Mitton, R. (1987). Spelling checkers, spelling correctors, and the misspelling of poor spellers. *Information Processing and Management, 23*, 495–505.

Morris, J. (1988). *Lexical cohesion, the thesaurus, and the structure of text.* Master's thesis, Department of Computer Science, University of Toronto. (Tech. Rep. No. CSRI-219.)

Morris, J., and Hirst, G. (1991). Lexical cohesion computed by thesaural relations as an indicator of the structure of text. *Computational Linguistics, 17*, 21–48.

Okumura, M., and Honda, T. (1994). Word sense disambiguation and text segmentation based on lexical cohesion. In *Proceedings of the Fifteenth International Conference on Computational Linguistics (COLING-94)*, vol. 2, 755–761. Association for Computational Linguistics.

Peterson, J. L. (1986). A note on undetected typing errors. *Communications of the ACM, 29*, 633–637.

Rada, R., Mili, H., Bicknell, E., and Blettner, M. (1989). Development and application of a metric on semantic nets. *IEEE Transactions on Systems, Man, and Cybernetics, 19*, 17–30.

Resnik, P. (1995). Using information content to evaluate semantic similarity in a taxonomy. In *Proceedings of the 14th International Joint Conference on Artificial Intelligence*, 448–453. San Francisco: Morgan Kaufmann.

Richardson, R., and Smeaton, A. F. (1995a). *Automatic word sense disambiguation in a KBIR application* (Working Paper CA-0595). Dublin: Dublin City University, School of Computer Applications. Available: ftp://ftp.compapp.dcu.ie/pub/w-papers/1995/CA0595.ps.Z

Richardson, R., and Smeaton, A. F. (1995b). *Using WordNet in a knowledge-based approach to information retrieval* (Working Paper CA-0395). Dublin: Dublin City University, School of Computer Applications. Available: ftp://ftp.compapp.dcu.ie/pub/w-papers/1995/CA0395.ps.Z

Rumelhart, D. E., and Norman, D. A. (1982). Simulating a skilled typist: A study of skilled cognitive-motor performance. *Cognitive Science, 6*, 1–36.

Sanderson, M. (1994). Word sense disambiguation and information retrieval. In *Research and development in information retrieval: Proceedings of the 17th ACM SIGIR Conference*, 142–151. New York: Springer-Verlag. Available: http://www.dcs.gla.ac.uk/~sanderso/papers/

Stairmand, M. (1994). *Lexical chains, WordNet and information retrieval.* Unpublished manuscript, Centre for Computational Linguistics, UMIST, Manchester.

St-Onge, D. (1995). *Detecting and correcting malapropisms with lexical chains.* Master's thesis, Department of Computer Science, University of Toronto. (Tech. Rep. No. CSRI-319.) Available: ftp://ftp.csri.toronto.edu/csri-technical-reports/319

Sussna, M. (1993). Word sense disambiguation for free-text indexing using a massive semantic network. In *Proceedings of the Second International Conference on Information and Knowledge Management (CKIM-93)*, 67–74. New York: ACM Press.

Voorhees, Ellen M. (1993). Using WordNet to disambiguate word senses for text retrieval. In *Proceedings of the 16th ACM SIGIR Conference on Research and Development in Information Retrieval (SIGIR'93)* [≡ *SIGIR Forum, 27*(2)], 171–180. New York: ACM Press.

Vosse, T. (1994). *The word connection: Grammar-based spelling error correction in Dutch.* Doctoral dissertation, University of Leiden, The Netherlands.

Chapter 14

Temporal Indexing through Lexical Chaining

Reem Al-Halimi and Rick Kazman

14.1 INTRODUCTION

As computerized repositories of information move increasingly away from traditional structured record- and field-oriented relational and hierarchical databases, to databases that include large bodies of unstructured data, new techniques will be needed to aid in the storage, indexing, and retrieval of this information (Kazman and Kominek 1993). The sources of such data are all around: televised newscasts, movies, videotaped lectures, requirements elicitation, computer-scanned photographs, computer-captured and computer-generated music. All of these new computer media types are either inherently unstructured or structured only within a limited domain (Zhang et al. 1995). The domain of interest for the research being presented here is videoconferences: conferences where the participants are physically remote and communicate through video and audio channels, as well as potentially sharing computer applications. Such conferences are already being used to reduce some of the need for business travel and to extend the reach of university courses to remote communities. However, the data resulting from such conferences are currently stored as a set of parallel streams of unstructured data.

Occasionally, videotaped meetings are indexed so that they may be queried like a database or browsed like an encyclopedia, but typically this indexing requires enormous amounts of manual labor (Salomon, Oren, and Kreitman 1989). There is little research into the management and *automatic* indexing of such repositories of information. Such research is clearly needed if the potential of distributed communication is to become a reality.

This chapter presents a method for indexing transcriptions of conference meetings by topic. The work described here is part of a research project that aims at designing and prototyping tools for transforming videoconferences into a repository of organizational memory and knowledge, but to do so with relatively little reliance on a semantic analysis of those videoconferences. The project has been based upon the assumptions that (1) such information is a valuable information resource and that (2) without tools to index and manage the information, it will be nearly useless. The research has also assumed that a true automatic semantic analysis of videoconferences is a distant goal, since it requires either sophisticated natural language recognition or sophisticated image recognition by a computer, neither of which will be possible in unrestricted domains in the foreseeable future.

We have been investigating ways to index the information based upon attributes of the data that are more easily derived (Kazman et al. 1996; Kazman, Hunt, and Mantei 1995): in particular,

1. indexing by intended content: both manually and automatically creating meeting agendas and associating them with meeting topics in real time;

2. indexing by temporal structure: viewing videoconferences as "contentless" simultaneous streams of data (the video and audio records of the participants) and indexing based upon the temporal relations of those streams;

3. indexing by topic: using speech recognition and lexical chaining to identify topics within the audio portion of videoconferences.

Furthermore, we have been investigating methods for presenting the analyzed information to a user:

4. in real time during a videoconference; and

5. post facto, in order to permit easier browsing of the stored contents based upon its semantic properties.

Topics 1, 2, 4, and 5 have been dealt with in the works just mentioned and will not be further discussed here. This chapter will primarily focus on our progress in indexing by topic, and the ways in which WordNet has been applied to this goal.

14.2 PREVIOUS WORK

Texts discussing a certain topic use words that are related to each other and to that topic. These words and relations form structures known as *lexical chains*. Hasan (1984) formulated lexical chaining as a measure for coherence of stories made up by children. Later, arguing that cohesive harmony reflects text coherence, she developed lexical chaining as a tool for measuring coherence of any text. Hasan's chains are linear linked lists consisting of text words and relations connecting these words. She defines seven types of these word-to-word relations: synonymy, meronymy, repetition, taxonomy, antonymy, co-taxonomy (two objects are taxonyms of the same object), and co-meronymy (two objects are part of the same object). In addition, she specifies six chain-to-chain relations: epithet-thing, medium-process, process-phenomenon, actor-process, process-goal, and process–location of process.

Morris and Hirst (1991) designed an algorithm to automatically build lexical chains using *Roget's International Thesaurus*. Unlike Hasan's lexical chains, however, Morris and Hirst's are groups of related words. They define six types of lexical relations: meronymy, synonymy, antonymy, taxonomy, repetition, and collocation. In addition, Morris and Hirst's lexical chains are not interrelated. St-Onge's LexC system (Hirst and St-Onge, this volume) is an implementation of Morris and Hirst's algorithm that uses WordNet instead of a thesaurus. LexC is the basis of LexTree, our implementation of the ideas presented in this chapter.

14.3 LEXICAL TREES FOR INDEXING

In order for lexical trees to reflect the semantic structure of the text, it is our assertion that we need to diverge from Hasan's and Morris and Hirst's notion of lexical *chains*—one-dimensional structures—and move to two-dimensional lexical *trees*. Our modifications to Hasan's and Morris and Hirst's schemes fall into two categories: chain structure and chain parameters. We will discuss each of these topics in turn.

14.3.1 Chain Structure

Previous work on lexical chaining has defined lexical chains as a linear linked list of words (see, e.g., Hasan 1984; Morris and Hirst 1991). These definitions do not account for the role of the chain's lexical relations in characterizing the chain. Lexical relations very in number within the text, thus conveying information about the text. For example, in an article that discusses growing roses, one is more likely to find words related to the main topic—namely, roses (words like *shrub, leaf, petal, root*, possibly *flower*, or even a scientific name such as *angiosperm*—than words related to a relevant but minor topic such as fertilizer. As a result, there are more instances of, and therefore more connections among, rose-related words than fertilizer-related words.

Therefore, the exact amount of text information a chain retains depends on the number and type of relations it contains. Hasan (1984) notes that any word in a chain can be related to multiple other words in that chain. If we preserve *all* lexical relations, we will quickly generate a graph of a possibly huge number of edges. Both building and traversing such a graph requires an $O(n^2)$ algorithm, where n is the number of words being considered. An algorithm of such high complexity precludes the possibility that lexical *graph* processing could be incorporated into a real-time system, as is required for indexing videoconferences. On the other hand, if we restrict the number of relations in a chain to any constant number N, where $N \geq 2$, we will be creating an artificial chain form that does not necessarily reflect the distribution of the lexical relations in the text since the actual density of connections to a word will be lost. Such a restriction on the form of a chain could have the effect of unintentionally culling important information about main text concepts.

In order to balance these competing concerns, we have decided to disallow cycles in the chain without restricting the number of relations per chain word, thus simplifying the structure—we create *trees*, not graphs—while retaining most of the inherent text information. Cycles of lexical relations contribute little *new* information (e.g., the fact that word A is a part of B, and B is a part of C, contributes no more information than knowing that A is a part of B, B is a part of C, and A is a part of C).

We do, however, consider the lack of cycles found while building a chain as an indicator of a sparse nonintuitive subtree such as that in figure 14.1. The subtree in this figure is part of LexTree's chains characterizing an article that discusses computer security. Some leaves in the subtree are either completely disjoint or so far apart in WordNet as to be pruned by

Figure 14.1
A sparse lexical tree

LexTree's algorithm (as will be discussed in section 14.3.3), producing a sparse subtree that contains several topics simultaneously.

Figure 14.2 shows an example of lexical relations, found in WordNet, which are used by LexTree to characterize the following text:

Inference is the process of creating explicit representations of knowledge from implicit ones. It can be viewed as the creation of knowledge itself. Deductive inference proceeds from a set of assumptions called axioms to new statements that are logically implied by the axioms. Inductive inference typically starts with a set of facts, features or observations, and it produces generalizations, descriptions and laws which account for the given information and which may have the power to predict new facts, features or observations. (Tanimoto 1987, 6)

Compare the tree in figure 14.2 with the graph in figure 14.3, where *all* lexical relations found in WordNet between the words are retained. The main concept in the above text, *inference*, is reflected in figure 14.2 by the inclusion of the *knowledge* subtree, which is in turn linked to a set of related features of knowledge and forms of knowledge, which are treated as synonyms of *knowledge*. Note that the word *set* has been wrongly disambiguated here, but this does not damage the overall effect of the tree. Note also that a cycle can exist between any set of related (but not necessarily reiterated) words.

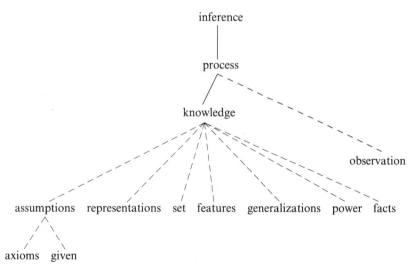

Figure 14.2
The lexical tree for the "inference" text. (— = hypernymy; --- = hyponymy.)

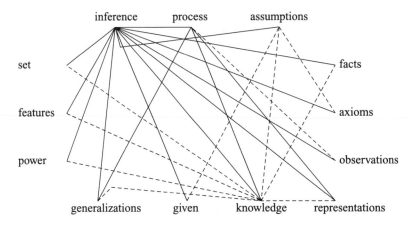

Figure 14.3
A lexical graph for the "inference" text. (——— = hypernymy; --- = hyponymy.)

14.3.2   Tree Parameterization

By restricting the form of the tree, we are forced into selecting a subset of relations from the set of all possible relations in the tree. Our selection is based on three criteria: relation informativeness, relation type compatibility, and word distance.

14.3.2.1   Relation informativeness   Relation informativeness deals with the amount of new information a relation type adds to the tree. This degree of informativeness is context independent. It is the same for a relation type regardless of other relation types in the tree. LexTree uses all noun relations defined in WordNet in addition to *repetition*, which is the relation between a noun and a different instance of the same noun. In LexTree we define five constants, each pertaining to the informativeness of a relation type:

1. *identity-value*, which reflects the informativeness of repetition;
2. *similarity-value*, which reflects the informativeness of synonymy;
3. *antonymy-value*, which reflects the informativeness of antonymy;
4. *holonymy-value*, which reflects the informativeness of holonymy; and
5. *hyponymy-value*, which reflects the informativeness of hyponymy.

The exact values of these constants can be set by the user. Currently these values are set in the order listed: identity highest, hyponymy lowest. (Hyponymy has the lowest level of informativeness because it generalizes the concept to be connected to the tree, thus introducing a less specific topic into the tree.) Note that we connect the concept to the tree node, not the other way around, so the relation goes from the concept to the tree node.

14.3.2.2 Relation Type Compatibility

Relation type compatibility, on the other hand, is context dependent. It reflects the fact that different relation types interact differently with each other, and these interactions affect the consistency of the information in the tree. For example, a tree that consists mainly of meronymy and synonymy relations, such as that for the "inference" text, as shown in figure 14.2, is more focused toward a certain aspect of the main topic than one that contains a mixture of meronymy and antonymy relations.

There are two types of relation type compatibilities: *within-connection compatibility* and *within-tree compatibility*. The compatibilities within a connection are what Hirst and St-Onge (this volume) call "allowable synset paths." These are paths that LexC allows between synsets of the two words it tries to connect. To form their set of allowable paths, Hirst and St-Onge define three relation directions: *right* for synonymy and antonymy,[1] *upward* for meronymy and hypernymy, and *downward* for hyponymy and holonymy. In LexTree we redefine the *right* direction for similarity, synonymy, and repetition only, and we introduce a *left* direction for antonymy. Using these directions, LexTree then applies the following synset path rules:[2]

1. Right directions are compatible with all other directions since synonymy, similarity, and repetition do not change the current meaning of the word.

2. Left directions are not allowed on the same path as any other direction except for the right direction; if they were, we would be allowing a more general or more specific form of the antonym that is not semantically related to the original word. For instance, *artifact* is the antonym of *natural object* in WordNet. If we were to allow left relations on the same path as an upward relation, we could relate *artifact* with *nest* since *natural object* is a hypernym of *nest*. Antonym coverage is slight in WordNet, and so this situation seldom obtains currently, but the rule makes sense and provides protection against future augmentations to WordNet's antonym coverage.

3. Opposite directions are incompatible (e.g., holonymy and meronymy) and cannot coexist on the same path. This condition guarantees that the

path found is consistent and accurately specifies the relation between the two connected words. For instance, *waste* is a kind of *material* and so is *rock*. If we allowed opposite directions on the path, we could connect *rock* to *material*, a downward direction, and then connect *material* to *waste*, an upward direction—an undesirable result.

Once a path is found, LexTree gives this path a relation type according to the following rules, in order:

1. If the path contins an antonymy relation, then the overall relation type is antonymy.
2. If the path contains any holonymy relations, then the overall relation type is holonymy.
3. If the path contains any meronymy relations, then the overall relation type is meronymy.
4. If the path contains none of the above relations, then the overall relation type is synonymy.

Whereas the within-connection compatibilities are concerned with compatibilities within a synset path, the within-tree compatibilities are concerned with the relations in the tree as a whole. This compatibility type takes into account the text content. The importance of this compatibility stems from the fact that some relations are more informative than others, and the degree of informativeness depends on the context. For example, if the discussion is about different means of communication, we learn more about the topic if we think of *letter* and *list* as different types of *communication*. On the other hand, if the discussion is about letters, it is more informative to relate *list* and *letter* through a part-whole relation.

When LexTree finds a relation between a word and a tree node, it checks this relation's compatibility with the other relations in the tree. Since each of the tree's existing relations is assumed to be compatible with all other existing tree relations, LexTree chooses the first relation in the path from the root to the current leaf that is neither a similarity nor a synonymy relation if one exists (since these relations carry the least information); if there is none, it chooses the synonymy relation. LexTree then checks the compatibility of this relation with the new relation. In LexTree we define five types of tree relation compatibility, in order of their priority starting with the highest:

1. *same direction compatibility* (when the new relation is of the same type as the tree relation);

2. *same right direction compatibility* (when one relation is synonymy relation and the other is a repetition relation);

3. *direction change compatibility* (when one relation is synonymy or repetition and the second relation is anything other than synonymy or repetition);

4. *mixed direction compatibility* (compatibility of relations, other than those in 1, 2, 3, or 5, with each other (e.g., meronymy with antonymy); and

5. *opposite direction compatibility* (when the two relations are of opposite types (e.g., synonymy and antonymy, holonymy and meronymy)).

LexTree modifies the weight (or value) of the new relation according to its direction compatibility (relation evaluation will be discussed further in section 14.3.3). These compatibilities are between different relations in the tree itself, not in the synset path between tree nodes. Although the two types—within-connection compatibility and within-tree compatibility— have several features in common, they differ in several important ways. First, mixed directions are not allowed within a synset path but are allowed within a tree. Second, a synset path cannot contain more than one antonymy relation, but there is no limit on the number of antonymy relations in a tree. Third, holonymy and meronymy cannot occur in the same synset path, but such co-occurrence is not a problem in a tree.

These differences derive from the different goals of the compatibility types. Within-connection, or synset path, compatibilities are meant to define as accurately as possible the relation type between the words to be connected. Within-tree compatibilities, however, are meant to produce a consistent and meaningful view of the text content through promoting the coexistence of certain relation types in the same subtree and penalizing the coexistence of other types such as opposite direction relations.

14.3.2.3 Word Distance   The final relation parameter to be considered is the distance between the words to be connected by the relation. The further the two words are from each other within the source text, the less likely it is that they belong to the same topic, and the weaker their relation. We use the number of intermediate syntactic connectives, words such as *which* and *who* that begin or join phrases, as a distance measure. Such a measure is independent of the text medium and depends only on the text content. Yet this measure captures the number of different contextual concepts that separate the two words. The set of syntactic connectives is predefined in LexTree and is simple to modify. No use of WordNet is being made for this criterion.

It is interesting to note that topics change more frequently at the prologue and epilogue of a text (spoken or written) than they do in its main body. As a result, the effect of distance on a relation is nonuniform (as well as nonlinear).

14.3.3 LexTree's Algorithm

Given a text file, LexTree builds a set of lexical trees that characterize the text's semantic structure. As shown in figure 14.4, building lexical trees involves several steps: first, the system selects text words to be included in the tree (stop words and words that have no noun sense are not selected); next, it determines the best relation between the chosen word and the tree node, for all trees if any exist; next, it chooses the trees to connect the chosen word to; if no trees are chosen, it creates a new tree whose root is the chosen word. In what follows we will describe LexTree's algorithm in more detail.

LexTree follows the same word selection strategy as LexC (step 2.2 in figure 14.4). It discards all words that do not have a noun sense from the tree-building process. It also ignores words that appear in the stop-word list since they are general words that do not make any significant contribution to the text's semantic structure.

If LexTree decides that a word is connectable, it then selects the appropriate trees to connect the word to (step 2.2.1). Unlike LexC, LexTree connects a word to *all* trees where the connection value between the word and the tree is higher than a preset threshold (step 2.2.1.2). Such a policy accounts for the possibility that a keyword will refer to more than one topic simultaneously. The *connection value* between a tree and a word is the best connection LexTree finds from among all possible relations between the word and the tree node (steps 2.2.1.1.1 and 2.2.1.1.2).

LexTree evaluates a relation using the parameters described in section 14.3.2. The weight of a relation is

$$Weight = R - M + \sum_{1}^{n} S_i + C + dist + T,$$

where

- R = relation informativeness value,
- M = maximum possible weight,
- S = within-synset direction compatibility for direction i,

```
REPEAT

1.  READ next word from input file

2.  IF word is a possible compound word component THEN

2.1     IF (word has a noun sense in WordNet) and
            (compound word buffer is empty) THEN
2.1.1       PUSH word in compound word buffer
        ELSE
2.1.2       IF (compound word buffer is not empty) THEN
2.1.2.1         attempt to join word and item in compound
                word buffer
            END IF
        END IF
    ELSE
2.2     IF (word is not a general word) and
            (word has a noun sense in WordNet) THEN
2.2.1       FOR all trees within a suitable span
2.2.1.1         FOR all words in the tree
2.2.1.1.1           CHECK WordNet for relations between word
                    and tree word
2.2.1.1.2           CHOOSE best relation
                END FOR
2.2.1.2         IF (best relation > connection threshold)
                    THEN
2.2.1.2.1           ADD word and best relation to tree.
                END IF
            END FOR
2.2.2       IF no relations are found THEN
2.2.2.1         MAKE word a node in a new tree
            END IF
        END IF
    END IF
UNTIL end of input file
```

Figure 14.4
LexTree's tree-building algorithm

- C = within-tree connection compatibility,
- *dist* = number of synsets between the word and the tree node, and
- T = number of syntactic connectives between the two words in the text.

The best relation is the relation with the highest weight. LexTree searches for paths between the text word and the tree node as long as the relation weight is higher than a preset minimum weight threshold. This means that synset paths that are longer than LexC's maximum of 5 are possible as long as the path's weight is higher than the minimum weight threshold.

One important distinction between LexC and LexTree's algorithm is that LexTree does not have LexC's three levels of relation strength: *extra-strong*, *strong*, and *medium-strong*. Instead, LexTree searches for the relation with the highest weight. Synonymy and repetition are no longer given absolute preference. Rather, they are weighted parameters in the relation weight equation. Their value is affected by all other relation parameters such as their text distance.

The trees produced by LexTree represent the topic semantic structure of the input. Therefore, a topic is represented by a lexical tree even though it might not be expressed explicitly in the tree.

14.3.4 Results

We conducted a preliminary study in order to verify the usability of our lexical trees for automatic indexing of arbitrary text. This study was aimed at demonstrating the existence of lexical trees in texts and comparing tree structures developed by humans to those developed by Lex-Tree. In the study, the subjects were given a journal article and asked to choose a set of text words that, in their opinion, characterized the article. The words the subjects chose from the text were constrained to be either single words or compounds. The subjects were then asked to group the words they had chosen from the text.

In order to allow the subjects to create trees that were most intuitive to them, we placed no restriction on the grouping criteria they could use. We also removed the article's title, since it would have provided extra information that is not necessarily available in spoken language and some forms of written text. The text we chose was an article from an electronic journal that the subjects were unlikely to have previously read (and which they had not in fact read), thus ensuring that their trees were produced entirely from their understanding of the text rather than from their previous experiences. In this way, their tree formation would be as constrained as possible to be a text comprehension task, in much the same way that LexTree has only the words of the text, and no context, to use in building its trees.

The trees built by subjects were similar to each other: there was a high degree of overlap in the keywords the subjects chose to characterize the text, as well as the grouping criteria they used. Moreover, even though they were restricted to using one-word keywords only, their trees were similar to the text's outline, as determined by us. This indicates that it is possible to build sound topic trees using one-word (or compound-word) text keywords only.

We then compared the subjects' trees with the trees produced by LexTree for the same text. Half of the text words the subjects used in characterizing the text's topics were found in a single tree of 160 words that LexTree produced (the text was about 1,800 words). We will call this tree the *characteristic tree* of the text. The rest of the words chosen by the subjects either connected to sparse trees or failed to connect to any tree.

Surprisingly, however, more than 75% of the subjects' grouping criteria were in the characteristic tree. This is surprising because the subjects were not required to use words from the original text in expressing their grouping criteria. Furthermore, even when they did use a word that was not used in the text, this word was found to be closely related to some other word in LexTree's tree. Since the subjects' grouping criteria were always important subtopics in the text, these preliminary results give a strong indication of the usefulness of lexical trees in text indexing and retrieval.

14.4 APPLICATIONS

Performing lexical chaining on transcripts of meetings, and in the future on recognized speech, allows us to search and query the text on the basis of *topics*—as identified by the lexical trees that are formed—rather than the basis of keywords, which is the most common form of search mechanism on text. For example, in a stored meeting regarding customer service, one might be interested in finding places where the participants discussed handing customer complaints, particularly responsiveness. Within the meeting, however, these words may not have been used, or they may have been used along with other, similar words. Our approach is to create a lexical forest from the user's query and match this to lexical trees that have been stored as indexes into the videoconference.

The failings of keyword searches have long been known in the information retrieval community. For example, Furnas et al. (1987) found that even within a constrained area of discourse people rarely agree on what to name things. In one experiment expert cooks were asked to extract keywords from recipes. The probability that two cooks applied the same term to an object was 18%. In another test 48 typists were shown typed pages with editorial markups and asked to devise names for each markup operation. Here the terminology overlap was only 7%. The operation of crossing out a word was variously called *delete, remove, change, spell, make into*, and so on. The authors found that heavy aliasing (using about 20 synonyms to describe the same concept) was required for moderate retrieval rates.

In a related study Freeman (1990) observed students using a commercial multimedia encyclopedia explicitly made for use in a classroom setting. Overall the students liked the product. Unfortunately, with no overview of the system, it was difficult for the students to get a sense of the encyclopedia's contents. Thus, they were unsure how to use the word-searching abilities of the program, the primary means provided for retrieving information. Lacking a model of how the information was partitioned and organized, the students had to use trial and error to discover those "sweet search words" that the encyclopedia makers happened to choose. Freeman recounts:

The fact that all the items, including pictures[,] were classified by keywords restricted the users to the vocabulary and perceptions of the editors and contributors. It has already been noted that a picture can convey so many messages and meanings according to the observer's own inclinations and preferences, which makes it well nigh impossible to classify a picture that will satisfy everyone's requirement. Certain words or phrases which achieve a desired result are passed on through the schools like precious nuggets. (p. 191)

By structuring our search software so that it looks for related trees, we give the user the ability to search a stored multimedia database by topic, rather than by keyword. We give the user not only the ability to search for concepts that are synonyms of the concepts specified in the query, but also the ability to search with the same lexical relations as those specified in the query.

Our current query-matching strategy measures the distance between the topics in the query and those in the text trees. The closer the concepts in the query are to those in the tree, the stronger the evidence of the relatedness between the query and the tree. Through such a measure, LexTree

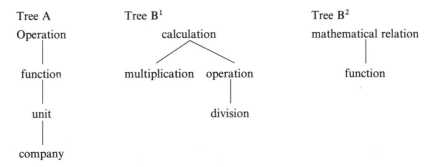

Figure 14.5
Sample trees A and B

finds the tree that is closest to the query. The text pertaining to this tree should be the system's response to the query. For example, assume that we have a business-related query with the following set of topics: *organization, administrative unit, function*. We would like to match these topics to all stored lexical trees, in order to find the texts that most closely match those trees. However, some of these words might match other trees. For example, *unit* and *function* could easily match terms from mathematics texts. Now, consider the following simple trees stored in our database, and represented in figure 14.5:

• Tree A consists of the following words indexed by LexTree from a text on business: *company, unit, function, operation*.
• Trees B[1] and B[2] consist of the following words indexed by LexTree from a text on mathematics: *function, mathematical relation, division, operation, multiplication, calculation*.

LexTree takes each topic in the query *organization, administrative unit, function* and determines the word with the minimum distance to that topic from each tree in its database. The tree with the closest matches (highest number of lexical relationships and minimum lexical distance) is returned as "matching" the query, provided that the number of lexical relationships is higher than a predetermined percentage of the topics in the query (currently set at 75%).

The semantic distances between the nodes of the two trees, as determined by LexTree, are given below:

Query
administrative_unit organization function

Comparison with trees in A
distance between function (0) and unit (0) = 3
distance between function (0) and function (0) = 0
distance between function (0) and operation (0) = 0
distance between organization (0) and company (0) = 4
distance between organization (0) and unit (0) = 1
distance between organization (0) and function(0) = 3
distance between organization (0) and operation (0) = 3
distance between administrative_unit (0) and company (0) = 4
distance between administrative_unit (0) and unit (0) = 1
distance between administrative_unit (0) and function (0) = 2
distance between administrative_unit (0) and operation (0) = 2

Comparison with trees in B
No connections

Since LexTree found two exact matches (zero distance) and several "near" matches (distance of 2–4) with tree A, it will prefer this tree over tree B, where no matches were found. This indicates that the text represented by tree A is more relevant to the query than that represented by tree B. Or, to be more precise, lexical relations inherent in the query match tree A better than they match either tree B^1 or tree B^2. The query matched many words in tree A; it matched neither of the "mathematics trees." An indication of the strength of this method is that no match was found between the query word *function* and the indexed word *function* in tree B^2, nor was a match found between *function* and *operation* in tree B^1, even though *function* exactly matched these same words in tree A. This is because the lexical relations in the query indicated a different sense of *function* than that used in trees B^1 and B^2.

14.5   CONCLUSIONS AND FUTURE WORK

We have encountered a number of challenges in creating LexTree and the system surrounding it. For example, WordNet's lexical coverage is inconsistent. Any corpus of lexical information has difficulty keeping up with the rate at which language changes, and this problem is particularly acute when the domain of interest is spoken language. This inherent problem is compounded by two additional factors: the purpose of a meeting, the domain being tested here, is often to describe or define new concepts; and the meetings we have been testing have addressed high-technology topics, a particularly rich source of neologisms. Thus, no lexical corpus will contain all of the relevant words or all of the relevant word associations. Concepts such as "smart card," "hyper link," "wearable computer," "virtual reality," or even "videoconference" may not be included or related in a lexical corpus. However, treating the words in these compounds as separate, unrelated words is a serious failing of a system that is attempting to discern word clusters and themes in a stored meeting.

Our approach to dealing with such neologisms is simple and takes advantage of the fact that such terms are typically used as rigid compounds. Although one might hear *smart card* in a conversation, one does not hear *smart green card, smart little card,* or *smart money card* (Di Sciullo and Williams 1987). Compounds of this sort most commonly have the form Noun Noun or Adjective Noun. Given this characterization, we can preprocess the text, looking for compounds of this form that are repeated throughout, and we can dynamically add these to our lexicon (although we cannot make any inferences about the lexical relations that such compounds enter into, other than knowing that a smart card is a type of card, virtual reality is a type of reality, a wearable computer is a type of computer, and a videoconference is a type of conference).

Lack of part-of-speech information also hinders creation of lexical trees. Many English words have, for example, verb, noun, and adjective senses. Currently we simply treat all such ambiguous words as nouns. In the future we intend to employ a naive "parsing" technique, such as a statistical part-of-speech tagger, to aid in narrowing the space of possibilities that LexTree considers for a given word. For example, if an ambiguous word follows a determiner, preposition, or adjective, we will feel relatively secure in treating that word as a noun. If the word is interposed between a determiner and a noun, we will treat it as an adjective.

We are also investigating the use of lexical relations in determining tree similarity. As shown in section 14.4, we can already make some surprisingly fine distinctions between senses of a word, merely by constraining the sense of the words found in its immediate vicinity. However, our way of determining the similarity of two trees is to treat each of them as a "bag" of words and to compare all words in the query with all words in a stored tree, irrespective of how they are connected. We feel that we can use tree relations to hone our tree-matching strategy even further (or, to be more precise, to move from "bag" matching to true tree matching). The major research issue here involves determining how to assign relative weights to similarity of relations and similarity of words in deriving an overall similarity metric.

Finally, we are still experimenting with usability testing and the proper parameterization of trees so that they correspond most closely to a human's subjective notion of lexical relationships. Although we can, through user testing, empirically determine the optimal parameters for building lexical trees given the parameter space that we have chosen, there is a much larger space of parameters that we have not been able to experiment with. For example, is our notion of tree distance the correct one?

Despite the problems inherent in this activity, we feel it is exciting an challenging and believe it has enormous potential benefits. Indexing through lexical chaining promises the ability to treat arbitrary multimedia data as an analyzable and queryable database. In addition, by transforming a user's query into a lexical tree and matching this to stored trees, it gives users the ability to query this database by topic, rather than being restricted to the vicissitudes of querying by keyword.

Notes

1. Actually Hirst and St-Onge call this direction "horizontal," but they show it as pointing rightward.

2. In a previous version of LexTree, left direction relations were allowed only once in the synset path. Such a restriction was meant to avoid meaning shifts throughout the path. (Consider, for example, that an antonym of *cool* is *excited*, but antonyms of *excited* are (in addition to *cool*) *calm, nonchalant, tame,* and *unreactive.*) However, we found that in practice such a restriction is unnecessary because the antonymy relation for nouns in WordNet is very restrictive, and thus LexTree was unlikely to produce wrong paths resulting from multiple antonymy relations in the path.

References

Di Sciullo, A. M., and Williams, E. (1987). *On the definition of word.* Cambridge, MA: MIT Press.

Freeman, D. (1990). Multimedia learning: The classroom experience. *Computers in Education, 15*(1–3), 189–194.

Furnas, G., Landauer, T., Gomez, L., and Dumais, S. (1987). The vocabulary problem in human-systems communications. *Communications of the ACM, 30*(11), 964–971.

Halliday, M. A. K., and Hasan, R. (1976). *Cohesion in English.* London: Longman.

Hasan, R. (1984). Coherence and cohesive harmony. In J. Flood (Ed.), *Understanding reading comprehension*, 181–219. Newark, DE: IRA.

Kazman, R., Al-Halimi, R., Hunt, W., and Mantei, M. (1996). Four paradigms for indexing video conferences. *IEEE Multimedia, 3*(1), 63–73.

Kazman, R., Hunt, W., and Mantei, M. (1995). Dynamic meeting annotation and indexing. In *Proceedings of the 1995 Pacific Workshop on Distributed Multimedia Systems*, 11–18. Skokie, IL: Knowledge Systems Institute.

Kazman, R., and Kominek, J. (1993). Information organization in multimedia resources. In *Procedings of SIGDOC '93*, 149–162. New York: ACM Press.

Morris, J., and Hirst, G. (1991). Lexical cohesion computed by thesaural relations as an indicator of the structure of text. *Computational Linguistics, 17*, 21–48.

Salomon, G., Oren, T., and Kreitman, K. (1989). Using guides to explore multimedia databases. In *Proceedings of the Twenty-Second Annual Hawaii International Conference on System Sciences*, vol. 4, 3–12. Los Alamitos, CA: IEEE Computer Society Press.

Tanimoto, S. (1987). *The elements of artificial intelligence: An introduction using Lisp*. Rockville, MD: Computer Science Press.

Zhang, H., Tan, S., Smoliar, S., and Yihong, G. (1995). Automatic parsing and indexing of news video. *Multimedia Systems Journal, 2*, 256–266.

Chapter 15

COLOR-X: Using Knowledge from WordNet for Conceptual Modeling

J. F. M. Burg and R. P. van de Riet

15.1   INTRODUCTION

In this chapter we will describe the role WordNet (Miller et al. 1993) plays in our linguistically based conceptual modeling environment (Burg 1996). The modeling method we are developing is called COLOR-X (**C**onceptual Linguistically Based **O**bject-Oriented **R**epresentation Language for Information and Communication Systems; ICS abbreviated to **X**) (Burg and van de Riet 1994, 1995a, b, c). It consists of several graphical modeling techniques that are all created using knowledge from WordNet interactively. In our view, WordNet is a source of *reusable* knowledge that can be used during conceptual modeling to ensure that the resulting models are correct. On the other hand, we are achieving a certain degree of consistency among the models and between the models and the original problem specification by paraphrasing the models into natural language sentences. This natural language generation process is also supported by WordNet.

The COLOR-X models are used to bridge the gap between the requirements analysis and software design phases of a software development process. By capturing the requirements in an adequate way, we are able to generate the more technical design models automatically.

This project is part of the LICS project (**L**inguistically Based **I**nformation and **C**ommunication **S**ystems), in which we investigate how linguistic knowledge can be used when building information and communication systems. In our view, the problem of controlling the *meaning* of words is becoming a key issue in developing information and communication systems, as in fields like database management systems, communication systems, and office automation. The systems offer highly sophisticated tools for efficient storage, processing, and transmission of data. However, transmission of data is useful only when the sender and the receiver agree on the meaning of the words. Database retrieval is successful only when the user knows where to look and what words to use. Although data dictionaries have existed for decades, and the best among them do contain meaning definitions of terms (Burg, van de Riet, and Chang 1993), they are of limited help, for several reasons worth noting. First, they lack any linguistic knowledge, making it difficult to sort out semantic and morphosyntactic aspects. Second, they lack a formal basis, making it impossible for the system itself to reason with the meaning descriptions. Third, they are usually closed systems, not integrated with the user interface, the CASE (Computer Aided Software Engineering) design environment, or other applications.

LICS itself is a subproject of the LIKE project (Linguistic Instruments in Knowledge Engineering), carried out by a consortium of researchers in three disciplines: linguistics, business administration, and computer science. Research in the LIKE project focuses on how linguistic instruments can be used profitably in the area of knowledge engineering (see van de Riet 1994). Preliminary research projects have shown the usefulness of this approach: a linguistically based data dictionary environment (Burg, van de Riet, and Chang 1993), a linguistic interpretation of entity relationship (ER) models (Buitelaar and van de Riet 1992b), and a general study of the feasibility of adding linguistic knowledge to the process of conceptual modeling (Buitelaar and van de Riet 1992a).

One of the main reasons for incorporating linguistic knowledge into conceptual modeling is to make the use of the words appearing in the models consistent. Among the obvious rules are these:

1. Class names should be nouns.
2. Relationship names should be verbs.

Less trivial, but more interesting and important, are the rules that hold between the meanings of words used in the model:

3. Certain relationship types require certain class types.
4. Certain class types cannot be related in some systems.

An example of rule 1 constrains the type of class required in the *buy* relationship to be (a descendant in the IS-A hierarchy of) *person*. An example of rule 3 forbids a *marry* relationship between two objects referring to people of the same gender.

Another reason to use linguistic knowledge in modeling techniques is to give those techniques more expressive power. We will show later that adding the roles objects play in a relation, such as AGENT or INSTRUMENT, makes the model easier to understand and to use. Adding modalities, like *must* and *permit*, clarifies the status of the relationships used.

Additionally, linguistically based modeling techniques allow relatively easy generation of natural language sentences, in order to give feedback to both system designers and end users. This feedback consists of sentences generated during the modeling phase in order to check whether the model is consistent with the requirements. Other kinds of feedback consist of explanation facilities, such as Gulla (1993) defines and uses in his CASE tool.

The integration achieved by using linguistic knowledge in the software-engineering process is both *vertical* and *horizontal*. To achieve a certain degree of vertical integration—integration between different phases of the software-engineering process (e.g., analysis, design, and implementation)—we have mainly focused on the correspondence of design models and analysis information. The reuse of knowledge from WordNet and the validation and verification of the design models, made possible by the linguistic base of the models, reduce the gap between these two phases considerably, The object-oriented paradigm, on which our approach is also based, facilitates this vertical integration in a natural way, by using the same concepts in each phase. As we will show in section 15.2, basing the different views modeled in the design phase on the same underlying formalisms integrates the design models horizontally; that is, it integrates several models in one phase of the software-engineering process.

Before we describe the use of WordNet as a source for this linguistic knowledge, we will introduce the COLOR-X models.

15.2   COLOR-X

At the moment COLOR-X consists of two kinds of models (Burg and van de Riet 1995c), which are both founded on formal (logical) specifications that have a linguistic base. (This underlying specification language, CPL (Conceptual Prototyping Language) is defined in Dignum 1989 and Dignum and van de Riet 1991.)

1. *COLOR-X Static Object Model* (CSOM) (Burg and van de Riet 1994, 1995b), which shows objects and classes of objects, the relationships between them, and static constraints upon them as they occur in a certain problem domain (or universe of discourse). This model is the central model because it defines the overall structure of the system to be built.

2. *COLOR-X Event Model* (CEM) (Burg and van de Riet 1995a), which shows the dynamic aspects of an information and communication system, in which all the occurring events and their dynamic and deontic constraints and restrictions are listed and ordered in time.

15.2.1   COLOR-X Static object Model

The aim of the CSOM, or object models in general, is to structure the static aspects of a system independently of the implementation environment. This means that we model the *logical* structure of the system, in which we define the stable, robust, and maintainable (i.e., also extendible) elements of the universe of discourse, about which information should be kept in the implemented system. We will not provide a complete introduction to the CSOM modeling technique, but we will explain it by giving an example and describing its component elements.

The example of a CSOM model, built for a simplified book-circulation system of a library, is shown in figure 15.1. Among the pieces of information contained in this figure are the following relationships:

- Zero or more users borrow at most seven books from a library.
- Zero or more users return at most seven books to a library.
- Novels and encyclopedias, which consist of more than zero parts, are subtypes of book.
- A library sends reminders to zero or more users.
- Zero or more users pay fines to a library.
- A library possesses zero or more books (including novels and encyclopedias).
- Users possess one and only one pass.
- Users have a name and address.

The CSOM (Burg and van de Riet 1994, 1995b) consists of the following elements:

I   *Objects:* An object is an entity occurring in the universe of discourse (problem domain), like *book* and *user*, that is able to save a state (information) and that offers a number of operations (behavior) to either examine or affect the state (Jacobson 1992). Objects (which, however, do not occur in figure 15.1) are drawn as boxes with rounded corners.

II   *Classes:* Classes represent templates for several objects and describe how these objects are structured internally. A class describes what is common to all the objects that are instances of this class. They are drawn as boxes in figure 15.1.

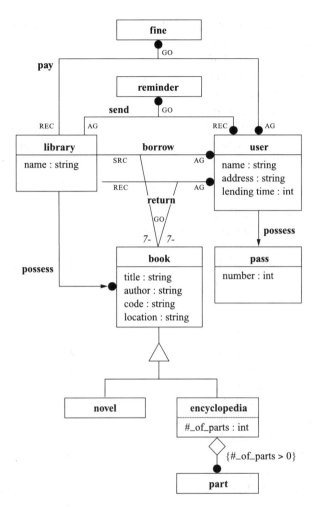

Figure 15.1
COLOR-X static object model

III *Relationships:* Relationships denote some static relations between two or more classes or objects. We distinguish two subsets:

A *Intra–state of affair* (or *user-defined*): These relations are represented as lines drawn from class to class, marked with

1. *label* (must be a verb; e.g., *borrow*),
2. *negation* (optional),
3. *cardinality* (black dot (≥ 0); no dot or number (exactly one); or a number, constraining the number of related objects),
4. *role* (AGENT, SOURCE, GOAL, etc.; describes for each connected class the role it is playing in the relationship as a whole).

B *Standard:* These relation ships are

1. *inheritance* (triangle on line),
2. *aggregation* (diamond on line),
3. *possession* (arrowed line),
4. *instantiation* (dotted, arrowed line from object to class).

IV *Constraints:* Constraints on cardinality of relationships, on values of attributes, and so on, are expressed between braces.

15.2.2   COLOR-X Event Model

In general, the purpose of dynamic modeling, of which the CEM is an example, is to show the time-dependent behavior of a particular part of the system or of the system as a whole. A CEM is merely a trace of the events that could and should be performed in the universe of discourse. This way of modeling the dynamic aspects of the universe of discourse links up very well with the way these aspects are described in the requirements document. However, so far there exists no automatic acquisition of conceptual models from these natural language sentences, as Black (1987) and Rolland and Proix (1992) propose. As with CSOMs, we introduce CEMs by way of an example, shown in figure 15.2, and we explain its elements.

The CEM (Burg and van de Riet 1995a) consists of the following elements:

I   *Event-boxes:* These are drawn as boxes, containing

A *modality* (PERMIT, NEC(ESSARY), MUST),

B *events* (numbered list of verbs and their objects and subjects, specified as CPL terms: [~] Verb [([$\langle Card[, Distr]\rangle$)]**Role** = [Var **in**]Noun)]+),

C *constraints* (predicates that events should obey; shown below a dotted line).

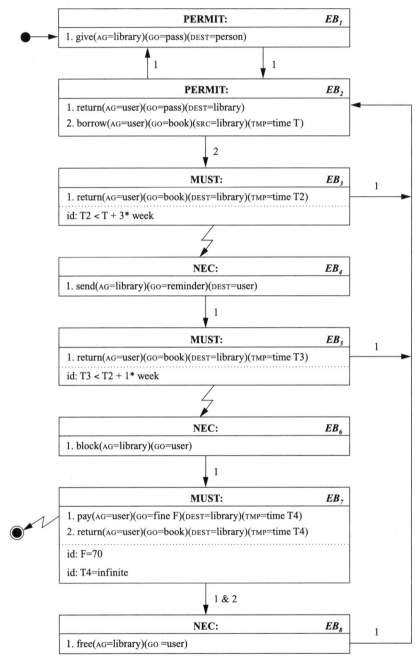

Figure 15.2
COLOR-X event model

II *Start and final nodes:* These are drawn as a black dot and black dot with circle, respectively.

III *Actual occurrence of event:* This is drawn as an arrow between event-boxes, labeled with the numbers of the events that occur.

IV *No occurrence of event at all:* This is drawn as a lightning-arrow between event-boxes, labeled with the numbers of the events that do not occur.

The event-box EB_1 of figure 15.2 expresses the *permission of a library to give a pass to a person.*

A violation of a NEC event leads the system into an inconsistent state and should therefore be prohibited by the system itself. MUST events may be violated, but the designer should specify the behavior of the (external) entity or (sub)system in the case of a violation. Because there are three modalities that can be used (permit, necessary, and must), there are three different kinds of event-boxes, the occurrences of which are triggered by words in the requirements document: for example, *can* and *is allowed to* trigger a PERMIT-box and *has to* triggers a MUST-box.

The existence of three modalities has led to the three standard building blocks, one for each. The events occurring in a NEC event-box cannot be violated, so no outgoing lighting-arrows are allowed. A MUST-box should always contain an expiration time (which may be infinite) as a constraint, in order to verify whether the obligation has been violated or not. A MUST-box should also have both a normal arrow and (violation) lightning-arrow for each event occurring in the box. A PERMIT-box may have a violation specification, but this is not obligatory. When only standard building blocks are used for creating models, the syntactic rules of the graphical modeling technique cannot be violated, since the building blocks are syntactically correct. By checking to see that there exists exactly one start and one final state, and that every arrow goes from one block into another, we can verify whether the model is syntactically correct.

A major novelty of both COLOR-X models is the possibility of handling and verifying their *semantic* correctness, by using WordNet on the one hand and by having a formal underlying representation on the other hand. By using WordNet as a source for reusable information and for parts of the models, we build our models out of semantically correct pieces, which may be adjusted to the needs of the modeler, but only according to certain rules. By augmenting and adjusting the models with additional or more specific information, we can guarantee the semantic correctness by formally describing the underlying relations between concepts occurring in models and the words that are allowed to be attached to these concepts (van der Vos and van de Riet 1994). To verify that the model as a whole is semantically correct and corresponds to the requirements as well, natural language sentences must be generated and checked against the original requirements (Burg and van de Riet 1994), or explanation facilities must be included (Gulla 1993).

The COLOR-X models and fully represented by formal CPL specifications, which are founded in several logics (e.g., dynamic, deontic, and temporal). Some other graphical conceptual modeling techniques have this formal foundation as well. Because we formalize the *roles* objects play in a relationship, the *constraints*, the *modalities* of static and dynamic relationships and events, and the relationships between *actions* and *events* (Mann and Thompson 1987), we are able to verify consistency and correctness inside and among the models. Additionally, we are able to make logical derivations out of these formalized specifications. The fact that both the static and the dynamic model have the same underlying formal representation integrates the models very strongly.

Unlike the developers of (for example) the Object Modeling Technique (OMT; Rumbaugh et al. 1991), we did not include a separate functional model (data flow diagram; DFD), because we have developed an algorithm and implemented a prototype that retrieves this kind of knowledge from the CSOM and CEM models. We are still improving and refining both the algorithm and its implementation.

An additional difference between our modeling technique and others (e.g., Feenstra and Wieringa 1993) is the absence in our model of separate object life-cycles. The information captured by models that incorporate object life-cycles is also generated automatically by the COLOR-X models. Possible outputs that have been implemented include state-transition diagrams (Burg and van de Riet 1995a) and Jackson structure diagrams.

15.3 WORDNET SUPPORTS CONCEPTUAL MODELING

In this section we provide a brief overview of the process of creating models according to the COLOR-X method, focusing chiefly on the support of, and the additional information retrieved from, WordNet.

To build a model of a certain universe of discourse, one must analyze it, retrieve the interesting information from it, and possibly add some other knowledge. We assume the existence of a requirements document that describes the universe of discourse and its problems (as well as proposed solutions). The next step is to analyze this document and to elicit the information to be put in the COLOR-X models. this results in lists of the following elements:

I   *Objects* (the entities playing an important role in the universe of discourse), which are identified by nouns
II   *Static relationships* (certain connections between two or more objects). We distinguish two kinds of relationships here:
     A *User-defined* (relationships introduced by the author of the requirements document, e.g., *lend* in a library book-circulation environment)
     B *Standard* or *conceptual* (relationships that relate objects in a conceptual way; e.g., a book IS-A (kind of) document)
III *Events* (all actions and events that can, may, will, or must happen in the universe of discourse)

As noted in section 15.2, objects and static relationships form the basis of the CSOM, and events, augmented with constraints and ordered in time, form the CEM. We will treat each of these three elements separately, to show exactly what kind of WordNet information is (or can be) used during the creation of conceptual models. We have implemented an environment that supports the selection of information from WordNet and its incorporation into the models. Examples of the implementations interface will be shown when we are explaining the selection of information from WordNet in the following sections.

15.3.1 Objects

The elements of the *object* list, retrieved from the requirements document of a universe of discourse, are grouped into *classes*, which contain objects with common properties and behavior. For the book-circulation department of a library, these include *book, library, user, reminder, fine,* and so on (see figure 15.1). The classes identified here will occur in the CSOM.

Because of the ambiguous nature of natural language, words can have several meanings (homonyms and polysemes), and many concepts are denoted by two or more words (synonyms). With the help of WordNet we try to find the right word meaning in each specific universe of discourse

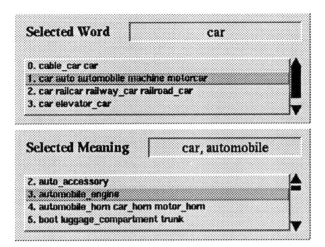

Figure 15.3
Specifying the meaning and attributes of *car*

(see figure 15.3). This approach is similar to the process of tagging pieces of text as described by Landes, Leacock, and Tengi (this volume). Polysemous word clashes are avoided by replacing these words with other ones that have similar meaning. If this search is successful, then for the rest of the development process we know that we are using the right meaning and that communication about the models will not be hampered by ambiguous word interpretations.

If we know which concept each word refers to, we are able to retrieve more general information about it from WordNet, using WordNet's substance, part, and member meronymy relationships. Examples of these relationships are *concrete* HAS-SUBSTANCE *cement*, *car* HAS-A *engine*, and *person* IS-MEMBER-OF *people*. The meronymy information will be translated into aggregation, possession, or attribute relationships in the CSOM, if they are useful and meaningful in the universe of discourse being modeled. The part and member meronymy information will be translated into aggregation relationships, and the substance meronymy information into class attributes (because substances are probably not identifiable).

15.3.2   User-Defined Relationships

Like the meaning of an object, the meaning of a certain relationship, denoted by a verb, can be ambiguous. The first step is to choose the right meaning (see figure 15.4). The next step is to choose the structure or

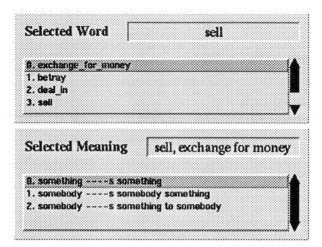

Figure 15.4
Specifying the meaning and selectional restrictions of *sell*

selectional restrictions of the verb: how many objects are involved and what kind of objects are allowed in the relationship (also see figure 15.4). The number of objects involved in a relationship is stored in WordNet in the form of verb frames. Unfortunately, WordNet discriminates only between *somebody* and *something* and therefore does not strongly restrict the kind of object. This limited discrimination is enough, however, to prohibit relationships like *a bike borrows a book*, because a *bike* is not a *somebody*. We have manually added a list that relates WordNet's verb frames to full verb specifications containing semantic functions. This addition considerably facilitates the generation of natural language sentences.

15.3.3 Standard Relationships

Both CSOM and WordNet contain standard relationships, and these are closely related (where by *standard relationships* we mean standard *conceptual* relationships; see section 15.2). The following information retrieved from WordNet points to a standard (conceptual) relationship:

- hyponymy/hypernymy: specialization/generalization (IS-A);
- part and substance meronymy: aggregation (HAS-A).

The possession and instantiation relationships are domain specific, and information about them is not available in WordNet.

15.3.4   Other Knowledge

Among the pieces of information we retrieve from WordNet are the antonym, entailment, and causal relationships between verbs. This knowledge is used to make the models more complete, by offering additional information about the events that may occur in the universe of discourse.

15.3.4.1   Antonym Events   Almost every current conceptual modeling method contains some step in which the events occurring in the universe of discourse are listed (e.g., OMT's event traces (Rumbaugh et al. 1991) or Jacobson's (1992) use cases). CEMs not only contain this kind of information, but also formalize it. Although the initial step, listing the events and ordering them in time in an informal way, should be done manually by the modeler, the creation of the CEM itself is embedded, and thus supported, by a CASE environment. The availability of standard building blocks was mentioned earlier. The event specifications are built up in the same way as the user-defined relationships of the CSOM, because they are both CPL specifications that differ only in their tense (active and passive, respectively). This means that the determination of the meaning, occurrence, and attributes of verbs and nouns is supported by WordNet. To end up with CEMs that are complete (to a certain degree), the *antonym events* of the events occurring in the requirements document are generated as well. Most of the time these antonym events occur in the universe of discourse, but they are not always explicitly included in the requirements document. In the library example, the *free* event was generated as the antonym of the *block* event and added to the CEM. By contrast, the antonym event of *borrow* (i.e., *return*) already appears in the model. The problem we discovered in using WordNet to find these antonyms was that in WordNet the antonym of *borrow* is not *return*, but *lend*. *Borrow-lend* is a perspective (or conversive) antonymy (the subject and object are switched) and not a complementary (or reversive) antonymy. Both relationships are important, but because WordNet does not distinguish them, their use is restricted.

15.3.4.2   Entailment and Cause-To Relationship   The entailment and cause-to relationships give more detailed information about what the exact contents of a certain event are. For example, the selling of a car to a customer means not only that the car is exchanged for money, but also that *possession of the car (something concrete or obstract) is transferred to the customer (somebody)*. This is a typical example of a dynamic effect on the static structure of an environment (the *sell* event entails a change in the possession relationship). The presence of the entailment relationship thus gives further insight into the meaning of events and the relations between events and static structures. The cause-to relationship is especially useful when relationships between events are being investigated (e.g., to take care of possible side effects of events).

15.3.5   Verification and Validation

By extending the conceptual model with linguistic features and by using WordNet as a lexicon, we have created more possibilities for validating and verifying the intermediate and resulting models. The following list summarizes the syntactic and semantic verifications we have computed so far:

• We have verified the kinds of nouns connected to a verb, relationships between nouns, standard building blocks, and consistency among specifications (i.e., parts of models).
• We have verified that the right category occurs in the right place in the model.
• We have constrained the combinations of labels and primitive modeling concepts at a metamodel level.
• We have incorporated reusable information and (parts of) models from the reusable knowledge base.

These verifications have led to models that are syntactically and semantically correct (i.e., the models are right), but there is still the possibility that the models do not express what is described in the requirements document (i.e., they are not the right models). This could easily happen as the result of misunderstandings, misjudgments, or miscommunication, and it should be recognized as a potential problem. Our solution is to generate natural language sentences expressing the contents of the models. These paraphrases and the models themselves should be compared with the requirements document to see if they are indeed an abstraction of this document.

Our natural language generation process is facilitated by the fact that we have based COLOR-X on CPL. Because CPL in turn is based on Functional Grammar (Dik 1978, 1989), the natural language generation is rather straightforward. Although we think that this kind of natural language processing processing should be supported with a lexicon that contains lexical information about words but also rules for generating derivational forms of words, WordNet was not built explicitly to facilitate natural language generation. Although we access the WordNet files directly, and therefore do not use WordNet's morphological processing functions, we also believe that inflectional forms of words should be generated by rules. We have created a lexicon that consists of WordNet augmented with new and optimized rules about verb inflection, plural and singular forms of nouns, numerals, adjectives, determiners, and so on. Our Prolog translator CPL2NL translates any form of CPL specifications into correct natural language sentences.

Certain aspects of the CPL specifications have an impact on the generated sentences. First, the modality determines the auxiliary verb of the sentence as follows: NEC, MUST, and PERMIT trigger *obliged to*, *should*, and *permitted to*, respectively. Second, the cardinality of the subject (agent or zero) of the relationship determines the singular (exactly one) or plural form (*n* (or more/less)) of the related verb. Third, the identification of the objects, which gives more detailed information about the nouns, is added as a subordinate clause that begins with *where* (see point 3 in the list below). Finally, the satellites of the CPL specification are translated into place or time adjuncts.

There are three basic forms of CPL specifications:[1]

1. *Unconditional*
   PERMIT:ACTION: borrow(AG = user)($\langle + \rangle$GO = book)
   ($\langle 1 \rangle$SRC = library)
   ```
   [an,user,is,permitted to,borrow,one or more,
   books,from,a,library]
   ```

2. *Conditional*
   MUST:PROSP: return(AG = user)($\langle + \rangle$GO =book)($\langle 1 \rangle$DEST = library)
   (sit: PERF: borrow(AG = user)($\langle + \rangle$GO = book)($\langle 1 \rangle$SRC = library))
   ```
   [if,an,user,borrowed,one or more,books,from,a,
   library,then,an,user,will have to,return,one or
   more,books,to,a,library]
   ```

3. *Identified*
   PERF: borrow(AG = user)(GO = book)(TMP = V1 in time) (id:
   V1 = yesterday)
   ```
   [an,user,borrowed,a,book,at,a,time,V1,where,V1,
   is,yesterday]
   ```

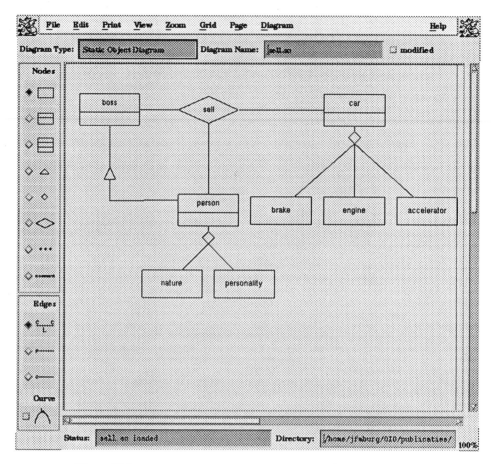

Figure 15.5
CSOM, generated from the WordNet consultations

15.3.6 Combining the Results

We have shown how, starting with a single verb, one can retrieve enough information from WordNet to completely build the corresponding CSOM (see figure 15.5). Here we summarize the steps required:

1. Choose the name of the relationship to be modeled from the requirements document (e.g., *sell*).

2. Consult WordNet to disambiguate the meaning of the verb (e.g., 'exchange for money') by examining synonyms.

3. Choose the selectional restrictions of the verb from the set of verb frames stored in WordNet (*somebody sells something to somebody*).

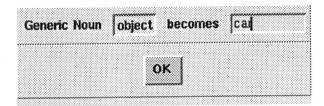

Figure 15.6
Specifying the elements of a verb frame (here, *something* becomes *car*)

4. If necessary, specify the elements of the verb frame (e.g., *something* becomes *car*, see figure 15.6).
5. Consult WordNet to find the right meaning for the nouns (e.g., *car* means 'automobile'; see figure 15.3) by examining synonyms.
6. Lists of possible attributes are given for some of the objects found in WordNet. If such a list is available for the object in question, choose from among the attributes those that are relevant to the intended sense (e.g., *car* HAS-A *engine*).
7. WordNet may contain relationships between nouns (e.g., *boss* IS-A *person*) that the modeler has not explicitly included. Add these relationships to the model.

15.3.7 An Alternative Approach

The approach we have described so far is to use the words retrieved from the requirements document in the analysis and design phase and find their meaning by consulting WordNet. In another small project we adopted an alternative way of using a lexicon during the conceptual modeling process—specifically, we consulted WordNet during the requirements analysis phase. We did this because (1) it is easier to retrieve the right meaning from the lexicon because the words that are examined can be found in their original context, and (2) it is desirable to know as early as possible exactly which concepts are described by the words from the requirements document.

We have built a small demonstration prototype that gives the opportunity to retrieve words denoting objects and relationships from the document, find all the occurrences of these words, and find the correct meaning of these words in WordNet. Figure 15.7 shows the interface of this prototype, including a part of the requirements document describing the library case, some retrieved objects and relationships, an alphabetically sorted list of all the words occurring in the document, and an interface

Chosen objects; Relations   Requirements document   Alphabetically sorted list of
                                          (*borrow* selected)   all words occurring in text

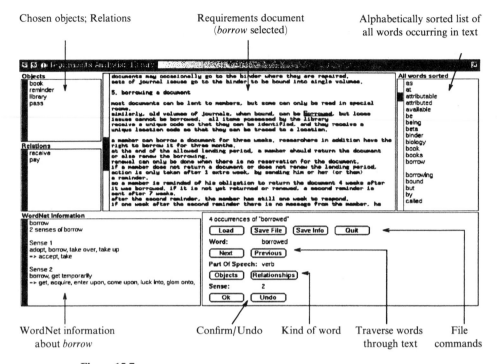

WordNet information   Confirm/Undo   Kind of word   Traverse words   File
about *borrow*   through text   commands

Figure 15.7
Using WordNet during requirements analysis

with WordNet. As mentioned earlier, the resemblance to tagging interfaces is clearly noticeable.

15.4   WORDNET AND A REUSABLE KNOWLEDGE LIBRARY

15.4.1   Kinds of Knowledge

As noted in section 15.3, we use WordNet as a source for reusable general
information for building conceptual models. In fact, we use WordNet as a
base for a much bigger, but more specific, *reusable knowledge library*. The
lexical knowledge from WordNet is applicable in every universe of discourse, but usually the meaning of a word used in a certain universe of
discourse is restricted.

We view the reusable knowledge library as a multilevel repository,
based on the specificity, or refinement, of the concepts found at each level.
One level stores *lexical knowledge* (WordNet), which is by and large

rather static and unchanging, but can be extended with new concepts or new insights. A second level stores *domain-specific knowledge*, consisting of concepts and relationships between these concepts, which are typical for the domain (e.g., a library) but whose specific meaning cannot be found in the lexical knowledge level.

The domain-specific knowledge level should be built from scratch, but lexical knowledge of course serves as a good starting point because domain-specific knowledge will be derived from it. Domain-specific knowledge is used when a new application is built; however, it in turn is extended if new knowledge is discovered during the construction of new applications that proves to be relevant throughout the domain or company as a whole. After some time, depending on the rate at which new applications are built and new definitions are elicited, the body of domain-specific knowledge will become rather static. It is probably not a good idea to include this knowledge in WordNet, because it might not be valid in other domains. A third level, *application-specific knowledge*, further refines the information available at the domain-specific level. The meanings of concepts and the relationships between concepts found at this level are not valid for the domain or company as a whole, but are specific to the application that uses them.

This last level of knowledge consists of different sets, which are not necessarily disjoint, belonging to separate applications. The knowledge can be reused when the application is revised or when a new version is constructed. Each set will be fairly static once construction of the application is finished. The number of words with several meanings (homonyms and polysemes) should be minimized to reach a certain level of standardization within a company. The amount of application-specific knowledge should therefore be as small as possible.

Because all levels of knowledge tend to become rather static after some time, the information remains valid and can be reused.

For example, the information available about *book* for the three different levels, where the domain is the book-circulation desk of a library, is as follows:

• *Lexical level*: A book is *a number of printed or written pages bound together* containing *text, chapters, foreword, contents, graphics, cover, and so on*.

• *Domain-specific level*: *All books possessed by the library have a unique code so that they can be identified, and they have a unique location code so that they can be traced to a location. Books can be lent to members of the library.*

• *Application-specific level: Most books can be lent to members, but some can only be read in special rooms.* (This leads to additional information about the lendability of books.)

15.4.2   Reusable Library: Models or Implementations?

In the software-engineering field, reusability is a very important issue. However, a tendency to shift from reusable software components to reusable models is visible (Francalanci and Pernici 1994; Castano et al. 1994) and usually focuses on reusable *object* specifications. An important addition to this reusable knowledge is knowledge about relationships between objects and about constraints on objects and relationships, as described in the previous section.

We have also carried out some research on reusable software components and a supporting reusable software library (Coudron et al. 1993). The incorporation of linguistic knowledge was a central theme. In particular, the search facilities, indexed by identified nouns and verbs, could be supported with lexical background knowledge (descriptions of components could be parsed, synonyms of search items were found as well, etc.).

We used our reusable knowledge library in a very nontraditional way, however. We did not search for models or software components directly; rather, we searched for knowledge describing a certain object, relationship, or event. If we found the desired piece of knowledge, we had the possibility of incorporating it into conceptual models or of translating it into descriptions of software components.

15.5   WORDNET EVALUATED FROM A CONCEPTUAL MODELING VIEWPOINT

We have been using WordNet in a conceptual modeling environment for some time now, and although we still feel a need for additions and adjustments, we think it is a very powerful supporting tool for the process of conceptual modeling. In this chapter we have described the use of WordNet during construction of the models. It can also be used after the models have been finished, as a way of verifying them; incorrect models would then be reconstructed. (We have used the WordNet information *during* the construction process precisely to avoid the possibility of finding out that an already constructed model is incorrect and then having to reconstruct it.)

Important strong points of WordNet as used in our environment include

1. the large number of words and concepts;
2. the determination of the meaning of words;
3. the "common knowledge" nature of the information about concepts, which frees the modeler from reinventing the wheel over and over again;
4. the availability of verb frames, which prevents the modeler from leaving parts of relationships unspecified or specifying the wrong type; and
5. the open architecture, which makes it possible to access information from every application.

For our purpose of supporting the process of conceptual modeling, WordNet would be even more powerful and useful if the following kinds of information (or knowledge) about words and concepts were available:

1. Semantic functions (or thematic roles), that is, the exact roles the elements of a verb frame play. For example, *somebody sells something to somebody* would be more powerful if it were stored as *sell* (AGENT = *somebody*) (GOAL = *something*) (RECIPIENT = *somebody*). The semantic functions and related satellites are defined well in the theory of Functional Grammar (Dik 1978, 1989).
2. More precise specification of what type the elements of the frame should have (i.e., the frame for *breastfeed* should specify that the subject must be + female). This improvement would be difficult, if WordNet were to remain as general as possible, because a more precise specification could restrict the frame's applicability to only a few situations. Some sort of leveling—such as we propose in our three-level reusable knowledge library, for example—could solve this problem.
3. Characteristic information (features) about concepts (e.g., durative, controlled, telic, dynamic). This improvement would be especially useful in combination with the previous two. To verify whether concepts could be combined, one would check to see whether their features match.
4. Additional "common knowledge" about concepts (e.g., "a person has a name" is commonly known to be true and is a very useful fact for conceptual modeling). (we should note, however, that it is very hard to determine what is commonly accepted and what is not. There is much disagreement on this question.)

5. The presence of rules for determining derivations of words (i.e., inflectional and derivational morphology)

6. The gender and [+human]/[−human] aspect of nouns (e.g., for determining relative pronouns during natural language generation)

7. A strict separation between perspective antonymy (e.g., *borrow-lend*) and complementary antonymy (e.g., *borrow-return*)

15.6   CONCLUSIONS AND FURTHER RESEARCH

As we have shown, introducing linguistic knowledge and theories into conceptual modeling is a viable process. The resulting models, mainly enforced by reusing information from WordNet and the related reusable knowledge library, tend to be syntactically and semantically correct; are consistent with the requirements documents, owing to generation of natural language sentences that paraphrase the models; and are mutually consistent. We have dealt successfully with two important integration orientations in the software-engineering life cycle, by using the same concepts for each phase and by using WordNet information and linguistic theories to adjust the analysis and design phase (vertical integration), and by using the same underlying formalism for both the static and the dynamic models (horizontal integration). Issues still under research include *rhetorical relationships* (e.g., WordNet's ENTAIL and CAUSE-TO relationships) (Mann and Thompson 1987). These could be used to relate events to other events and states of the system as whole. The dependencies between natural language specifications in the requirements document and the code that is generated also need to be worked out (an example: the promise to do something in the future will have consequences for the implemented code, which should include a list of such promises that trigger certain events when they are not fulfilled in time). The COLOR-X project focuses mainly on natural language generation out of models, which increases the communicative properties of the models. The generated sentences are also used for validating the models, as we and others have described (Burg and van de Riet 1994, 1995a,b; Dalianis 1992). Natural language parsing, on the other hand, could be used for creating models (Rolland and Proix 1992). The output of this parsing process could be an ER model (Tseng, Chen, and Yang 1992) or a NIAM-like schema (Natural Language Information Analysis Method; Black 1987). The parsing of the requirements document could be a useful addition to the creation of COLOR-X models.

At the moment we are working on a system that is being developed for planning and scheduling educational activities at the Vrije Universiteit in Amsterdam. Although we are still in a preliminary phase, the results are promising.

Notes

1. Because no phonetic analyzer is used in generating the natural language sentences, the initial consonant sound of *user* is not noticed and the article *an* is generated rather than *a*.

References

Black, W. J. (1987). Acquisition of conceptual data models from natural language descriptions. In *Proceedings of the 2nd Conference of the European Chapter of the ACL*, 241–248. Association for Computational Linguistics.

Buitelaar, P., and van de Riet, R. P. (1992a). *A feasibility study in linguistically motivated object-oriented conceptual design of information systems* (Tech. Rep. No. IR-293). Amsterdam: Vrije Universiteit.

Buitelaar, P., and van de Riet, R. P. (1992b). The use of a lexicon to interpret ER diagrams: A LIKE project. In *proceedings of the 11th International Conference on the Entity-Relationship Approach (ER '92)*, 162–177. New York: Springer-Verlag.

Burg, J. F. M. (1996). *Linguistic instruments in requirements engineering*. Doctoral dissertation, Vrije Universiteit, Amsterdam. Tokyo: Ohmsha, and Amsterdam: IOS Press.

Burg, J. F. M. and van de Riet, R. P. (1994). *COLOR-X: Object modeling profits from linguistics* (Tech. Rep. No. IR-365). Amsterdam: Vrije Universiteit.

Burg, J. F. M. and van de Riet, R. P. (1995a). COLOR-X: Linguistically-based event modeling: A general approach to dynamic modeling. In *Proceedings of the 7th International Conference on Advanced Information Systems Engineering (CAiSE '95)*, 26–39. New York: Springer-Verlag.

Burg, J. F. M., and van de Riet, R. P. (1995b). COLOR-X: Object modeling profits from linguistics. In N. J. I. Mars (Ed.), *Towards very large knowledge bases: Knowledge building & knowledge sharing (KB&KS'95)*, 204–214. Tokyo; Ohmsha, and Amsterdam: IOS Press.

Burg, J. F. M., and van de Riet, R. P. (1995c). The impact of linguistics on conceptual models: Consistency and understandability. In *First International Workshop on Applications of Natural Language to Data Bases (NLDB '95)*, 183–197. AFCET.

Burg, J. F. M., van de Riet, R. P., and Chang, S. C. (1993). A data-dictionary as a lexicon: An application of linguistics in information systems. In *Proceedings of the 2nd International Conference on Information and Knowledge Management (CIKM-93)*, 114–123. New York: ACM Press.

Castano, S., De Antonellis, V., Francalanci, C., and Pernici, B. (1994). A reusability-based comparison of requirement specification methodologies. In *Proceedings of the IFIP 8.1 Conference, CRIS*, Maastricht. IFIP.

Coudron, M. G. H., Eerbeek, J. A. M., de Jong, M. W. G., and Leckie, A. G. (1993). Reusable software library: design and implementation. Unpublished master's thesis, Vrije Universiteit/GAK, Amsterdam.

Dalianis, H. (1992). A method for validating a conceptual model by natural language discourse generation. In *Proceedings of the 4th International Conference on Advanced Information Systems Engineering (CAiSE '92)*, 425–444. New York: Springer-Verlag.

Dignum, F. P. M. (1989). *A language for modelling knowledge bases. Based on linguistics, founded in logic.* Doctoral dissertation, Vrije Universiteit, Amsterdam.

Dignum, F. P. M., and van de Riet, R. P. (1991). How the modelling of knowledge bases can be based on linguistics and founded in logic. *Data and Knowledge Engineering Journal, 7*, 1–34.

Dik, S. C. (1978). *Functional Grammar.* Amsterdam.

Dik, S. C. (1989). *The theory of functional Grammar.* Part I: *The structure of the clause.* Dordrecht: Foris.

Feenstra, R. B., and Wieringa, R. J. (1993). *LCM 3.0: A language for describing conceptual models–syntax definition* (Tech. Rep. No. IR-344). Amsterdam: Vrije Universiteit.

Francalanci, C., and Pernici, B. (1994). Abstraction levels for entity-relationship schemas. In *Proceedings of the 13th International Conference on the Entity-Relationship Approach.* New York: Springer-Verlag.

Gulla, J. A. (1993). *Deep explanation generation in conceptual modeling environments.* Doctoral dissertation, University of Trondheim, Norway.

Jacobson, I. (1992). *Object-oriented software engineering: A use case approach.* Reading, MA: Addison-Wesley.

Mann, W. C., and Thompson, S. A. (1987). Rhetorical structure theory: Description and construction of text structures. In G. Kempen (Ed.), *Natural language generation: New results in artificial intelligence, psychology and linguistics*, 85–95. Dordrecht: Nijhoff.

Miller, G. A., Beckwith, R., Fellbaum, C., Gross, D., Miller, K., and Tengi, R. (1993). *Five papers on WordNet* (Tech. Rep. No. 43). Princeton, NJ: Princeton University, Cognitive Science Laboratory.

Rolland, C., and Proix, C. (1992). A natural language approach for requirements engineering. In *Proceedings of the 4th International Conference on Advanced Information Systems Engineering (CAiSE '92).* New York: Springer-Verlag.

Rumbaugh, J., Blaha, M., Premerlani, W., Eddy, F., and Lorensen, W. (1991). *Object-oriented modeling and design.* Englewood Cliffs, NJ: Prentice-Hall.

Tseng, F. S. C., Chen, A. L. P., and Yang, W.-P. (1992). On mapping natural language constructs into relational algebra through E-R representation. *Data and Knowledge Engineering, 9*, 97–118.

van de Riet, R. P. (1994). Linguistic instruments in knowledge engineering: A research proposal and some experiments. In K. Fuchi and T. Yokoi (Eds.), *Knowledge building and knowledge sharing*, 200–207. Tokyo: Ohmsha, and Amsterdam: IOS Press.

van der Vos, A. J., and van de Riet, R. P. (1994). *A first semantic check based on linguistic information for state transition diagrams* (Tech. Rep. NO. IR-372). Amsterdam: Vrije Universiteit.

Chapter 16

Knowledge Processing on an Extended WordNet

Sanda M. Harabagiu and Dan I. Moldovan

16.1 VERY LARGE KNOWLEDGE BASES AND WORDNET

16.1.1 Desirable Features and What WordNet Can Offer

Commonsense reasoning requires extensive knowledge. In order to be useful for practical artificial intelligence problems, a knowledge base needs to have millions of concepts and relations. The nature of knowledge is such that even solutions to relatively small, narrow artificial intelligence problems require a great deal of knowledge. Unfortunately, knowledge cannot be modularized or partitioned. WordNet contains almost all English words, grouped into a hundred thousand synsets, which in turn are linked by semantic relations. But most importantly, each synset has a gloss that, when disambiguated, may increase the number of semantic relations by an order of magnitude.

It takes a large effort to build a very large knowledge base. Because of this, it is highly desirable that the knowledge base be generally applicable, such that it can be adapted to a particular problem with as little effort as possible. If the knowledge base is to be generally applicable, then its relations must always hold. WordNet was built on such a principle. Its relations apply broadly throughout English and are concept and context independent.

Another desirable feature of a knowledge base is to have a rich concept connectivity while using only a small set of relation types. The richer the connectivity in the knowledge base, the more inference is possible. This conflicts somehow with the other goal of having fewer types of relations that keep the number of inference rules small and thereby simplify the reasoning mechanism. There are endless possible relations between concepts; the challenge is to find only the basic ones that support inference rules and that can help generate many other relations through inference. WordNet has a small set of relations that provide structure and support property inheritance.

16.1.2   Plausible Inferences

In this chapter we discuss the way in which a large knowledge base may be implemented using WordNet and extensions. The goal is to create an environment that supports text inference, which in turn is the key to exploiting the expressive power of natural language.

Text inference refers to the problem of extracting relevant, unstated information from a text. The implied information contributes to the understanding of the context of the text and also accounts for text coherence. There are also other inferences that are required in order to understand a text. They cover lexical disambiguation, reference resolution, and the recognition of predicate arguments. Consider (1):

(1) Jim was hungry.
     He opened the refrigerator.

The explicit inferences needed to understand this text include word sense disambiguation and pronoun reference. A human also concludes (among other things) that the *intention expressed in this text* is eating, that most likely the event takes place at home, and that the text is coherent since being hungry is a cause for opening the refrigerator where food is stored. These latter inferences are plausible since an average reader finds them highly probable. A great deal of knowledge is needed in order to be able to extract such inferences. WordNet 1.5 has this information in the glosses that define concepts. For example:

hungry has the gloss '(feeling a need or desire to <u>eat</u>)'
eat has the gloss '(take in solid <u>food</u>)'
refrigerator has the gloss '(an appliance in which <u>foods</u> can be stored at low temperature)'

We show below that *semantic paths* between the concepts expressed by words such as *hungry* and *refrigerator* may be established and that many inferences involving the concepts along the paths are possible.

16.1.3   Related Work

WordNet (Beckwith et al. 1991; Miller 1995) is the largest machine-readable dictionary, with approximately 168,000 words, 91,600 synsets expressing as many concepts, and 345,000 relations. Although using machine-readable dictionaries for natural language processing is hardly a new idea (Wilks, Slator, and Guthrie 1996), at present they are not widely used in work on artificial intelligence. Perhaps the most used machine-readable dictionary is the *Longman Dictionary of Contemporary English* (LDOCE) (Procter 1978). Although it has only 41,000 entries, less than half the size of WordNet, it associates syntactic categories to words, a function that is useful for classification and other applications. LDOCE's categories were used by Walker and Amsler (1986) to do topic recognition of newswire stories from the *New York Times*. Slator (1988) used LDOCE to extract knowledge structure from text.

LDOCE was also the starting point for building a variety of knowledge bases, many of them used in systems that were part of the DARPA-funded TIPSTER project, aiming at producing document classification, analysis, and retrieval. The New Mexico State University–Brandeis University system's lexical knowledge base consists of generative lexical structures (Pustejovsky 1991) automatically extracted from LEXBASE (Stein et al. 1993), the machine-tractable version of LDOCE containing syntactic codes and selectional information. Pathtrieve is an information retrieval system developed at New Mexico State University that uses contextually organized semantic structure derived from LDOCE (Fowler and Dearholt 1989; Fowler and Slator 1989).

In order to improve LDOCE's flat subject code hierarchies, a connectionist representation of LDOCE was envisioned by assembling genus hierarchies (Amsler 1980; Chodorow, Byrd, and Heidorn 1985). WordNet, using only a small number of lexical relations, provides a better connectivity. By far, the largest connectivity is found in CYC (Lenat 1995), but at the expense of a weak structure that reduces its applicability to general-purpose reasoning.

WordNet glossaries, viewed as dictionary definitions, induce supplementary information. Disambiguated glosses, transformed in network representations, can significantly increase the connectivity of the lexical knowledge base. Automatic disambiguation of definitions, first proposed by Amsler, was also attempted on LDOCE entries (Bruce and Guthrie 1992). A large body of research deals with the problems of deriving semantic primitive relations (Guo 1992), meaningful patterns (Alshawi 1989), and defining formulae (Evens 1988) from dictionary definitions.

16.2   KNOWLEDGE REPRESENTATION ON EXTENDED WORDNET

16.2.1   Semantic Relations in WordNet

The semantic relations that link the synsets are the building blocks to our solution for knowledge processing. Table 16.1 summarizes the relations that exist in WordNet 1.5. For each relation, table 16.1 indicates the parts of speech connected by the relation, the number of occurrences, an example, and some properties. Altogether there are 345,264 links. Some of the relations are asymmetric and transitive; others are symmetric. As we will show, this plays a role in the type of inference they support. Most relations hold between words belonging to the same syntactic category. Since in a knowledge base it is highly desirable to link nouns with verbs and adjectives, and verbs with adverbs and adjectives, we have to look for this information inside the concept glosses.

16.2.2   Synset-Defining Features

Almost each WordNet synset has a gloss expressed in English that defines that synset. A synset's gloss may also contain comments and/or one or more examples of how the words in the synset are used. In order to make a knowledge base out of WordNet, we must use its glossary information. The idea is to transform each synset's gloss into a defining feature directed acyclic graph (DAG), with synsets as nodes and lexical relations as links.

Although highly desirable and feasible, this is not an easy task. It is useful to note that glosses are expressed in stereotyped phrases, whose structure is often the same and which use a simpler grammar than that used in general English. To build defining features from glosses, we must deal first with lexical disambiguation, then with semantic disambiguation and the problem of identifying case and lexical relations between words expressing concepts. For example, the word *interaction* has the gloss '(a mutual or reciprocal action)', which uniquely parses into a noun phrase. Therefore, the problem of whether *reciprocal* in this gloss is a noun or an adjective is easily solved. In a noun phrase, the adjectives describe attributes of the nouns; thus, in the example gloss the relations are immediately identified: *interaction*—GLOSS→*action*—ATTRIBUTE→*mutual* and *action*—ATTRIBUTE→*reciprocal*.

A defining feature is not complete unless the words are semantically unambiguous. Heuristics contribute to this endeavor. In the example gloss and many others, the head noun is a hypernym (subsumer) of the concept itself. This observation is sufficient to select the right sense for the noun

Table 16.1
WordNet 1.5 relations

Relation	Connects	Number	Examples	Comments
HYPERNYM	n_synset-n_synset	61,123	{oak}→{tree}	IS-A, asymmetric, transitive
	v_synset-v_synset	10,817	{hit}→{propel, impel}	
HYPONYM	n_synset-n_synset	61,123	{tree}→{oak}	REVERSE_IS-A
	v_synset-v_synset	10,817	{propel, impel}→{hit}	
HAS-MEMBER	n_synset-n_synset	11,472	{family, family unit}→{child, kid}	asymmetric, transitive
IS-MEMBER-OF	n_synset-n_synset	11,472	{child, kid}→{family, family unit}	REVERSE_HAS-MEMBER
HAS-STUFF	n_synset-n_synset	366	{tank, army tank}→{steel}	asymmetric, transitive
IS-STUFF-OF	n_synset-n_synset	366	{steel}→{tank, army tank}	REVERSE_HAS-STUFF
HAS-PART	n_synset-n_synset	5,695	{torso, body}→{shoulder}	asymmetric, transitive
IS-PART-OF	n_synset-n_synset	5,695	{shoulder}→{torso, body}	REVERSE_HAS-PART
ENTAIL	v_synset-v_synset	435	{snore, saw wood}→{sleep, slumber}	asymmetric, transitive
CAUSE-TO	v_synset-v_synset	204	{develop}→{grow, become larger}	asymmetric, transitive
PAST-PARTICIPLE	adj-verb	89	developed→develop	asymmetric
ATTRIBUTE	adj_synset-n_synset	636	{hypocritical}→{insincerity}	asymmetric
SYNSET	n_synset-n	107,484	{place, property}→place	from synsets to words
	v_synset-v	25,768	{travel, journey}→travel	
	adj_synset-adj	28,762	{glad, happy}→happy	
	adv_synset-adv	6,203	{well, much}→well	
PERTAINYM	adj-n	3,458	academic→academia	asymmetric
	adj-adj	3,539	universalistic→universal	
	adv-adj	2,894	reasonably→reasonable	
ANTONYM	n-n	1,713	presence→absence	symmetric
	v-v	1,025	rise→fall	
	adj-adj	3,748	active→passive	
	adv-adv	704	always→never	
SIMILAR-TO	adj-adj	20,050	abridge→shorten	symmetric
SEE-ALSO	v-v	840	touch→touch down	symmetric
	adj-adj	2,686	inadequate→unsatisfactory	symmetric

action out of eight possible senses encoded in WordNet 1.5. Another useful observation is that in many cases adjectives describing attributes of the same noun are semantically related. In this case the second WordNet sense of the adjective *mutual* is similar to the single sense of the adjective *reciprocal*. The construction of defining features is not always that easy, but with a large body of heuristics operating on WordNet, the task is feasible.

Table 16.2 illustrates the relations we used to transform WordNet glosses into semantic networks. Most of these are case relations and their inverses, defined in Fillmore 1968, Alterman 1985, and other papers. By introducing these new relations in WordNet, we enhance the connectivity between synsets, although requiring that such relations exist only in the environment of defining features.

For example, the gloss for the first WordNet sense of the noun *pilot* is '(a person qualified to guide ships through difficult waters going into or going out of a harbor)'. We transform this gloss into the network representation illustrated in figure 16.1. The concept "pilot" is connected to nine other concepts: "person," "qualified," "guide," "water," "difficult," "go in," "go out," "ship," "harbor." The links between the concepts reflect the lexical relations between the disambiguated words of the gloss. In addition, the figure shows the inheritance chain: "pilot" IS-A "mariner," who IS-A "sailor," who IS-A "skilled worker," who IS-A "person."

The concept "pilot" is directly linked to the concept "person" through a GLOSS relation, meaning that a *pilot* is a *person* who has the properties and attributes defined by the chain of lexical relations that are connected to *person*. The first such property is the adjective concept "qualified," an attribute of *person* in this context. "Qualified" is further specialized by the verb concept "guide," whose location is defined by "waters" with the attribute *difficult*. Furthermore, the purpose of "guide" is to "get in" or "get out" the object "ship" from a place defined by the concept "harbor."

16.2.3　Microcontexts

An important and extremely useful property of each defining feature is that it provides *context* for its concept. In the case of the concept "pilot," the context is defined by nine other concepts and their semantic connections.

One can think of these defining features as miniframes or scripts. But since they were provided as basic descriptions of concepts, they are generally applicable.

Table 16.2
Relations derived from WordNet concepts' glosses

Relation	Connects	Concept	Gloss	Example
GLOSS	n_synset-n_synset	{doctor, physician}	(a licensed medical practitioner)	{physician}—GLOSS→{practitioner}
	v_synset-v_synset	{tease, harass}	(annoy persistently)	{tease}—GLOSS→{annoy}
	adj_synset-adj_synset	{alert}	(vigilantly attentive)	{alert}—GLOSS→{attentive}
	adv_synset-adv_synset	{fully, well}	(completely)	{fully}—GLOSS→{completely}
AGENT	v_synset-n_synset	{culture}	(all the knowledge and values shared by society)	{share}—AGENT→{society}
OBJECT	v_synset-n_synset	{glass}	(container for holding liquids)	{hold}—OBJECT→{liquid}
INSTRUMENT	v_synset-n_synset	{chop, hack}	(cut with tool)	{cut}—INSTRUMENT→{tool}
BENEFICIARY	v_synset-n_synset	{ratables}	(property that provides tax income for local government)	{provide}—BENEFICIARY→{government}
PURPOSE	v_synset-v_synset	{fork}	(something used to serve or eat)	{use}—PURPOSE→{serve} {use}—PURPOSE→{eat}
ATTRIBUTE	n_synset-adj_synset	{doctor, physician}	(licensed medical practitioner)	{medical practitioner}—ATTRIBUTE→{licensed}
	v_synset-adv_synset	{browse}	(shop around)	{shop}—ATTRIBUTE→{around}
	n_synset-n_synset	{apharesis, aphaeresis}	(omission at the beginning of a word)	{word}—ATTRIBUTE→{beginning}
	v_synset-v_synset	{carry}*	(move while transporting)	{move}—ATTRIBUTE→{transport}
REASON	v_synset-n_synset	{treasure}	(something prized for beauty)	{prize}—REASON→{beauty}
STATE	v_synset-n_synset	{create}	(bring into existence)	{bring}—STATE→{existence}
LOCATION	v_synset-n_synset	{earth}	(hide in the earth)	{hide}—LOCATION→{earth}
THEME	v_synset-n_synset	{lecture}	(teaching by giving a discourse on some subject)	{discourse}—THEME→{subject}
TIME	v_synset-n_synset	{monthly}	(a periodical that is published every month)	{publish}—TIME→{month}
MANNER	v_synset-v_synset	{cook}	(change by heating)	{change}—MANNER→{heat}

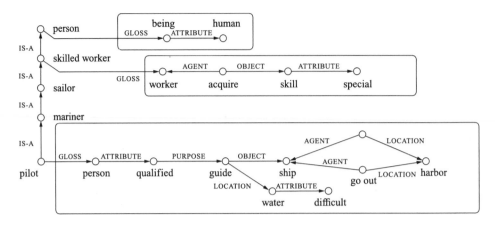

Figure 16.1
Representation of the defining features for the noun concept "pilot"

When a concept belongs to a hierarchy, it inherits the properties of its hypernyms. As illustrated in figure 16.1, the concept expressed by *pilot* connects through IS-A and GLOSS links to the concepts expressed by *worker* and *human being*, and inherits their properties. Furthermore, a concept inherits properties through some of its defining feature concepts. Each of the concepts that create the defining features of another concept may have its own defining features. They also may have superordinate concepts, with their own defining feature concepts. Thus, the number of concepts that relate to a given concept may be very large. The context of a concept may be calibrated with different degrees of precision, depending on how many defining features were imported from superordinate concepts, the semantic distance, and the types of relations.

16.3   INFERENCE RULES

16.3.1   Combinations of Two Semantic Relations

A principle that guides our design of inference rules is to make them independent of the concepts to which they apply. The inference rules are implemented as chains of relations. First, we form some *primitive rules* by pairing two semantic relations. They may be further combined to generate more complex rules. Since the relations we use are unambiguous, the inference rules are unambiguous. The rules may be more or less plausible, but they are not a source of ambiguity, unlike the plausible inference rules described in Cohen and Loiselle 1988.

The relations that are asymmetric and transitive are more useful for inference than others since they often support deductions. For example, moving up an IS-A hierarchy of nouns or verbs, one goes from more specific to more general concepts, and inferences make sense. The same can be said for many of the entailment or causation verb relations. For example, WordNet 1.5 includes the following chain of entailments: if a defendant is sentenced, then that person has been convicted, and further, that person must have been judged.

However, inferences sometimes need to go against these transitive relations, and conclusions are not precise. In a sense, these are abductions. For example, if one is sleeping, it is possible that one is snoring.

Now let us look at the inference rules that result from pairing two verb concept relations and their inverses. Figure 16.2 illustrates all possible pairs of two semantic relations from WordNet 1.5 (see table 16.1) that link three concepts. They are grouped according to the parts of speech they connect. For example, the relation pairs in the first set connect the three verb concepts VC_1, VC_2, and VC_3. The number to the right of each pair indicates all possible combinations that can be formed with two relations and their inverses. When both relations are symmetric, there are eight possible combinations; when one relation is symmetric and the other is asymmetric, there are four combinations; and when both relations are symmetric, there are two combinations. These numbers exclude cases where a relation is combined with itself. An asymmetric relation can link to itself in four distinct combinations, but a symmetric relation produces only one combination. Overall, these pairings result in 314 distinct inference rules, a few of which we analyze in detail in the next section.

16.3.2   Rules Formed by Pairing IS-A and ENTAIL

Figure 16.3 shows the 16 inference rules resulting from pairing the relations IS-A, ENTAIL, REVERSE_IS-A, and REVERSE_ENTAIL, and figure 16.4 illustrates the logical expressions of these inference rules. Figure 16.3 includes some useful statistics that indicate how often a rule occurs in WordNet 1.5. Variable c measures the number of occurrences in WordNet of a particular synset relation chain. In order to determine how often a rule applies to English words, we looked at the synonyms pointing to these synsets. Let $s(j)$ be the number of synonyms of a synset j. For each rule we measured the sum of all synonyms for VC_1 and VC_3 as $n_1 = \sum_{j=1}^{c} s_1(j)$, and $n_3 = \sum_{j=1}^{c} s_3(j)$. The sum of products $np = \sum_{j=1}^{c}$

CONCEPTS : VERB→VERB→VERB

Relations	Number of combinations
IS-A + ENTAIL	8
IS-A + CAUSE-TO	8
ENTAIL + CAUSE-TO	8
IS-A + ANTONYM	4
ENTAIL + ANTONYM	4
CAUSE-TO + ANTONYM	4
SEE-ALSO + IS-A	8
SEE-ALSO + ENTAIL	8
SEE-ALSO + CAUSE-TO	8
SEE-ALSO + ANTONYM	4

CONCEPTS : NOUN→NOUN→NOUN

Relations	Number of combinations
IS-A + IS-PART	8
IS-A + IS-MEMBER	8
IS-A + IS-STUFF	8
IS-PART + IS-MEMBER	8
IS-PART + IS-STUFF	8
IS-STUFF + IS-MEMBER	8
IS-A + ANTONYM	4
IS-PART + ANTONYM	4
IS-MEMBER + ANTONYM	4
IS-STUFF + ANTONYM	4

CONCEPTS : ADJ→NOUN→NOUN

Relations	Number of combinations
ATTRIBUTE + IS-A	4
ATTRIBUTE + IS-PART	4
ATTRIBUTE + IS-MEMBER	4
ATTRIBUTE + IS-STUFF	4
ATTRIBUTE + ANTONYM	2
PERTAINYM + IS-A	8
PERTAINYM + IS-PART	8
PERTAINYM + IS-MEMBER	8
PERTAINYM + IS-STUFF	8
PERTAINYM + ANTONYM	4
SIMILAR + IS-A	4
SIMILAR + IS-PART	4
SIMILAR + IS-MEMBER	4
SIMILAR + IS-STUFF	4
SIMILAR + ANTONYM	2

CONCEPTS : ADJ→ADJ→ADJ

Relations	Number of combinations
SIMILAR + ANTONYM	2
SEE-ALSO + ANTONYM	3
SIMILAR + SEE-ALSO	4
SEE-ALSO + PERTAINYM	8
SIMILAR + PERTAINYM	4
PERTAINYM + ANTONYM	4

CONCEPTS : ADJ→VERB→VERB

Relations	Number of combinations
PAST-PARTICIPLE + IS-A	8
PAST-PARTICIPLE + ENTAIL	8
PAST-PARTICIPLE + CAUSE-TO	8
PAST-PARTICIPLE + ANTONYM	4

CONCEPTS : ADJ→ADV→ADJ

Relations	Number of combinations
PERTAINYM + SIMILAR	2
PERTAINYM + SEE-ALSO	2

CONCEPTS : ADJ→ADJ→VERB

Relations	Number of combinations
SIMILAR + PAST-PARTICIPLE	4

CONCEPTS : ADJ→ADJ→VERB

Relations	Number of combinations
PERTAINYM + PAST-PARTICIPLE	4

CONCEPTS : ADV→ADJ→NOUN

Relations	Number of combinations
PERTAINYM + ATTRIBUTE	4

Figure 16.2
Pairs of relations used for inference rules

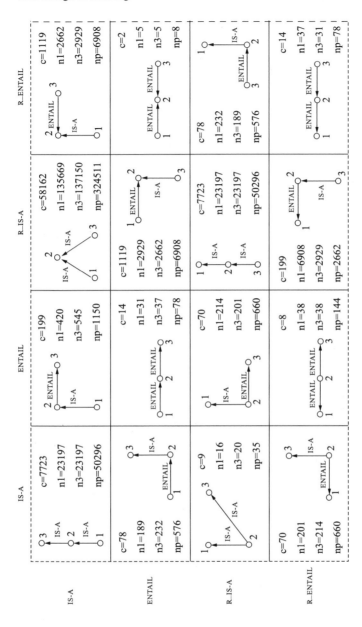

Figure 16.3
Sixteen possible pairs of IS-A, ENTAIL, and their reverses

Rule 1	Rule 2	Rule 3	Rule 4
VC_1 IS-A VC_2	VC_1 IS-A VC_2	VC_1 IS-A VC_2	VC_1 IS-A VC_2
VC_2 IS-A VC_3	VC_2 ENTAIL VC_3	VC_2 R_IS-A VC_3	VC_2 R_ENTAIL VC_3
VC_1 IS-A VC_3	VC_1 ENTAIL VC_3	VC_1 PLAUSIBLE (not VC_3)	VC_1 EXPLAINS VC_3
Rule 5	Rule 6	Rule 7	Rule 8
VC_1 ENTAIL VC_2	VC_1 ENTAIL VC_2	VC_1 ENTAIL VC_2	VC_1 ENTAIL VC_2
VC_2 IS-A VC_3	VC_2 ENTAIL VC_3	VC_2 R_IS-A VC_3	VC_2 R_ENTAIL VC_3
VC_1 ENTAIL VC_3	VC_1 ENTAIL VC_3	VC_1 BACKGROUND-OF VC_3	VC_1 PLAUSIBLE VC_3
Rule 9	Rule 10	Rule 11	Rule 12
VC_1 R_IS-A VC_2	VC_1 R_IS-A VC_2	VC_1 R_IS-A VC_2	VC_1 R_IS-A VC_2
VC_2 IS-A VC_3	VC_2 ENTAIL VC_3	VC_2 R_IS-A VC_3	VC_2 R_ENTAIL VC_3
VC_1 PLAUSIBLE (not VC_3)	VC_1 PLAUSIBLE VC_3	VC_1 PLAUSIBLE VC_3	VC_1 PLAUSIBLE VC_3
Rule 13	Rule 14	Rule 15	Rule 16
VC_1 R_ENTAIL VC_2	VC_1 R_ENTAIL VC_2	VC_1 R_ENTAIL VC_2	VC_1 R_ENTAIL VC_2
VC_2 IS-A VC_3	VC_2 ENTAIL VC_3	VC_2 R_IS-A VC_3	VC_2 R_ENTAIL VC_3
VC_1 PLAUSIBLE VC_3	VC_1 PLAUSIBLE (not VC_3)	VC_1 PLAUSIBLE (not VC_3)	VC_1 PLAUSIBLE (not VC_3)

Figure 16.4
Inference rules corresponding to figure 16.3. (VC = verb concept)

$s_1(j)s_3(j)$ represents the total number of applications of that rule for English words in WordNet.

The semantics of the rules is as follows. Rule 1 is a deduction; it is always true, owing to the transitivity of IS-A. Rule 2 is also a deduction, owing to the transitivity of both relations. Because VC_1 inherits all of the properties of VC_2 and some of them determine the entailment of VC_3 from VC_2, then the same properties account for the entailment between VC_1 and VC_3. Rule 3 indicates that VC_1 most likely differs from VC_3, or if VC_1 is true, then VC_3 is not, and vice versa. This is because both VC_1 and VC_3 are subsumed by VC_2. Rule 4 shows that VC_1 is a possible explanation for VC_3, a special form of plausibility. For example, consider (2):

(2) The criminal apologized.
He confessed his crime.

As shown in figure 16.5, *confess* is a form of *admit*, which is entailed by *apologize*; *confess* explains the way in which he *apologized*. Rule 5 is a deduction; VC_1 entails VC_3. Consider (3):

(3) The king rewarded his men for bravery.

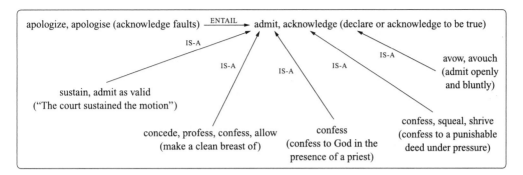

Figure 16.5
Example for rule 4

Reward entails *approve*, which is subsumed by *authorize*, and by this rule, *reward* entails the subsumer *authorize*. Rule 6 is a deduction owing to the transitivity of ENTAIL. For example, {*save, spend less*} entails {*buy, purchase, take*}, which entails {*pay, make a payment*}. Rule 7 is the reverse of rule 4; VC_1 provides background for VC_3. In figure 16.5, for example, *apologize* provides background for *confess*. Rule 8 indicates the plausibility between two verb concepts that both entail the third one. Although the structure of rule 8 is similar to that of rule 3, the implication is different. In WordNet there are examples of rule 8 in which VC_1 makes VC_3 plausible, owing to the nature of the ENTAIL relation. An example is provided by *snore* and *dream*, which both entail *sleep*.

Rule 9 shows that VC_1 plausibly excludes VC_3, since they have a common subsumee VC_2, For example, both *sit* and *stand* subsume *sprawl*, as shown in figure 16.6, and if one is sitting, one is not standing. Rule 10 indicates that VC_1 subsumes VC_2; thus, VC_1 makes VC_2 plausible, which further entails VC_3. In WordNet *breathe* subsumes *snore*, which entails *sleep*; given that, if one breathes, it is plausible that one sleeps. Rule 11 links two REVERSE_IS-A relations; VC_1 makes VC_2 plausible, which makes VC_3 plausible. Rule 12 engenders plausibility resulting from reverse relations; VC_1 makes VC_2 plausible, and VC_2 is entailed by VC_3.

In figure 16.7 *improve* subsumes several verb concepts, one of which is lexicalized by *repair*, and *modernize* entails *repair*. When the sense of *improve* is 'repair', *modernize* is implied; however, when *improve* takes the meaning of another subsumee, *modernize* may not be implied, as figure 16.7 indicates.

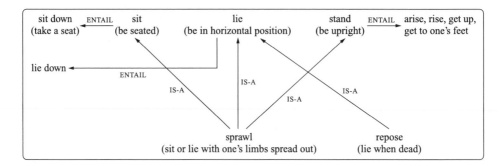

Figure 16.6
Example for rule 9

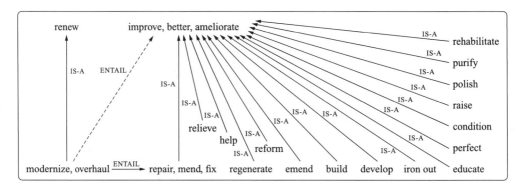

Figure 16.7
Example for rule 12

Rule 13 engenders plausibility arising from REVERSE_ENTAIL. Figure 16.7 shows that *repair* is entailed by *modernize*, which is linked to *renew* by an IS-A relation. In rule 14 VC_2 entails both VC_1 and VC_3; thus, VC_1 makes VC_3 highly plausible. An example is provided by *chew* and *swallow*, both entailed by *eat*.

In rule 15 the REVERSE_ENTAIL relation is inherited by VC_3. An example is shown in figure 16.6: *sit down* makes *sprawl* possible. Rule 16 is the reverse of rule 6. REVERSE_ENTAIL is a plausible relation, and chaining REVERSE_ENTAIL retains plausibility. An example is *judge*, which is entailed by *convict*, which is entailed by *sentence*.

16.3.3 Factors Affecting Plausibility

Plausibility is mainly affected by (1) the nature of relations, (2) the number of relations in a chain, and (3) the number of subsumees of concepts to which a rule is applied.

The plausibility of REVERSE_IS-A relations is generally weaker than the plausibility of REVERSE_ENTAIL relations. Also, since each reverse relation brings a degree of plausibility, the longer the chain of reverse relations, the weaker the plausibility. Although these two factors are related to the inference rules themselves, we have observed that the plausibility of a rule is also affected by the concepts to which that rule is applied. The explanation is that the more subsumees a concept has, the weaker the plausibility of implying these subsumees. A heuristic for the plausibility factor in this case is $1/n$, where n is the number of subsumees of a concept.

16.4 RULE CHAINING AND MARKER PROPAGATIONS

16.4.1 Rules with More Than Two Relations

Rules can be chained by letting the conclusion of one be the premise of the other. For example, rules 1 and 2 can be chained without difficulty. Furthermore, inferences may be expanded with rules like this:

Rule 17

VC_1	PLAUSIBLE	VC_3
VC_1	IS-A	VC_4

VC_1	PLAUSIBLE	VC_4

An example of this is shown in figure 16.7. By applying rule 12 and considering *improve* true, we derive the result that *modernize* is plausible; then applying rule 17, we further derive that *renew* is plausible. The reverse is also plausible, by rules 10 and 17.

Figure 16.8 illustrates several cases where an inference can be drawn from a chain of four relations: IS-A, CAUSE-TO, ENTAIL, and REVERSE_IS-A. To *dine*, *lunch*, and *bottlefeed* are different manners of *feeding* people, which is a cause of *eating*, which further entails two activities: *swallow* and *chew*. A form of *swallowing* is to *bolt*; thus, it is probable that a form of feeding might imply *bolt*. Everyone *chews* when *eating*, but only sometimes do we *crunch*. Again, it is plausible that *dining* implies *crunching*.

The same figure illustrates come inferences that are not true. One is the chain *inject*—IS-A→*feed*, *give food to* —CAUSE-TO→*eat*—ENTAIL→*chew*—REVERSE_IS-A→*mumble*. What goes wrong? To *inject* is a form of *feeding*,

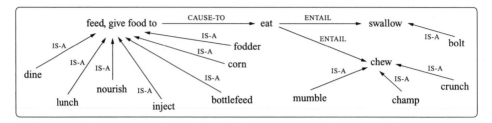

Figure 16.8
Example of chaining four rules

but it doesn't cause *eating*. In this case the causation is inexact, because case constraints in the glosses are violated. The gloss of *inject* is '(feed intravenously)', where *intravenously* is '(in the vein)'; thus, the INSTRUMENT of *feed* is *vein*. The gloss of *eat* is '(take in solid food)'. From this gloss, we cannot find the filler of the INSTRUMENT case for *take in*. However, by searching for the pattern *take in*—OBJECT→*food* in other glosses, we discover that the synset {*mouth, oral cavity*} has the gloss '(the opening through which food is taken in and vocalizations emerge)'. Thus, *mouth* may be taken as an INSTRUMENT of *eat*. Having therefore determined a discrepancy between INSTRUMENT of *inject* and INSTRUMENT of *eat*, we can conclude that the causation does not hold. Moreover, in the case of *inject*, the food is not solid.

Another inference that does not hold is *dine*—IS-A→*feed, give food to*—CAUSE-TO→*eat*—ENTAIL→*chew*—REVERSE_IS-A→*champ, chafe_the_bit*. The reason why the inference doesn't hold is that *dine* refers to people, whereas *champing* is typical of horses.

These examples have proved that long chains of different relations lead to plausible inferences. An important point is that the degree of plausibility may be measured by the degree to which constraints such as case restrictions are satisfied.

16.4.2 Marker Propagations

The underlying mechanism for forming chains of relations is marker propagation. In a networklike knowledge base, a marker is placed on a node, and it is programmed to propagate from that node only along some selected relations. The concepts along the propagation path relate to the original node via the inference rule, or the marker propagation rule.

A marker propagation computational paradigm is especially suitable for applications where control flow is incompletely specified. Reasoning on knowledge bases falls into this broad category. The markers presented in this chapter may be called "smart" markers because they are able to follow complex propagation rules. This contrasts with spreading activation models used by Charniak (1986), Norvig (1989), or Hendler (1988), where markers propagate along all links, thus generating a large number of false conclusions. The inferences generated by "smart" markers are as good as the inference rules.

The marker propagation model can be briefly described as a network consisting of *nodes* and *links*, and a set of *markers* moving through the network according to some propagation rules. The nodes can independently execute a set of functions, store data, and communicate with other nodes. Nodes may have several identities or labels simultaneously. The links are directional, connecting source nodes to destination nodes. A link has a name, indicating the link type, and it may have associated functions that are executed when some markers are propagated along it. This is the static part of the model.

The markers are process threads that carry a variable number of fields. Thy reside inside the nodes and propagate to other nodes through links using user-defined propagation rules. The required marker fields include, among others, the marker type, the propagation function, and the node where the marker originated. The arguments of a propagation rule may be node labels, regular expressions of link labels, and/or functions that govern the interactions between a marker and other markers or nodes. In addition to the required fields, the user may define any other fields. A set of functions is normally included to specify the behavior of markers inside nodes.

16.4.3 Semantic Paths

In this section we describe a marker propagation algorithm for finding relational paths between concepts in a knowledge base. Markers are placed on some initial concepts and then are set free to propagate through the knowledge base to establish semantic connections.

The input to the algorithm is a semantic knowledge base as described above. The output of the algorithm consists of semantic paths that link pairs of input concepts. To each path correspond certain inferences that explain how the two concepts are logically related.

Step 0. Create and load the knowledge base. The extended WordNet knowledge base in the form of semantic network consisting of nodes and relations is loaded into the computer memory.

Step 1.   Place markers on knowledge base concepts.   This step consists
of creating markers and placing them on the knowledge base nodes corresponding to the input concepts. The markers are created by selecting
and filling the marker fields with the values provided by the input.

A typical marker format contains (among other items) fields that indicate the sentence and the concept where that marker originated, a marker
propagation function, the processing functions called by the marker, and
the colliding markers.

Step 2.   Propagate markers.   After markers are placed on nodes, they
start to propagate according to their propagation rule. New markers are
spawned every time a node contains more than one outgoing link that is
part of its propagation rule. Whenever a marker reaches a node that does
not have an outgoing relation as part of its propagation rule, the marker
stops. The propagation trail of a marker becomes part of that marker's
history; thus, markers become fatter as they propagate. For reasons that
will become evident in the next step, nodes keep a copy of each passing
marker.

An example of a propagation rule for markers placed on verbs is
any combination of the relations IS-A, CAUSE-TO, and ENTAIL. According to
figure 16.4, this rule provides plausible inferences. Markers continue to
propagate as long as the propagation rule allows them to. The algorithm
detects and avoids cycles by simply checking whether or not a marker has
already visited a node.

It is important to realize that a marker does not have to wait in a node
for its colliding pair. Instead, it leaves a copy on each node along its path
and moves on. In this model we opted for a flexible, asynchronous operation at the expense of using additional memory necessary to hold copies
of propagating markers.

Step 3.   Detect collisions.   After all marker propagations cease, the collisions that took place during marker propagations are detected. To each
marker collision corresponds a path. The path is found simply by inspect-
ing the path history of the colliding markers and linking the two halves.
Each marker participating in a collision provides half of the path.

Step 4.   Extract inferences.   Once a semantic path has been established
in the knowledge base between a pair of concepts, the concepts along the
path are easily retrievable since they are marked with the same marker
as the originating concept. Some simple inferences may be concluded

by listing the concepts retrieved from the paths. The examples given in section 16.3.2 with inference rules fall under this category.

It is possible, however, to draw more complex inferences by considering an originating concept as part of its clause syntactic structure. In that case, by propagating syntactic relations along the path, one can find new connections between the original clause concepts and the concepts that are part of the path. Some simple examples are given in the following section.

16.5   KNOWLEDGE-PROCESSING APPLICATIONS

16.5.1   An Inference Example

Inference is the key to may knowledge-processing problems. Here we show how inferences may be extracted by applying the path-finding algorithm to extended WordNet. Let us reexamine example (1):

(1) Jim was hungry.
     He opened the refrigerator.

We assume that the text is first semantically disambiguated. A path between the concepts expressed by *hungry* and *refrigerator* is established by placing markers on these two concepts and having their propagation controlled by their propagation rules. The propagation rules are in the form of regular expressions as follows:

marker m_1 on *hungry* with propagation rule [*gloss*⋆]
marker m_2 on *refrigerator* with propagation rule [*gloss*⋆]

The marker originated at *hungry* collides with the marker originated at *refrigerator* in the node *food*. This indicates that a path exists between the two input concepts. Figure 16.9 shows the path, here called path 1, and the concepts along the path that provide the context. Inferences are extracted by carrying case structures along the path, as shown in table 16.3.

Many other semantic paths can be established between the two sentences by using different marker propagation rules. Figure 16.10 shows two other paths. Path 2 from *hungry* to *open* is produced by the collision of markers m_3 and m_4 at the node *get*:

marker m_3 on *hungry* with propagation rule [*gloss*⋆ R_IS-A *gloss*⋆ IS-A⋆]
marker m_4 in *open* with propagation rule [CAUSE-TO *gloss*⋆ IS-A⋆]

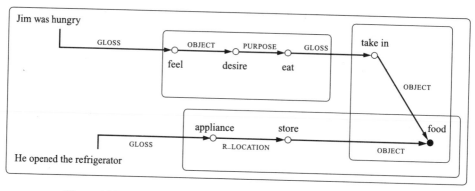

Figure 16.9
A semantic path between *hungry* and *refrigerator*

Table 16.3
Inferences resulting from coherence path 1, figure 16.9

Inference sequence
Jim was hungry.
Jim felt a desire to eat.
Jim felt a desire to take in food.
COLLISION: Jim = he felt a desire to take in food, stored in an appliance, which he opened.
He opened an appliance where food is stored.
He opened the refrigerator.

Path 3 from *hungry* to *refrigerator* is produced by the collision of markers m_5 and m_6 at the node *possess*. Note that this path and path 1 differ because they arise from different propagation rules.

marker m_5 on *hungry* with propagation rule [*gloss* ⋆ R_IS-A *gloss* ⋆]
marker m_6 on *refrigerator* with propagation rule [*gloss* ⋆ IS-A]

The propagation rules consist of sequences of relations that encompass both WordNet relations and relations derived from the glosses. We denote by *gloss* any of the relations illustrated in table 16.2 and their reverses. The inferences that result from paths 2 and 3 are shown in table 16.4.

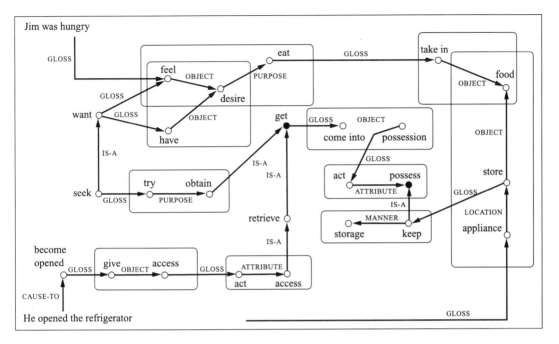

Figure 16.10
Path 2 (from *hungry* to *open*) has a marker collision at *get*, and path 3 (from *hungry* to *refrigerator*) has a marker collision at *possess*.

16.5.2   Intentions and Context

One way of detecting intentions is to search the semantic paths for concepts accessed by the PURPOSE relation. This relation may appear in some
concepts' defining feature. In path 1 *eat* expresses such a concept, and this
is indeed the main intention of the text *Jim was hungry. He opened the
refrigerator.* In path 2 *obtain* (*food*) expresses another concept accessed
by the PURPOSE relation. This may be regarded as an intention that supports the dominant intention of the text: Jim's intention is to *eat*. The fact
that *obtain* is subordinated to *eat* is established by the presence of an IS-A
relation between *seek* and *want*.

Although at this moment neither WordNet nor its proposed extensions
support plan representations, partial plans can be recovered from the
information provided by the semantic paths. For example, a step in the
plan to eat is to obtain food. A mode of obtaining food (thus another
subplan) is to access it from a refrigerator.

Table 16.4
Inferences resulting from path 2 and path 3, figure 16.10

Inference sequence for path 2	Inference sequence for path 3
Jim was hungry.	**Jim was hungry.**
Jim felt a desire to eat (food).	Jim felt a desire to eat (food).
Jim wanted to eat (food).	Jim wanted to eat (food).
Jim sought to eat (food).	Jim sought to eat (food).
Jim tried to obtain food.	Jim tried to obtain food.
Jim tried to get food.	Jim tried to get food.
COLLISION: Jim = he tried and got food.	Jim came into possession of food.
He retrieved food.	COLLISION: Jim = he came into possession of food.
He accessed food.	
The refrigerator gave him access (to food).	He opened the appliance to possess food.
The refrigerator became open to him.	He opened the appliance where food is kept in storage.
He opened the refrigerator.	He opened the appliance where food is stored.
	He opened the refrigerator.

Every text conveys information about the context in which actions or events take place. The context may be as simple as a location or time, or as complicated as the whole background of a story narrated in the text, depending on the narrator's point of view.

There is little agreement in the artificial intelligence community about the definition of context, although many consider it an important notion (McCarthy 1993). We regard a context as the totality of concepts along the semantic paths—in other words, the totality of inferences that can be drawn from a text. The more we know beforehand about a context, the more we can filter the relevant inferences related to that context. If the context is not known beforehand, and the goal is to identify a narrow context, this can be done by identifying those concepts that are crossed by many paths. Once the context is known, the inference plausibility must be reevaluated, since the same inference may be true or false in different contexts.

16.5.3   Text Coherence

The existence of logical between the sentences of a text makes that text coherent. In our model these logical relations become semantic paths between sentences. Path 3, for example, explains how the goal of obtaining food is satisfied by opening an appliance where food is stored. The more such semantic paths there are between sentences, the more coherent the text is. Our method avoids the difficulty inherent in the traditional method of recognizing coherence from a predetermined set of relations (Hobbs 1985; Mann and Thompson 1988).

16.5.4 Questions and Answers

The answers for some questions become obvious from the inferences generated by the coherence paths. For example, the answer to "What is the relation between *hungry and refrigerator?*" is the entire context along paths 1 and 3. The answer may be more elaborate, or brief.

To answer "Why would someone open a refrigerator?" we make use of the deep structure generated by the paths. The answer is found along a path from *open* to *refrigerator* that is a combination of paths 2 and 3, namely, "to access food stored in the refrigerator."

16.5.5 Case Propagation

Semantic cases usually associated with verbs can play a major role in narrowing proper inferences. Unfortunately, current versions of WordNet do not have cases associated with concepts. However, many glosses provide rich information about cases. Many verb senses are disambiguated by the case function they support. For example, in *change1* (e.g., *The discussion has changed my thinking about the issue*) and *change2* (e.g., *Her thinking changed completely after the discussion*) the action is the same, but the senses are different, because they use different case functions. For *change1*, the determiner (or the agent) of the action is explicit, whereas *change2* does not have an agent. Furthermore, *change1* causes *change2*.

It is interesting to observe how cases propagate on different relations. The case structure is preserved along hierarchical relations such as IS-A. This can be seen in figure 16.11, where the AGENT relation between the verb concepts and *John* and the OBJECT relation between the verb concepts and *ball* hold for the whole hierarchical chain *hit1*—IS-A→*propell*—IS-A→*move2*. When the inference path enters into the defining feature of *propel*, the case functions for *move1* change: namely, the ball becomes the experiencer of moving forward.

16.5.6 Reference Resolution

As cases propagate along paths, their fillers are unified when markers collide, producing referents for pronouns or identifying antecedents for

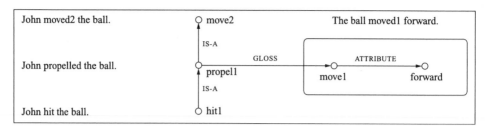

Figure 16.11
Case propagation

noun anaphora. Tables 16.3 and 16.4 illustrate the resolution of the pronoun *he* to *Jim*, which takes place at the collision nodes. This reference
seems trivial, because Jim is the only human present in the text. But the
paths remain the same even when other sentences are placed between
these two sentences, and the pronoun reference still holds. Of course, reference resolution may benefit from some recency constraints that can
prioritize or even discard semantic paths.

16.6   WHAT WORDNET CANNOT DO

From the knowledge-processing point of view, both WordNet 1.5 and our
inference method currently have many substantial limitations. The major
WordNet limitations are (1) the lack of compound concepts, (2) the small
number of causation and entailment relations, (3) the lack of precondi-
tions for verbs, and (4) the absence of case relations.

To construct a powerful knowledge base for commonsense reasoning,
WordNet needs to be augmented in several directions. Although 52% of
the noun synsets and 49% of the verb synsets contain groups of words
such as *flea market, inside trading,* or *joint venture,* WordNet does not
include many compound words used in everyday English.

Many more entailments could be added. For an excellent classification
of the entailments rendered by WordNet, see Fellbaum 1990. New classes
of entailments may be added, which will enlarge the general number of
entailments provided in WordNet. For example, the synset {*fly, aviate,
pilot*} could entail two other verb concepts that are necessary for any
piloting routine: the synset {*take off, lift off*}, which initiates the flight,
and the synset {*land, put down, bring down*}, which terminates it.

WordNet provides no information regarding the conditions necessary
for an action to take place. For example, driving a car requires (among

other things) a driving license and ownership of the car. Depending on the purpose of the knowledge base, many more relations could be added that are usually, but not always, true. For example, dropping a glass often results in breaking the glass.

Perhaps one of the most useful additions to WordNet would be case relations associated with verbs. As discussed earlier, case constraints play an important role in the inference process.

The inference method proposed in this chapter is still very simplistic, because (1) it cannot quantify the plausibility of inference rules, (2) there is no mechanism for ranking the goodness of the semantic paths, and (3) the method operates at the concept level and thus does not take into consideration relations between higher discourse entities, such as discourse segments.

A thorough analysis of each inference rule is required in order to understand its general applicability. Although we have identified some factors that affect plausibility, other sources, such as the nature of the relations, need to be explored.

References

Alshawi, H. (1989). Analysing the dictionary definitions. In B. Boguraev and T. Briscoe (Eds.), *Computational lexicography for natural language processing*, 153–170. London: Longman.

Alterman, R. (1985). A dictionary based on concept coherence. *Artificial Intelligence, 25*, 153–186.

Amsler, R. A. (1980). *The structure of the Merriam-Webster Pocket Dictionary* (Tech. Rep. No. TR-164). Austin: University of Texas.

Beckwith, R., Fellbaum, C., Gross, D., and Miller, G. A. (1991). WordNet: A lexical database organized on psycholinguistic principles. In U. Zernik (Ed.), *Lexical acquisition: Exploiting on-line resources to build a lexicon*, 141–170. Hillsdale, NJ: Erlbaum.

Bruce, R., and Guthrie, L. (1992). Genus disambiguation: A study in weighted preference. In *Proceedings of the 14th International Conference on Computational Linguistics (COLING-92)*, 1187–1191. Association for Computational Linguistics.

Charniak, E. (1986). A neat theory of marker passing. In *Proceedings of the Fifth National Conference on Artificial Intelligence (AAAI-86)*, 584–588. Menlo Park, CA: AAAI Press, and Cambridge, MA: MIT Press.

Chodorow, M., Byrd, R., and Heidorn, G. (1985). Extracting semantic hierarchies from a large on-line dictionary. In *Proceedings of the 23rd Annual Meeting of the Association for Computational Linguistics*, 299–304, Association for computational Linguistics.

Cohen, P. R., and Loiselle, C. L. (1988). Beyond ISA: Structures for plausible inference in semantic networks. In *Proceedings of the Seventh National Conference on Artificial Intelligence (AAAI-88)*, 415–420. Menlo Park, CA: AAAI Press, and Cambridge, MA: MIT Press.

Evens, M. (Ed.). (1988). *Relational models of the lexicon.* Cambridge, England: Cambridge University Press.

Fellbaum, C. (1990). English verbs as a semantic net. In *Five papers on WordNet* (Tech. Rep. No. CSL-43). Princeton, NJ: Princeton University, Cognitive Science Laboratory.

Fillmore, C. J. (1968). The case for case. In E. Bach and R. Harms (Eds.), *Universals in linguistic theory*, 1–88, New York: Holt, Rinehart and Winston.

Fowler, R. H., and Dearholt, D. W. (1989). *Pathfinder networks in information retrieval* (Tech. Rep. No. MCCS-89–147). Las Cruces: New Mexico State University, Computing Research Laboratory.

Fowler, R. H., and Slator, B. M. (1989). Information retrieval and natural language analysis. In *Proceedings of the Third Annual Rocky Mountain Conferences on Artificial Intelligence*, 129–136. The Rocky Mountain Society of Artificial Intelligence.

Guo, C. M. (Ed.). (1992). *Machine tractable dictionaries: Design and construction.* Norwood, NJ: Ablex.

Hendler, J. A. (1988). *Integrating marker-passing and problem solving: A spreading activation approach to improve choice in planning.* Hillsdale, NJ: Erlbaum.

Hobbs, J. R. (1985). *On the coherence and structure of discourse* (Tech. Rep. No. CSLI-85-37). Stanford, CA: Stanford University, Center for the Study of Language and Information.

Lenat, D. B. (1995).CYC: A large-scale investment in knowledge infrastructure. *Communications of the ACM, 38*(11), 32–38.

Mann, W. C., and Thompson, S. A. (1988). Rhetorical Structure Theory: Toward a functional theory of text organization. *Text, 8*, 219–281.

McCarthy, J. (1993). Notes on formalizing context. In *Proceedings of the 13th International Joint Conference on Artificial Intelligence (IJCAI-93)*, 555–560. San Francisco: Morgan Kaufmann.

Miller, G. A. (1995). WordNet: A lexical database for English. *Communications of the ACM, 38*(11), 39–41.

Norvig, P. (1989). Marker passing as a weak method for text inferencing. *Cognitive Science, 13*, 569–620.

Procter, P. (Ed.). (1978). *Longman dictionary of contemporary English.* Harlow, Essex, England: Longman Group.

Pustejovsky, J. (1991). The Generative Lexicon. *Computational Linguistics, 17*, 409–441.

Slator, B. M. (1988). Constructing contextually organized lexical semantic knowledge-bases. In *Proceedings of the Third Annual Rocky Mountain Conference on Artificial Intelligence*, 142–148. The Rocky Mountain Society of Artificial Intelligence.

Stein, G. F., Lin, F., Bruce, R., Weng, F., and Guthrie, L. (1993). *The development of an application independent lexicon: LEXBASE* (Tech. Rep. No. MCCS-93-247). Las Cruces: New Mexico State University, Computing Research Laboratory.

Walker, D. E., and Amsler, R. A. (1986). The use of machine readable dictionaries in sublanguage analysis. In I. R. Grishman and R. Kittredge (Eds.), *Analyzing language in restricted domains*, 223–279. Hillsdale, NJ: Erlbaum.

Wilks, Y. A., Slator, B. M., and Guthrie, L. M. (1996). *Electric words: Dictionaries, computers, and meanings.* Cambridge, MA: MIT Press.

Appendix

Obtaining and Using WordNet

Although most of the work reported on in this book is based on WordNet 1.5, the currently distributed release is version 1.6.

Packages are available for using WordNet on various Unix platforms and PC and Macintosh computers. Each WordNet package consists of the WordNet lexical database files, interface software, source code, and documentation. The Semantic Concordance package contains semantically tagged files for the Standard Corpus of Present-Day American English (the Brown Corpus), the Escort browsing program, and documentation. All of these packages can be downloaded using anonymous FTP from the following sites: ftp.cogsci.princeton.edu, ftp.ims.uni-stuttgart.de. A CD-ROM for PC and Macintosh systems containing both the WordNet and Semantic Concordance packages can be ordered from MIT Press.

A WordNet World Wide Web site is located at www.cogsci.princeton.edu/~wn/. Users can access the WordNet database on-line from this site and can download any of the packages.

A list of users is maintained for the purpose of informing them of new releases and serious bugs. Users who download WordNet are encouraged to send e-mail to wordnet@princeton.edu. They may also choose to have their names added to the wn-users@princeton.edu discussion group. Mail addressed here is automatically distributed to all addresses in the group.

Index